W9-ADM-450

Northerners at War

CIVIL WAR IN THE NORTH
Series Editor, Lesley J. Gordon, University of Akron

ADVISORY BOARD

| | |
|---|---|
| William Blair | Pennsylvania State University |
| Peter S. Carmichael | West Virginia University |
| Stephen D. Engle | Florida Atlantic University |
| J. Matthew Gallman | University of Florida |
| Elizabeth Leonard | Colby College |
| Elizabeth Varon | Temple University |
| Joan Waugh | University of California Los Angeles |

# Northerners at War

*Reflections on the
Civil War Home Front*

J. Matthew Gallman

The Kent State University Press
KENT, OHIO

© 2010 by The Kent State University Press, Kent, Ohio 44242

ALL RIGHTS RESERVED

Library of Congress Catalog Card Number 2010000358

ISBN 978-1-60635-045-4

Manufactured in the United States of America

LIBRARY OF CONGRESS CATALOGING-IN-PUBLICATION DATA

Gallman, J. Matthew (James Matthew)

Northerners at war : reflections on the Civil War home front / J. Matthew Gallman.

p.   cm.

Includes bibliographical references and index.

ISBN 978-1-60635-045-4 (hardover : alk. paper) ∞

1. United States—History—Civil War, 1861–1865.   2. United States—History—Civil War,
1861–1865—Social aspects.   3. United States—History—Civil War, 1861–1865—Economic aspects.   4. Philadelphia (Pa.)—History—Civil War, 1861–1865.   5. Philadelphia (Pa.)—Social
conditions—19th century.   6. Philadelphia (Pa.)—Economic conditions—19th century.
7. Dickinson, Anna E. (Anna Elizabeth), 1842–1932.   I. Title.

E468.G354 2010

973.7—dc22                2010000358

British Library Cataloging-in-Publication data are available.

14  13  12  11  10      5  4  3  2  1

For Joan, Gary, Lesley, and Jim

# Contents

# Introduction

## TWO SEMINARS

In an odd sort of way, this book owes its existence to the meetings of two graduate seminars, separated by just over two decades. The first took place in Morton Keller's Cambridge, Massachusetts, living room, sometime in 1981, when I was a young graduate student. The second seminar was more than two decades later, in Gainesville, Florida.

I had arrived at Brandeis in 1979, with a focus on colonial America, an outside interest in economic history, and a passion for the new social history. I had a deeply held belief that our task as historians was to uncover the lives of ordinary Americans. The goal was to give voice to the voiceless. Those dead white men who wrote speeches, owned companies, left diaries, and won elections were of no interest to me. The historians I most admired had painstakingly reconstructed the daily lives of early American communities, teasing living history out of tax records, probate records, demographic profiles, and the tiniest pieces of everyday life.[1]

In those days we all admired Robert Gross's *The Minutemen and Their World*. In this brilliant book, Gross had examined the daily life of late eighteenth-century Concord, Massachusetts, and then considered how the American Revolution shaped the history of that small New England town. Gross had attempted to uncover how everyday people, and an everyday community, responded to cataclysmic events. Between those covers, the new social history met political history.[2]

Back to Morton Keller's living room. The seminar was a broad readings course in American history. That week, we were discussing the American Civil War. Somebody asked why it is that there was no *Minutemen and Their World* for the Civil War. Why hadn't social historians tried to dissect a Civil War community the way Gross had tackled Concord during the Revolutionary War? The idea stuck with me. Later, after passing my qualifying exams, I decided to abandon my earlier work on colonial America and become a historian of the Civil War era. So I went to see Morton Keller. I had taken two seminars with Keller but had never worked very closely with him. He was an intimidating, ironic, brilliant, no-nonsense scholar who was known largely as a political and institutional historian. I felt that he saw me as a visitor from some other shore. I was a devotee of the new social history, and, more specifically, I was a "cliometrician": an historian who embraced quantitative methods. Fortunately, Keller agreed to take me on.

I began my new life as a Civil War historian by reading Allan Nevins's magisterial four-volume history of the war.[3] Meanwhile, I settled on Philadelphia as my "community" to study. I wanted to work on a community where I could find lots of diaries and letters and a range of newspapers, so, I thought, why not go with a city rather than a small town? New York was out because the city's draft riots were about the only home front event that had attracted scholarly attention. Boston, where I was living at the time, felt too isolated from military threat. Philadelphia seemed like a good choice because it was close enough to the seat of war that perhaps the city's civilians had occasionally feared for their safety. So I decided to take the city's largest circulation daily newspaper, the *Public Ledger*, and read it for the span of the entire war. As I recall, I approached this huge task with the very open mind of the social historian who was simply interested in how—if at all—the Civil War "affected" life on the home front. And as a quantifier, I was particularly attuned to any bits of evidence that might be counted. I took copious notes, jotted down themes, and identified and tracked patterns.

Let me skip ahead just over twenty years. I was at the University of Florida, teaching a graduate seminar on nineteenth-century America for first-year students. I had come to Gainesville in 2003, having spent the previous 17 years teaching at liberal arts colleges. I had made the move for many reasons, but largely because I wanted to be in just that sort of environment: working with talented graduate students. On this particular day, early in the fall semester, one of my students raised her hand and asked if I could say something about the new social history. There was something about the way she framed the question that made it seem as if she was asking me to explain what it was like to land on Normandy Beach, or perhaps just to recall the heady days when televisions were first invented. (First-year graduate students have a charming way of making one feel like a dinosaur.) If the question raised in that first Keller seminar meeting roughly explains how it was that I came to work on the Civil War home front, the innocent question posed in that second seminar explains part of the impulse behind this book.

. . .

This collection is really the product of two impulses. The first is the most obvious. Since I began working on the Civil War, I have published quite a few essays on aspects of the Northern home front. With the passage of time, some of those articles have become less easy to find, or at least they have become less likely to find their intended audiences. There are various forces at work here. Although we might speak of the Civil War home front as a cohesive field of study, the questions raised by the war attract the interest of scholars from various discrete fields. Thus, for instance, a piece on Civil War entrepreneurs published in a collection on American economic history will likely escape the notice of specialists in the war. An essay on gender and voluntarism in a Civil War collection might elude the woman's historian. And so on. Two of these articles were prepared for volumes honoring distinguished scholars: Morton Keller and my father, Robert Gallman. It is a great honor to be in those two collections, but neither volume has much to do with the Civil War, and thus I am pleased to have the chance to present those essays to a wider audience.

The second impulse behind this collection is less about the specific essays and more about how they might illustrate a professional trajectory. I hope that this volume might be read as an autobiographical reflection. But whereas most autobiographies claim to tell a particularly distinctive tale, I am hoping that there might be some interest in these essays as a narrative—at least to students— because they suggest pretty common patterns and perhaps illustrate some of the ways the discipline has evolved over the last quarter century or so.

## QUESTIONS, CONVERSATIONS, AND METHODS

I began my work on Civil War Philadelphia with an exceedingly broad question: How did the Civil War affect life in Philadelphia? In other words, I was asking the classic historian's questions about change and about causality. What, if any, changes did Philadelphians experience? Were those changes the result of the war? Given the huge significance of the Civil War in our nation's history, and the massive casualties suffered, the default assumption, I thought, must surely be that the war "changed everything" for all who lived through it. But as I embarked on the project, I had a few reasons to be skeptical, or at least to be open to grand continuities. First off, for several years I had been study- ing American economic history. For a generation or so, the new economic historians—including my father—had been applying economic theories and quantitative methods to familiar historical problems, uncovering new sources and reconsidering old evidence. (They were, in a sense, the intellectual first cousins of those new social historians who had been measuring mobility rates, demographic patterns, and the like.) One of the most intriguing arguments was that the Civil War had not really produced a grand "takeoff" into postwar economic growth and industrial development. In fact, shifts in growth predated the war, and military demands had a far less substantial and more ambiguous impact on the economy than had been previously supposed.

A further source of skepticism came from Morton Keller himself. Keller loved to point out the grand continuities in history that so often lie just below the tumult of daily life. His brilliant *Affairs of State* examined American public life in the decades after the Civil War, concluding that despite the war's upheavals, the postwar period was in many senses a time of retrenchment. When I read his book as a first-year graduate student, I was not buying much of that argument; but to paraphrase Mark Twain, as I got further into my research, I was pleased to discover how smart he became.

Finally, somewhere buried fairly deep in my consciousness was the war in Vietnam. I was 18 when the final helicopters left Saigon—too young to face the draft but old enough to be aware of the odd mix of experiences that characterized life on a wartime "home front." Among other things, I wanted to uncover how everyday folks lived life in the midst of that much larger conflict, much closer to home.

Today I stress to my graduate students that new monographs are almost always in conversation with other books. Sometimes they build upon previous insights; sometimes they argue against received wisdom. The good ones frequently borrow an idea or a question but move it onto entirely new terrain. When I started thinking about the Northern home front, I did not feel as if I was in conversation with anyone at all. The standard scholarly treatment of the topic had been published in 1910![4] In addition to the mounds of military studies, there was a large body of scholarship on wartime politics, but almost nothing existed on social and economic issues beyond the work on the war's economic impact. I read a bit here and there on other wars, and as my project crystallized into a series of topical chapters, I generally found useful theoretical and empirical work upon which to draw. Still, at the time there was no ongoing "conversation" about the Civil War home front at the time.

I suppose that this has something to do with what many young scholars thought about war itself. People who were drawn to the questions of social historians, and particularly to those of quantitative historians, sought long-term patterns, often anchored in census records and comparable statistical indices that did always not lend themselves to the close analysis of a few tumultuous years. Moreover, the pursuit of the everyday experiences of anonymous people seemed somehow at odds with a focus on the inherently unusual years of the war. And no doubt there was probably some post-Vietnam resistance to studying war at all.

My research method was ambitious to the point of foolishness. I defined my research agenda by what I was *not* going to address. I was not interested in battles or elections, except insofar as they framed attitudes, opinions, and experiences on the home front. I would steer clear of national debates over political issues like emancipation, civil liberties, conscription, and banking legislation, except where those debates found their way onto the streets of Philadelphia. (And they often did.) Apart from that, everything was pretty much fair game. I read widely, although certainly not exhaustively, in the city's newspapers. I read every diary and letter written by a Philadelphian that I could lay my hands on. I considered how Philadelphians responded to the war's ebbs and flows and how individual citizens handled the strains of separation and death. I went through the annual reports of societies formed to address a myriad of wartime concerns, but I also looked at the reports of societies that were unrelated to the war. I looked at the papers of labor unions, asking how the particular challenges of wartime shaped labor strategies and outcomes.

As a good cliometrician, I was ever alert for things that I might count. How did arrest patterns change over time? What sorts of crimes might have reflected the economic challenges posed by war? What disorders might have been caused by the movement of troops or the threat of a draft? I spent many months visiting Harvard's Baker Library, where I read the huge folio volumes of the R. G. Dun Credit Company, recording information on every local firm with any remote connection to the war and assembling a large sample of firms with no obvious wartime links. From this material I experimented with applying the insights of demography to the life expectancies of individual firms. I grew fascinated with maps of the city and started to think spatially (long before I thought theoretically about physical space). I mapped where volunteers from various philanthropic and fund-raising organizations lived. I asked whether military recruits followed the dictates of neighborhood, occupation, or both. I traced patriotic parade routes to see if I could distinguish some underlying message in their paths.

When I describe it this way, the research method sounds like a complete mishmash of approaches. I was essentially following the evidence in a host of directions, framed in some general way by a few key questions. As the project evolved, I came to believe that the wartime changes were not as dramatic as one might have expected. Thus, I built an interpretive framework arguing that throughout the war Philadelphia and its citizens engaged in a series of "adjustments" to the conflict, building upon past experience while rarely overturning established practice.

I was—both by method and training—being very empirical, even while I was doing my best to be rather creative. The changes and continuities I was finding were almost exclusively of the sort that could be seen with the naked eye and measured in some sense. Thus, I asked: What specific duties did women and men have in various organizations? Where did their names appear in the broadsides? Who worked the fundraising desks, and who counted the money? I looked at mourning practices by examining specific observable rituals, like cutting off locks of hair or recording last words. I compared (as best I could manage) the amount of fireworks fired off on successive Independence Day celebrations. I even tracked the number of violent altercations recorded in the *Public Ledger* that seemed to be prompted by political arguments. I was thinking like an empirical social historian.

As I was writing my dissertation, I made no effort to publish any parts of it, although its structure lent itself to that kind of treatment. In fact, I did not even give a conference paper on the project until very late in the game, and that was really grounded in the entirety of the dissertation rather than a particular theme.[5] (This runs counter to the advice I generally give my students.) My only excuse is that I had been very fortunate in my earlier work on colonial demography: I had already given several conference papers and I had a few articles in print, so the professional gamble was that my resume would be in good enough shape when I entered the job market.

This collection includes several pieces that emerged from the project that would become my first book, *Mastering Wartime: A Social History of Philadelphia during the Civil War*. None is precisely a chapter from that book, but all three rely on my dissertation research.[6] "Preserving the Peace: Order and Disorder in Civil War Philadelphia" examines the relationship between recruiting and wartime disorder. "Voluntarism in Wartime: Philadelphia's Great Central Fair" makes a comparable effort to bridge distinct wartime themes in a single essay—in this case, centralization and gender roles. "Entrepreneurial

Experiences in the Civil War: Evidence From Philadelphia" goes well behind the arguments and evidence I used in *Mastering Wartime* several years earlier.[7]

After *Mastering Wartime* was published in 1990, I was casting around for a new major project. By this point I was in a tenure-track position at Loyola College in Maryland, and I concluded that I could afford to be pretty ambitious in my future plans. Once again I thought it might be interesting to try to yoke a few different issues together. When I was a graduate student at Brandeis, the history department had two distinct doctoral programs: one in the history of American civilization, and the other in comparative history. My colleagues in the comparative program all worked on some aspect of European history, but their training—and by extension the training of the Americanists—included substantial attention to the virtues of thinking comparatively. It seemed to me that although American historians often wrote about the need for more comparative work across national boundaries, we rarely attempted to carry out that work. That sounded like an interesting challenge. Meanwhile, in my work on Philadelphia I came to conclude that the keys to Philadelphia's success in navigating the Civil War lay in the antebellum decades. Perhaps, I wondered, the city responded to the war's challenges so adroitly because it had an institutional history of dealing with exogenous shocks?

My interest in understanding how Philadelphia became the city it was in 1861 became intertwined with this notion that comparative history might be challenging and rewarding. Still thinking very much like a cliometrician, I tried to imagine an appropriate comparative "laboratory," preferably one that could let me draw upon my graduate field in Victorian England. What sort of challenge did antebellum Philadelphia share with British cities? Between 1830 and 1860, cities on both sides of the Atlantic struggled with a host of challenges associated with dramatic growth: crime, disease, poverty, sectarianism, and so on. It did not take long for me to conclude that the Irish famine migration represented an ideal laboratory. After some extensive contemplation of various options, I concluded that Liverpool and Philadelphia made for an excellent point of comparison.

I take this detour from my Civil War story for several purposes. First, I wish to point out that once again the interest in a broader historical question had led me to a new field of study. Before long I found myself knee-deep in several topical subfields, and in the history of a city I had never visited. More importantly, I had inadvertently given myself a new professional identity as an historian of immigration. I would have preferred to define myself as a comparative urban historian, or perhaps as a "crisis historian." But although I was really interested in how Irish immigration was a trigger for public policy responses in England and the United States, some of that subtle distinction was commonly lost in translation. In truth, I was naively not thinking much at all about professional identities one way or the other. I just thought that this sounded like an interesting project. It eventually resulted in my second book, *Receiving Erin's Children: Philadelphia, Liverpool, and the Irish Famine Migration, 1845–1855.*[8]

Another thing I did not think much about was that while I was plugging away on the 1840s and early 1850s, my colleagues in the field were only aware of my work on the Civil War home front. Shortly after I had begun work on *Receiving Erin's Children,* I received an invitation to write a broad, synthetic history of the Northern home front for Ivan R. Dee's American Ways series— what eventually became *The North Fights the Civil War.*[9] It was an interesting professional opportunity. Like many first authors, I think I was feeling a bit discouraged, because my first book seemed terribly expensive and thus the number of potential readers seemed small. Publishing a book for the American Ways series would give me a chance to expand my own thinking while perhaps allowing me to reach a broader audience. And having written my dissertation so close to my evidence, I thought it would be an interesting and even liberating experience to paint with a much broader brush.

## An Emerging Subfield

My work on *The North Fights the Civil War* also gave me a good excuse to keep reading the steady flow of new scholarship on the social history of the Civil War. And what an explosion it was. It turns out that while I was working on wartime Philadelphia, other young social historians were applying their own analytic lenses to the Civil War. At the end of *The North Fights the Civil War,* I included a short bibliographic essay, running about six printed pages. Today that essay is an excellent illustration of the pace of scholarly change. Only a handful of the books I cited had been published at the time I defended my dissertation. Over twenty of the most important titles appeared between 1990 and 1993. Suddenly a whole new subfield on the social history of the Civil War soldier emerged, with new books by Reid Mitchell, Gerald Linderman, and Joe Glatthaar.[10] Phillip Paludan completed the first overview of the Northern home front since Emerson David Fite's wonderful 1910 study, *Social and Economic Conditions in the North;* new monographs examined the wartime history of New York City, Chicago, the Pennsylvania coal fields, and the New York City draft riots.[11] Moreover, several scholars—including Mary Ryan, Lori Ginzberg, and Wendy Hamand Venet—tackled the lives of Northern women; Maris Vinovskis assembled a collection of essays on the Northern home front; and Catherine Clinton and Nina Silber published a pioneering collection of essays on gender and the war.[12] I did my best to come to terms with the main lines of this new work, although I felt as if I was trying to capture a subject in motion.

The *North Fights the Civil War* came out in 1994, four years after *Mastering Wartime*. Although by then I was thoroughly absorbed with Irish immigrants on both sides of the Atlantic, my colleagues in the field saw me as a home-front historian. That meant that I had a steady stream of interesting opportunities to write small pieces on aspects of the home front, while much of the latest scholarship found its way to my desk in the form of manuscripts to evaluate or books to review. And at Loyola my teaching rotation now included courses on the American Civil War and on American women's history.

In sum, as my scholarship concentrated on crime, cholera, quarantines, and sectarian violence, I was reading and admiring an impressive array of new work on the Civil War era. The emerging scholarship explored new topics and experimented with underexamined sources and—to me—unfamiliar methods. Quantitative techniques fell out of favor, and the already expansive notion of social history evolved to consider issues that fell under the rubric of cultural history. I was particularly interested in new work on nineteenth-century women, and especially those studies that expanded and complicated our notions of public participation. Several scholars—including Nina Silber, Lyde Clyde Sizer, and Alice Fahs—had applied sophisticated gender analysis to hitherto neglected novels and popular culture.[13] Others—most notably Stuart McConnell, David Blight, and Carol Reardon—had posed complicated challenges to our understanding of the meaning of legacy, history, and memory.[14] Twenty years earlier, it seemed as if the most interesting scholarship had simply ignored the Civil War as a bloody, uninteresting, historical aberration. Now the military historians were doing fascinating stuff and, more shockingly, the social and cultural historians were engaging their military historian colleagues.[15]

My own narrative took two turns at about the same time. In 1998 I accepted an appointment at Gettysburg College, where I was charged with creating and administering two interdisciplinary programs: a minor in Civil War Era Studies for Gettysburg College undergraduates and a Gettysburg Semester for visiting students. This meant that my teaching and administrative work concentrated almost exclusively on the diverse ways that scholars in various disciplines contemplated the Civil War era. Meanwhile, I had nearly completed *Receiving*

*Erin's Children* and I had begun work on a new project: a biographical study of the nineteenth-century orator, Anna Elizabeth Dickinson.[16]

In some senses the Dickinson project returned me to familiar terrain. Dickinson was a Philadelphian who rose to fame during the Civil War. I had first encountered her during my dissertation research. But for me the real appeal was that this project promised me the opportunity to engage with the exciting new scholarship on women in the public arena. I also thought it would be interesting to try writing a biography of a celebrated person after so many years of studying the anonymous and largely inarticulate.

My work on Dickinson drew me far away from the questions and methods of the new social history. Rather than trying to uncover the elusive life experiences of ordinary people living in extraordinary times, I was trying to figure out what we could learn by examining the life of an extraordinary woman. A quarter century earlier, I would have been appalled at the idea of studying the famous, but in fact I found the work to be great fun and the results interesting. It was particularly challenging to interweave a complex personal history with a significant public life, all the while trying to write for a general audience. I learned a tremendous amount by reading, and consulting with, the impressive lineup of scholars who had been working on nineteenth-century women. I also found myself thinking quite a bit about the nature of public discourse and the construction of fame. Dickinson, the individual woman, was in an ongoing conversation, in words and symbols, with the American public who defined her, celebrated her, and eventually lost interest in her. The project drew me into cultural history, studies of sexuality, discussions of the commodification of fame, some considerations of memory and the Civil War, and even some struggles with the nature of insanity. As I was researching the Dickinson biography, I had several opportunities to explore various related themes in invited lectures or essays. Several of those pieces appear in this collection.

At the time, I was responding to particular invitations and opportunities, but upon reflection I would claim that I was intentionally selecting topics out of the larger project that spoke to particular methodological issues and scholarly audiences. One essay, written in honor of Morton Keller, considers Dickinson as the subject of gendered political discourse. Another shifts the lens to consider Dickinson as the center of a swirl of friendships and relationships. Thanks to an invitation from my friends and colleagues Joan Waugh and Alice Fahs, I used Anna Dickinson's experiences in 1872 to offer my own take on the complex history of Civil War memory. Finally, as the project was coming a close, I wrote an essay that stitched together several topics of personal interest: Dickinson as orator and abolitionist; the wartime intersection of race, rhetoric, and masculinity; the military significance of black soldiers; and the underexamined Battle of Olustee, the largest Civil War battle fought in Florida. (Olustee had become particularly interesting to me because I had once again changed positions, moving to my current job at the University of Florida.)

The essays in this collection are snapshots about particular questions, bodies of evidence, and theoretical issues. Taken together, they map out a portion of my own professional evolution, from the questions that absorbed my attention when I was first thinking about the Civil War home front, to the issues that have seemed most interesting to me in the last few years. They also, I hope, offer an illustration of how our profession has evolved in the past several decades.

It should be obvious from reading this volume that I have accumulated many scholarly debts while preparing these essays. Some of those are acknowledged in the introductions to the individual pieces or in the accompanying notes. In preparing this collection my debts mounted. Thanks to Lesley Gordon, the editor of the Kent State University Press's Civil War in the North series, and to Joanna Craig and Joyce Harrison at the Kent State University Press. Thanks as well to Joan Waugh, Louise Newman, and Gary Gallagher for reading over this Introduction.

I suppose that I keep returning to the Civil War era because the period's questions continue to fascinate and challenge me. But I attend the conferences and seminars for the good times and the wonderful friendships. This volume is dedicated to four scholars who have each had some hand in what appears here. I dedicate it to them for all the laughter they have brought me along the way, and all the laughter yet to come.

J. MATTHEW GALLMAN
Gainesville, Florida

## NOTES

1. The pathbreaking trio of New England community studies were John Demos, *A Little Commonwealth: Family Life in Plymouth Colony* (New York: Oxford Univ. Press, 1970); Philip Greven, *Four Generations: Population, Land, and Family in Colonial Andover, Massachusetts* (Ithaca: Cornell Univ. Press, 1970); and Kenneth Lockridge, *A New England Town: The First Hundred Years, Dedham, Massachusetts, 1636–1736* (New York: Norton, 1970). Since I was working on colonial North Carolina, I was also drawn to the slightly more recent studies of the Chesapeake by Lorena Walsh, Lois Green Carr, Russell Menard, and Allan Kulikoff.

2. Robert Gross, *The Minutemen and Their World* (New York: Hill and Wang, 1976).

3. Allan Nevins, *The War for the Union,* four volumes (New York: Scribners, 1959–1971).

4. Emerson David Fite, *Social and Industrial Conditions in the North during the Civil War* (New York: Macmillan, 1910).

5. "Did the Civil War Accelerate Urban Centralization? Evidence from Philadelphia." *Organization of American Historians,* Reno, 1988.

6. The introductions to each essay will say a few words about the specific history behind the article.

7. *Mastering Wartime: A Social History of Philadelphia during the Civil* War (New York: Cambridge Univ. Press, 1990).

8. *Receiving Erin's Children: Philadelphia, Liverpool, and the Irish Famine Migration* (Chapel Hill: Univ. of North Carolina Press, 2000).

9. *The North Fights the Civil War: The Home Front* (Chicago: Ivan R. Dee, 1994).

10. Gerald Linderman, *Embattled Courage: The Experience of Combat in the American Civil War* (New York: Free Press, 1987); Reid Mitchell, *Civil War Soldiers* (New York: Viking, 1988); Joseph Glatthaar, *Forged in Battle: The Civil War Alliance of Black Soldiers and White Officers* (New York: Free Press, 1990).

11. Phillip Paludan, *A People's Contest: The Union and Civil War, 1861–1865* (New York: Harper and Row, 1988); Ernest McKay, *The Civil War in New York City* (Syracuse: Syracuse Univ. Press, 1990); Iver Bernstein, *The New York City Draft Riots: Their Significance for American Society and Politics in the Age of the Civil War* (New York: Oxford Univ. Press, 1990); Theodore Karamanski, *Rally 'round the Flag: Chicago and the Civil War* (Chicago: Nelson-Hall, 1990); Grace Palladino, *Another Civil War: Labor, Capital, and the State in the Anthracite Regions of Pennsylvania, 1840–68* (Urbana: Univ. of Illinois Press, 1990).

12. Mary Ryan, *Women in Public: Between Banners and Ballots, 1825–1880* (Baltimore: Johns Hopkins Univ. Press, 1990); Lori Ginzberg, *Women and the Work of Benevolence: Morality, Politics, and Class in the Nineteenth-Century United States* (New Haven: Yale Univ. Press, 1990); Wendy Hamand Venet, *Neither Ballots nor Bullets: Women Abolitionists and the Civil War* (Charlottesville: Univ. of Virginia Press, 1991); Maris Vinovskis, ed., *Toward a Social History of the American Civil War: Exploratory Essays* (New York: Cambridge Univ. Press, 1990); Catherine Clinton and Nina Silber, eds., *Divided Houses: Gender and the Civil War* (New York: Oxford Univ. Press, 1992).

13. Nina Silber, *The Romance of Reunion Northerners and the South, 1865–1900* (Chapel Hill: Univ. of North Carolina Press, 1993); Lyde Cullen Sizer, *The Political Work of Northern Women Writers and the Civil War, 1850–1872* (Chapel Hill: Univ. of North Carolina Press, 1993); Alice Fahs, *The Imagined Civil War: Popular Literature of the North and South, 1861–1865* (Chapel Hill: Univ. of North Carolina Press, 2001).

14. Stuart McConnell, *Glorious Contentment: The Grand Army of the Republic, 1865–1900* (Chapel Hill: Univ. of North Carolina Press, 1992); Carol Reardon, *Pickett's Charge in History and Memory* (Chapel Hill: Univ. of North Carolina Press, 1997); Lesley Gordon, *General George E. Pickett in Life and Legend* (Chapel Hill: Univ. of North Carolina Press, 1998); David Blight, *Race and Reunion: The Civil War in American Memory* (Cambridge: Harvard Univ. Press, 2001).

15. In fact, at the 1999 annual meetings of the Organization of American Historians in Toronto, a distinguished group of social, cultural, and military historians held a roundtable discussion on the thorny question, "What do military and cultural histories of the Civil War have to say to each other?" I was in the audience that day. As I recall, the panel included Stuart McConnell, Alice Fahs, Joan Waugh, Gary Gallagher, and Joe Glatthaar.

16. *America's Joan of Arc: The Life of Anna Elizabeth Dickinson* (New York: Oxford Univ. Press, 2006).

Northerners at War

# Voluntarism in Wartime

## Philadelphia's Great Central Fair

A few years after I completed my dissertation on Philadelphia during the Civil War, I received a letter from Maris A. Vinovskis. Vinovskis had just published an important article in the *Journal of American History* in which he asked, "Have social historians lost the Civil War?" Now he was assembling a collection of essays by social historians who were in a sense answering that question, and he wanted to know if I would take part. I jumped at the chance. The resulting volume, *Toward a Social History of the American Civil War* (Cambridge University Press, 1990), included Vinovskis's *JAH* piece and six essays by very young scholars, like myself.

My essay, on Philadelphia's 1864 Great Central Fair, was a compressed version of a much longer chapter from my dissertation, combined with some additional material on voluntarism from a different chapter. I was trying to use the fair to test two familiar aspects of the home front narrative: the notion that the war accelerated national centralization and the idea that wartime voluntarism propelled women into expanded public roles. The result is a highly empirical approach, perhaps too dense in the details even in this abbreviated version. But I do think that the two main threads stand up well. The fair was a huge event, but it did not just reflect "persistent localism" at its finest (the national United States Sanitary Commission had almost no role), it was also a highly decentralized event with labor scattered across the city and relatively little centralized control even at the local level. And although women were involved in great numbers, I argued that the fair's structure did little to challenge received gender norms, nor did it deviate much from antebellum practices.

The real point here was that something very large, like a huge wartime fundraising fair, is not in and of itself evidence of change. On the one hand, I am particularly pleased that I managed to get in several pages about the 1870s, raising the possibility that some of the most interesting changes in gender roles in voluntarism took place a decade after the war. On the other hand, I regret that some of the prose erases important racial, ethnic, and class differences within wartime Philadelphia. The efforts of the city's African Americans—who made up 4 percent of the city's population—are entirely invisible here (although they do appear elsewhere in the book).

*Toward a Social History of the American Civil War* has remained in print since 1990. Many of the essays have been staples in footnotes and bibliographies for years. My piece was reprinted—in an even more abbreviated form—in the second edition of Michael Perman's fine collection, *Major Problems in the Civil War and Reconstruction* (Houghton Mifflin: 1998).

.  .  .

In September 1864 Philadelphian John J. Thompson penned a lengthy description of America's "fearful ordeal" to a cousin overseas. Although there had been "gloomy and discouraging periods," as the conflict came to a close the iron manufacturer found cause for pride:

> The progress of our war has of course worked great changes in military and naval matters—but it has also developed an amount of sympathy, active, earnest and working, with suffering sick & wounded soldiers, such as has no parallel in the history of the world—The amount of volunteer labor on the battle fields, and in the Hospitals, has been extraordinary and the voluntary contributions by our citizens through the Sanitary Commissions amount to many millions of dollars in money & hundreds of tons in merchandize etc![1]

This enthusiasm for Civil War voluntarism was especially marked in Philadelphia. Soldiers passing through the City of Brotherly Love repeatedly paid tribute to its particularly benevolent citizenry.[2] As one French traveler reported, "Philadelphia has not lost her religious character; she remains equally faithful to her philanthropic traditions."[3]

## CIVIL WAR VOLUNTARISM

Thousands of Philadelphians took part in the "peoples' contest" from behind the lines by working at sewing circles, visiting hospitals, staffing refreshment saloons, or raising money for one of the score of local and national soldiers' aid organizations.[4] Philadelphia supported its own array of voluntary groups, but two national organizations—the United States Sanitary Commission (USSC) and the United States Christian Commission (USCC)—dominated the national scene. In the war's first months a New York group, led by Unitarian minister Henry W. Bellows, organized the USSC to improve health conditions for Union soldiers. Although military authorities initially disapproved of civilians on the battlefield, the Sanitary Commission soon gained official recognition and blossomed into an enormous national organization, bringing clothing and medical supplies to Union field hospitals. While the USSC was strongly conservative and militantly secular, the YMCA–sponsored Christian Commission, launched in November 1861, dispensed Bibles and evangelical enthusiasm with their blankets and bandages.[5]

Despite their differences, the two national commissions shared a common structure: Each had a central executive committee, regional branches based in major cities, and hundreds of local affiliates.[6] At the local level, both bodies were dominated by female volunteers.[7] As he closed the first of his four-volume *War for the Union*, Allen Nevins considered Northern society after a year of war and observed that "[a]ll over the map . . . voluntary effort had exhibited a vision and strength which shamed inertia and self-seeking. It was already clear that women could write a lustrous page in public affairs . . . and [the Sanitary Commission's] success was to show that a new era of national organization was opening." Three volumes later Nevins concluded that "[p]robably the greatest single change in American civilization in the war period . . . was the replacement of an organized nation by a highly organized society—organized, that is, on a national scale."[8]

These two interpretive threads—that the Civil War accelerated America's evolution toward "a highly organized society" and that the experience of women in the war's voluntary organizations helped thrust them into "public affairs"—are woven, usually independently, through much of the scholarship on American social history. In his analysis of the Sanitary Commission, George Fredrickson argued that "[i]ts success and the public acceptance of its policies . . . symbolized this new willingness of Americans to working large, impersonal organizations."[9] Anne Firor Scott has suggested that women's "long apprenticeship in [antebellum] voluntary associations" left them better prepared to orchestrate affairs on the home front than their male counterparts were to fight on the battlefield.[10] This wartime experience, in turn, she claims, aided women in the "process of inventing a public role" in the postwar decades.[11] Nancy Hewitt, in her study of women's activism in Rochester, New York, found that their voluntary experiences "led wartime workers into wider public service when the [Soldier's Aid Society] disbanded."[12]

## THE GREAT CENTRAL FAIR

### *Organization*

Between June 7 and June 28, 1864, Philadelphia held its Great Central Fair, which raised over $1 million to replenish the Sanitary Commission's dwindling funds. This grand event was the product of months of labor by thousands of Philadelphians. Its organization and character are an excellent lens through which to view life on the Philadelphia home front. Moreover, the fair offers an opportunity to examine the centralizing forces underlying wartime voluntarism and to investigate the role of women within the newly fashioned patriotic organizations.

The Sanitary Commission's "fair movement" began in Chicago in late 1863 with a ten-day fund-raising fair for its Northwestern Branch. This event earned nearly $80,000, a figure that was almost doubled one month later in Boston. Soon Cincinnati, Cleveland, Albany, Brooklyn, and St. Louis followed suit. New York's Metropolitan Fair, which cleared $1,183,505 in April 1864, was the most successful of these ventures, topping Philadelphia's total by about $150,000.[13] By the end of the war, roughly thirty "sanitary fairs" had been held, earning about $4.4 million. Some raised money for regional branches of the USSC; others collected funds for supplies to be sent to the home troops through Sanitary Commission channels. Over 80 percent of the $2.7 million funneled directly into the USSC's coffers came from the New York and Philadelphia fairs.

The Great Central Fair extended established practices. Antebellum Americans had often turned to fund-raising fairs to support civic charities, and as the Civil War progressed Philadelphians learned to rely on festive affairs to stir the patriotic sentiments of a war-weary citizenry.[14] But the sanitary fairs melded entertainment and benevolence in events that eclipsed anything in America's experience, in both scope and design. Like London's Great Exhibition of 1851, these fairs enticed their visitors with a wide array of manufacturing and artistic exhibits displaying local accomplishments and foreign curiosities. But whereas Prince Albert conceived of the Crystal Palace to showcase the marvels of industrial progress, the sanitary fairs' organizers devoted their ingenuity to creating diverse methods for extracting money from their guests' pockets.[15]

The initial impetus for Philadelphia's fair came from the highly patriotic Union League, which passed a resolution on January 11, 1864, asking the Philadelphia associates of the Sanitary Commission to join the nationwide fair movement. Two weeks later the USSC's local branch voted to put on a fair, under the supervision of an executive committee headed by prominent merchant John Welsh.[16] On February 20 the committee announced the coming fair in the city's newspapers. Its open letter set the tone for the ensuing months:

> We call on every workshop, factory, and mill for a specimen of the best thing it can turn out; on every artist, great and small, for one of his creations; on all loyal women for the exercise of their taste and industry; on farmers, for the products of their fields and dairies. The miner, the naturalist, the man of science, the traveler, can each send something that can at the very least be converted into a blanket that will warm, and may save from death, some one soldier who the government supplies have failed to reach.

The organizers sought to touch everyone by emphasizing that no gift would be too small.[17]

The Philadelphia fair's organizational structure was enormously complex, with over 3,000 volunteers in nearly 100 different committees, ranging from the 5-member Committee on Gas Fixtures to the roughly 330-strong Committee on Schools.[18] Most committees were organized around a particular craft or branch of manufacturing. A member visited each of the city's establishments in search of donations of cash or goods to be sold at the fair. Other committees solicited flowers, fruit, handmade items, or "Relics, Curiosities, and Autographs." Tea merchant L. Montgomery Bond's Committee on Labor, Income, and Revenue adopted a massive advertising campaign encouraging all Philadelphians to donate the proceeds of a day's work to the fair.[19]

## Volunteers

One of the first orders of business for the executive committee was to recruit people to chair the various committees. The burden of chairing a committee was large, and more than 40 nominees refused to serve.[20] Nevertheless, the executive committee enlisted many of Philadelphia's business leaders. J. B. Lippincott headed up the Committee on Book Publishers, Booksellers, and Bookbinders; David S. Brown, one of the region's largest textile manufacturers, chaired the

Wholesale Dry Goods Committee; William J. Horstmann, the proprietor of the city's foremost military uniform and regalia establishment, led the Committee on Military Goods.[21]

It was up to the chairs to form their own committees;[22] once formed, individual groups adopted quite different structures. The members of the Ladies' Committee on Boots, Shoes and Leather visited stores individually, only meeting periodically to report their progress and to discuss plans for decorating their display. The official list includes 26 women on the committee, but the minutes show that only 3 came to all six meetings, one-half came to four or more, and 2 never attended.[23] The minutes of the Women's Committee of the Children's Department of Toys and Small Wares reveal a far more complex infrastructure. Initially, this group of 33 women split into six subcommittees to visit local dealers. Later they formed seven topical subcommittees, which met separately (each keeping its own minutes) for the next month.[24] The all-male Wholesale Dry Goods Committee also had poor attendance at committee meetings, with most of the serious work being accomplished in smaller subcommittees.[25]

As with many peacetime organizations, the fair's committee structure divided men and women into separate but parallel bodies. Although the women's committees enjoyed substantial autonomy, their tasks often reflected different concerns and circumscribed gender roles. The Wholesale Dry Goods Committee voted to leave the designing of a suitable badge to their ladies' committee; the women's committee of the Children's Department of Toys and Small Wares left the construction of a Maypole to their male affiliates. The women's committees generally devoted special attention to determining the appropriate apparel for committee members to wear at the fair.[26]

Despite its enormous scale, the Great Central Fair was a notably decentralized, individualized event. At each level citizens sought to mold the fair to their own desires. Much of recording secretary H. H. Furness's time was devoted to sorting out squabbles among committee heads. These battles reflected the difficulties inherent in forcing independent-minded volunteers into a large cooperative structure.

Mrs. George Plitt, secretary of the Committee of Women and chair of the Women's Committee on Internal Arrangements, peppered the executive committee with notes on a wide range of issues. On March 15 she suggested to Furness that a Miss Blanche Howell should be removed from the published list because she was too young. Later she insisted on removing a woman's name from a chairwomanship because "no lady should be published as [chair] of

2 [committees]." As opening day approached, Mrs. Plitt suggested a Turkish Department to Mr. Welsh, demanded more stamps from Mr. Furness, and continued her efforts at "keeping the names of *sweet young girls* from the public eye" by excluding them from published committee lists.[27]

While Mrs. Plitt sought to have a hand in all of the fair's activities, other committee chairs were directing their groups like well-drilled armies battling for territory. The most violent controversy swirled around S. Montgomery Bond and his Labor, Income and Revenue Committee. This group used extensive newspaper advertising and personal visitation to solicit one day's wages or profits from every Philadelphian. When rival chairmen accused Bond of stealing their thunder, he complained that he was being victimized by "the carpings of others." He maintained that his methods earned more but said that he left certain territories alone when asked.[28]

Bond's usurpations led Alexander R. McHenry, the chairman of the Oil Committee, to dissolve that committee.[29] Soon after, McHenry wrote to the executive committee, this time wearing the hat of chairman of the Receiving Committee, to complain of further indignities. His committee had recently sold a gift of several dozen eggs and placed the receipts in the general funds rather than passing the profits on to the Restaurant Committee. The chair of the Restaurant Committee complained so bitterly about this slight that the executive committee passed a resolution barring similar actions in the future. McHenry became furious at the implication of this decision and wrote, "I will not consent to be placed in an unpleasant position again—I had enough of this in Mr. Bond's case." Although the executive committee rescinded what McHenry termed the "vote of censure," the damage was done. He kept his formal position but refused to reenter the fairgrounds.[30]

These battles suggest that within the fair's hierarchical structure, committees enjoyed a wide latitude and chairpersons acted as individuals, not as cogs in a patriotic machine. Similarly, many Philadelphians who were outside the fair's administrative structure viewed the event as their own. Both executive committee chairman Welsh and receiving secretary Furness regularly received letters from townspeople suggesting ways to improve the fair. One inventive writer argued that the executive committee should send a wagon through the city to collect rags, old shoes, and newspapers. He believed that such a venture "would raise $20,000 to $30,000." Another citizen took note of the annual infestation in Logan Square's trees and suggested that "a *committee on worms* is very much wanted." Other correspondents proposed separate committees for soaps and candles, auctions, fireworks, architects, ship owners, and engravers.[31] These people took their fair seriously, and sought to do their part, however small, to make it a success.

In her diary entry for April 4, 1864, Anna Ferris reported the opening of New York's Metropolitan Fair, noting that "every effort will be made to equal it in Phila. & everybody is at work to do what they can for the cause." She added that "the unselfish devotion to a great purpose makes life better."[32] Anna Blanchard shared Ferris's selflessness. As a member of the Restaurant Committee, she worked six-hour shifts and usually stayed late, "always finding there was something to be done."[33] Joseph Harrison, businessman and inventor, chaired the Fine Arts Committee, which put together the fair's Art Gallery. Several weeks before the fair opened, Harrison explained to a neglected business associate that "I have *much* to do in arranging my department of the Fair." A few days before the opening, he could only manage a hurried note to his friend while sitting in the middle of the Art Gallery, surrounded by busy workers. Soon Harrison put aside business entirely, explaining that "my time has been so much taken up with the Sanitary Fair . . . that I [have] little time to think of or do anything else." The results lightened his burden, however, because Harrison found the fair "a great success, particularly the Art Gallery, which has never been equalled in modern times."[34]

Whereas Harrison and Blanchard devoted long hours to the fair, others offered special talents to the cause. Dr. S. M. Landis volunteered to serve as a lecturer on phrenology, and Jonathan M. Thompson made his bookkeeping skills available.[35] Joseph Boggs Beale contributed his artistic talents by drawing an eagle for the Boys' Central High School Display; James Tyndale Mitchell lent his time to the Music Committee and his voice to several fund-raising concerts; Sydney George Fisher penned a poem "on the part woman plays in this war" for a poet's album to be sold at the fair.[36]

Like other wartime relief organizations, the fair relied on donations of money and goods. In some cases the gift entailed only a small sacrifice, but in other instances the offering was—to the giver—quite significant. Individuals flooded the Receiving Department with all manner of heirlooms, trinkets, handicrafts, and farm products. One Union League member donated a deed to a downtown plot of land valued at $500; another man offered to share the proceeds from a holding in Iowa worth $1,500. A Wilmington inventor wanted to raffle off his patent for coal-oil burners (splitting the profits with the Sanitary Commission), and a second inventor hoped to display his new gas stove. If these latter gifts appeared partly self-serving, the same could not be said for the man who sent pieces of wood he had collected at Gettysburg or the New Yorker who contributed 5 gallons of water from the Amazon River.[37]

Perhaps the most interesting assortment of gifts came to the Department of Singing Birds and Pet Animals. One poor woman wrote that since her husband would not give her any money she was sending six kittens. The offerings from the countryside included a pet donkey that purportedly had served in the War of 1812 and two white mice from China. One 10-year-old boy had only his black terrier to offer; the committee chairwoman gratefully accepted the donation, bought it herself, and returned it to its young owner. Finally, the chairwoman reported, there were "thirty-six parrots, well accustomed to low company," with vocabularies befitting their background.[38]

Numerous organizations and labor groups sent contributions to the fair. The employees of John Bromley's carpet factory gave $41.50; the city's policemen donated over $1,000 in wages; the men aboard the steamer *Ladona* offered a day's pay; members of Philadelphia's Anderson Troop collected items in the field; and the officers and crew of the ship of war *Constellation* sent $842.75 all the way from Italy. The fair also enjoyed one day's profits from an all-star baseball game; a traveling circus; the Chestnut Street Theater; several local railways; and Bird's Billiard Saloon.[39] Small businesspeople, such as dressmaker Mrs. E. C. Tilton and grocer Joshua Wright, offered part of their revenues; the Great Valley Association for the Detection of Horse Thieves sent $30.[40] The range of donations was limited only by the reach of citizens' imaginations. The Carpenters and Bricklayers helped construct the Logan Square buildings, and representatives of various fire departments agreed to cooperate to protect the fair from fire.[41]

Many businesses used the festivities for publicity. Newspapers reported on a fierce competition between sewing-machine companies, each seeking the title of most generous establishment in the city. The Singer Sewing Machine Company donated $300; three days later the Florence Sewing Machine Company matched that figure. The American Button Hole Machine Company gave two of its machines (valued at $650) and $50 in cash, which the Bulletin acknowledged as "the largest contribution of any sewing machine company so far."[42]

### Visitors

The 15,000 Philadelphians who attended the fair's opening ceremonies on June 7 viewed a scene that was "possibly the most imposing ever witnessed in Philadelphia." The procession to the speaker's stand consisted of the executive committee (which included many of Philadelphia's most prominent citizens); Mayor Alexander Henry; Bishop Matthew Simpson, of the Methodist Episcopal

Church, who represented President Lincoln during the ceremonies; selected clergy; the governors of Pennsylvania, Delaware, and New Jersey; General George Cadwalader and other military officers; members of the city council and several committee chairmen.[43]

The ceremony was marred by the sudden collapse of a hastily installed platform for the choir, but after a few moments of confusion the program continued.[44] In his welcoming speech Mayor Henry applauded the work of both national relief commissions, which, he said, had jointly provided "wide channels through which the oil and wine of soothing kindness and of strengthening cheer may flow." Governor Andrew Curtin added that "the work before this great nation is big enough for all."[45]

The visitor to the fair who made his way to the center of the Logan Square buildings found his senses assaulted by the smells from two large, canvas-domed rotundas housing the restaurant and the Horticultural Department.[46] From that central location, Union Avenue presented a crowded display of tables and flags for half a block in each direction. On the far side of the Horticultural Department stood the 500-foot long Art Gallery, featuring what was repeatedly referred to as the greatest collection of its kind in the nation's history.[47]

If the guest walked down Union Avenue, toward the Eighteenth Street exit, she passed displays of items such as umbrellas, glassware, and shoes; hallways on either side housed the exhibits built by the city's public and private schools, and the popular Arms and Trophies room. At the end of Union Avenue, she could choose between the Delaware display to her right and the New Jersey effort on the left. If she chose to turn around and meander back up Union Avenue, she found some of the most crowded exhibits, including the Pennsylvania Kitchen, the William Penn Parlor, the machinery and shipbuilding display, and a wide assortment of sewing machines.

While enjoying the splendor of the surroundings, the visitor had innumerable opportunities to give to the cause. Ticket sales earned nearly $180,000. Many visitors purchased items on sale at the committees' tables. Others spent $2 to vote on the recipient of one of the elegant gifts donated to the fair. And most took time to sample the restaurant's bill of fare, which ranged from mock turtle soup and lobster salad to an assortment of Hungarian wines.[48]

To do the fair justice required several days, and many Philadelphians returned frequently during the fair's three weeks. The city's newspapers—as well as the official *Our Daily Fare*—provided meticulous coverage of each department and event, seemingly competing to achieve the loftiest heights of hyperbole. The *North American and United States Gazette* promised that "[t]he exhibition will be . . . infinitely superior to all ordinary displays which have taken place in this city." The *Evening Bulletin* praised the "display of baby houses [as] without a parallel in the history of baby architecture."[49]

The evidence of contemporary diaries suggests that nearly every Philadelphian was aware of the fair, that most visited it, and that almost all were strongly enthusiastic. As early as March 10, Anna Blanchard wrote that "the town is in excitement in relation to [the] Great Central for the Sanitary." A month later Henry Benners noted that the fair buildings were progressing rapidly and that workers in his glass factory had each given a day's wage to the cause. And by the time opening day arrived, Anna Ferris reported that it "occupies the thoughts & interests of the public to the exclusion of most other things."[50]

Some were less pleased. George W. Fahnestock, who had already refused to serve as a committee member, complained bitterly of being "beset with circulars begging for everything," claiming—rather ironically—that "of course we need no such reminder of incentive to duty." Later he visited the fair buildings, recording his view that the whole affair seemed like "childs play particularly when the Sanitary Commission do not need the money." After he visited the fair, Fahnestock's litany of dissatisfaction included the crowds, the high prices, the "uncouth dances" of the "savages" at the Indian display, and the quality of the horticultural exhibit. But even this great cynic found himself swept up in the enthusiasm, and four days later he returned for four evening hours.[51] Another naysayer, 75-year-old Jacob Elfreth, Sr., dismissed the whole fair as a "waste of money." But although he never went himself, Elfreth's son and daughter were regular visitors, and he soon admitted that it "appears to be very attractive."[52]

Most Philadelphians needed no convincing. Joseph Boggs Beale visited the fair at least ten times; Susan Trautwine mentioned four visits; James Tyndale Mitchell went almost every day; Mary Dreer often went twice a day. Dr. Lewis Walker found it such a "magnificent display" that he bought season tickets and returned after dark to see the fair by gaslight. Sydney George Fisher called the event a "miracle of American spirit, energy, & beauty." Anna Ferris added that it was "the most wonderful display of everything under the sun." After his first visit, an enthusiastic Jacob Elfreth, Jr., made a lengthy journal entry in which he called the Horticultural Department the "most magnificent I ever saw," the Art Gallery the "largest collection of Pictures I ever saw," and the entire fair "the greatest collection of curiosities that ever was exhibited in this city." It was certainly, as Anna Blanchard put it, "an Exhibition of which [Philadelphia] may well be proud."[53]

On June 16 President and Mrs. Abraham Lincoln visited the city. Their short stay brought together public officeholders, civic leaders, and spontaneous crowds in a series of celebrations that reflected the complexity of both the war's rituals and its voluntarism. The Lincolns' carriage rolled down Broad Street toward the Continental Hotel amid cheering throngs, enjoying a general business holiday, massed on both sides.[54] In the afternoon, several Union League members met the city council at the Continental to escort Lincoln to the fair. Sydney George Fisher joined this group and "[w]as much pleased by [Lincoln's] contenance, voice and manner. He is," Fisher continued, "not awkward & uncouth as has been represented." But Jacob Elfreth, Jr.—who viewed the president from outside the hotel—found him "very tall and ungainly looking and not at all showy."[55]

The president pleased the throng waiting at the fair by vowing to fight for three more years, if necessary, and by applauding all the "voluntary contributions, given freely, zealously, and earnestly, on top of all the disturbances of business, the taxation, and burdens [of] the war." That evening Lincoln visited the Union League and the National Union Club, before returning to the Continental around midnight. There he found more crowds, a band, and a fireworks display. Lincoln later recalled that by the end of the day "I was the most used up that I ever remember to have been in my life."[56]

The fair's doors stayed open for a week after Lincoln's visit, but some of the novelty had worn off, and many of the best displays had been picked clean. On June 27 and 28 the committee lowered ticket prices from $1 to $.25, but still the turnout remained low. By the time the fair closed, 253,924 ticket holders had made an estimated 442,658 visits, an average of 29,510 visitors each day.[57]

Over 250,000 people bought tickets to the fair.[58] There were roughly 608,000 Philadelphians in 1864.[59] Even allowing for thousands of visitors from out of town, the fair attracted a large proportion of the city's population. Most accounts of the Great Central Fair stress that all segments of Philadelphia society combined to make it a success. Two months before the fair began George Fahnestock wrote, "Everybody is working for it, talking about it, begging for it. The newspapers are full of it—advertising columns and all—and everybody in town, male and female, is on some committee—self appointed or otherwise."[60] The *North American and United States Gazette* marveled at "how thoroughly this Great Fair has worked into the popular sympathy," and the *Bulletin* noted the "thousands of men, women and children" who worked for its success and the further "thousands who contributed money, labor, time, gifts or loans."[61] *Forney's War Press* made the case even more directly: "There

Although women numerically dominated many of the Great Central Fair's committees, the executive committee was entirely male, and where men and women formed parallel subcommittees the men consistently received top billing. In fact, the fair's organizers seemed particularly proud of this structure. As the event came to a close, *Our Daily Fare* looked back on the successful venture and concluded that "[o]ne of the distinguished features of this fair is that its management is more under the control of the gentlemen than any one which had preceded it."[80]

When the doors opened, the relationship between male and female volunteers seemed reminiscent of the gender roles within the Union Benevolent Association. Whereas in the peacetime organization men "managed" and women "visited," during the fair the men managed and the women attended to the selling. Certainly these efforts earned Philadelphia's women substantial notice. *Forney's War Press* applauded the efforts of women, who, "forbidden to fight or to vote for the Union," took this opportunity to aid the cause. "There is scarcely a department of the Fair," the editorial continued," [to] which the hand of woman has not added a charm."[81]

But generally such accolades revealed unflattering gender stereotypes. As opening day approached, the *Press* reported that "[t]he ladies are in a state of excitement about all the little details of the great display."[82] A male committee member wrote, "[W]e have agreed with every female member of our committees on every suggestion that they have made, and when you consider the variety of the suggestions, and their utter inconsistency . . . you may imagine the mental strain upon us."[83] *Our Daily Fare* consistently spoke condescendingly of female volunteers, who were "sending palpitations to the masculine heart" while selling their wares, and predicted "extra orders for wedding-cake and white stain, 'when this cruel fare is over.'" One observer described how enthusiastic committeewomen ignored all the "formalities of social intercourse" and, on occasion, bullied men like "accomplished overseer[s]."[84] And in response to those who questioned the fair's utility, *Our Daily Fare* pointed out that it had improved young ladies' skills in darning socks, sewing buttons, and writing with a graceful hand.[85]

In private some men appeared even less complimentary. One Philadelphian insisted on turning over his gift to a man, because "[a] woman is a woman" and should not be trusted with "property."[86] L. Montgomery Bond endorsed a proposed mock presidential election for women as an "amusing scheme" that would delight local women by given them "an opportunity for once in their lives to be heard on the great question of the Presidency" while also pleasing "the 'womens rights' people."[87]

As a large, citywide event designed to support a national patriotic organization, Philadelphia's Great Central Fair is a reasonable place to look for evidence of the Civil War's centralizing impulses. The widely recognized role of women in ensuring its success also makes the fair a logical starting point in a search for a widening role for women in the public sphere. But in both cases the signs of change seem outweighed by the evidence of persistent localism and gender divisions. A glance into the following decade emphasizes the point.

## The Centennial City

Eight years after Appomattox, the panic of 1873 sent the United States into a crippling depression, and philanthropy-minded Philadelphians faced a challenge reminiscent of 1861. As the city's existing charities did their best to meet the new demands, many Philadelphians followed tradition by forming emergency relief associations. Like their antebellum and wartime counterparts, these groups typically organized at emergency meetings to meet local needs. In most wards male officers and managers directed the local relief association and female visitors distributed relief to the needy. Thus, long after the war these new organizations turned to traditional gender differentiation, as well as to decentralized control, in response to crisis.[88]

But if Philadelphia's benevolent world in 1873 looked much as it had in 1860, the next several years saw signs of change. Although the established organizations did not alter their practices, the annual reports reveal slight shifts in the recognition of women's activities. For instance, in 1874 the PSEIP's report introduced a new page listing the Ladies' Auxiliary Committees and a separate "Report of the Ladies' Board of Managers."[89] The UBA's male managers dispensed with their report in 1874, deferring instead to the ladies' reports. The following year the managers' reports ran a short page and a half, whereas the ladies' report covered thirteen pages.[90]

The PSEIP's lists of managers also indicate continuity through the war decade and then a shift in the mid-1870s. Of 21 lady managers in 1871, 5 had been managers since before the war, 10 had served since at least 1863, and only 1 woman had been a manager for less than four years. Four years later, in 1875, only one of these 21 lady managers remained on the PSEIP's rolls. Among the society's 22 male managers in 1871, 10 had joined the ranks by 1863 and 14 had served for four years or more. But whereas the female membership turned over almost completely between 1871 and 1875, 14 male managers remained by the middle of the decade.[91] Were the PSEIP's new lady managers veterans of Civil War benevolence? None appears among the extensive committee lists for the 1864 sanitary fair. Perhaps they were active among the rank and file but deemed too young to have their names published.[92]

In 1876 Philadelphia hosted the nation's Centennial Exhibition. The exhibition's planning and organization followed some of the patterns set by the 1864 sanitary fair. But the two events were different, suggesting how circumstances had changed in the postwar decade.

In 1870, Philadelphia's Select Council officially resolved to hold an international exhibition to mark the centennial of the Declaration of Independence, and soon afterward the state legislature voted its support of the proposal. In the following year, Congress passed a bill naming Philadelphia the official site of the Centennial Exhibition and providing for the selection of exhibition commissioners from each state. In 1872 Congress authorized the creation of a Centennial Board of Finance to sell stock in the exhibition.

The Board of Finance, which was dominated by the same core of Philadelphia elites who had orchestrated the sanitary fair and Philadelphia's other wartime activities, had to raise $10 million to ensure the exhibition's success. In early 1873, the City Council appropriated $500,000 to the fund; eventually the city donated a total of $1.5 million. The state legislature added $1 million to finance the construction of a permanent Memorial Hall on the exhibition site. Philadelphians held numerous fund-raising mass meetings; the city's coal, railroad, and lumber companies made large donations, as did local publishers, fraternal societies, and various other economic and social organizations. But by mid-1874, only $1.5 million in stock had been sold. The federal government resisted requests that it provide financial support for the project, until finally, as the exhibitions opening day approached, Congress lent the Board of Finance $1.5 million to guarantee that the celebration would open.[93]

The Centennial Exhibition, modeled on the world's fairs held in London (1851), Paris (1855 and 1867), New York (1853), and Vienna (1873), featured displays of industrial progress from across the globe, filling more than two hundred buildings that covered 450 acres of Fairmount Park. Between May and November more than 10 million visitors came to Philadelphia to share in the celebration.[94]

How did the 1876 exhibition compare with the Great Central Fair of 1864? The exhibition's physical design was much like that of its wartime predecessor but on a grander scale. Both fairs featured special horticultural, art, and manufacturing displays. Each had a section reserved for guns and military regalia. Both boasted elaborate restaurants and oddities from around the world. For the visitor, the biggest difference was that the 1876 exhibition was much more ambitious than the earlier fair and included many more international displays. And while the sanitary fair was completely dismantled after a few weeks, the exhibition lasted for half a year, and some of its buildings remained as permanent structures.[95]

Apart from its scale and international aspect, one display in particular set the Centennial Exhibition apart from the wartime fair. In 1876 the Citizens' Centennial Finance Committee formed a women's committee headed by 13 prominent Philadelphia women. This body carried out a grass-roots fund-raising campaign that quickly collected $40,000. When it became evident that the Centennial Exhibition's male organizers had made no plans to display women's work, the women's committee collected an additional $30,000 to finance the construction of a women's building. The Women's Pavilion housed an eclectic assortment of displays, ranging from a 6-horse-power engine to a head carved out of butter, all produced by women. In a fair that heralded the nation's progress, this exhibit—unlike those of its wartime predecessor—explicitly acknowledged women's role in that development.[96]

A further difference between the two fairs was in their organization. Whereas the executive committee of Philadelphia's sanitary fair acted independently of the national Sanitary Commission and without any government aid, the 1876 exhibition received large donations from the city, state, and federal governments as well as financial support from foreign nations.[97] Still, both fairs relied on the direction of a handful of Philadelphia elites, the voluntary efforts of hundreds of local men and women, and the financial support of the city's businesses, fraternal societies, and private citizens.

In 1879 the formation of the Philadelphia Society for Organizing Charitable Relief and Repressing Mendicancy (PSOCR) marked a major milestone in the city's benevolent history. The organization, which had been formed to eliminate the evils of overlapping philanthropies, gave Philadelphia charities the centralized agency that the war years had lacked. The PSOCR's complicated structure included a wide array of subcommittees and an entirely male board of directors, which supervised the activities of affiliated organizations in each ward.[98]

The PSOCR and its ward associations introduced greater efficiency and organization into Philadelphia's benevolent world and also reflected an increased recognition of the role of Philadelphia's charitable women. The original plan followed tradition by placing women in circumscribed roles, attending to visitation and the like, while men served in the highest offices and controlled

the funds. But the *2nd Annual Report* included a call for increased "Coopera-
tion of Men and Women Workers" and even indicated that "in some wards
women had been placed on the Board of Directors."[99] By 1884 the Eighth
Ward Association had 5 male and 5 female directors; in 1888 the combined
Thirteenth and Fourteenth Wards Association reported an evenly balanced
board of directors and a woman superintendent.[100]

By the end of the 1870s Philadelphia's charities were increasingly centralized
and efficient, as well as more open to putting women in positions of authority.[101]
Those changes emerged in the postwar years, however. The city that set out
to stage a three-week fund-raising fair in 1864 relied on traditional practices
rather than recasting familiar ways.

## NOTES

Most of the material in this chapter appears, in a somewhat different form, in J. Matthew Gallman, *Mastering Wartime: A Social History of Philadelphia during the Civil War* (New York:
Cambridge University Press, 1990).

1. John J. Thompson to (cousin) John Thompson, September 26, 1864, Society Misc. Collection, Historical Society of Pennsylvania, Philadelphia (hereafter *HSP*).

2. See Emil Rosenblatt, ed., *Anti-Rebel: The Civil War Letters of Wilbur Fisk* (Croton-on-Hudson,
N.Y., 1983), 56; Christopher Pennell to "Migonne" [Sabra Snell], July 14, 1864, Christopher Pennell
Papers, Frost Library Archives, Amherst College, Amherst, Mass., transcribed by Daniel Cohen.

3. Auguste Laugel, *The United States During the Civil War*, ed. Allan Nevins (1866); reprint,
Bloomington, Ind., 1961), 177.

4. For a detailed discussion of these varied forms of wartime voluntarism, see J. Matthew
Gallman, *Mastering Wartime: A Social History of Philadelphia during the Civil War* (New York,
1990), Chapter 5.

5. See George M. Fredrickson, *The Inner Civil War: Northern Intellectuals and the Crisis
of the Union* (New York, 1965), 98–1112; Robert H. Bremner, "The Impact of the Civil War on
Philanthropy and Social welfare," *Civil War History*, 12 (September 1966), 293–307; Robert H.
Bremner, *The Public Good: Philanthropy and Welfare in the Civil War Era* (New York, 1980),
39–46, 54–62; William Q. Maxwell, *Lincoln's Fifth Wheel: The Sanitary Commission* (New York,
1956); [Linus Pierpont Brockett], *The Philanthropic Results of the War in America* (New York,
1984), 33–76, 96–164.

6. See Bremner, *Public Good*, esp. 58.

7. See Mary Elizabeth Massey, *Bonnet Brigades* (New York, 1966); Agatha Young, *The Women
and the Crisis* (New York, 1959); Frank Moore, *Women of the War; Their Heroism and Self-sacrifice*
(Hartford, Conn., 1866).

8. Allan Nevins, *The War for the Union*, 4 vols. (New York, 1959–71), 1:416; 4:395. See also 1:v.

9. Fredrickson, *Inner Civil War*, 111.

10. Anne Firor Scott, "On Seeing and Not Seeing: A Case of Historical Invisibility," *Journal
of American History*, 71 (June 1984), 12.

11. Anne Firor Scott, "Women's Voluntary Associations in the Forming of American Society," *Making the Invisible Woman Visible* (Urbana, Ill., 1984), 281–2.

12. Nancy A. Hewitt, *Women's Activism and Social Change: Rochester, New York, 1822–1872* (Ithaca, 1984), 201. Mary Ryan, in her study of Utica, New York, found that after their wartime voluntary experiences "it seemed that women were poised to make an assault on the male sphere and were determined to take direct control of municipal services." See Ryan, *Cradle of the Middle Class: The Family in Oneida County, New York, 1790–1865;* (New York, 1981), 213.

13. For good general background information on the fair movement, see William Y. Thompson, "Sanitary Fairs of the Civil War," *Civil War History,* 4 (March 1958), 51–67. Also see Philadelphia's official fair newspaper, *Our Daily Fare* (hereafter *ODF*).

14. On antebellum fairs, see Bremner, *Public Good,* 20; Catherine Clinton, *The Other Civil War: American Women in the Nineteenth Century* (New York, 1984), 81. For a good account of an 1841 fund-raising fair, see Isaac Mickle, *A Gentleman of Much Promise: The Diary of Isaac Mickle, 1837–1845,* ed. Philip English Mackey, 2 vols. (Philadelphia, 1977), 2:254, 291, 293–5. On wartime fund-raising, see Gallman, *Mastering Wartime,* Chapter 5.

15. Thompson, "Sanitary Fairs of the Civil War," 51–67; R. K. Webb, *Modern England* (New York, 1968), 278. For an excellent study of postwar expositions, see Robert W. Rydell, *All the World's a Fair: Visions of Empire at American International Expositions, 1876–1916* (Chicago, 1984).

16. *ODF,* June 20, 1864.

17. Furness Scrapbook, Box 1, H. H. Furness Papers, HSP.

18. *List of Committee Members of the Great Central Fair for the U.S. Sanitary Commission Held in Philadelphia* (Philadelphia, 1864). A copy of this pamphlet is in Box 5, F-1, Furness Papers.

19. *ODF,* September 11, 1865. This particular appeal, which netted $247,500, seems to have been a Philadelphia innovation. For a good description of Bond's visit to the Manayunk woolen mills, see *Germantown Telegraph,* June 15, 1864.

20. Box 5, F-2–F-5, Furness Papers.

21. *List of Committee Members.*

22. For a good description of the experiences of a committee chairman, see "Autobiography of William F. Miskey," 58, HSP.

23. Ladies' Committee on Boots, Shoes and Leather—Account Book and Minutes, Box 1, Furness Papers. Despite this poor attendance record, the committee collected $1,517.15 in cash, twelve morocco skins to be sold at the fair, and a wide assortment of shoes.

24. "Minute Book of the Children's Department of Toys & Small Wares—Great Central Fair, 1864," Minute Book, HSP.

25. Minute Book of the "Wholesale Dry Goods Department—Sanitary Commission Fair," HSP. The minutes of the Newspaper Committee and the Sword Committee reveal similar patterns of procedure, with various tasks being turned over to subcommittees, so that the committee as a whole met less frequently. See Society Misc. Collection, Leland Papers, HSP.

26. "Minute Book of the Children's Department of Toys & Small Wares"; Minute Book of the "Wholesale Dry Goods Department."

27. Box 7, F-1, F-2, Box 8, F-2, Furness Papers.

28. Bond to Furness, April 18, 19, 1864. Box 7, F-2, Furness Papers.

29. McHenry to Furness, April 22, 1864, Box 7, F-2, Furness Papers.

30. McHenry to Welsh, May 7, 9, 1864; Welsh to McHenry, May 9, 1864; McHenry to Furness, May 23, 1864, Box 8, F-2, Furness Papers.

31. Unsigned to Furness, April 18, 1864, Box 7, F-2, Furness Papers; Susan R. Barton to Furness, March 23, 1864, Box 7, F-1, Furness Papers; miscellaneous letters, Box 7, Furness Papers.

32. Anna Ferris diary, April 4, 1864, Film Ms-F, Swarthmore College, Swarthmore, Pa.

33. [Anna Blanchard] diary, June 1864, Anna Day Papers, HSP. This diary is not signed and is not identified by HSP. I have been able to attribute it to Anna Blanchard because of her position on the Restaurant Committee.

34. Joseph Harrison to Thomas Luders, May 17 and June 21, 1864, and undated June note, Harrison Letterbook, HSP.

35. S. M. Landis to Furness, undated, Box 5, F-1, Furness Papers; Thompson to Furness, March 16, 1864, Box 7, F-1, Furness Papers.

36. Joseph Boggs Beale diary, June 3, 1864, HSP; James Tyndale Mitchell diary, 1864, privately owned; Nicholas B. Wainwright, ed., *A Philadelphia Perspective: The Diary of Sydney George Fisher* (Philadelphia, 1967), 471, entry for April 25, 1864.

37. *ODF*, June 11, 1864; unsigned letters, June 22, 1864, Box 8, F-2; May 6, 1864, Box 8, F-2; undated, Box 7, F-2, all Furness Papers; USSC and Fair Papers, Box 1, F-2; Box 1, F-3, HSP.

38. *ODF*, June 11, 1864.

39. *Philadelphia Evening Bulletin,* June 4, 1864 (hereafter *EB*); Furness Scrapbook, Furness Papers; Suzanne Colton Wilson, ed., *Column South with the Fifteenth Pennsylvania Cavalry* (Flagstaff, Ariz., 1960), 62; *EB,* June 13, 1864; Philadelphia *Press*, May 25, 30, 1864; Furness Scrapbook.

40. *Press,* May 2, 3, 1864; *EB,* June 13, 1864.

41. *Press,* May 7, 1864; Furness Scrapbook.

42. *Press,* May 28, 31, 1864; *EB,* June 3, 1864.

43. *ODF*, June 8, 1864. The fair was actually less crowded for the inaugural ceremonies than it was on later days, because the admission price had been doubled to $2 for the day.

44. *EB,* June 8, 1864.

45. *ODF*, June 8, 1864.

46. This description of the fair is from a combination of newspaper and diary accounts, *ODF*, and *Godey's Lady's Book* (August 1864), 179 and (September 1864), 262. A map of the fairgrounds is on the frontispiece of the bound collection of *ODF*, which was printed immediately following the fair.

47. Wainwright, ed., *a Philadelphia Perspective,* 474, entry for June 12, 1864.

48. The gifts to be voted on included a sword valued at $2,500, to be presented to a Union general; a silver trumpet, for the most popular fire company; and a bonnet, for the city's favorite general's wife. *ODF.* For the restaurant menu, see Helena Hubbell, "Civil War Scrapbook," Book 2, *HSP.*

49. *North American and United States Gazette,* June 3, 1864, *EB,* June 9, 1864. The account went on to refer to the play houses as "palatial juvenile establishments."

50. Blanchard diary, March 10, 1864; Benners diary, April 12, 1864; A. Ferris diary, June 8, 1864. For an excellent firsthand account in a published form, see Wilson, ed., *Column South,* 163–4.

51. George W. Fahnestock diary, 1864, *HSP.*

52. Jacob Elfreth, Sr. diary, June 7, 11, 1864, Haverford College Library, Haverford College.

53. Lewis Walker diary, June 17, 1864, *HSP*; Wainwright, ed., *A Philadelphia Perspective,* 473, entry for June 7, 1864; A. Ferris diary, June 9, 1864; Jacob Elfreth, Jr., diary, June 15, 1864, Haverford; Blanchard diary, June 1864.

54. For descriptions of Lincoln's visit, see *ODF*, June 17, 18, 1864; Maxwell Whiteman, *Gentlemen in Crisis: The First Century of the Union League of Philadelphia, 1862–1962* (Philadelphia, 1975), 71–76; *EB,* June 16–18, 1864; and Kenneth A. Bernard, *Lincoln and the Music of the Civil War* (Caldwell, Idaho, 1966), 216–18.

55. Wainwright, ed., *A Philadelphia Perspective*, 475, entry of June 16, 1864; Jacob Elfreth, Jr. diary, June 18, 1864.

56. *EB*, June 16, 17, 1864; Bernard, *Lincoln and the Music*, 217.

57. *EB*, June 25, 1864; *ODF*, September 11, 1864.

58. *ODF*, September 11, 1864.

59. Roger Lane, *Violent Death in the City: Suicide, Accident and Murder in Nineteenth Century Philadelphia* (Cambridge, Mass., 1979), 11.

60. Fahnestock diary, April 5, 1864.

61. *North American and United States Gazette*, June 4, 1864; *EB*, 4, June 25, 1864.

62. *Forney's War Press*, June 11, 1864, in Furness Scrapbook.

63. *Press*, May 17, 1864. The decision to reduce the admission fee to $.25 for the last two days was made explicitly to accommodate "the poor" in Philadelphia. See *EB*, June 15, 1864.

64. Circular of the Committee on Labor, Income and Revenue, dated March 28, 1864; Circular of the Committee on Looking Glasses, Picture Frames and Gilt Ornaments, dated March 15, 1864; Circular of the Committee on Sewing Women, undated. All circulars in the Great Sanitary Fair—Misc. File, HSP.

65. *Philadelphia Public Ledger*, May 6, 1864 (hereafter *PL*); *Press*, May 12, 1864; *ODF*, June 8, 1864; *EB*, June 10, 1864. See also *PL*, June 7, 1864, and numerous other newspaper editorials for discussions of patriotism and the fair.

66. Furness Papers; *EB*, June 2, 1864.

67. *ODF*, June 13, 1864.

68. *EB*, June 18, 1864. Also see *PL*, May 14, 1864, and *EB*, June 3, 1864. In a speech to the committee chairmen, the Sanitary Commission's Dr. Henry Bellows challenged Philadelphians to beat the standard established by other Northern cities. "Miskey Autobiography," 58.

69. *List of Committees*. The occupations are taken from *McElroy's City Directory*. The same pattern holds true for the Bakers Committee and presumably for the other committees organized around trades.

70. Isaac Collins and John Powell, *A List of Some of the Benevolent Institutions of the City of Philadelphia* (Philadelphia, 1859); Eudice Glassberg, "Philadelphians in Need: Client Experiences with Two Philadelphia Benevolent Societies, 1830–1880," Ph.D. diss., University of Philadelphia, 1979, 4. For a discussion of the variety of antebellum benevolent societies, see Bremner, *Public Good*, 14–34.

71. *Constitution of the Union Benevolent Association* (Philadelphia, 1831); Union Benevolent Association, 25th–29th *Annual Reports* (Philadelphia, 1856–60). *Constitution of the Philadelphia Society for the Employment and Instruction of the Poor* (Philadelphia, 1847, 1852); Glassberg, "Philadelphians in Need," 147–51, 258, 272–4. See also Gallman, *Mastering Wartime*, Chapter 5. The PSEIP began with a Board of Managers that included both men and women, but soon the female managers became relegated to an auxiliary board.

72. See Gallman, *Mastering Wartime*, Chapter 5.

73. Citizens' Volunteer Hospital Association, *2nd Annual Report* (Philadelphia, 1864).

74. Allan Nevins used the quoted phrases as the subtitles to his four-volume *War for the Union*, for (respectively) volumes 1 and 2 and volumes 3 and 4.

75. Fredrickson, *Inner Civil War*, 98–112. In her study of benevolent women, Lori Ginzberg accepts Fredrickson's argument that the USSC dominated wartime giving and acted as a force for both efficiency and centralization. "Women and the Work of Benevolence," Ph.D. diss., Yale University, 1984, Chapter 5.

76. Gallman, *Mastering Wartime*, Chapter 5.

77. *ODF*, June 20, 1864. In fact, the local members of the Sanitary Commission had resisted

joining the fair movement because they felt that the flow of donations from Philadelphians was already adequate. It is also telling that the histories of the various city fairs reveal a wide range of origins and structures. See *ODF.*

78. The sanitary fair was also an entirely private event. Local politicians participated in the opening ceremonies, but no public monies went to supporting the fair. See Gallman, *Mastering Wartime,* Chapter 6.

79. See L. P. Brockett and Mary C. Vaughan, *Women's Work in the Civil War: A Record of Heroism, Patriotism, and Patience* (Philadelphia, 1867); Moore, *Women of the War;* [Brockett], *Philanthropic Results.* For a particularly glowing description of the activities of Philadelphia's women, see Septima M. Collis, *A Woman's War Record, 1861–1865* (New York, 1889), 12–13.

80. *ODF,* June 20, 1864. In other cities this was not the case. The Chicago, New York, and Poughkeepsie fairs were all sparked by women. *Our Daily Fare's* Boston correspondent was proud to describe that city's fund-raiser as "a Ladies' Fair." *ODF,* June 9, 13, 15, 16, 1864.

81. *Forney's War Press,* June 11, 1864. Clipping in Furness Papers, Box 2, HSP.

82. *Press,* May 17, 1864. Two weeks later the paper added that "[t]he women are in a state of delightful excitement." *Press,* May 31, 1864.

83. *ODF,* June 9, 1864.

84. Ibid., June 9, 10, 1864. References to the "attractive" and "charming" saleswomen appear in nearly every issue of the fair's official newspaper.

85. Ibid., June 8, 1864.

86. Ibid., June 11, 1864.

87. Montgomery Bond to Welsh, April 28, 1864, Furness Papers, Box 7.

88. See *Report of the Tenth Ward Citizens' Association* (Philadelphia, 1874); *Report of the Executive Committee of the Fourteenth Ward Relief Association* (Philadelphia, 1874); *The Germantown Relief Society* (Philadelphia, 1875) (this is a four-page pamphlet describing the society's aims); *Fourth Annual Report of the Board of Managers of the Germantown Relief Society* (Philadelphia, 1877).

89. The society's next two annual reports continued these new features and took particular care to acknowledge the efforts of the Ladies' Branch. PSEIP, *27th Annual Report* (Philadelphia, 1875) and *28th Annual Report* (Philadelphia, 1875); *29th Annual Report* (Philadelphia, 1876).

90. UBA, *43rd Annual Report* (Philadelphia, 1875) and *44th Annual Report* (Philadelphia, 1875). Of course this slight shift in the annual reports does not suggest a movement toward balanced gender roles in the UBA or the PSEIP.

91. PSEIP, 4th–28th *Annual Reports* (1851–75).

92. Seventeen of the PSEIP's 22 lady managers in 1875 were unmarried. Thus, their absence from the sanitary fair committee lists does not merely reflect postwar name changes through marriage. The wartime committee lists did include younger women, but the correspondence suggests that younger girls were sometimes kept off the lists. The membership lists of the all-female Indigent Widows' and Single Women's Society also suggest strong continuities over the war decade. Twenty of 24 officers and managers in 1859 were still serving in 1866 (2 others were unmarried in 1859 and might have appeared in 1866 under married names). By 1873, 14 of the 1859 officers and managers remained, *22nd Annual Report* (Philadelphia, 1859); *49th Annual Report* (Philadelphia, 1866); *55th Annual Report* (Philadelphia, 1873).

93. Faith K. Pizor, "Preparations for the Centennial Exhibition of 1876," *Pennsylvania Magazine of History and Biography,* 94 (April 1970), 213–19, 2.13, 228, 231; Whiteman, *Gentlemen in Crisis,* 132; Dorothy Gondos Beers, "The Centennial City, 1865–1876," in *Philadelphia: A 300-Year History,* ed. Russell F. Weigley (New York, 1982), 460–70. John Welsh—who had headed the executive committee of the sanitary fair—served as president of the Board of Finance, which had 15 Philadelphians among its 25 members. Welsh and 7 other board members had been founding members of the

Union League. For an excellent description of the exhibition, see James D. McCabe, *The Illustrated History of the Centennial Exhibition* (1876; reprint, Philadelphia, 1975). Rydell's *All the World's a Fair* devotes a chapter to the Centennial Exhibition but does not address the issues discussed here (9–37).

94. Beers, "Centennial City," 213–14. For visitors' descriptions, see William Randel, ed., "John Lewis Reports the Centennial," *Philadelphia Magazine of History and Biography*, 79 (July 1955), 365–74; William H. Crew, ed., "Centennial Notes," *Pennsylvania Magazine of History and Biography*, 100 (July 1976), 410–13.

95. The events also differed in that each part of the Great Central Fair was designed to raise money, while the Centennial Exhibition's organizers sought to celebrate the national anniversary by displaying America's technological progress to the world. Whereas the sanitary fair had been stocked with tables of items for visitors to purchase, the exhibition's displays were not for sale.

96. Beers, "Centennial City," 461; McCabe, *Illustrated History*, 218–20; Randel, ed., "John Lewis Reports the Centennial," 369.

97. Of course the Centennial Exhibition enjoyed such broad support because it was not a local event but a national celebration hosted by Philadelphia.

98. Philadelphia Society for Organizing Charitable Relief and Repressing Mendicancy, *1st Annual Report* (Philadelphia, 1879); *Suggested By-Laws for Ward Associations* (Philadelphia, 1878).

99. PSOCR, *2nd Annual Report* (Philadelphia, 1880).

100. Eighth Ward Association of the Philadelphia Society for Organizing Charity, *6th Annual Report* (Philadelphia, 1884); Thirteenth and Fourteenth Wards Association of the Philadelphia Society for Organizing Charity, *8th Annual Report* (Philadelphia, 1888). The evidence is too spotty to detect a shift in the practices of any particular ward association, but in 1881 the Tenth Ward Association reported a more traditional structure, with men serving as officers and directors and women acting as officers of their own "Corps of Visitors," *3rd Annual Report*.

101. But gender differentiation did persist. The women in the Society for Organizing Charitable Relief still did the bulk of the visiting, much as they had for decades in the UBA. In 1881 the ladies of the Indigent Widows' and Single Women's Society reported that extensive repairs to their building had been made, "under the wise direction of an efficient committee of gentlemen." Twenty-eight years before, they had thanked a similar body of gentlemen for almost identical assistance. *64th Annual Report* (Philadelphia, 1881); *36th Annual Report* (Philadelphia 1853).

# *Preserving the Peace*

## Order and Disorder in Civil War Philadelphia

Like "Voluntarism in Wartime," this essay represents a distillation and reorganization of material from one chapter in *Mastering Wartime,* framed around a set of questions that I found particularly interesting. But in this case, the path to publication was more circuitous, and a bit strange.

The year after I defended the dissertation, my old friend Cheryl Greenberg—who had just defended her dissertation on Harlem during the Great Depression at Columbia University—and I decided to put together the panel "Cities Under Crisis" for the 1987 meetings of the Social Science History Association. (This seemed like a good idea since the meetings were going to be held in New Orleans.) I was particularly pleased because Roger Lane, the great historian of crime and violence, attended our session and made a few suggestions from the floor. Shortly afterwards, I received a notice that the journal *Pennsylvania History* had some unexpected openings, leading them to solicit proposals for immediate consideration. I rushed off my unedited paper with a cover letter promising further revisions if the journal was interested. Many months later they wrote that there had been some mix-up and in fact it was not the journal that had been soliciting contributions but the annual meetings of the Pennsylvania Historical Association. But the folks at the PHA had kindly sent my contribution on to *Pennsylvania History.* Many more months after that, I heard from the journal and was appalled to learn that Roger Lane was one of the readers. I was appalled because—as he noted in his letter—what he had read was word for word what he had heard in New Orleans nearly a year earlier, unrevised based on his earlier suggestions! Fortunately, Roger was very understanding when I explained the essay's peculiar history.

"Preserving the Peace" really discusses two themes that I found particularly interesting: recruiting and policing. Although there had been no systematic study of wartime rioting, quite a few scholars had written case studies of particular draft riots, and of course New York City's draft riot had produced quite a bit of work. And there were some first-rate institutional histories of recruiting and conscription in the North. Meanwhile, some of the most interesting scholarship on nineteenth-century cities had considered the rise of American police departments. This essay attempted to bridge those topics by asking why Philadelphia, with its long history of urban violence, was relatively calm during the Civil War.

This essay is a good illustration of some of the larger themes in *Mastering Wartime*. It is a piece trying to explain what Sherlock Holmes called the dog that doesn't bark. Given all the sources of tensions in wartime Philadelphia, and the city's reputation for disorder, how did Philadelphia survive four years of conflict with relatively little domestic violence? I offer a few explanations, including a very successful recruiting campaign (which reduced the need for conscription) and an unusually savvy mayor. But I argue that the real answer lay in antebellum Philadelphia. The famed 1844 riots that had branded the City of Brotherly Love with a violent reputation had also left it with an unusually well-organized and violent police force. Or, to put the argument more broadly, I was arguing in this essay that the keys to Philadelphia's wartime experience could be found in its antebellum history. Thus, although the war years presented unprecedented challenges, the city's wartime experiences included broad continuities with the prewar decades.[1]

If I were to write this essay today, I would use the occasion to blur the lines between battlefield and home front even further. Here I emphasized the relationship between local voluntarism and military recruiting, but in the broader scheme of things the story of wartime recruiting and conscription illustrates how events at home were intrinsically linked to success on the battlefield.

## NOTES

1. Much later I would try to explore these issues more fully by writing a book about Philadelphia (and Liverpool) during the 1840s and 1850s, *Receiving Erin's Children: Philadelphia, Liverpool, and the Irish Famine Migration, 1845–1855* (Chapel Hill: Univ. of North Carolina Press, 2000).

. . .

After nearly 125 years of scrutiny, the American Civil War remains a fertile ground for historical inquiry. But while we know much about political developments, military strategies and battlefield experiences, our knowledge of life on the Northern home front remains meager. One aspect of the home front experience has attracted widespread notice. Numerous scholars have noted that the wartime tensions in general, and those surrounding conscription in particular, led to periodic outbreaks of rioting, with the bloodiest occurring in New York in July 1863. This essay will use those disorderly episodes as a backdrop to explore a less dramatic facet of Philadelphia's wartime experience: Despite ample provocation, serious rioting never disrupted the City of Brotherly Love.[1]

It is a bit tricky to claim that a particular place and time was "orderly." How does an historian ask the historical record such a question? Newspapers or diarists rarely note that a city is unusually orderly. Those who are likely to make public statements on the issue generally have an axe to grind. Mayor Alexander Henry—a gentleman who emerges as something of a hero in this piece—noted the "almost uninterrupted order and quiet of the city" in the war's first year and added similar pronouncements in his next three annual reports.[2] But we probably should not hang a judgment on the words of the man charged with keeping the city calm. While Henry's optimistic words support the point, the conclusion that wartime Philadelphia was relatively calm rests on a broad reading of sources—both newspapers and personal papers—that *should* have revealed unusual disruptions.[3]

Of course such a conclusion implies some frame of reference. How much disorder must there be before a city is no longer "orderly?" Wartime Philadelphia appears orderly when measured against antebellum Philadelphia or against other wartime cities. On the eve of the Civil War Philadelphia had a long tradition of rioting. One historian, noting battles involving Irish immigrants, handloom weavers, rival fire companies and anti-abolitionist mobs, has called the three post-war decades "the bloodiest period Philadelphia has known."[4] The city's most violent mobs roamed the streets during the 1844 riots which stemmed from rising hostilities towards the city's Irish. Two altercations, in May and July, left at least eighteen dead, as many as ninety wounded, and an enormous amount of property destroyed.[5] In New York's July 1863 riot mobs of predominantly Irish New York workers responded to the Draft with four days of violence which left roughly 120 dead and 200 seriously wounded.[6] In numerous other Northern cities and towns citizens responded to conscription with serious, if less devastating, violence.[7] As we shall see, although potentially disruptive tensions often flared up in Philadelphia, apparently the various war-related conflicts claimed only one victim.[8]

APRIL 1861

The story begins in the hours after the firing on Fort Sumter. As news filtered into the city, Philadelphians took to the streets in search of more information. Soon crowds formed on streetcorners and in front of newspaper office bulletin boards. Although many in the city had favored peaceful compromise with the South, once war began Philadelphia's streets were dominated by ardent patriots. As tensions mounted, anyone who seemed to support the young Confederacy risked mob violence. One citizen's comments on the "alleged wrongs of the South" attracted a substantial mob, forcing him to take refuge in a Chestnut Street drug store. Later that evening a crowd forced an intoxicated Southern sympathizer to raise his hat and give three cheers for the Union. A third secessionist had his clothes ripped from his back, mobs threatened another with lynching, and several others were roughed up in the first days after Fort Sumter's fall.[9]

But such actions were only incidental to the mob's larger agenda. On April 15th, the day after Sumter's fall, crowds gathered at the Chestnut Street office of the strongly pro-Southern *Palmetto Flag*. From there they rushed to the homes of several wealthy Southerners (whose names and addresses were conveniently listed in a local newspaper) demanding shows of patriotism. For the next several days mobs swept through Philadelphia's streets visiting hotels, colleges, newspaper offices and other prominent institutions.[10]

Many local diarists noted the wandering mobs and feared for their city, but despite rising tensions the disorder did not really amount to very much.[11] On April 18th one citizen passing through the city found "the streets all a flutter with flags" and confidently reported that "we are not likely to suffer from the greater evil of partisan war among ourselves."[12] In fact, several days of tension resulted in very little damage. Buildings were visited, but none were burned to the ground; secessionists were harassed, but none were killed and apparently no one was seriously injured. In short, by the standards of the nineteenth century city, Philadelphia's April 1861 disorders appear almost trivial. What explains this relative calm? Four forces combined to maintain calm in the war's first few days; the first three depended on Mayor Henry for their success.

At the first appearance of danger the Mayor used his own powers of persuasion to mollify the crowd. When the mob threatened the *Palmetto Flag's* offices, Henry personally appeared at an upstairs window waving a small flag and deftly calmed the crowd with a spirited speech.[13] On the second day of rioting Henry once again stepped in to restore order, but this time he turned to preemptive actions to make his point. When a crowd gathered at the home of prominent Democrat William Reed, Henry arrived with a squad of policemen and announced that they would shoot to maintain the peace. Faced with this threat the mob quickly dispersed.[14] Finally, Philadelphia's intrepid Mayor turned to official threats to encourage citizens to return to their homes. On April 17th the newspapers printed a mayoral proclamation announcing that both individuals suspected of aiding the enemy and those guilty of "assembly in the highways of the city, unlawfully, riotously, or tumultuously" would be subjected to arrest.[15]

With these three techniques—personal appearances, preemptive police activity, and threatening announcements—Henry managed to maintain calm in the face of extreme tensions. To these we should add a fourth force: mob intimidation. While many Southerners and Southern sympathizers lived in Philadelphia, that April the streets were ruled by rabid anti-secessionists. Most who supported the infant Confederacy quietly slipped out of town, joined the *Palmetto Flag* (which shut down its operations) in judicious silence, or decorated their homes and offices with flags and banners. As one man put it: "It is at the risk of any man's life that he utters publicly a sentiment in favor of secession or the South."[16] Thus, public pressure helped maintain order by silencing the opposition.

The first days after Fort Sumter's fall established several patterns which were to mark Philadelphia's experience for the next four years. Frequently tensions precipitated widespread concern for order in the city, but rarely were these fears realized. And those tools which kept the city calm in April 1861 served it well in the years to come.

## ORDERLY PHILADELPHIA

In 1861 Philadelphia had numerous traits that could easily have provoked violent disorder in the years to come. Many members of the city's elite were of Southern stock and much of the local economy relied on trade with slave states. Philadelphia also combined a greater proportion of blacks, four percent, than any other Northern city,[17] with a widespread antipathy to abolition. In the pivotal election of 1860, Lincoln received only 52% of the Philadelphia vote as compared with 57% statewide. Moreover, local candidates spurned the Republican label (opting to run as the People's party), while stressing tariff issues and ignoring abolitionism.[18]

If the city's population contained the "preconditions" for disorder, the war's events certainly provided numerous potential catalysts. On several occasions inflammatory tensions developed when crowds gathered at the city's various newspaper bulletin boards to learn the latest news from the battlefield. After Confederate soldiers routed Union troops at the Second Battle of Bull Run, for instance, Philadelphians were greeted with posted headlines from the New York *Tribune* (incorrectly) reporting that the Union army had been destroyed and Lincoln had denounced McClellan as a traitor. In the resulting confusion, one diarist reported "quarrels & fighting in the streets" while the *Ledger* described angry assaults on several anti-McClellan men.[19] The offices of the Democratic *Age* attracted an angry mob in May 1863 by posting headlines applauding General Hooker's defeat at Chancellorsville.[20]

While losses on the battlefield led angry citizens to cast about for a victim on whom to vent their rage, political contests combined equally dramatic passions with immediately apparent enemies. As the war progressed, Lincoln's policies—arbitrary arrests, greenbacks, conscription, emancipation, taxation—provided ample fuel for the loyal and disloyal opposition within the North. By the fall of 1862 Philadelphia's Copperheads were openly in dissent. When, in January 1863, the *Evening Journal's* Albert Boileau was arrested for publishing an editorial criticizing Abraham Lincoln, many in the city feared the worst. A worried Sidney George Fisher wrote that he "should not be surprised if trouble grew out of this act" and George Fahnestock surveyed the situation and concluded: "we are bordering upon anarchy."[21] A month after Boileau's seizure, a jeering crowd turned out to assail Ohio Copperhead Clement Vallandigham as he spoke at the Girard House.[22]

While partisan political meetings were frequently the occasion for angry rhetoric, some of the most tense wartime moments accompanied election campaigning. The strongest upsurge of Democratic fervor, and the greatest threat to Philadelphia's wartime public order, occurred in the weeks before the 1864 elections. On September 26th the *Public Ledger* warned: "Political excitement and partisan feeling are so high that, unless cool judgement is sprinkled over this passion, the contending parties are likely to come into serious collision at every public assemblage."[23] From mid-September to early November torchlight processions lit Philadelphia's nights and on several occasions political displays disintegrated into brawls. On October 29th the Democrats held the largest torchlight procession the city had ever seen.[24] When the Democrats passed the Republican headquarters on Chestnut Street a bystander was killed by an object reportedly thrown by a man sporting a McClellan button.[25] From a window at the *Age* office, Anna LaRoche, the daughter of a prominent Democrat, watched the parade and later wrote: "we dread blood in the streets."[26]

As Republican policies enraged local Democrats, wartime inflation placed a particularly heavy burden on Philadelphia's workers, prompting them to turn to unionization and strikes to bring wages closer to antebellum levels. Such actions created several moments when problems could have led to violence, and the general inflationary climate could easily have molded an angry working class ready to respond to an unrelated incendiary incident.[27]

One particular subgroup, Philadelphia's blacks, clearly feared that local tensions would bring violence down upon their heads. In August arsonists destroyed the home of a black Harrisburg man and in Philadelphia rumors circulated that hostile whites had prepared lists of leading black citizens destined for similar treatment.[28] Following the March 1863 anti-black rioting in Detroit, Philadelphia's black newspaper, the *Christian Recorder,* reported that "[e]ven here, in the city of Philadelphia, in many places it is almost impossible for a respectable colored person to walk the streets without being assaulted."[29] Then in July, with Philadelphia's draft only a few days away, New York City erupted into massive anti-draft and anti-black rioting. The *Christian Recorder's* readers felt the dangers most acutely:

> Our citizens are expecting every day that a mob will break out here, in Philadelphia. And if so, it is thought, they will not only resist the draft, but will pounce upon the colored people as they did in New York, and elsewhere, and if so, we have only to say this to colored citizens of Philadelphia and vicinity: Have plenty of powder and ball in your houses, and use it with effect, if necessary, in the protection of your wives and children.[30]

In addition to exacerbating political, class and racial tensions, the war also introduced a new disruptive force into Philadelphia: unruly soldiers. Philadelphia's size and location made it a critical depot for soldiers bound for the front as well as wounded and furloughed men on their way home. Throughout the war the city served as campground, training site, hospital and recreational haven for thousands of Union soldiers. By taking young men out of their homes the war unleashed a body with an enormous potential for mayhem.[31] Frequently overzealous soldiers raised popular ire by battling in public places or, worse, shooting at deserters as they fled through city streets. But the greatest public outcry came when soldiers brawled with angry locals or stray bullets found innocent citizens.[32]

While such strains certainly raised potentially disruptive tensions in Philadelphia, the principle cause of controversy, and the major catalyst for violence in other Northern cities, was conscription. The Northern draft rules were controversial both because Americans had relatively little experience with conscription and because the provisions of the Enrolment Act were widely viewed as biased in favor of the wealthy. The initial law allowed able bodied draftees to avoid service by hiring a substitute or by paying a $300 commutation fee. Vehement complaints helped lead to the removal of the commutation fee in 1864 (for all but conscientious objectors), but the substitute rule remained in place. (And with the commutation fee option removed, the market price for substitutes climbed rapidly.)[33]

Dissent with government policies, dissatisfaction with the Enrolment Act, and occasional rumors that the drawings were fixed by the party in power helped turn many a draft day into a violent affair. In Philadelphia the first federal draft in July of 1863 was particularly tense, but while the enrolling officers ran into trouble in some wards and the provost marshals frequently had difficulties serving draft notices, the provost marshals reported no major violent incidents associated with the draft.[34] On the final day of drafting the *Evening Bulletin* expressed its pride in Philadelphia for having withstood the draft with order and good humor.[35] The next three draft days also passed quietly in Philadelphia, but this was largely owing to the city's vigorous recruiting efforts which filled most ward quotas without any need for conscription.[36]

In sum, Philadelphia had every reason to break out in violence. The city had a long history of ethnic, racial and labor violence as well as a population with divided sympathies. Military setbacks, political conflicts, inflation, racial tensions, unruly soldiers and unpopular conscription all could have provided the tinder to set the city ablaze. Moreover, in many instances two or more of these catalysts came to a head at the same time, enhancing the chances for disaster. But although there was quite a bit of smoke, the record reveals precious little fire. The newspapers occasionally reported a fistfight or spontaneous crowd action in response to some ill chosen words by a Copperhead. Political contests regularly became heated, but apparently the only casualty came when a bystander at a Democratic torchlight parade was hit in the head by a rock. Some neighborhoods harassed draft enrollers, but when draft days rolled around the crowds who turned out for the public drawings were consistently calm and cooperative. In fact, probably the greatest violence attributable to the war must be laid at the feet of the Union soldiers who poured into the city. But even such episodes were infrequent, and they cannot really be attributable to wartime "tensions" *per se*.

## UNDERSTANDING PHILADELPHIA'S CALM

Should Philadelphia's wartime calm surprise us? Certainly other Civil War cities were not so fortunate. An examination of several violent episodes on the home front will help explain this paradox.

Often violence exploded at the confluence of several wartime tensions. In New York an unlucky draft day drawing ignited essentially anti-black rioting.[37] Rising job competition between blacks and whites, Lincoln's Emancipation Proclamation, and the new class-biased Enrolment Act helped make Detroit a powderkeg in early 1863; but it was the arrest of a local mulatto for raping two girls which sparked racial violence in the Michigan city.[38] Irish stevedores in Cincinnati battled blacks in racial rioting touched off by the bitter struggle for jobs.[39] Draft day rioting in one Wisconsin town pitted Luxembourgers against German Protestants.[40] Charleston, Illinois Copperheads used draft riots to repay a body of unarmed soldiers for repeated indignities at the hands of the military.[41] The Confederacy, faced with much greater hardship, suffered through its own urban riots, many stemming from food shortages.[42]

The accounts of these Civil War riots suggest that they reflected a wide range of long-term frictions—racial, ethnic, economic, political—which often combined with draft day tensions to disrupt local harmony. As we have seen, Philadelphians' lack of violence was not for want of tensions. Of course some of the conflicts which tore apart other cities were relatively less powerful in Philadelphia. For instance, secession temporarily crippled the local economy and rapid inflation certainly caused discomfort as the war progressed, but the war years were generally prosperous times in Philadelphia. And vigorous recruiting spared the city from substantial conscription in all but the July 1863 call-up. But this is only half the story. Philadelphia's wartime tensions were quite real and substantial. In several senses—history, racial and ethnic make-up, political climate, location—the city was a particularly strong candidate for violent upheaval. A full explanation for its orderly experience must consider what forces maintained that order.

Let us return for a moment to April 1861. In those anxious days Mayor Henry used personal persuasion, preemptive measures and shows of force to keep calm in his city. In a sense he was aided by the mobs themselves, who dominated the streets and effectively silenced dissent. These forces combined to keep local violence to a minimum.

In the years to come the same forces continued to serve Philadelphia well. When bad news from the battlefield threatened to divide the city, Copperhead voices were consistently silenced by the "patriotic" crowds who continued to rule the streets, forcing antiwar voices indoors. Those who did speak in public (often brave from drink) were frequently hustled off to jail by policemen before the mobs could do them much harm. More importantly, whenever planned events threatened local order, Mayor Henry positioned his police force ahead of time assuring that things never got out of hand. When Philadelphia's increasingly brazen Copperheads organized several large political rallies in mid-1863, the local police force massed outside and successfully kept angry hecklers at bay. Many expected a repeat of New York's disorders during the July 1863 drafts, but Philadelphia—profiting from its Northern neighbor's experience—kept calm with an impressive display of police and military forces at each drafting site. And when in May 1863 a thousand angry citizens massed before the offices of *The Age,* Mayor Henry, who had no time for a carefully orchestrated preemptive strike, personally came to the scene (accompanied by a large police force) and quelled the crowd much as he had two years before at the *Palmetto Flag* offices.

To these familiar means of preserving order were added new devices, rooted in federal power. Thus Federal troops joined local forces in preserving draft day order. And on several occasions federal marshals stepped in to arrest vocal Southern sympathizers and silence dissenting newspapers. But such arbitrary methods served to stir up disorder as well, as when Philadelphia Democrats used Constitutional arguments to stoke dissenting fires. In this same fashion, the military kept its own men in order with armed guards and provost patrols, but not without creating disorder and violence through their own overexuberance. And while provost guards were charged with arresting deserters, they were aided by hired civilian agents and private citizens who brought in deserters in exchange for government rewards. Thus, while the Civil War certainly yielded new methods for maintaining order, traditional means and players were most responsible for keeping disorder in check.

Of course the "public quiet" that Henry proudly noted in his annual reports should not be confused with civic harmony. The police force assembled in the mid-1850's "battled" disorder quite literally. Henry's predecessors had filled the force with tough veterans of Philadelphia's street gangs who were quick to use familiar strong-arm tactics to maintain the peace.[43] Thus, when the Mayor threatened violence his audience knew he could back up his words. And if the police force maintained order through intimidation, the citizenry certainly followed a similar formula. The mobs that demanded shows of patriotism in April 1861 and again four years later performed their own form of civic ritual, enhancing group solidarity while forcing community standards upon perceived enemies. Such demonstrations, coupled with the occasional street corner assaults on vocal Rebel sympathizers, assured relative order even when individual feelings ran high.

In April 1865 news of Lincoln's assassination shocked the North. Philadelphia navigated the stormy waters that followed much as it had four years before. While most of the city joined in mourning, some were not so sorrowful. As in the days after Fort Sumter's fall, several forces combined to assure order. First, the threat of mob violence encouraged many to keep their counsel. Second, police officers spirited away several loose-tongued Southern sympathizers before angry mourners could do much damage. Third, Mayor Henry anticipated assaults at the *Age* offices and ordered his police to protect the Democratic newspaper. And finally, Henry acted both publicly and behind the scenes to ease tensions. The *Public Ledger* applauded his "personal efforts" in calming the streets. And recognizing that he and his police force could not be everywhere, Henry sent notes to prominent Democrats advising them to display mourning bows in their windows. Most heeded his advice and escaped unscathed. In short, when it came to maintaining order in the city, little seemed to have changed in four years of war.[44]

Let us now return to the other Civil War riots. The scholars who have examined these episodes have tended to focus on how particular events acted as catalysts, pushing underlying social tensions into open violence. But in each case there is another side of the story. Repeatedly the local forces for maintaining order proved insufficient and, more important, they were directed ineptly.

After a calm first day of drafting, New York City officials, expecting no trouble, left only a small police force at the draft office. When rioters overcame these men, inadequate reinforcements were sent. Once the riot got out of hand, a much larger force was required to restore order.[45] The March 1863 riot in Detroit only broke out after the Provost Guard sent to escort the suspected rapist was removed from the scene.[46] And similarly, the Cincinnati police successfully put down racial rioting until 120 of 160 available police officers were pulled away to help stop Confederate raider John Hunt Morgan.[47] The

Charleston, Illinois, mob was led by the county sheriff, a prominent Democrat who relished the opportunity to attack unarmed soldiers.[48] The draft commissioner in Port Washington, Wisconsin, could not calm Luxembourger rioters because he himself was a hated German Protestant.[49] And perhaps the most prominent case of official ineptitude came when Richmond's women, furious at food shortages, began looting the Virginia city. Despite widespread rumors of disorder, no police were on the scene as the crowd gathered. And when the violence started Mayor "Old Joe" Mayo (in stark contrast to the politically savvy Alexander Henry) stood atop a makeshift platform reading the riot act to a disinterested audience.[50]

What does all this add up to? In each case sufficient police or militia forces were probably available to calm crowds before they rioted, and in most instances local officials were aware of rising hostilities. The riots were not simply the result of uncontrollable tensions combining with unpredictable catalysts. Rather, these incidents could have been controlled with the tools at hand.

Certainly other cities managed to maintain calm under stress, but two such episodes reinforce the conclusion that Philadelphia's success was particularly striking. Boston, like Philadelphia, held its first 1863 draft in the wake of New York's bloody rioting. In that city a North End mob assaulted two assistant provost marshals and a policeman who came to their rescue. The local police, who arrived unarmed, were soon overwhelmed and sought refuge in the station house until Mayor Lincoln arrived with military reinforcements. These combined forces soon dispatched the mob with far less carnage than New York had suffered.[51]

While Bostonians applauded their mayor and police for heroism under fire, the following year New Yorkers were, perhaps, spared further rioting through effective preemptive measures. As the 1864 elections approached, New York City braced for rumored sabotage by pro-Confederate forces. But election day passed peacefully as Major General Benjamin Butler—remembering the city's inefficiency the previous July—deployed a large force in boats around lower Manhattan, leading one historian to credit Butler's "unobtrusive yet ubiquitous presence" with maintaining calm.[52]

These two examples demonstrate that Philadelphia was not alone in diffusing potentially volatile situations. But each incident also underscores Philadelphia's particular success. While Boston's Mayor Lincoln showed bravery under fire, an armed police force might have silenced the mob without reinforcements while perhaps a better placed military force could have caught the riot before it got out of hand.[53] The New York example reflects the power of an intimidating show of force, but whereas local forces generally preserved order in Philadelphia, the Secretary of War's decision to deploy troops outside of New York was an explicit recognition that the civic authorities could not be entrusted with keeping the peace.[54]

Why was Philadelphia particularly successful? First, its police force was stronger and performed better than in other cities.[55] And second, Mayor Alexander Henry was particularly adept at using the tools at his disposal. In so doing he artfully combined the skills of a "modern" mayor, directing a uniformed police force, with those of a traditional city mayor, relying on his own powers of persuasion to soothe an angry crowd.[56]

This success is partly owing to good fortune, but the fuller explanation lies in Philadelphia's disorderly past. The two ethnic riots of 1844 had rocked the city. In the first instance the local militia hesitated too long; in the second case they acted decisively, but foolishly, producing more violence. The resulting loss of life generated a strong law and order backlash. On July 11, 1844, thousands of Philadelphians joined in a mass meeting in the State House Yard to promote civil order. During the next 15 years a Philadelphia police force took form to further that end. In 1850 the legislature replaced the inefficient system of sheriffs and constabulary by a daytime "Marshal's Police" with jurisdiction over all of Philadelphia County. Four years later the city council of the newly consolidated city created the first Philadelphia Police Department.[57]

When Alexander Henry became mayor in 1858, one of his top priorities was an improved police force. In his first years in office Henry appointed a citizen board to oversee appointments, organized a special Detective Department, and put his force into new uniforms. By 1861, Philadelphians enjoyed a far more structured and efficient police force than during the riotous 1840's.[58] Thus, while successful recruiting and federal troops certainly helped matters, the key to Philadelphia's wartime calm lay in its recent disorderly history.

## Notes

An earlier version of this article was delivered at the 1987 meetings of the Social Science History Association in New Orleans. The author would like to thank Morton Keller, Arnold Hirsch, Roger Lane, and Allen Steinberg for helpful suggestions.

1. The findings in this essay are part of a larger study of the Civil War home front in Philadelphia. See James M. Gallman, *Mastering Wartime: A Social History of Philadelphia During the Civil War* (forthcoming, Cambridge University Press).

2. Alexander Henry, *Fourth Annual Report* (Philadelphia, 1862), p. 26; Henry, *Fifth-Seventh Annual Reports* (Philadelphia, 1863–1865).

3. This includes a complete reading of the Philadelphia *Public Ledger* from January 1861 through December 1865 and an extensive reading in several other local newspapers as well as in the available personal papers. The *Ledger,* which was published 6 days a week, was the city's largest circulation newspaper. See Elwyn B. Robinson, "The Public Ledger: An Independent Newspaper," *Pennsylvania Magazine of History and Biography* (January, 1940): 43–55.

4. Michael Jay Feldberg, "The Philadelphia Riots of 1844: A Social History" (Ph.D. dissertation, University of Rochester, 1970), p. 2 and *passim.* See also Elizabeth M. Geffen, "Violence in Philadelphia in the 1840's and 1850's," *Pennsylvania Magazine of History and Biography* 36 (October, 1969): 381–410; David R. Johnson, "Crime Patterns in Philadelphia, 1840–1870," in Allen F. Davis and Mark H Haller, editors, *The Peoples of Philadelphia: A History of Ethnic Groups and Lower Class Life, 1790–1840,* pp. 89–110, Bruce Laurie, "Fire Companies and Gangs in Southwark: The 1840s," in Davis and Haller, eds, *The Peoples of Philadelphia,* pp. 71–87.

5. Feldberg, "The Philadelphia Riots of 1844," pp. 77–109, 151–182; Feldberg, *The Turbulent Era: Riot and Disorder in Jacksonian America* (New York, 1980), pp. 9–32.

6. See Adrian Cook, *The Armies of the Streets: The New York City Draft Riots* (Lexington, 1974).

7. *Official Records,* Series III, volume 2, p. 903; volume 3, pp. 324–4, 330–32, 351–2, 357, 382, 588–96.

8. By "war related violence" I mean conflicts over politics, conscription, emancipation and the like. Several individuals were killed in altercations involving soldiers or deserters.

9. Philadelphia *Public Ledger,* April 15, 1861 (hereafter PL); John Scharf and Thompson Westcott, *History of Philadelphia, 1609–1884* three volumes (Philadelphia, 1912), 1:753; William Dusinberre, *Civil War Issues in Philadelphia, 1856–1865* (Philadelphia, 1965), p. 118.

10. PL, April 16, 1861; Dusinberre, *Civil War Issues,* pp. 117–118; Russell F. Weigley, "The Border City in Civil War, 1854–1865," in Weigley, editor, *Philadelphia: a 300-Year History* (New York, 1982), p. 394; Scharf and Westcott, *Philadelphia* 1:753.

11. For comments by onlookers see Joseph Boggs Beale Diary, April 15, 1861, Historical Society of Pennsylvania, Philadelphia (hereafter HSP); J. A. Culley letter, April 15, 1861, manuscript room, Library of Congress, Washington, D.C.; Fanny Kemble Wister, "Sarah Butler Wister's Civil War Diary," *Pennsylvania Magazine of History and Biography* 102 (July, 1978): 274–276. Wister noted that the mob was "in the utmost state of excitement & the least thing would have fired them, & then riots must have followed."

12. Nicholas B. Wainwright, ed. *A Philadelphia Perspective: The Diary of Sidney George Fisher* (Philadelphia, 1967), p. 387.

13. PL, April 16, 1861.

14. PL, April 17, 1861.

15. PL, April 17, 1861.

16. Wainwright, ed., *A Philadelphia Perspective,* p. 385, entry for April 18, 1861. Also see Wister, "Sarah Butler Wister's Civil War Diary," pp. 280–281; Dusinberre, *Civil War Issues,* p. 119; Edward G. Everett, "Contraband and Rebel Sympathizers in Pennsylvania in 1861," *Western Pennsylvania Historical Magazine* 41 (Spring 1958): 35.

17. Scott Campbell Brown, "Migrants and Workers in Philadelphia: 1850 to 1880," (Ph.D. dissertation, University of Pennsylvania, 1981), p. 27, Dusinberre, *Civil War issues,* pp. 20–21.

18. Weigley, "The Border City in the Civil War," p. 392; Erwin Stanley Bradley, *The Triumph of Militant Republicanism: A Study of Pennsylvania and Presidential Politics, 1860–1872* (Philadelphia, 1964), chapter 2.

19. Scharf and Westcott, *Philadelphia,* 1:802; Diary of Jacob Elreth, Sr., September 1, 1862, HSP; PL, September 2, 1862.

20. PL, May 9, 1863; Dusinberre, *Civil War Issues,* p. 158.

21. Wainwright, *A Philadelphia Perspective,* p. 447; Diary of George W. Fahnestock, January 31, 1862, HSP; Arnold Shankman, "Freedom of the Press During the Civil War: The Case of Albert D. Boileau," *Pennsylvania History* 42 (1975): 305–315.

22. Scharf and Westcott, *History of Philadelphia,* 1:807.

23. PL, September 26, 1864.

24. See Auguste Laugel, *The United States During the Civil War,* edited by Allen Nevins (1866; Bloomington, 1961), pp. 71–72.

25. In the weeks to come, Campbell, the only Philadelphian to die during wartime rioting, became a celebrated figure. Scharf and Westcott, *History of Philadelphia,* 1:819; PL, October 31, November 2, 4, 7, 19, 1864.

26. Diary of Anna LaRoche, October 31, 1864, Columbia University Archives, New York.

27. This issue is discussed in Gallman, *Mastering Wartime,* chapter 9. While real wages declined through most of the war and employers actively resisted the efforts of organized labor, Philadelphia's workers enjoyed a very low unemployment rate.

28. "Documents," Jacob A. White to Joseph C. Bustill, August 19, 1862, *Journal of Negro History* 11 (January, 1926): 83; Frederick M. Binder, "Pennsylvania Negro Regiments in the Civil War," *Journal of Negro History* 37 (1952): 396.

29. *Christian Recorder,* March 4, 1863 (hereafter cited as CR).

30. CR, July 25, 1863.

31. See Eric Monkkonnen, *Police in Urban America, 1860–1920* (London, 1981), pp. 78–82.

32. See Gallman, *Mastering Wartime,* chapter 8.

33. For a discussion of the draft laws and Philadelphia's recruiting see Eugene C. Murdock, *One Million Men: The Civil War Draft in the North* (Madison, 1971); Gallman, *Mastering Wartime,* chapter 2.

34. Provost Marshals, Pennsylvania Districts One–Five, "Historical Reports," September 6, 1865, microfilm M1163, reel #4, National Archives.

35. *Evening Bulletin,* August 4, 1863. Scharf and Westcott say that the draft was "never interrupted by the slightest disturbance." *History of Philadelphia,* 1:809. The *Public Ledger* only reported one arrest. PL, July 21, 1863.

36. See Gallman, *Mastering Wartime,* chapter 2.

37. Cook, *The Armies of the Streets,* p. 56 and *passim.*

38. John C. Schneider, "Detroit and the Problem of Disorder: The Riot of 1863," *Michigan History* 38 (Spring, 1974): 4–24.

39. Leonard Harding, "The Cincinnati Riots of 1862," *Bulletin of the Cincinnati Historical Society* 25 (October, 1967): 229–239.

40. Lawrence H. Larsen, "Draft Riot in Wisconsin," *Civil War History* 7 (December, 1961): 421–7.

41. Charles H. Coleman and Paul H. Spence, "The Charleston Riot, March 28, 1864," *Journal of the Illinois State Historical Society* 33 (March, 1940): 7–56. These riots left 10 dead.

42. For a description of the Richmond food riots see Michael Chesson, "Harlots or Heroines? A New Look at the Richmond Bread Riot," *Virginia Magazine of History and Biography* 92 (April, 1984): 131–175.

43. Weigley, "The Border City in Civil War," pp. 370; David R. Johnson, *Policing the Urban Underworld* (Philadelphia, 1979), pp. 139–140; Johnson, "Crime Patterns in Philadelphia," p. 102.

44. PL, April 17, 1865; Glossman and Welch (editors of the *Age*) to Henry, April 15, 1865, F-2, Henry Letters, HSP. On April 15th Sidney Fisher wrote that an assault on the *Age* seemed "very likely" and perhaps even justifiable. Wainwright, *A Philadelphia Perspective,* p. 493.

45. Cook, *Armies of the Streets,* pp. 53–63, 199.

46. Schneider, "The Detroit Riot of 1863," pp. 16–18, 23–24.

47. Harding, "The Cincinnati Riots," p. 231.

48. Coleman and Spence, "The Charleston Riot."

49. Larsen, "Draft Riot in Wisconsin."

50. Chesson, "Harlots or Heroines?" pp. 143–151.

51. Roger Lane, *Policing the City, 1822–1885* (New York, 1975), pp. 133–134.

52. Edward G. Longacre, "The Union Army Occupation of New York City, November, 1864," *New York History* 65 (April 1984): 133–158.

53. Lane notes that Mayor Lincoln summoned "regulars from outside the city." Lane, *Policing the City*, p. 133. When Philadelphia held its July 1863 draft the city's policemen were reinforced by both militia and federal troops. Of course this large preemptive force reflected Philadelphia's critical strategic position and was not entirely the mayor's responsibility. For communications concerning the July 1863 draft see *Official Records*, series III, volume 3, pages 491, 497, 499, 518–19, 532–33, 543, 573. In June a group of local citizens, dissatisfied with the troop build-up, appealed to President Lincoln. See Roy P. Basler, editor, *The Collected Works of Abraham Lincoln*, eight volumes (New Brunswick, 1953), 6:279.

54. Longacre, "The Union Army Occupation of New York City," p. 131. Even when federal troops were used to protect order in Philadelphia, as they were in July 1863, such plans were made in concert with local police preparations.

55. Of course by "better" I mean that they were particularly successful at maintaining order, it is quite likely that disruptive citizens were less satisfied with the police force's methods.

56. John C. Schneider argues that by the mid-nineteenth century the traditional mayoral role as a "'moral' power . . . was becoming increasingly irrelevant to the growing cities . . . " "Mob Violence and Public Order in the American City, 1830–1865," (Ph.D. dissertation, University of Minnesota, 1971), pp. 81–111.

57. Feldberg, "The Philadelphia Riots", pp. 186–199; Feldberg, *Turbulent Era*, p. 115.

58. Howard O. Sprogle, *The Philadelphia Police, Past and Present* (Philadelphia, 1887), pp. 114–123; Alexander Henry *1st–3rd Annual Messages* (Philadelphia, 1859–1861); Schneider, "Mob Violence and Public Order," 30–51; Weigley, "'A Peaceful City': Public Order in Philadelphia from Consolidation Through the Civil War," in *The Peoples of Philadelphia*, pp. 155–173.

# Gettysburg's Gettysburg

## What the Battle Did to the Borough

### (with Susan Baker)

This essay began with an invitation from Gabor Boritt, the director of the Civil War Institute at Gettysburg College. Each summer Gabor runs a weeklong institute for Civil War enthusiasts, combining guest lectures and battlefield tours around a selected theme. Gabor was planning to revisit the Battle of Gettysburg, and he invited me to prepare a piece on the town of Gettysburg. The assignment was to write a public lecture, with the distinct possibility that the product would appear in one of Gabor's popular edited volumes.

At the time I had a student, Susan Baker, who was casting around for a thesis topic. I suggested that she work on Gettysburg for her thesis and we could collaborate on the eventual essay.[1] This, then, was a commissioned piece of scholarship, although I had complete freedom of analysis and interpretation. Susan (and then I) worked through several local newspapers and the treasure trove of diaries and reminiscences collected at the Adams County Historical Society. Gabor offered the use of a database he had created from the 1860 and 1870 censuses.

My first visit to the CWI was a great time, although I fear that I did not pitch my talk at just the right level. Like a good adherent of the new social history, I came equipped with a stack of tables, and I offered analytic themes grounded in social history. Nearly all of the other speakers addressed military topics that were probably better matched to the interests of the paying audience. At the close of my talk, the first question came from a man at the back of the room who—as I recall—said something like, "I am afraid I came in late. Could you explain why you were talking about women?" But several women who were regulars at the CWI came to me afterwards and expressed appreciation of the unfamiliar themes I had raised.

The published essay follows themes that I had explored for Philadelphia and in my broader survey of the North, but the compelling thing here is that

Gettysburg was both extraordinarily typical and wildly distinctive. No other Northern community had been the scene of such carnage. That opened up interesting questions about the true nature of continuity and change during the Civil War era. The narrative also presented Northern women in unfamiliar roles, coming face to face with the enemy. For a few days in the summer of 1863, these Northern civilians had experiences that many Southerners endured over and over again.

In reading over the piece I am struck by how much new work on Gettysburg has come out in the decade since it appeared in print, including Gabor Boritt's own *The Gettysburg Gospel*.[2] Still, I am pleased with the essay's attention to the first two years of the war, when Gettysburg was just another small town in Pennsylvania and not yet an iconic community.

## NOTES

1. As it turned out, Susan's life—both a car accident and then a wedding—interfered with these plans and the final product was essentially mine. But I saw no harm in sticking with the previous agreement.

2. See especially Jim Weeks, *Gettysburg: Memory, Market, and an American Shrine* (Princeton: Princeton Univ. Press, 2003); Margaret S. Creighton, *The Colors of Courage: Gettysburg's Hidden History: Immigrants, Women, and African-Americans in the Civil War's Defining Battle* (New York: Basic Books, 2004); Gabor Boritt, *The Gettysburg Gospel: The Lincoln Speech that Nobody Knows* (New York: Simon and Schuster, 2006).

. . .

History has an odd way of elevating relatively unknown locales into positions of prominence. The luck of geography or some strange twist of fate can suddenly turn a nation's eyes onto an unsuspecting community, forever linking its name with a single major episode. Gettysburg, Pennsylvania, in 1863 was hardly an obscure backwater. This bustling county seat of roughly 2,400 people boasted a vibrant commercial center, several hotels and taverns, a railroad depot, the county prison and a new courthouse, a Lutheran Theological Seminary, and a college. Nonetheless, few Americans were familiar with Gettysburg before the first days of July, when nearly 170,000 armed men converged upon the borough. By battle's end, the two armies had suffered over 51,000 casualties; Gettysburg would never be quite the same.

When we think of the Battle of Gettysburg, we do not imagine bloody street fighting. Indeed, the Union's famed fishhook stretched along the hills to the south of town. Still, the residents who opted to stay in Gettysburg saw the war firsthand, in a way that few Northern civilians would. At different points in the battle, both Yankee and Rebel troops occupied the streets. For years to come, the residents of the town would tell harrowing tales of terrifying escapes, hidden Union soldiers, suspicious Confederate patrols, and—most disturbing—thousands and thousands of the dead, dying, and wounded.

Historians who set out to reconstruct Civil War battles quickly learn that participants know little beyond the limited range of their own senses, obscured by clouds of smoke and deafening noise. To understand a battle's panoramic aspects, one must piece together dozens of small stories. Surely much of the enduring fascination with the battle of Gettysburg is in these smaller, personal stories. We never tire of the tales of heroic figures, such as Joshua Lawrence Chamberlain, or timeless relationships, such as that between Lewis Armistead and Winfield Scott Hancock.

Gettysburg's townspeople had their own array of battle tales, ranging from the highly celebrated to the barely documented. Even the casual observer of history has probably heard of Jennie Wade and John Burns. Virginia (Jennie) Wade became the town's only casualty when a stray bullet passed through two doors, mortally wounding her as she tended a kitchen fire. On July 1, John Burns—far too old to serve in uniform—grabbed a gun and went out to face the invaders, where he sustained three wounds. Most locals survived the battle in relative obscurity. Sarah Broadhead spent much of the three days in cellars, hidden from both stray bullets and hostile Confederates. Her terror did not subside until July 4, when she wrote in her diary: "For the first time for a week I shall go to bed feeling safe."[1] In the days after the battle, young schoolteacher Salome Myers threw herself into nursing the wounded soldiers, a passion she sustained into her later life. Neither woman enjoyed much fame either before or after the battle; we only have knowledge of their thoughts and actions because both kept diaries throughout the crisis.

For those in more public positions, the Confederate invasion brought particular difficulties. David Buehler, the town postmaster, watched Lee's progress north with special concern, fearing that his government post might result in his capture. When the Rebels approached Gettysburg, Buehler took several horses and fled the town, leaving his wife Fannie and their children to fend for themselves. Henry Stahle edited the *Gettysburg Compiler*, a vigorously Democratic weekly. During the battle, Stahle took in a wounded Union officer, Colonel William W. Dudley of Indiana. When the Colonel took a turn for the worse, Stahle left his home in search of a surgeon. Soon after the battle the controversial editor was arrested and incarcerated in Baltimore's Fort McHenry, charged with giving information to the enemy.[2]

Many Gettysburg citizens only reached the historic record indirectly, through the comments of other observers. For the town's African-American population, the Confederate invasion brought with it the specter of capture and forced enslavement, prompting many to abandon their homes and flee the neighborhood. Years after the battle, Albertus McCreary described the mass exodus of African Americans from the western portion of the town. McCreary particularly remembered the story of an African-American woman who apparently had worked for his family and fell into Rebel hands. "We never expected to see 'Old Liz' again," he wrote, "but the day after the battle ended she came walking in, exclaiming, 'Thank God, I's alive yet.'"[3]

Hundreds of individual stories such as these are embedded in Gettysburg's history. For the historian of the Northern home front, Gettysburg's experience is particularly compelling. On the one hand, most of its wartime experience was so "typical" that the town can nearly serve as the analytic proxy for towns across the North. On the other hand, neither the townspeople nor the historian can forget the thousands of men who fell in those three days. The task before us is to come to terms with Gettysburg, both as a perfectly normal Northern town that experienced the tremendous challenges of the American Civil War, and as a community that fate elevated to a special status. In the process, we must remain cognizant of the events that framed the town's wartime history and the narratives that defined its memory.

The Civil War's human costs still stagger the modern observer. The conflict's estimated 618,000 military deaths nearly equal America's combined losses in every other war before Vietnam. The death rate—more than 180 out of every 10,000 Americans—was more than six times as high as that of World War II and well beyond the 118 per 100,000 of the American Revolution.[4] It is only natural to assume that such tremendous casualties dramatically reshaped the United States. In some fundamental ways that assumption is correct: America after Appomattox was indeed a different place than it had been before Fort Sumter. Slavery had at long last been abolished. Following decades of debate and uncertainty, the nation had finally established the primacy of the Union against the constitutional claims of states' rights advocates. In the South, the economy and social structure faced years of acrimonious Reconstruction while the legacy of rebellion muted the region's political voice in national affairs for decades to come. And in dozens of ways—both large and small—the war fought on the battlefields of 1864 and 1865 would hardly have been recognized by military participants at the First Battle of Bull Run.

In other senses, the war's effects are less easily gauged, particularly insofar as they touched the North. Scholars have now agreed that the war had only a modest impact on long-term patterns of economic growth and development. The case for a rising centralized state driven by the war's unprecedented demands appears powerful on the surface when we consider the array of innovative war measures addressing conscription, banking, taxes, and civil liberties; but on deeper reflection the lasting effects no longer seem quite so compelling.

We may also measure the war's effect on the home front by considering the experiences of ordinary citizens. How did they mobilize to support, or resist, the war? What changes did the conflict force on their everyday lives? How, for instance, did they weave local and personal voluntaristic impulses into the emerging tapestry of state and national benevolent organizations? How did the war's new political and administrative challenges fit into established partisan conflicts? Wars commonly challenge, and occasionally recast, existing social hierarchies. What became of racial and gender hierarchies under the strain of war?

A survey of the Northern home front would reveal ample evidence of a world in flux, but the larger story is one of broad continuities. Citizens threw themselves into all manner of war-related activities, but they generally did so within the context of time-honored traditions and beliefs. Perhaps this should come as no surprise. After all, most communities north of the border states never saw an enemy soldier. And after a brief downturn during the secession crisis, the Northern wartime economy boomed. Since existing resources and traditions could meet the war's challenges, there was little reason for Northerners to pursue dramatic change. The contrast with the Confederacy is considerable. Southerners fought the war with far fewer men and materials, and most of the conflict's carnage fell on Southern soil. White Southerners on the home front lived in a world of invading armies, food shortages, and the gradual destruction of slavery. Confederate women faced new challenges—and opportunities—as the vast majority of military-aged white men were drawn into uniform. Slaves in the Confederate states experienced uncertainty and hardship as well as tremendous possibilities. For those and other reasons, Southerners felt the war's impact far more than their Northern counterparts.

As long as we paint with a broad brush, the contrast between the prosperous North and the embattled South is dramatic. In this context, Gettysburg becomes particularly interesting because the borough was distinctly Northern in all respects, *except* that it endured a moment of invasion and destruction akin to that experienced in the South. If the historian wants to find evidence of a Northern community transformed by war, Gettysburg is a logical place to look.

On the eve of the Civil War, Gettysburg was a thriving county seat with 2,391 residents, including 190 (8 percent) African Americans. While certainly not a major city, the borough was a substantial local center, with about 8 percent of the Adams County population. In fact, only about a quarter of Northerners lived in larger communities in 1860. Although only a short distance from Maryland, Gettysburg's population had a distinctly Northern character. More than four out of five residents were born in Pennsylvania (1,976) and an additional 44 were born in other Northern states. Only 185 (8 percent) came from Maryland and a mere 22 (1 percent) residents were born in states that would become part of the Confederacy (all but one of these came from Virginia). Nearly a third (59) of the 207 residents who were born south of Pennsylvania were African Americans. About one in fourteen (164) Gettysburg residents listed European birthplaces. This percentage of immigrants was roughly twice that for the Southern states (3.5 percent) although well below the aggregate Northern figure of 20 percent, which included the major East Coast cities.[5]

Located in the midst of Adams County farmland, Gettysburg supported a variety of local businesses catering to agricultural and mercantile needs, reflecting its strategic position at the hub of several major roads and, more recently, as a stop on the Hanover and Gettysburg Railroad. The town had several tanneries and a thriving carriage manufacturing industry. Twenty-two shoemakers appear on the 1860 census; however, despite the rumors, there was no local shoe factory or storehouse of shoes awaiting the Rebel raiders in 1863. Roughly half of the residents with occupations listed in the 1860 census were in some sort of craft or artisanal position; nearly a quarter were professionals, merchants, or retailers. Most of the remaining employed citizens were unskilled laborers.

By most measures, Gettysburg's African Americans lived in a separate, and largely unequal, world. In the decades before the war, the town had been a stop on the "Underground Railroad," providing refuge for runaway slaves. Although roughly 8 percent of the population, the real estate owned by Gettysburg's blacks in 1860 was valued at only about 1 percent of the town's total. Only three African Americans held professional positions in 1860, seven more were craftspeople. The remaining thirty-eight blacks with occupations listed in the census worked as some type of laborer or servant. As was common in the North, the local

African-American community supported separate churches, cemeteries, and other institutions. Black children attended a separate "colored" school.[6]

The hotly contested elections of 1860 proved to be important political litmus tests at the local, county, and state levels. The Republicans and Abraham Lincoln carried Pennsylvania with 57 percent of the vote, largely by stressing economic issues while playing down any discussion of slavery's future. In Adams County, Lincoln edged Illinois Democrat Stephen Douglas by a mere eighty votes. Gettysburg voters showed slightly more enthusiasm for the Republican ticket, giving Lincoln and Hannibal Hamlin 54 percent of the vote.

Local and national politics were the focus of spirited partisan debate in two weekly newspapers: the pro-Republican *Sentinel*, edited by Robert G. Harper, and Henry Stahle's staunchly Democratic *Compiler*. The debates over the 1860 election revealed both sharp political divisions and a shared distrust of abolitionism. Stahle's *Compiler* took every opportunity to paint Lincoln (and the *Sentinel*) as the voice of "Black Republicans" intent on forcing abolitionism down Americans' throats; the *Sentinel* denied such charges with equal vehemence.[7]

Abraham Lincoln's election triggered a series of events that would lead the United States into civil war. Between the firing on Fort Sumter in April 1861 and Robert E. Lee's invasion in the summer of 1863, the citizens of Gettysburg experienced the Civil War much like any other Northern community. The student of the home front is struck less by the borough's special characteristics than by the sense that this relatively small community was like the entire Union writ small.

Before the war began, Gettysburg, and most of the North, divided over how to treat the seceding states. All that ended with news of the firing on Fort Sumter. For at least a brief time, partisan disputes took a back seat to patriotism. In cities and towns across the North, flags flew, cannon roared, and local dignitaries delivered impassioned speeches at hastily assembled town gatherings. On April 16, the citizens of Gettysburg staged a "large and enthusiastic" Union Meeting "irrespective of party differences." The assembly attacked the treasonous South and resolved to set aside all party feeling to defend the Union.[8]

Immediately following the fall of Fort Sumter, Abraham Lincoln issued a call for ninety-day volunteers. For a time, fervent military recruiting seemed to absorb all attention. Gettysburg's patriotic young men flocked to emergency companies with exhilarating names and enticing uniforms: the Independent Blues, the Adams Rifles, and—most spectacular—the Gettysburg Zouaves. As these filled, new companies and regiments enlisted men from Gettysburg and across Adams County. Meanwhile, the town named a Committee of Safety to organize a Home Guard for local defense and a public gathering appointed seven men to raise money for the families of military volunteers. The rhetoric from these first few days is particularly telling. As the county mobilized to meet the state's quota, the *Compiler* declared: "Men of Adams County, your country calls." At the time, no further inducements seemed necessary.[9]

After a few weeks of drilling, the emergency troops departed for the front, sent on their way with enthusiastic public displays. Gettysburg's volunteers often were escorted to the train station by the colorfully garbed Zouaves. Crowds lined the street and gathered at the station to see their loved ones off. Such carefully constructed rituals sealed the bonds between the regiments and the communities left behind. In the months and years to come, citizens on the home front followed the exploits of local regiments with particular care. In addition to personal letters from family and friends, Gettysburg's newspaper readers received a steady diet of stories following the local companies and published letters from soldiers in the field.

The initial enthusiasm for mustering volunteers into uniform was matched by a surge of benevolent voluntarism at home, particularly among the women of Gettysburg. On May 6 a group of women gathered at the Methodist Church "to organize a Union Relief Society." Before long, the Ladies' Union Relief Society was hard at work sewing flannel shirts, havelocks, and other military garments. The women of Gettysburg responded repeatedly to specific requests from neighboring towns or benevolent groups.[10]

By mid-summer of 1861, wartime Gettysburg had settled into a routine of sorts, much like the patterns established across the North. Near the end of July, the first ninety-day recruits began returning home, prompting more martial displays and another round of public celebration.[11] Even before the First Battle of Bull Run, the President issued calls for three-year recruits, leading many ninety-day volunteers to reorganize into three-year regiments. In these early days, the patriotic spirit was still generally sufficient to fill the ranks, but Gettysburg's recruiters were already experimenting with added incentives. Young men considering Captain Buehler's new company were promised a $100 bounty and were assured that "comfortable houses are to be erected" for winter quarters.[12] On April 20, Gettysburg's Town Council voted to contribute $500 to the fund for families of volunteers. That June the County Commissioners passed a modest property tax to fund more substantial assistance to the families of volunteers.[13]

In August, Gettysburg hosted a Grand Military Review of Adams County troops, with several thousand citizens and roughly 350 soldiers in attendance.[14] Throughout the fall, local regiments departed for the front, and the two local newspapers continued to follow their exploits with care. As 1861 came to a close, the War Department ordered the Tenth New York Cavalry to winter quarters outside Gettysburg. The troops took up temporary quarters in several vacant buildings throughout the town. Gettysburg staged a reception in the New Yorkers' honor and their commander, Colonel James C. Lemmon, issued a statement requesting that any breaches of the peace by his men be reported directly to him.[15]

For several months, the 776 members of the 10th NY Cavalry, known as the Porter Guards, were the talk of the borough. Residents regularly attended the troop's afternoon parades and individual soldiers soon became part of the borough's social world. As the *Compiler* put it, "Our place is far more lively than usual, but good order prevails all the while." When new barracks were finally completed a mile east of town, the citizens staged a formal ceremony at which local women presented the Porter Guards with a banner. On their departure the *Sentinel* grew wistful: "We miss the lively Bugle in our Square . . . as well as the music of the Band, and the handsome military display." But even after the Porter Guards had left town, local citizens made regular sorties to the camp to watch the parade drilling. When the regiment finally left for the front, the *Compiler* noted that "many pleasant associations have been formed" during their stay.[16]

Diarist Salome Myers would certainly long remember the men from New York. From their first days in town Salome routinely attended gatherings with men from the Porter Guards. In fact, Ed Casey became such a consistent companion that Salome's ex-beau—an ailing local man named Snyder—charged that she had been the subject of town gossip. Salome never revealed a particular affection for Ed until mid-March, after the Porter Guards had left for Perryville. Then she wrote: "It is just a week since the Porter Guards left Gettysburg, i am beginning to miss them or rather Ed, for I knew him better than any other one in the Regiment., May God be with him *wherever* he goes." In the months to come, Salome's romantic plot thickened as she continued to alternatively see and reject Snyder while carrying on an intense correspondence with Ed Casey.[17]

Gettysburg's "adoption" of the Porter Guards is an interesting variation on the localistic theme that characterized Gettysburg's first few years of war. When the regiment departed, the *Sentinel* promised that "we shall follow the 'Porter Guards' as they go onwards." After their departure the local papers, like Salome Myers, followed their recent guests much as they traced the activities of Gettysburg's volunteers.[18] In this fashion, the local (and personal) became intermingled with the war's regional and national aspects.

The borough's wartime voluntarism also continued this combination of local sensibilities with an increasingly national perspective. The Ladies' Union Relief Society continued to orchestrate the borough's benevolent efforts. In October 1861, both newspapers published appeals from the U.S. Sanitary Commission to the "Loyal Women of America" calling on them to form local organizations of patriotic women. The *Sentinel* addressed these words to the women of Adams County:

> You are among the *loyal women of America,* who are called upon— while your sons, husbands and fathers are exposing themselves to great hardships, and death itself upon the battle-field—to come to the aid of the sick and wounded, and to do *what is in your power* to maintain our country—OUR EARTHLY ALL—against the traitorous hands that have been lifted up to destroy it!

The paper went on to make the Sanitary Commission's point more explicit:

> You have already done great service to those who have gone from our immediate neighborhood; and now you are urged to send as many of the articles mentioned in the Appeal of the Secretary of War, as you are able—that those who are SUFFERING, FAR FROM HOME, MAY BE MADE AS COMFORTABLE AS POSSIBLE."[19]

The *Sentinel* was joining the national umbrella organization in calling on Adams County women to look beyond their borders for objects of patriotic benevolence. In the next few weeks, "the Ladies of Gettysburg" answered this call by sending several boxes of food, clothing, and blankets to military hospitals in Baltimore, earning the profound thanks of the USSC's Washington branch.

Despite these highly publicized appeals from the Sanitary Commission, Gettysburg's Ladies' Union Relief Society seems to have carried on pretty much as it had before. Under the continuing leadership of Mrs. R. G. Harper (the wife of the *Sentinel's* editor), the Relief Society moved from project to project. Throughout December 1861, they shipped packages to the wounded soldiers in Baltimore. The following June, they answered a new appeal from the female volunteers at the military hospital in York, Pennsylvania. When Lee invaded the North the next fall, the women of Gettysburg mailed bandages and food to Keedysville and Antietam. In February 1863, the Ladies' Relief Association issued a call for donations to the sick and wounded in Washington. In response to each of these special calls, the Relief Society published requests for donations of goods and money to be delivered to Mrs. Harper. If these periodic emergencies led the volunteers to look beyond their community borders, they never really had to look very far. In the meantime, the group apparently met regularly to prepare materials for local volunteers in the field.

This array of voluntary efforts suggest something about the public position of women in wartime Gettysburg. Nearly all the fairs, festivals, and voluntary societies active during these two years were formally designated as efforts by local "Ladies." Whereas male voices dominated the U.S. Sanitary Commission and U.S. Christian Commission at the national level, Gettysburg's Ladies' Relief Society—like many local bodies across the Union—had an entirely white female membership. The women and men of Gettysburg clearly viewed these war-related activities as the logical extension of women's proper sphere. Did these early efforts also extend the public position of women? Certainly their voluntaristic efforts received widespread recognition. Public calls for assistance were aimed at local women; announcements that packages were in the mail typically praised the efforts of "the ladies" of the town. In a particularly interesting public acknowledgment of women's warwork, the *Sentinel* took to publishing an extensive column of benevolent notices under the heading, "The Ladies."

The public role—and recognition—of Northern women extended beyond the philanthropic to the ceremonial. Departing troops routinely received hand-sewn banners or flags from local women's groups. At one gathering honoring the 10th New York Cavalry, Colonel Lemmon offered public thanks to the local women who had cared for the regiment's sick members and then the Porter Guards offered "three cheers for the Ladies of Gettysburg."[20] Such rituals suggest an appreciation for women, but largely in a symbolic context. The borough's 1861 Independence Day celebration was particularly telling. That afternoon a group of local women presented the Zouaves with a flag. This was followed by a military parade and a series of public toasts. Each toast—to the Union, the flag, leading public institutions, and major (male) figures both living and dead—was followed with a formal response. The final toast was offered to "Woman":

The light of the world—God's noblest gift to man. The talisman of all our joys, and the sympathetic friend in all our distresses. Her beauty only excelled by her virtues and her devotion steadfast and pure as the Northern Star.

The official response was delivered by J. C. Neely, Esq., a leading male in the community.[21] On this grand public occasion, "Woman" was to be praised, but women were neither seen nor heard.

As the war entered its second year, the rising manpower demands put new strains on Northern communities. In July 1862, Lincoln called for 300,000 new three-year volunteers. Disheartened by the slow response to this latest appeal, Congress passed the 1862 Militia Act, laying the groundwork for state militia drafts. The following month the President asked for 300,000 nine-month recruits, to be conscripted if necessary. At the national level, this series of events, and the complex negotiations and calculations that followed, revealed a government inching toward federally controlled conscription. In the process, local communities faced new recruiting demands.

Gettysburg responded with several large "war meetings" to raise bounty funds. These voluntary contributions, which quickly amounted to over $1,400, were supplemented by appropriations from the County Commissioners.[22] Throughout August and early September, enrollers collected names and the people of Adams County braced for a draft. The Provost Marshal set the County quota at 1,645 men, including 157 for Gettysburg. Several weeks before draft day the newspapers announced that Gettysburg had been credited with 159 men in Pennsylvania service and another 18 who had volunteered in other states, giving the town an excess of 20 men beyond its quota. Therefore, while the county was still nearly a thousand men short of its quota, Gettysburg would be spared a draft. Nonetheless, the borough still remained in the thick of the conscription process. In early August, conscripted men from across the county converged on "Camp Gettysburg" where they were quartered awaiting medical inspection and official mustering into the army. In a sense, their presence was reminiscent of the Porter Guards. Local citizens ventured to the camp to watch the draftees drill; military officials asked Gettysburg's women to provide blankets, sheets, and even a flag for the new recruits. There were, however, important differences between these conscripted soldiers and the enthusiastic volunteers of the previous winter. Armed guards were posted around Camp Gettysburg to discourage deserters; $5 rewards were offered for help in capturing those who got away. And occasional newspaper stories suggest that these new visitors were not as universally orderly as their predecessors. Finally, in mid-December, the draftees boarded three railroad cars and departed for the seat of war.

Gettysburg's general enthusiasm for the war effort, reflected in both enlisting and voluntarism, masked deep political divisions. Whereas most Northerners claimed to support the Union, they split over crucial Republican policies. Once again, Gettysburg's experience during the first two years of war reflected larger national political patterns played out in a local arena.

From the outset, Stahle's *Compiler* served as a persistent critic of administration policies nationally and Republican sentiments closer to home. The *Sentinel* followed a more cautious path, emphatically supporting the Union while distancing itself from radical abolitionism. This approach was typical of Pennsylvania Republicans, who renamed themselves the "Union" party. In the fall of 1861, the *Sentinel* celebrated Union victories in the Adams County elections. The following March, the party triumphed in the borough elections, although the *Compiler* pointed out that the margins were smaller than customary. By the close of 1862, both parties were gearing up for a heated set of national, state, and local elections. The *Compiler* warned its readers of the dangers of imminent emancipation, claiming to unmask its opponents as closet abolitionists. When the votes were counted, the Democrats had swept to victory in Adams County, but Gettysburg voters continued to support the Union candidates in their losing efforts. The following March the slate of local Republicans once again controlled the borough elections.

These political battles were fought in an atmosphere of rising partisan tension, amid acrimonious charges and countercharges. Soon after the Independent Blues returned from the field in August 1861, the company published a lengthy document beginning with the following preamble:

> Information having been communicated to us in regard to certain persons in the Borough of Gettysburg, and in different portions of the County, who by their words and actions have given indubitable evidence of *disloyalty;* and whereas, things have come under our observation, since our return, to satisfy us that such is the case.

These words were followed by a series of resolutions attacking treasonous talk and action and threatening ominous consequences for all those who persisted in such behavior. The Blues took particular care to include "those who *print* as well as those who speak and act—or in any other way give aid and comfort to the rebels."[23] The *Compiler,* perhaps feeling the sting of such threats, routinely insisted on its loyalty, going so far as to print warnings about the proliferation of treasonous "Dark Lantern Societies" in other parts of the country.[24]

In August 1862, as political tensions were heating up and the county braced for the upcoming draft, the *Sentinel* warned: "It would, perhaps, be well for some individuals in this community to remember that there is a law on our statute books imposing heavy penalties on those who discourage enlistment." Editorials in the same issue chastised the *Compiler* editor for his insufficient patriotism and applauded government officials for political arrests in nearby Frederick, Maryland.[25]

By the following spring, the combined tensions of emancipation, conscription, and military failure had brought the North's political conflicts into the open. Partisans on both sides turned to new political organizations. On April 25, 1863, a gathering of Gettysburg men launched a chapter of the national Loyal Union League, an organization that they insisted was nonpartisan but which the *Compiler* dismissed as merely an abolitionist body. The previous month the *Compiler* described a "Festival of the 'Americans of African descent'" which was "largely and liberally patronized by 'black spirits and whites.'" The Democratic paper added that "it is supposed that the 'Union League' made it a point to have the Festival a more than ordinary success, because on the same night 'white folks' had a Promenade Concert at Sheads & Buehler's Hall."[26] This intriguing story indicates that local Republicans had an informal "Union League" in place before April.

In May several men from the surrounding towns were arrested as suspected members of the Knights of the Golden Circle, a secret organization with Confederate sympathies. When several Westminster men were arrested a few weeks later, Stahle's *Compiler* called the action the work of a "few low curs of the Abolition party."[27] One can only imagine what charges must have been made in more private settings.

In the first two years of the war, Gettysburg had evolved from fervent enthusiasm to a more organized, business-like approach to the conflict. Recruits responded to cash bounties as much as patriotic rhetoric. Voluntary societies had established regular routines to answer each new call for assistance. Nevertheless, the world had not changed very much. A few weeks in mid-summer would provide a new host of challenges.

In June 1863, Confederate General Robert E. Lee opted to head north for a second time. By this point, the citizens of Gettysburg had become accustomed to invasion scares and it was not until late June that most locals began taking the threat seriously and bracing for the worst. Farmers drove their animals to safety, merchants packed up their retail stock for shipment to more distant towns, and some citizens—including many local African Americans—fled the borough.

On June 19, Company A of the 26th Pennsylvania Emergency Volunteer Infantry, all men from Gettysburg, were mustered in for service. On June 22, a group of Gettysburg men—including Sarah Broadhead's husband—who had journeyed west of town to fell trees to impede the Rebels' progress rushed home to report that the Confederates were on their way. On June 26, the 26th Pennsylvania Emergency Troops made an unsuccessful stand against a Confederate contingent outside Gettysburg. That day, Confederate General Early arrived in town and demanded various supplies, including flour, meat, groceries, shoes, hats, and ten barrels of whiskey; he and his troops left the following morning. On June 28, Union cavalry were spotted just outside town, but they left the next day. By June 30, Gettysburg civilians could see Confederate pickets and officers on Seminary Ridge. That same day, Union cavalry leader Buford and his troops arrived in town to an enthusiastic greeting, and many soldiers were invited to dinner at Gettysburg homes. Finally, on the morning of the 1st, Buford's cavalry made contact with Confederate infantry on McPherson's Ridge to the west of the town. The battle had begun.

Although most of the battle was fought outside the town limits, Gettysburg civilians did come into repeated contact with soldiers from both armies. On the morning of July 1, people in the northwest section of town heard the first sounds of battle; a few young boys climbed up on the Seminary's cupola to watch the action while civilians gathered along Seminary Ridge or sought vantage points on rooftops in town. In late morning, the Union's 11th Corps marched up Washington Street to meet the enemy north of the College. But that afternoon the 11th Corps passed through again, this time in full retreat toward Cemetery Hill. Several civilians immediately began tending to the wounded, but soon Union officers rode through town warning everyone to take refuge in their cellars. From their hiding places, many reported hearing sounds of fighting between the retreating Union forces and the pursuing Confederate troops. By the evening, Confederate troops occupied the town.

On the evening of July 1 and throughout July 2, Gettysburg civilians faced the threat of Confederate vandals and stray bullets. Rebel soldiers searched houses for hidden Union soldiers and demanded food from civilians. Meanwhile, the occupying troops built barricades in the streets against possible Union attacks from Cemetery Hill to the south. In the southern part of town, sharpshooters targeted any vaguely suspicious people. Rebel marksmen commandeered homes with promising windows, drawing Union fire toward civilian targets. Mary McAllister was nearly shot when she ventured to the store to get whiskey for medicinal purposes. The town was literally split between Union and Confederate forces, the latter occupying much of it. At John Rupp's house,

Confederates occupied the back of the house while Union men fought from the front porch.

By July 3, life inside the town had settled into a routine for most civilians: they stayed inside as much as possible. Loud cannonading continued through the late afternoon, and the danger from sharpshooters continued. Jennie Wade, the only civilian killed during the battle, was hit by an errant bullet. In a Confederate-controlled section of town, Agnes Barr left her house for the first time since the battle began. As she returned with supplies, she had to run to avoid Union sharpshooters. In the afternoon the tremendous artillery duel that preceded Pickett's charge seemed, to Sallie Broadhead, "as if heaven and earth were crashing together." That evening, citizens in their cellars could hear the creaking of Confederate wagons in retreat. It was the evening of July 4—Independence Day—that a relieved Sallie Broadhead wrote: "For the first time for a week I shall go to bed feeling safe." By the end of the day, many civilians correctly suspected that the Confederate forces would be defeated soon, but when the Confederates sent in a flag of truce the next day, some civilians feared it was a warning that they were going to shell the town.[28]

During the days of the battle, local citizens filled various roles. On the first day, many townspeople managed to observe some of the fighting from rooftops until the Confederates entered the town. During and immediately after the battle, Gettysburg civilians provided food, lodging, and care for the wounded of both sides. Citizens set up hospitals in public buildings and took wounded soldiers into their homes. Agnes Barr, for instance, aided wounded Union soldiers in her home and at a nearby church. Mary McAllister also helped with wounded soldiers, even venturing outside of the hospital to find doctors for them. Some Gettysburg civilians harbored Union soldiers despite threats of punishment from the Confederates. Catherine Foster managed to keep Confederate soldiers from discovering a Union soldier hidden in her home. The Forney family disguised a Union soldier in civilian clothes during the Confederate occupation. Some civilians found more direct ways to assist the Federal forces. John Burns, the aging veteran of the War of 1812, rushed to the battlefield to stand alongside the Union troops. Tillie Pierce Alleman recalled that two Gettysburg College professors "point[ed] out to the Union officers the impregnable positions of the locality"—that is, readily defendable positions.[29]

Black Gettysburg civilians experienced the battle differently from the white citizens. Although much of the battle was fought near the black section of town in the southwest, no black homes were used to house the wounded during or after the battle. Many African Americans had left Gettysburg before the battle.

In her diary late that month, Salome Myers wrote that "[t]he town is pretty clear of darkies. . . . Darkies of both sexes are skedaddling and some white folks of the male sex." Some who stayed behind were hidden by their white employers. Jacob Taughenbaugh's mother hid her two African American servants in the cellar. "Old Liz," who had been captured by Confederate troops, managed to escape the Rebels on the first day of battle and hid in a church belfry for the next two days.[30]

The battle of Gettysburg and the invasion scares in June exacerbated previously existing local conflicts. Tillie Pierce Alleman described how tension between her family and their neighbors resulted in angry accusations in the tense days before the battle. Her father was described to a Confederate colonel as a "black Abolitionist" by a woman who blamed their family for her son's near capture. Shortly after the battle ended, Henry Stahle, the editor of the Democratic *Compiler,* was arrested for purportedly directing the Confederates toward hidden Union troops. That accusation, which stemmed from Stahle's efforts to find a doctor for a wounded Union soldier, likely reflected his controversial political stances.[31]

White citizens' experiences during the battle (and recollections after the fact) reflected continued assumptions about gender roles. Women were celebrated for being nurturers: nursing wounded soldiers, cooking, and providing lodging. Fannie Buehler wrote that after the battle started, "The wounded were brought in. Here was women's work, and they did it nobly." Agnes Barr and many other women remained busy providing food for the wounded soldiers they hosted in their homes. In one instance, Confederate soldiers killed Harriet Bayly's chickens, then brought the chickens to her to cook. Gettysburg's men were also engaged in tending to the wounded, but contemporary accounts consistently stressed the contributions of women. Commenting on the praise lavished on Gettysburg women for their nursing efforts, the *Compiler* was moved to add: "Some of our male citizens were active in rendering all the aid in their power to alleviate the suffering wounded."[32]

The personal accounts emphasized that Gettysburg men were responsible for protecting goods, home, and family, even when these roles came into conflict. One week before the battle, Harriet Bayly's husband and son left town to remove their horses and some valuables from the Confederates' reach. Harriet Bayly stressed that her husband returned by the first day of the battle, "being anxious about the welfare of his family." William Bayly, thirteen years old during the battle, later wrote, "Our skedaddling trips were entirely for the protection of our stock and not for personal safety, as my father was too old for military service and I too young." Other men, such as Liberty Hollinger's father, attempted to keep Confederate soldiers out of their homes and tried to retain their supply of food despite Confederate demands. Even when men acted for their own protection, the published narratives stressed their heroic aspects. For example, Fannie Buehler wrote that she persuaded her husband, David, "much against his will, to prepare for flight should the enemy make an invasion into Pennsylvania," as he was a staunch, outspoken Republican as well as a postmaster.[33]

The most telling challenges to gender roles occurred when local women were temporarily left alone to defend their families and homes. Fannie Buehler's husband was unable to return through the army lines until after the battle ended. As Sarah Broadhead wrote, "I was left entirely alone, surrounded by thousands of ugly, rude, hostile soldiers, from whom violence might be expected." Several narratives described local women brazenly confronting Confederate soldiers or demanding help for the wounded. In other cases, women defied Confederate orders by helping to harbor Union soldiers. Although they cared for the wounded from both sides, Gettysburg's women explicitly identified with the Union soldiers. On July 11, Broadhead wrote, "[t]his day has been spent in caring for OUR men."[34]

Any talk of historic "turning points" is almost inherently misleading: the past has few right angles. Nonetheless, the first few weeks of July 1863 were certainly crucial in shaping the course of the Civil War. The day after Pickett's disastrous charge in the fields outside Gettysburg, Vicksburg fell to Federal forces, giving the Union control of the vital Mississippi. Nine days later, New York City erupted in bloody draft rioting, underscoring the North's conflicts about conscription, race, and the progress of the war. In hindsight, it is easy to argue that the South had little chance of achieving a purely military victory after the summer of 1863. For the next two years, Gettysburg had a strange dual identity. As the site of the Confederacy's "high water mark," the borough took a special place in the nation's consciousness. As a Northern community, Gettysburg continued to experience the war's evolutions much like the rest of the North. Our task is to sort out both how the battle affected Gettysburg and how the larger patterns of change touched this small Pennsylvania town.

For weeks after the battle, Gettysburg was dramatically different from all other Northern towns. Contemporary accounts describe evidence of the "ravages of war" for miles in all directions. Fences and crops had been destroyed, animals were lost, and—above all—thousands of dead and wounded remained to be tended to. Scores of benevolent volunteers, including the famed Dorothea Dix, descended on the town. Both the USSC and the USCC established bases of operation, complementing the ongoing relief efforts by local citizens. Private homes became emergency hospitals, prompting the local papers to declare: "We feel satisfied that Gettysburg and its loyal citizens will not be forgotten when the history of this War is written by the future historian." As Sarah Broadhead noted ten days after the battle ended, "The old story of the inability of a village of twenty-five hundred inhabitants, overrun and eaten out by two large armies, to accommodate from ten to twelve thousand visitors, is repeated almost hourly."[35]

Soon calm returned to Gettysburg. Trains carried the many wounded soldiers to distant hospitals. Others were moved to a temporary General Hospital outside of town. Before long, the citizens began discussing how the battle should be commemorated, eventually settling on a proposal for a grand National Cemetery near the battlefield. After months of detailed planning, the cemetery's official consecration day was set for November 19. Once again, the nation's eyes turned to the Pennsylvania community as Abraham Lincoln and a huge assembly of dignitaries took the train to Gettysburg. Edward Everett, the leading American orator, delivered a lengthy address, which was followed by a few carefully chosen words by the President. The event, the *Sentinel* declared, "made Gettysburg famous for the second time."[36]

Throughout the weeks after the battle, the local voluntary organizations carried on their familiar routines, but the national benevolent societies began playing an expanded local role. In early August, a group of Gettysburg men, identifying themselves as the "Local Committee of the USCC," issued an appeal for food, clothing, and blankets for the wounded soldiers. The following month, several "ladies of the town," joined with USSC and USCC workers to entertain the soldiers at the General Hospital.

By early 1864, the local branch of the Christian Commission had taken on new prominence. In late March, the committee called for donations, suggesting "that our citizens collect and contribute relics and mementoes from our battlefield, by the sale of which in the city fairs, considerable sums can be realized." The Ladies' Aid Society for the Christian Commission formed a few weeks later. The Society's seventeen members included the wives of five of the six men on the local branch of the USCC. The Gettysburg branch of the USCC raised $1,132 in the town and the surrounding county.

In the final year of war, the two national benevolent societies grew in stature, often competing for limited resources. The Sanitary Commission responded by staging a series of fund-raising "sanitary fairs" across the North, with Philadelphia hosting the second largest in June 1864. Planning for the Philadelphia fair quickly became a statewide effort. In April, the Adams County subcommittee called on towns to form their own organizations to raise money and collect goods for the fair. Gettysburg's citizens were especially asked to collect trophies from the battlefield and local women were "earnestly solicited to prepare articles from the mosses, grass, ferns, pines, &c, taken from the Gettysburg battlefield." For the next several weeks, the local committee made repeated requests for assistance, often stressing the historic significance of battlefield memorabilia.

On one level it would seem that Gettysburg became a battleground between these two competing national agencies. In mid-April, local papers reprinted the following appeal from the Christian Commission: "In these days when 'Sanitary Fairs' are engrossing the public attention and absorbing immense sums of money, we ask the Christian public to remember and aid the society whose unpaid delegates are upon the battle field." This request, which included a thinly veiled slap at the Sanitary Commission's *paid* agents, reflected the tensions between the two national agencies. Yet three of the ten Adams County women on the Sanitary Fair committee also served on Gettysburg's branch of the USCC's "Ladies' Aid Society," and a fourth was the daughter of a USCC committee member. The Fair Committee also included Mrs. R. G. Harper, who continued to direct Gettysburg's local Ladies' Union Relief Society.

In the summer after the battle, Gettysburg once again braced for a new Confederate invasion. In mid-July, the tension within the borough mounted as the streets filled with refugees and animals from farms and towns to the south. The initial scare turned out to be a false alarm and calm slowly returned. A few weeks later, word reached Gettysburg that Confederate raiders had entered Pennsylvania and burned Chambersburg. Following lessons learned the previous year, farmers fled with their animals, local merchants packed their goods off to distant towns, and a hundred armed volunteers stepped forward for home defense. When the immediate threat subsided, Gettysburg's philanthropic machinery eased into motion. A town meeting named a "Committee of Ladies" to assemble goods to ship to Chambersburg and an affiliated men's committee assembled to collect cash donations.

Neither the experiences following the battle nor the changing nature of benevolence in its aftermath seems to have had much of an effect on the perception or reality of Gettysburg's benevolent gender roles. Both the local and national societies separated men and women into different bodies, with men in positions of greater national authority and with appeals for assistance reflecting gendered assumptions. The committees named to assist the Chambersburg victims were quite typical: the women collected goods and packed boxes, whereas the men's group was charged with receiving cash donations. Other public roles reflected similarly persistent divisions. When patriotic occasions called for civic ritual, Gettysburg's "ladies" were still called on to present flags or serve similar ceremonial functions.

Recruiting practices, like voluntarism, took on new characteristics in the final years of the Civil War. By mid-1863, Northerners grew increasingly desperate to find volunteers to meet Federal quotas without holding drafts. The grim story of New York City's rioting only exacerbated such concerns. In August 1863, after months of recruiting and anticipation, the names of forty-nine Gettysburg men—including seven African Americans—were drawn to meet the borough's new quota.[37] That October, Abraham Lincoln called for another 500,000 men, with the draft to occur in March. As draft day approached, the town adopted newly aggressive measures. In January, the borough held a large meeting and named an official recruiting committee. The Town Council approved a motion to borrow $4,000 to fund $100 bounties for local recruits (to be grafted onto existing state and federal bounties). When draft day arrived, Gettysburg had already filled its quota.

The town had little opportunity to rest on its recruiting laurels. Lincoln issued three more major calls in 1864. On each occasion, communities were given ample opportunity to fill their quotas before draft day. These drafts are best viewed as recruiting incentives, rather than measures designed to put conscripts into uniform. Gettysburg responded to each call in typical fashion: with aggressive lobbying to reduce their assigned quotas and increasingly frenetic bounty-fund drives. By September, the town committee had raised $14,500 in voluntary subscriptions to go along with an $8,000 appropriation from the Town Council, providing recruits with sizeable $500 local bounties. These efforts enabled the town to escape each of the Union's remaining drafts. The three 1864 drafts yielded over 484,000 names drawn and 120,507 men "held to service." In contrast, Gettysburg met all its 1864 quotas without resorting to a draft.

Meanwhile, Gettysburg continued to link the Union's military successes with distinctly local concerns. Newspapers published letters from local soldiers and paid particular attention to the exploits of Gettysburg companies. The town celebrated the return of three-year regiments with familiar rituals, featuring parades, speeches, and receptions. Such celebrations mirrored rituals in communities throughout the North. The soldiers who returned home discovered that they had changed far more than the worlds they left behind.

The political tensions that festered through the first two years of war, and led to editor Stahle's arrest immediately following the battle, continued to divide Gettysburg for the rest of the war. Stahle's one week incarceration in Baltimore's Fort McHenry turned out to be only the first part of his ordeal. Immediately on returning to Gettysburg, he was arrested—and quickly released—a second time. The following week he returned to Fort McHenry to face new charges. Stahle insisted that he had acted innocently (and bravely) to assist the wounded Union colonel and that leading Republican lawyer David McConaughy was behind the charges.

Stahle's story suggests that political antagonisms persisted even in the midst of the fighting. In fact, he claimed that local "abolitionists" directed Union search parties toward Democratic homes and that his political enemies tore down the *Compiler's* flag under cover of battle. The following year the issue resurfaced when the state House of Representatives debated a motion to limit reimbursements for military damage claims to those citizens who could "furnish positive proof of their loyalty." Democrats attacked this assault on their loyalty, insisting that they had been equally involved in assisting the Union troops.[38]

In 1863, Democrats had grown more open in their attacks on emancipation, conscription, and the suppression of civil liberties. After the battle, Gettysburg remained a Republican—or Union—Party stronghold in a largely Democratic Adams County. That fall the County supported the Democratic challenger to Governor Curtin, but Gettysburg backed the incumbent Republican 265 to 169. The following March the *Sentinel* celebrated as the Union ticket swept the Borough elections. Partisan political discourse heightened in the fall of 1864 when the Democrat George McClellan mounted a serious challenge to President Lincoln. The two parties staged large rallies in Gettysburg on consecutive September evenings. The language in speeches, letters, and editorials grew increasingly bitter as election day approached. Local Democrats delighted in playing the race card, accusing their adversaries of supporting Lincoln's most controversial abolitionist plans. Pennsylvania Democrats won victories in the crucial state elections, which preceded the national Presidential election, but Gettysburg continued to support Republican candidates for Congress and various local and county offices. A few weeks later, Lincoln defeated McClellan with the support of Pennsylvania voters. Once again, Gettysburg supported the Republican candidate by a 259 to 178 margin. The following March, as the war was in its final stages, Gettysburg Democrats managed to win three local offices, including one of three positions on the Council. These modest victories led Stahle to declare that "The People [are] Getting Tired of Abolitionism."[39]

The wartime history of Gettysburg's African Americans, both before and after the battle, remains largely elusive. The March 1863 "Festival of the 'Americans of African descent'" reported in the *Compiler* indicates the continuation of separate civic rituals into the war years. As we have seen, many African Americans temporarily fled the town when Lee's troops advanced; others were captured and carried off by the Confederates. Those who returned after the battle often found property missing or destroyed. When the Union allowed African Americans to serve in uniform, several local men stepped forward and others appeared on the conscription lists. By one estimate, forty-three African Americans from the vicinity served in the Union Army. Despite such efforts, local whites clearly had little enthusiasm for racial equality, and both political parties were anxious to resist any taint of abolitionism.

In December 1864, Solomon Devan, a seventeen-year-old student at Gettysburg's "Colored School," drew a revolver and fired two shots at a teacher who had tried to "correct [him] . . . with a rod." Fortunately, Devan's shots missed their mark and thus he was only charged with assault and battery. The local court found the young man guilty, sentencing him to thirteen months in the state penitentiary. One can only guess at the untold story behind this episode. Perhaps Devan resisted because he saw his teacher's attitude as that of a master toward a slave. The two local papers reported the facts of the case, with the *Compiler* adding that "Abolitionism is costing more than it will come to."⁴⁰

The Civil War's effect on Gettysburg's economy was generally quite modest. After a brief economic downturn during the secession crisis, the Northern economy prospered for the war years. Unemployment was extraordinarily low; demand for goods and services—partially stimulated by military need—was generally high. Whereas the Confederacy suffered from serious shortages and crippling inflation, most Northerners enjoyed the fruits of prosperity. The greatest exception were those unskilled or semiskilled workers who were hit hard by inflation and lacked the negotiating strength of their better organized brethren.

The anecdotal evidence from the local newspapers suggests that Gettysburg's businesses generally fared well during the war. Some local stores added military-related goods to their stock or used patriotic rhetoric in their advertising. A few individuals offered their services to citizens or veterans in search of pensions or bounties. Only a handful of local companies earned direct war-related profits. Two firms profited by building the barracks for the Porter Guards; the Gettysburg Railroad routinely reported modest profits from transporting military units; and, in October 1863, two local men won the contract to disinter bodies

and move them to the new national cemetery. Periodically, Northern war contractors became embroiled in complex scandals involving shoddy equipment
or illegal kickbacks. Adams County had its own small scandal during the war's
first winter, when several farmers contracted with the War Department to board
government horses. In the byzantine discussions that followed, it came to light
that certain individuals were making exorbitant profits while subcontracting
out the work to unsuspecting third parties.

The evidence from Adams County's Poor-House Accounts also tells a tale
that is similar to the North as a whole. The auditor's annual report included a
summary of residents in the almshouse as of the first of the year. Between 1858
and 1865, this population fluctuated between 107 and 118 people, suggesting
that the almshouse probably ran at close to capacity. However, the number of
transients assisted annually fluctuated dramatically. In 1860 and 1861—in the
midst of the secession crisis—the county assisted 1,990 and 1,738 transients.
By 1863 this figure had dropped to 814; the following year it fell to 430.[41]

In the war's final winter, the citizens of Gettysburg gathered for an emergency meeting "to adopt measures to relieve the wants of the destitute." The
meeting named a "Relief Committee" composed of representatives from seven
local church congregations and nine two-man "visiting committees" to visit
the poor in their homes. They also named a parallel committee of "ladies of
the Borough." Two months later, the Relief Committee called a public meeting
to discuss their progress. But despite public announcements and bell ringing,
only five committee members and no other citizens appeared.

What does the story of the Relief Committee indicate about wartime Gettysburg? Certainly it suggests unfamiliar demands for poor relief in the war's final
months. The Committee's structure shared much in common with war-related
philanthropies, with a steering committee of men and an auxiliary committee
of women. Most of the members of the seven-man committee were drawn
from the same pool of leaders that directed the town's benevolent and political
organizations: three had been on the committee formed in April 1861 to assist
the families of volunteers; three had run for local office (two Republicans and
one Democrat); two had served on recruiting committees; and two served on
the local branch of the USCC. Five of the eight members of the women's committee had served on at least one of the war-related benevolent committees
and the remaining three were also from very active local families. Four years
of war had done little to change the community's leadership structure.[42]

. . .

The events of April 1865 sent the Northern states through a bewildering series of emotional highs and lows. Early in the month, news arrived of the fall of Petersburg and Richmond, signaling the imminent end of the Confederacy. On April 4, the *Sentinel* reported: "Our town was quite jubilant last evening over the glorious intelligence. The flags, the ringing of bells, the firing of salutes, bonfires, and the cheering of the crowds, were evidences of the general rejoicing." With victory within reach, schools and public buildings closed and the town gathered for song, speeches, and celebration.[43] The revelry was to be short-lived. On the evening of April 14, Abraham Lincoln was shot while attending Ford's Theater. Newspapers across the North printed black-bordered accounts of the President's final hours. Gettysburg held a special town meeting that passed formal resolutions of sorrow and requested that citizens don black crepe armbands for the month to come. Before long, the Northern soldiers began filtering back home. In May, the returned Union troops staged a Grand Review in Washington. In early July, two years after the Battle of Gettysburg, the town's surviving volunteers paraded through the flag-lined streets to enthusiastic cheers.

How had the Civil War and the Battle of Gettysburg altered the borough? By many measures Gettysburg, like the rest of the North, was surprisingly unchanged by four years of carnage. Whereas the South faced major physical damage, the destruction of slavery, and the concomitant demise of the plantation system, the North—and Gettysburg—experienced no comparable economic shocks (although of course some individuals suffered property losses from the invasion and battle). Certain local businesses profited from war contracts, but there was no need for substantial economic adjustments in response to the war's demands. In the long run, the town's notoriety as the site of the famous battle would dramatically alter its economic and cultural world. The evidence from the other end of the economic spectrum suggests a steady decline in the county's transient poor through most of the war, but a short-term increase in the demand for local poor relief during the war's final winter. One of the war's economic legacies that Gettysburg shared with many Northern communities was an expanded municipal debt. In 1869, the Town Council voted to implement a special Bounty Tax to repay subscribers who had invested in the town's 1864 bounty fund.

The best available demographic portrait comes from the census of 1870. In the decade of the 1860s Gettysburg's population climbed from 2,389 to 3,072, a rate of increase quite comparable to that of the national population. The military losses left some Southern states with a short-term "man shortage." Georgia, for instance had about 30,000 more women than men over the age of eighteen in 1870. No such shortage struck the more populous North. Gettysburg males made up roughly 51 percent of the population in 1870, a slight increase from 49 percent in 1860. The number of African Americans in Gettysburg increased from 190 to 223 over the decade, but the percentage of blacks in the population declined from 8 to 7 percent. One scholar has estimated that fewer than a third of the African Americans in the town in 1860 remained in 1870, perhaps owing to the dislocations accompanying the Rebel invasions. As in 1860, the vast majority of residents were born in Pennsylvania (82 percent) while an additional 271 (9 percent) were from Maryland. The African-American population included 63 (28 percent) people from Maryland and 24 (11 percent) from reconstructed Confederate states. The most substantial demographic shift was a decline in immigrants from 164 (7 percent of the total) to 127 (4 percent).

Of course, wars often have effects that resist quantitative measures. Some American conflicts, the American Revolution and World War II, for instance, affected the economic and social positions of women. The military experiences of African Americans have sometimes been connected to subsequent peacetime gains. Certainly both groups experienced important challenges during the Civil War. But the best evidence for concrete wartime changes—for blacks certainly, but for women as well—occurred in the Confederacy. The women of Gettysburg earned fame for their efforts after the battle, but such acclaim rarely challenged established gender norms.

Gettysburg's leadership structure seemed equally unaffected by four years of war. Periodically over the course of the conflict the borough selected men and women for special committees to address recruiting or philanthropic needs. A comparison of these committee lists reveals a handful of names appearing time and again. Moreover, these local leaders were drawn disproportionately from the town's economic elite. For instance, in the first days of the war, Joel B. Danner served on both the Central Relief Committee, to raise money for families of volunteers, and the Committee of Safety, which organized the Home Guard. In the next four years, the Gettysburg merchant, who had been listed with $6,000 in personal wealth in 1860, twice served on emergency recruiting committees and also on the local organizing committee for the Sanitary Commission's Great Central Fair. William A. Duncan, an attorney with $15,000 in real estate and another $8,000 in personal wealth, joined Danner on both April 1861 committees and later served on the 1864 recruiting committee and the 1865 Poor Relief Committee. Mary Carson served on the Ladies' Relief Society, on committees associated with both the USSC and the USCC and on the 1865 Poor Relief Committee. Her husband, T. D. Carson, was a local banker.

Another way to measure the war's impact is to consider the rising role of national institutions, both public and private, in everyday life. This was, after all, a war fought by national armies over the meaning of the Union. Gettysburg shared fully in many of the war's centralizing impulses, particularly after July 1863. In the war's final two years, the town threw itself into recruiting, stimulated by new federal conscription legislation. Both national benevolent societies played enlarged local roles after the battle, as did the patriotic Union League. And the wartime emphasis on national military and political affairs naturally drew the attention of citizens beyond their immediate surroundings. On the other hand, localism still prevailed in each of these areas: the Ladies' Relief Society maintained its autonomy; recruiting depended on local energies and fund-raising; and national political debates were viewed through the prism of local personalities and concerns.

We are left, then, with an almost troublesome conclusion. Although it was the scene of unimaginable carnage, Gettysburg survived the battle with surprisingly few effects. As traumatic as the events of July 1863 may have been, they did not last long, and when they were over the invading army had been vanquished. Communities across the South faced more serious challenges that were measured in months and years, rather than hours and days. In this sense, Gettysburg shared much more in common with the rest of the Northern home front than with the beleaguered Confederacy.

Perhaps the battle's true legacy is found less in the events than in their retelling. Immediately following the battle, the townspeople began seeing themselves as caretakers of an historically vital place. The creation of the National Cemetery in November 1863, spurred on by local citizens and sealed by Lincoln's famed visit, elevated Gettysburg into a new symbolic importance. The organizers of Philadelphia's Great Central Fair called on Gettysburg to provide battlefield "relics" rather than more routine donations. The town reflected its own shifting self-image in its annual celebration of Independence Day. The town celebrated July 4, 1862, in a traditional, highly localized fashion. In contrast, in preparing for the first Independence Day after the battle, the local organizers insisted on giving the celebration "a National character." Gettysburg's first postwar Independence Day featured a visit by President Andrew Johnson, who observed the laying of a cornerstone at the Soldiers' National Monument. The "great national celebration" that day included the President, the Cabinet, the Supreme Court,

Ulysses S. Grant, and various other national dignitaries. Meanwhile, the town and the battlefield had already become a major tourist attraction, with visitors venturing from all over the North and South.

Gettysburg's civilians provided their own version of the battle's significance by telling their individual tales. Some citizens grew famous shortly after the battle concluded. Jennie Wade quickly became the subject of legend and controversy. John Burns survived his wounds to become a national hero. For other individuals, like editor Henry Stahle, the act of telling his story was part of his almost obsessive pursuit of vindication. In 1864, Sarah Broadhead printed her diary of the events between June 15 and July 15. In an almost apologetic preface Broadhead stressed that she was having her words "printed (not published) for distribution among [her] kindred and nearest friends" with seventy-five copies to be presented for sale at Philadelphia's Great Central Fair. She hoped that "these statements [would] disarm severe criticism" from those who objected to her rushing her "feeble efforts into print." As a woman, Broadhead felt the need for such disclaimers before placing her words in the public eye.

For a half-century and more, Gettysburg's citizens published diaries, memoirs, and interviews detailing the events during those three days in July 1863. By writing these personal "narratives," the civilian participants defined the battle as a momentous event in their individual lives. Their stories stressed the minutiae, not the grand themes. Perhaps this is because the North approached the battle, as it approached the Civil War, to protect what had previously been in place rather than to produce broad changes. For Gettysburg, victory ensured continuity. But in the process of remembering the battle, the borough helped shape itself into something quite new: a local community with a distinctive sense of its own national significance.

## NOTES

1. Sarah Broadhead, *The Diary of a Lady of Gettysburg, Pennsylvania,* July 4, 1863. Typescript in the Adams County Historical Society [hereafter ACHS].

2. *Gettysburg Compiler,* Oct. 9, 1865.

3. Albertus McCreary, "Gettysburg: A Boy's Experience of the Battle." Type script at ACHS. Also published in *McClure's Magazine* (July 1909).

4. Maris Vinovskis, "Have Social Historians Lost the Civil War? Some Preliminary Demographic Speculations," in Vinovskis, ed., *Toward a Social History of the American Civil War: Exploratory Essays* (New York: Cambridge University Press, 1990), 3–7. Of course America's losses during the Civil War include men who fell on both sides.

5. United States Census of 1860, Gettysburg, Pennsylvania. (All calculations in this chapter are from computer databases created at the Civil War Institute, Gettysburg, Pa.) Despite the borough's clear Northern sympathies, William Frassanito has unearthed evidence of several antebellum residents or Gettysburg College alumni who went on to serve with the Confederacy. See William A. Frassanito, *Early Photography at Gettysburg* (Gettysburg: Thomas, 1995), 124–28, 368–83.

6. Peter C. Vermilyea, "'We Did Not Know Where Our Colored Friends Had Gone': The Effect of the Confederate Invasion of Pennsylvania on Gettysburg's African-American Community." (Unpublished independent study, Gettysburg College. Gettysburg, 1994); Census of 1860.

7. *Adams Sentinel,* Oct. 3, 1860.

8. *Compiler,* Apr. 22, 1861 and *passim; Sentinel,* Apr. 24, 1861.

9. *Sentinel,* Apr. 24, 1861 and *passim; Compiler,* Apr. 29, May 6, 13, 27, June 17, 1861.

10. *Compiler,* May 6, 13, 20, June 3, 17, 1861; *Sentinel,* June 12, 1861; Bloom, 185–86. On May 20, for instance, the *Compiler* reported that the Ladies' Union Relief Society was preparing goods to send to York, Pennsylvania.

11. *Sentinel,* July 31, 1861; *Compiler* Aug. 5, 1861.

12. *Compiler,* Sept. 9, 1861.

13. The Town Council ended up paying the Relief Committee $204.58 of the appropriated $500; the remainder of the Committee's 1861 expenses were covered by the County Commissioners. "Excerpts of the Minute Book of the Gettysburg Town Council," Apr. 20, Sept. 30, 1861, GNMPL; *Compiler,* July 1, 1861. The County Commissioners reinstated the tax at a reduced level the following April. *Compiler,* Apr. 28, 1862.

14. *Compiler,* Aug. 26, 1861; *Sentinel,* Aug. 28, 1861.

15. *Compiler,* Dec. 30, 1861; *Sentinel,* Jan. 1, 1862.

16. Corner, Jan. 6, Feb. 10, Mar. 3, 10, *1862; Sentinel,* Jan. 29, Feb. 12, 1862.

17. Salome Myers Stewart Diary, 1862, ACHS. Quotation from Mar. 14, 1862.

18. *Sentinel, Mai.* 12, 1861.

19. Ibid., Oct. 23, 1861. The United States Sanitary Commission and the United States Christian Commission were two national bodies with local auxiliaries in communities across the North. Both raised tremendous funds to send supplies to soldiers at the front. The two bodies were different in several ways, the most obvious being the Christian Commission's delivery of bibles and religious tracts along with other necessities. See J. Matthew Gallman, *The North Fights the Civil War: The Home Front* (Chicago: Ivan Dee, 1994).

20. *Compiler,* Jan. 6, 1862; *Sentinel,* Jan. 8, 1862.

21. *Compiler,* July 8, 1861.

22. Ibid., July 21, 28, Aug. 4, 11, 1862; *Sentinel,* Aug. 12, 1862.

23. *Sentinel,* Aug. 28, 1861.

24. *Compiler,* Apr. 21, 1862.

25. *Sentinel,* Aug. 12, 1862.

26. *Compiler,* Mar. 2, 1863.

27. Ibid., May 18, June 1, 1863; *Sentinel,* May 19, 26, 1863.

28. Broadhead, *Diary,* July 3–4, 1863.

29. Tillie Pierce Alleman, *At Gettysburg: Or What a Young Girl Saw and Heard of the Battle* (New York: Borland, 1889), 16, 90.

30. Fannie Buehler, *Recollections of the Great Rebel Invasion and One Woman's Experiences During the Battle of Gettysburg* (ACHS, 1896), 11; McCreary, "A Boy's Experience"; Stewart, "Recollections of the Battle of Gettysburg," Diary entry for June 21, 1863, ACHS; Jacob Taughenbaugh, "In Occupied Pennsylvania," edited by T. W. Herbert, *Georgia Review* (Summer 1950): 104–105.

31. Alleman, *At Gettysburg*, 26; *Compiler*, July 13, 20, 27, Aug. 17, 1863, Oct. 9, 1865; *Sentinel*, July 14, 28, 1863.

32. Buehler, *Recollections*, 17; *Compiler*, July 20, 1863.

33. Buehler, *Recollections*, 5; Harriet Bayly, "Story of the Battle," ACHS, 1; William Bayly, "Memoir of a Thirteen-year-old Boy Relating to the Battle of Gettysburg" (typescript 1903), 2–3, ACHS.

34. Broadhead, Diary, June 27, July 11, 1863.

35. Ibid., July 9,13,1863.

36. *Sentinel*, Nov. 24, 1863.

37. *Compiler*, Aug. 24, 1863. Men selected on draft day still had several routes to avoid service. They could demonstrate one of a long list of personal or medical exemptions or, failing that, they could furnish a substitute. Thus, the number drawn does not reflect the actual number of men who ended up serving in uniform. The draft and recruiting appeared regularly in both newspapers from June through August.

38. *Compiler*, July 13, 1863, Mar. 21, 28, 1864.

39. *Sentinel*, Oct. 25, Nov. 8, 15, 1864; *Compiler*, Oct. 31, Nov. 7, 14, 1864, Mar. 20, 1865. In 1864 Adams County backed McClellan 2,886 to 2,362.

40. *Sentinel*, Dec. 13, 1864, Jan. 24, Apr. 25, 1865; *Compiler*, Dec. 12, 1864. Neither newspaper offered any comment at the seemingly light sentence.

41. The Poor-House Accounts were published several times each year in the local newspapers, generally beginning in the first week of March.

42. Three women were on the local branch of the USCC; three served on the Sanitary Fair committee; and two were on the Ladies' Relief Society. Several women served on more than two of these organizations.

43. *Sentinel*, Apr. 4, 11, 1865.

# Urban History and the American Civil War

When I wrote my dissertation on Civil War Philadelphia, there were very few studies of the Northern home front and almost no scholarly works on Civil War cities. Since then, when new home front studies came down the pike, they often ended up on my desk, either in manuscript form or for review. This essay is my response to seven of the more recent urban histories, with some more general thoughts on Civil War cities in general. I think that the topic is particularly interesting because it represents the confluence of two very different areas of study: urban history and Civil War history. These seven scholars, with very different backgrounds and goals, brought a fascinating array of tools and perspectives to their task.

. . .

LOUIS S. GERTEIS, *Civil War St. Louis.* Lawrence: University of Kansas Press. 2001, pp. 410, illustrations, notes, bibliographic essay, index, $34.95 cloth.

THEODORE J. KARAMANSKI, *Rally 'Round the Flag: Chicago and the Civil War.* Chicago: Nelson-Hall, 1993, pp. xiii, 292. illustrations, maps, notes, index, $31.95.

STEPHEN J. OCHS, *A Black Patriot and a White Priest: André Cailloux and Claude Paschal Maistre in Civil War New Orleans.* Louisiana State University Press, 2000, pp. 304, illustrations, appendix, bibliography, index. $39.95 cloth.

THOMAS H. O'CONNOR, *Civil War Boston: Home Front & Battlefield.* Boston: Northeastern University Press, 1997, pp. xvi, 313, illustrations, notes, bibliography, index, $42.50 cloth.

WILLIAM WARREN ROGERS, JR., *Confederate Home Front: Montgomery During the Civil War.* Tuscaloosa: University of Alabama Press, 1999, pp. xiv, 208, illustrations, notes, bibliography, index, $29.95 cloth.

EDWARD K. SPANN, *Gotham At War: New York City, 1860–1865.* Wilmington, DL: Scholarly Resources, 2002, pp. xiv, 213, illustrations, notes, bibliographic essay, index, $17.95 paper.

STEVEN ELLIOTT TRIPP, *Yankee Town, Southern City: Race and Class Relations in Civil War Lynchburg.* New York: New York University Press, 1997, pp. xviii, 344, illustrations, notes, bibliography, index, $45.00 cloth.

It is probably the nature of our discipline that most historians believe that their particular area of interest is poised—delicately—at the intersection of a host of vital scholarly discussions, thus elevating even the most modest micro-study into a work of tremendous significance. Why, we each ask—if only in the privacy of our own minds—have scholars across the historiographic landscape failed to grapple with the larger implications of my findings? None of these authors betray such secret musings, but collectively they could be forgiven for claiming that their shared topic—Civil War cities—has a rightful place in several of the most interesting conversations occupying nineteenth-century American historians. And, indeed, the assembled volumes do speak, albeit unevenly and sometimes disappointingly, to a host of broader issues.[1]

Let me suggest four ways in which the study of a Civil War city might address larger questions and perhaps point to broader analyses. First, city studies can flesh out the familiar Civil War chronology, adding detail and coherence to portions of a narrative that remain underexplored, while providing further evidence of how local developments—particularly in larger urban areas—shaped the fate of both the Union and the Confederacy. Second, this scholarship speaks directly to the broader concerns of the urban historian. What role did the Civil War play in the life of American cities? Did the war stimulate the growth of some metropolitan areas while retarding the development of other urban centers? Did it change how cities functioned politically or economically? A third cluster of questions places these urban studies within the booming literature on the social history of the Civil War. Although that scholarship certainly addresses the meaning of the American Civil War, many home front studies are as interested in using the conflict to explore broader social, political, and cultural topics. Civil War cities—with their ample newspapers, annual reports, court records, city directories, and occasional juicy diaries or collections of letters—are fertile ground for the social and economic historian.

To these three broad interpretive categories, I would add a fourth, more traditional form of urban history with its own set of questions and concerns: the city biography. In the same way that the discipline needs good biographies of Salmon P. Chase or Stonewall Jackson, there is much to be said for the volume that lays out, in clear no-nonsense fashion, the story of how major cities passed through the four years of war. Not coincidentally, two of these books—Spann's *Gotham at War* and O'Connor's *Civil War Boston*—were authored by emeriti scholars who have published extensively on their chosen cities,[2] while both Gerteis and Karamanski are senior scholars with established publication records and academic homes close to their subjects. It is a fair bet that all four surveyed the terrain and concluded—quite rightly—that each city deserved a solid Civil War history. Rogers's study of Montgomery generally fits within this urban biography tradition, whereas Steven Tripp—whose book began as a dissertation—organizes his study around specific interpretive questions, and Stephen J. Ochs uses Civil War New Orleans as a backdrop for a very different sort of volume.

I first started thinking about Civil War cities over two decades ago. I came to the task as a social historian, influenced by the great colonial community studies of the early 1970s.[3] I was inspired more by Robert Gross's marvelous study of Concord during the Revolutionary War than by Margaret Leech's older Pulitzer Prize–winning history of Civil War Washington.[4] When I dove into the urban studies of the middle period, I found much methodological inspiration in the works of the new social historians, but surprisingly little scholarship on the Civil War years themselves. It was as if a new generation of social historians had become so intent on mining the sources for the long sweeps of history, especially as experienced by the voiceless and powerless, that they had collectively turned their backs on those political and military events that dotted the traditional time line.[5] I felt as if, as we used to joke in graduate school, I had stumbled upon the perfect "curiously neglected topic."[6]

In the past two decades, Civil War historians have paid much more attention to the home front, and cities in particular; urban historians have thought more about the impact of the Civil War on their discipline. Consider two indices of these shifts. One of my favorite single-volume surveys of American urban history is Howard P. Chudacoff's *The Evolution of American Urban Society*. First published in 1975, the third edition of this popular text, co-authored by Judith E. Smith, appeared in 1988. That edition, like its predecessors, makes absolutely no reference to the Civil War, apart from the occasional use of the conflict as a chronological marker in transitions from one paragraph to the next. Even New York's draft riots go unnoticed. But six years later, in the fourth edition, Chudacoff and Smith added a three-page section entitled "Cities and the Civil War."[7] Similarly, for many years one of the most popular Civil War texts was *The Civil War and Reconstruction,* first authored by James David Randall in 1937 and later coauthored with David Herbert Donald in 1961. The Randall-Donald edition certainly paid attention to the Confederate and Union home fronts, including a chapter devoted to "The North in Wartime," but cities as a separate topic received no attention, and few individual cities appeared in the index. Forty years later, Jean Baker and Michael Holt joined Donald in a thorough revision of *The Civil War and Reconstruction.* This new volume included a wealth of changes reflecting two generations of new scholarship, including a section on "Urban Society" and numerous other references to cities.[8] And, in an interesting episode of art inadvertently imitating (or ignoring) scholarship, recently Hollywood offered its own distorted version of the urban home front in Martin Scorsese's "Gangs of New York."[9]

The seven volumes under review provide further testimony that Civil War cities are no longer curiously neglected, although I would stop well short of declaring the issues covered or the terrain too crowded. In fact, even where each author succeeds in meeting his own objectives, collectively these books fail to extend the discussion as far as one might wish, and perhaps reasonably expect.

The four northern studies are all fairly traditional, highly successful biographies of Civil War cities. In *Rally 'Round the Flag: Chicago and the Civil War,* Theodore Karamanski charts a challenging path. As the subtitle suggests, *Rally 'Round the Flag* is not so much a history of the Windy City during the Civil War as it is a broader narrative of both Chicago and its citizens during the conflict. Karamanski wishes to "[focus] on those personalities and incidents that reflect how Chicagoans affected the struggle for the Union and how the war shaped the city" (xii). The result is neither fish nor fowl. Several early chapters trace the national narrative through the lens of local politics and people, starting with the 1860 Republican Convention in Chicago, and including Lincoln's postelection visit to the city; the exploits of Chicago detective Alan Pinkerton; and the heroic death of Elmer Ellsworth in Alexandria, Virginia. All good material, interestingly rendered, but sometimes the city itself seems little more than backdrop.

Once the war is underway, Karamanski turns his attention more productively to the war's impact on the booming metropolis. The Civil War found Chicago well-situated to profit from the conflict's unusual economic opportunities even while it faced those internal conflicts that divided much of the northern home front. By 1860, Chicago—a city of 109,000—had nearly quadrupled in population over the previous decade and was "poised to begin the second stage of its urban development" (175) as a manufacturing center. Local boot makers, shipbuilders, and machinists—to name just a few—provided the Union army with manufactured goods, while the western city became a major supplier of meat, grain, horses, and the other raw materials of warfare. In the process, the war provided Chicago with the opportunity to parlay its geographic advantages into economic ascendancy over rivals St. Louis and Cincinnati.

Other sections sketch out the familiar themes that compose the home front story: recruiting and conscription, emancipation and racial tensions, voluntarism and fund raising, inflation and labor strife, politics and dissent. Even the familiar occasionally took on a distinctive shape in Chicago. Nowhere else in the North do we find a tandem of women as active and influential as Chicago's Mary Livermore and Jane Hoge, who proved instrumental in shaping the local branch of the Sanitary Commission and in orchestrating the highly successful Northwestern Sanitary Fair. Karamanski also devotes considerable attention to Camp Douglas, a military camp on the outskirts of the city that eventually became a major prison camp for captured rebels, and—in the war's final year—the focus for an elaborate failed Confederate conspiracy.

Whereas Chicago prospered through four years of war, three hundred miles to the south St. Louis faced a more awkward set of challenges. In *Civil War St. Louis,* Louis S. Gerteis is most interested in how the Missouri city was affected by, and helped shape, national political developments. As an outpost of free labor sentiment in a border slave state, antebellum St. Louis was home to powerful Democratic Senator Thomas Hart Benton and his circle of antislavery friends. When Lincoln was inaugurated in Chicago two years after Benton's death, Frank Blair and Gratz Brown were among the St. Louis delegation to the Republican convention. Once elected, Lincoln turned to St. Louis politicians Montgomery Blair and Edward Bates to join his cabinet. Shortly after the war began, Lincoln named Benton's son-in-law—explorer-turned-general John C. Frémont—as commander of Department of the West, which included Missouri. The radical Frémont soon antagonized the President with his abolitionist proclamations, prompting Jessie Benton Frémont's celebrated journey east to meet with the President. These are the characters and episodes that occupy much of Gerteis's attention.

While the state of Missouri was frequently a thorn in Lincoln's side, St. Louis remained loyal to the Union, but not without a tense early showdown between federal forces and pro-southern state militia over control of the local arsenal.

And although the city remained in Union hands, charges of disloyalty, political arrests, and occasional banishments revealed divisions beneath the patriotic surface. Gerteis appears most engaged in his descriptions of politics and civil liberties, but much like *Rally 'Round the Flag*, *Civil War St. Louis* includes extended discussions of voluntarism (emphasizing the roles of women), war contracting (and specifically the Carondelet shipyard), racial tensions over emancipation, and labor strife. And, unlike Karamanski, Gerteis's somewhat longer volume devotes some attention to the postwar years, with particular emphasis on the battles by women and African Americans to win a political voice.

Thomas H. O'Connor's history of *Civil War Boston* is another lively read that is likely to please a general audience as well as local specialists. And, very much like Karamanski, O'Connor's subtitle—*Home Front & Battlefield*—seems designed to suggest a large umbrella under which much history can fit. At one level *Civil War Boston* is a broad political and military narrative of the entire Civil War, as seen through the eyes of Bostonians. Thus, O'Connor summarizes important battles and elections, with particular attention to the exploits of local leaders or Massachusetts regiments in the field. The stories of William Lloyd Garrison, Charles Sumner, Dorothea Dix, Robert Gould Shaw, Susan B. Anthony, and a host of other famous figures fill the pages. At another level it is a well-written chronology of the main events on the Boston home front. Once again we learn of recruiting, voluntary societies, conscription and dissent, debates over emancipation, war contracting, and labor strife. One cannot help but be struck by how much cities and communities across the North shared similar subnarratives despite their differing circumstances.

In his introduction, O'Connor raises a set of questions and themes that work their way through *Civil War Boston*. Did the war "produce changes that had transforming effects upon the general population during the postwar years" (xv)? He promises to pursue this broader question by concentrating on four specific communities: businessmen, Irish-Americans, women, and African Americans. In practice, all four communities do appear periodically: the Irish rally around several Irish regiments and, later, respond angrily to the Emancipation Proclamation; African Americans jump at the opportunity to join the 54th Massachusetts, and the folks back home, except the Irish, follow their exploits with enthusiasm; Susan B. Anthony and Elizabeth Cady Stanton organize the Women's Loyal National League to lobby for emancipation, while other women form sewing circles or volunteer as nurses; and leading members of the conservative Boston business community, while initially opposed to the fight, eventually throw themselves into the cause and in the process they rethink their resistance to emancipation. In a concluding chapter, O'Connor returns to each of these communities in some detail, but the scope of the research makes it difficult to propose convincing answers to the original question about the war's "transforming effects."

When he set out to write a history of wartime New York, Edward K. Spann had a slightly different task before him. Ernest McKay's *The Civil War in New York City* covered the same factual terrain barely a decade earlier while failing, as Spann correctly explains, "to incorporate his findings into a coherent study of New York as an urban society" (xii). Meanwhile, several recent volumes dissected the city's famed draft riots.[10] Much more than the volumes on Chicago, St. Louis, and Boston, *Gotham at War* is a self-conscious work of urban history. Unlike those other books, national events provide a narrative context without competing with Gotham's own story; celebrated individuals appear where appropriate, but Spann does not go in for extended biographical sketches and lively episodic excursions. The result is a short, tightly woven study that succeeds as both description and interpretation.

Politically, New York was hugely significant as a Democratic metropolis within a Republican nation. In 1860, Lincoln won the state while losing every ward in the city. When the South seceded, flamboyant Democratic Mayor Fernando Wood openly supported peaceful separation. In the crucial 1862 elections, seventy percent of the city's voters supported Democrat Horatio Seymour in his victorious gubernatorial campaign. Two years later Abraham Lincoln captured only a single ward as General George McClellan swept the rest of the city. Locally, the city government used its resources creatively in response to the crisis: distributing funds to families of volunteers and appropriating huge sums for bounties to enlistees. Gotham also figured prominently in the North's larger benevolent and organizational history. The crucial Woman's Central Relief Association was founded at Cooper Institute; the United States Sanitary Commission—which emerged out of the WCRA—was run out of the city, under the leadership of several prominent New Yorkers; the Union League Club played a central role in promoting patriotism.

New York's size and location ensured the city a major role in the northern war effort, which in turn guaranteed Gotham a prosperous war. The city's shipyards produced vessels for the highly successful Union blockade. While the loss of Southern commerce and cotton certainly hurt, local contractors supplied the army, the city's railroad companies profited from an exploding demand to move goods west, and the war years witnessed a huge increase in the transatlantic petroleum trade through the port city. According to Spann, these economic shifts produced "a new economic order dominated by Gotham" (196). But such prosperity was only half the story. Following a brief treatment of the infamous draft riots, Spann presents a broader survey of New York's tremendous diversity and internal tensions, including its complex ethnic and racial dimensions and the huge economic disparities that characterized the wartime city.

When placed alongside these large cities, Montgomery, Alabama—the subject of William Warren Rogers, Jr.'s *Confederate Home Front*—hardly seems to merit the same label. With fewer than nine thousand residents in 1860 half (more than of those enslaved) Montgomery was about one-twentieth the size of New Orleans and only a twelfth the size of Chicago, the smallest of the four northern cities represented here. Still, as a political and distribution center Montgomery functioned as an important Confederate city. Prior to the war, Montgomery was a thriving commercial city, a vital player in the region's cotton trade and the center of state politics. In 1860, local voters lined up strongly behind John C. Breckinridge, and when the deep South seceded, Montgomery became the provisional capital. Soon after the shooting started, the Confederate government shifted its base of operations to Richmond, but Montgomery remained an important economic and political capital. As a railroad hub, the city became a center for Confederate medical care, with makeshift hospitals dotting the landscape. In the meantime, Montgomery took on the aspect of an armed camp, with soldiers passing through town and periodically causing unruly disruptions.

Montgomery did not see the ravages of battle that decimated communities closer to the seat of war, and in fact the city remained out of enemy hands until the final days of the conflict. Thus, Rogers portrays a world of ongoing entertainment, religious observance, economic activity, and various efforts at normalcy. Still, while northern cities generally enjoyed prosperity, even Montgomery's fortunate citizenry suffered through shortages, heavy inflation, and the absence of many white men. As in the North, patriotic citizens did their best to support the war effort, organizing fund-raising fairs and other activities, but they did so under severe financial constraints. Local women volunteered at the city hospitals and threw themselves into benevolent work. Montgomery, like the northern cities, was not immune from political dissent. Despite the city's overarching patriotism, Rogers finds pockets of enduring Unionism, including the occasional secret meeting. Surprisingly, the city's 4,500 African Americans do not figure in the chapter on "Dissenting Voices," and in fact Montgomery's black community barely appears in the narrative at all; they are entirely absent in the final chapter when the city finally surrenders.

Stephen L. Ochs's *A Black Patriot and a White Priest* is both a dual biography and an innovative history of Civil War–era New Orleans. At the core of this fascinating study are the lives of two very different and very distinctive men. André Cailloux was born into slavery in Louisiana's Plaquemines Parish. From his birth in 1825 until his legal manumission in his twenty-first year, Cailloux lived within Louisiana's complex society of slaves and masters, enduring a host of jarring transitions that characterized so many lives in that world. Between 1846 and the eve of the Civil War, Cailloux became something of a leader in New Orleans' largely Catholic Afro-Creole community. Through a series of carefully researched chapters, Ochs unravels the details of Cailloux's antebellum life while placing that narrative within New Orleans's broader Afro-Creole world.

With the outbreak of hostilities, the free black men of New Orleans formed a militia regiment and offered their services for home defense, selecting Cailloux as their First Lieutenant. Ochs argues that the Native Guard were not really voicing their support for the Confederacy, but they hoped to parlay military service into enhanced civil liberties and political status. When the Union Army occupied New Orleans in 1862, Cailloux and many of his comrades gladly tossed their lot in with the conquering heroes, eventually reforming as the 1st Louisiana Native Guard. The following May, Captain Cailloux fell while leading an abortive charge on Port Hudson. In his death, Cailloux became a hero in both the black and white communities. His funeral was an elaborate citywide ritual; even northern newspapers, anxious for a black military martyr, covered the event. The logical man to officiate on such an important occasion was Father Claude Paschal Maistre, the other half of Ochs's dramatic duo. Dedicated to racial justice, the French-born Maistre was rumored to have committed various sexual and financial improprieties prior to his arrival in North America. In Louisiana, Maistre continued his independent ways, repeatedly butting heads with his pro-Southern archbishop, who eventually suspended the troublesome cleric. For years after his suspension Maistre defiantly ran an unauthorized ministry for New Orleans Afro-Creoles, and even after his formal reconciliation with the church, Maistre remained an independent voice until his death in 1875.

In *A Black Patriot and a White Priest* Ochs explores not only these two separate lives but the larger urban universe of race, status, ethnicity, and religion that defined Civil War–era New Orleans. It is a story of positive transformation, but also frustration and disappointment. Following Cailloux's heroic death, his surviving comrades still chafed at unfair treatment by the Union army. And, despite emancipation and Union victory, Maistre continued to struggle with a city, and a church, that failed to embrace African Americans as equals.

Steven Tripp's study of Lynchburg, Virginia, provides another valuable point of contrast to the traditional urban biographies. Tripp—like Ochs—emphasizes the impact of the war on race and class relations, but *Yankee Town, Southern City* aspires to a much more complete portrait of its urban subject. Located in western Virginia, a hundred miles upstream from Richmond, Lynchburg, on the eve of the Civil War, was a small city of fewer than seven thousand residents. As Tripp notes, Lynchburg was in many senses an atypical southern community. Nearly forty percent of the city's residents were enslaved; another five percent were free African Americans; and a tenth were foreign-born whites. While Montgomery was built on commerce, a large percentage of Lynchburg's laborers, both free and enslaved, worked in one of several prosperous tobacco factories.

The Civil War produced tremendous changes in Lynchburg. Even prior to emancipation, lower-class whites and free blacks had begun to challenge long-established elite hegemony, undercutting a tradition of paternalism. After the war, Lynchburg's black workers clashed with employers, established their own vibrant institutional world, and withdrew from predominantly white churches. As he weighs the evidence, Tripp sides with those historians who see the middle period as a time of discontinuity rather than continuity, "but not by much" he cautions.

Several traits set *Yankee Town, Southern City* apart. First, this is a book shaped by its questions, rather than by a topic or location. Tripp hopes to uncover how the forces of continuity and change played themselves out in the Civil War south. His interest in class and race leads him to explore a diversity of subjects, thus producing a fairly complete study of Lynchburg, but his central concerns remain in focus throughout. Second, the emphasis on class and race as *interpretive* categories, is a refreshing change from the treatment of workers and African Americans merely as demographic groups or as sources of conflict. Finally, while all these authors have mined the local newspapers and various other published and manuscript materials, *Yankee Town, Southern City* reflects the most extensive research. Here, finally, we have an author who has assembled substantial hard data on occupations, crime, church membership, court records, and the like. Similarly, Tripp's analysis reveals a much greater familiarity with the relevant scholarship on a range of subjects. In short, *Yankee Town, Southern City* reads like a thoroughly revised dissertation, and that is not always a bad thing.

Unfortunately, the news is not all good. Tripp asks interesting questions and uses original sources, but too often his use of evidence presents cause for concern. Space permits only two illustrations. Early in the book we learn that in 1860 Lynchburg had "about eight hundred house servants, nurses, cooks, and domestics . . . virtually all of whom were female slaves" (17). But in a note we discover that in the face of incomplete data Tripp "assumed that all slave women between the ages of fifteen and sixty were domestics—except those owned by the tobacconists and seamstresses" (278). That seems a fair assumption, but it appears to have created a rather remarkable methodological tautology in which he assumed that most slave women were domestics and then discovers that "virtually all" domestics were female. Later, Tripp supports the argument that merchants were highly selective in distributing credit by consulting the will of Nathan Kabler, a dry goods merchant, who died with 140 debtors. Of these, Tripp was able to identify eighty-nine in the census or city directory, of which only "19 were skilled laborers who owned their own business, 10 were skilled laborers who worked for someone else, and 2 were unskilled." This leads him to conclude that the merchant "did not think it his responsibility to extend assistance to all whites—only those he did not view as serious credit risks" (40). Presumably we are to assume that the remaining fifty-eight *identified* debtors were higher up the socioeconomic pecking order than these thirty-one, illustrating how selective the merchant was. But even if those fifty-eight were all bankers and lawyers (and I can find nothing in the text that identifies their occupations) the fact remains that fifty-one other debtors did not appear in the census or the city directory. It would be quite reasonable and judicious to conclude that the missing fifty-one were—collectively—younger, poorer, more transient, and worse credit risks than those who Tripp could identify. But of course such a conclusion would undermine the analysis. Time and again, Tripp introduces interesting data only to undercut the analysis with problematic readings of his evidence.

So, where does this leave us? Let us glance back to those four interpretive categories for a moment. Two are pretty straightforward. The newest wave of Civil War city studies is certainly valuable for what the studies reveal about their respective cities. They also add useful dimensions to our understanding of the grand Civil War narrative. Certainly the individual case studies illuminate how communities raised troops, formed benevolent organizations, and responded to the war's economic demands and opportunities. In St. Louis and New York, we see the important impact of divided local, state, and national politics in the midst of the war. Meanwhile, the histories of Chicago, St. Louis, and New York include tantalizing tales of subterranean disloyalty, planned prison escapes, and murky Confederate plots, all of which are worth broader scrutiny. The varied studies of New Orleans. Montgomery, and Lynchburg demonstrate the diversity of the South's wartime experience, cutting against easy generalizations about the Confederate home front and particularly the character of southern cities.

How do these Civil War studies contribute to our larger understanding of American urban history? At the macro level, they point to the war's impact on established urban hierarchies. Karamanski, whose *Rally 'Round the Flag* includes the most extensive analysis of economic evidence, finds that the combination of economic demands and geographic location gave Chicago important advantages over its more southern competitors. Meanwhile, Spann argues that New York successfully emerged from the conflict at the top of a "new economic order." Still, there is more work to be done. Too often, anecdotal evidence or case studies of particular contractors or industries—sometimes accompanied by more sweeping statements that seem unsupported by the data—stand alone, where one would hope to find more ambitious analyses of broader economic evidence, including quantitative data that can assess the war's true long-term impact. Further, some authors conflate local and national (usually, really New York) price and wage data, undermining the value of a local study. None compares his or her findings with other cities.[11]

Civil War studies are potentially fertile ground for a variety of other under-explored urban topics. For instance, how did these city governments compare in their political response to the war's financial challenges? Spann notes that New York's municipal authorities devoted substantial funds to aid to families of volunteers and bounties for prospective recruits, and that the postwar developments paved the way for the rise of William Marcy "Boss" Tweed, but the other studies are largely silent on these political concerns.[12] Urban geographers might find much to discover about how the war recast the shape of cities and perhaps patterns of internal movement. For the duration of the war, cities became homes to training camps, military hospitals, makeshift prisons, sanitary fairs, and refreshment saloons. Shipyards and railroad stations took on new functions and boomed in the process. How did these new and redrawn physical spaces recast movements within cities? Did these innovations leave lasting legacies, either on the permanent maps of cities or in the assumptions of their inhabitants about the nature of travel within and between cities?

This last observation suggests the final cluster of questions: how do these studies contribute to nineteenth-century social history? What do we learn about the wartime role of women? How did the conflict change the position of African Americans in urban society? Did the economic and military events of the war recast ethnic and class relationships? Once again, the record is mixed. The good news is that all of these volumes address each of these traditionally marginalized issues, sometimes at length, suggesting how the profession has evolved over the last generation of scholarship. Clearly there is a consensus that a proper Civil War urban study must stretch beyond the lives of politicians, generals, entrepreneurs, and the occasional elite white woman. But even where the coverage is broad (and that is not always the case), the analysis is too often thin and rarely informed by the relevant scholarship. In the northern studies, African Americans tend to appear as targets of white hostility, recipients of white generosity, and controversial—but heroic—volunteers in the Union army. (Spann's short volume extends the furthest beyond this template.) To the south. Ochs and Tripp are much more successful at putting blacks at center stage as active participants and three-dimensional figures, but Rogers has lengthy sections in which he completely neglects half of Montgomery's population. Meanwhile, white women generally appear as stock characters: benevolent volunteers and organizers, nurses, impoverished sewing women. We learn about the famous, but rarely about how the war affected the rank and file, particularly those who did nothing extraordinary. Even those authors who devote the greatest attention to the experiences of women—particularly Karamanski and Gerteis—generally neglect the burgeoning scholarship in the field. Thus, for instance, in his discussion of female nurses Gerteis leans heavily on the autobiography of a male doctor, unfiltered by recent research exploring the sometimes adversarial relationship between men and women in Civil War hospitals.

Although Civil War cities are no longer a curiously neglected topic, the time is ripe for a new round of monographs. The challenge for the next generation of scholars will be to tell the local story with the entertaining flair of those who came before, but with a broader contemplation of the lessons of comparative analysis, much more attention to the important findings in a wealth of relevant subdisciplines, and a fuller exploration of the insights that can be gleaned by a thorough contemplation of the available quantitative and qualitative evidence.

## NOTES

1. I would like to thank Jeffrey S. Adler and Timothy J. Gilfoyle for their helpful suggestions.

2. Edward K. Spann is emeritus professor of history at Indiana State University. His many books include *The New Metropolis: New York City 1840–1857* (New York, 1981) and *Ideals and Politics: New York Intellectuals and Liberal Democracy 1820–1880* (Albany, 1972). Thomas H. O'Connor is emeritus professor of history at Boston College and author of *Boston Catholics: A History of the Church and its People* (Boston, 1998), *Fitzpatrick's Boston, 1846–1866* (Boston, 1984), *The Boston Irish: A Political History* (Boston, 1995), and various other studies of Boston history.

3. John Demos, *A Little Commonwealth: Family Life in Plymouth Colony* (New York, 1970); Philip J. Greven, *Four Generations: Population, Land, and Family in Colonial Andover, Massachusetts* (Ithaca, 1970); Kenneth A. Lockridge, *A New England Town: the first hundred years. Dedham, Massachusetts, 1636–1736* (New York, 1970).

4. Robert A. Gross, *The Minutemen and Their World* (New York, 1976); Margaret Leech, *Reveille in Washington* (Garden City, NY, 1945).

5. Two prominent exceptions among these early-nineteenth-century community studies were Michael H. Frisch, *Town into City: Springfield, Massachusetts, and the Meaning of Community, 1840–1880* (Cambridge, Mass., 1972) and Don Harrison Doyle, *The Social Order of a Frontier Community: Jacksonville, Illinois, 1825–70* (Urbana, 1978).

6. My own early research produced *Mastering Wartime: A Social History of Philadelphia during the Civil War* (New York, 1990). That same year Iver Bernstein published his *The New York City Draft Riots* (New York, 1990). Although these two volumes ask very different questions of their cities, they are perpetually yoked together in bibliographic essays as early, home-front city studies.

7. Howard P. Chudacoff and Judith H. Smith, *The Evolution of American Urban Society* (third edition, Englewood Cliffs, New Jersey, 1988); Chudacoff and Smith, *The Evolution of American Urban Society* (fourth edition, Englewood Cliffs, New Jersey, 1994), pp. 80–83.

8. James G. Randall, *The Civil War and Reconstruction* (New York, 1937); James G. Randall and David Donald, *The Civil War and Reconstruction* (1961; revised New York 1969); David Herbert Donald, Jean Harvey Baker, Michael F. Holt, *The Civil War and Reconstruction* (New York, 2001).

9. For two scholarly responses to "Gangs of New York" see J. Matthew Gallman, "Gangs of New York," *Journal of American History* (December 2003), pp. 124–5; and Timothy Gilfoyle, "Scorsese's Gangs of New York: Why Myth Matters," *Journal of Urban History* (July 2003), pp. 620–630.

10. Ernest A. McKay, *The Civil War in New York City* (Syracuse, 1990); Adrien Cook, *The armies of the Street* (Lexington, K.Y. 1974); Bernstein, *The New York City Draft Riots*. Spann apparently finished *Gotham at War* before the publication of Sven Beckert, *The Monied Metropolis: New York City and the Consolidation of the American Bourgeoisie, 1850–1896* (New York, 2001).

11. This absence of comparative analysis, with a very few limited exceptions, extends to almost every topic under investigation.

12. These political topics are not ignored in the larger literature. See, for instance, Robin Einhorn, *Property Rules: Political Economy in Chicago, 1833–1872* (Chicago, 1991) and Einhorn, "The Civil War and Municipal Government in Chicago," in Maris Vinovskis, editor, *Toward a Social History of the American Civil War* (New York, 1990). Although his book appeared three years after Einhorn's fine essay, Karamanski never mentions her findings.

# The Civil War Economy

## A Modern View

### (with Stanley L. Engerman)

This essay, like "Gettysburg's Gettysburg," began as a commissioned piece, but there the similarities end. The German Historical Institute sponsors occasional conferences of leading scholars on selected topics, many of which result in published volumes. On this occasion, the conference conveners had contacted Stanley L. Engerman, one of the nation's leading economic historians, to contribute to a conference comparing the American Civil War and the German Wars of Unification, particularly around the thorny issue of "total war." Almost thirty years earlier, Stan had published one of the most important statements on the economic impact of the Civil War.[1] This invitation presented him with the opportunity to revisit these themes in a new context. Stan was one of my father's oldest friends, and we had known each other for years. He had read and commented on nearly all of my published work, and as luck would have it, I had been working on some of these economic themes in my home front work. So Stan generously invited me to coauthor his contribution.

In this age before email, Stan and I communicated by phone, mail, and fax. After deciding on a general structure, we divided up pieces for preliminary drafting, with Stan taking on the heavy economic sections while I took a stab at the policy issues, the introduction, and the conclusion. Stan is an incredibly thorough researcher, a remarkably hardworking scholar, and a marvelous editor. I did my best to keep up with his amazing pace. The conference itself was a fascinating experience. Since I was tagging along with Stan, I was one of the most junior scholars in attendance. The papers were circulated in advance, and everyone met around the same seminar room for long days of discussion and argument. I had the opportunity to meet many people who I had admired for years, some of whom remain friends to this day.[2]

I think that the resulting volume, *On the Road to Total War*, has received insufficient attention from Civil War historians. Quite a few important pieces on the Civil War are hidden in this large volume. I am particularly proud of the essay that Stan and I contributed. Readers will find a few things that might be of interest. First, we present a broad theoretical perspective on the idea of "total war" and "modern war"—terms that I think are sometimes used imprecisely. Second, we offer an up-to-date analysis of the war's economic impact on both the North and the South, including some arguments that may seem counterintuitive. Finally, we argue that the war produced a fundamental irony, in that the side that was least industrialized and least "modern" actually ended up adopting measures that were in many senses most centralized and government controlled.

## NOTES

1. Stanley L. Engerman, "The Economic Impact of the Civil War," *Explorations in Economic History* 3 (Spring/Summer 1966): 176–99.

2. More than thirty scholars contributed to this volume. Historians of the American Civil War will find gems by a host of historians, including Phillip S. Paludan, Reid Mitchell, Earl Hess, Michael Fellman, Reid Mitchell, Joe Glatthaar, Herman Hattaway, James McPherson, Mark Neely Jr., and Jörg Nagler.

. . .

## I. INTRODUCTION: WHEN IS THE CIVIL WAR A TOTAL WAR?

Perhaps more so than any other episode in American history, the main lines of the Civil War story are familiar to Americans. Insofar as today's discussion of total war is concerned, that conventional wisdom proceeds through three logical stages. First, we all recognize that this war was a tremendously destructive war. Second, accounts of the conflict often characterize it as the world's first excursion into *total war* or *modern war*, terms sometimes, although not necessarily, used interchangeably. Some approach that conclusion more gingerly, suggesting that this was a transitional war, with one foot in modern, total war and the other in some sort of traditional world. The third stage in this common analysis acknowledges the North as the side most ready to engage in total war. This conclusion builds on the North's industrial superiority, emphasizing the link between the Industrial Revolution and the global transition to a new kind of warfare. The North was the more modern, industrialized state and thus best prepared to win a total war.

Although this chain of logic makes some sense, it blurs distinctions and can lead to imprecise conclusions. The first point—the Civil War was tremendously destructive—is certainly true.[1] But before we take the next step and locate the Civil War on war's grand evolutionary scale, we should define our terms more clearly. When we do so, we are left with a paradox: The industrial North may have adopted fewer of the trappings of total war than its more agrarian opponent.

Our intention in this essay is to hone the issues a little more sharply, particularly as they relate to economic concerns. The first step will be to distinguish between *modern war* and *total war* in preparation for considering how each side approached the conflict. We also hope to examine the various assumptions concerning the relationship between industrialization and the Civil War. Specifically, this will involve distinguishing between, on the one hand, industry's role in the fighting of the Civil War and, on the other, the importance of the Civil War in the United States' subsequent industrial development.

## II. Total and Modern War

The literature touching on these terms is certainly vast, although often the discussions seem to be running at cross purposes. Our first task is to sketch out some generalizable definitions. We begin with a simple observation. *Modern war* generally implies specific characteristics associated with a modern, or modernizing, society and economy.[2] Conversely, the measurement of a nation's movement toward total war is relative rather than absolute.

The progress toward modern war reflects changes in three areas: (1) the behavior of the state; (2) the pattern of economic growth; (3) and the level of military technology. A nation engaged in modern war will see an expansion in the government bureaucracy and a concomitant shift of powers toward the central state. This political process is accompanied by industrial development, reflected in economic shifts such as an expanded manufacturing output and movement toward an urban economy. On the battlefield, modern wars feature an increased reliance on new military technologies in the form of munitions, transportation, and the like. These new technologies, in turn, spur on strategic innovations. These characteristics are certainly connected. The military technology required to sustain modern war depends on a strong industrial base and the governmental mechanisms necessary to bring that power to bear on a military objective. Similarly, the military demands of a strong central state may spur technological and industrial adjustments.

Whereas modern warfare is generally best seen as a post–Industrial Revolution phenomenon, some scholars have treated total war in more relative terms. Thus, total war may be viewed as the opposite of *limited war*. Or, if we shift from hard dichotomies to a seamless continuum, various characteristics may place a particular war effort on a spectrum between the most limited war and full total war. Three broad questions are commonly associated with total war. First, what is the magnitude of the nation's commitment to the conflict? That is, what share of productive manpower and economic output are mobilized to fight the conflict? The second question—or cluster of questions—concerns military strategy. What are the strategic intentions? How are those intentions enacted in battlefield strategy? We associate total war with attacks on civilians, destruction of property, and the strategic aim of destroying the enemy's "will to fight." In this sense, the totality of a war effort could be described either by the declared goals or the actual effect of that strategy on the enemy. Third, moving beyond matters of mobilization and strategy, we may ask about the nature of the nation's war aims. A country engaging in limited war may have quite circumscribed objectives in mind, whereas total war might emerge out of a broader array of conflicts in which at least one combatant insists on the right to reshape dramatically the future of its opponent if victory is won.

These three questions really identify different, although certainly related, aspects of what historians have described as total war. In discussing the American Civil War, many scholars have emphasized strategic considerations, particularly William Tecumseh Sherman's famed march to the sea.[3] Others add a focus on the North's war aims, pointing to Lincoln's insistence on unconditional surrender.[4] Still others place the Civil War in the long-term development of warfare by concentrating on the movement toward heavy mobilization of resources.[5]

Each of these approaches concentrates on events during the war years, perhaps linking them to long-term patterns of military development. A further measure of total war could look beyond the conflict to gauge the lasting effects of wartime measures. In the political arena, this would encompass the long-term shifts in the balance of powers among branches. If wartime mobilization led to an expanded central government, did this shift last into the postwar decades? Similar questions could be asked about the legacy of military and economic policies. Did the nation continue to support an expanded military into the peacetime decades? Did the economic mobilization associated with war yield long-term sectoral shifts within the economy?

Let us shift now from the general to the specific. How can we build the case for the Civil War as either a modern war or a total war? The case for the war's modernity can be made both in terms of economic patterns and governmental initiatives. By the eve of the Civil War, the United States could—by most measures—be described as in the midst of modern economic growth.

The previous half-century had witnessed high rates of growth in total output and in output per capita, accelerated by a post-1840 shift toward industrial production in the North. This economic growth was built in part on a steady pattern of development in transportation and communications so that by mid-century the major urban areas were linked by rail and telegraph. And as the nation's economic infrastructure matured, America's financial network emerged as one of the world's leaders. At a bureaucratic level, there is ample room to argue that the North, at least, had achieved the status of a modern state. As the conflict progressed, the Union demonstrated the capacity to collect taxes and issue bonds to fund the effort while developing the institutional apparatus to direct a region-wide conscription system. Moreover, although the Civil War dwarfed all previous American military ventures, the North did have a military in place that had won the Mexican War barely a decade before. In short, the nation that had divided in Civil War could certainly be treated as a modern nation capable of engaging in modern war.

But we are really more concerned with fitting our discussion of total war to the Civil War case. On the face of it, there is room to argue that the conflict was a total war (or at least toward that end of the total war–limited war spectrum) according to any of the three aforementioned criteria: commitment, strategy, or objectives. The commitment to war, or mobilization, could be measured in manpower terms or by military expenditure. About 2.1 million soldiers fought for the Union, and between 850,000 and 900,000 fought for the Confederacy. Taken together, roughly 40 percent of military-aged whites served in the war, including over 60 percent of Southerners.[6] The direct costs of the Civil War can be presented in a variety of ways, all pointing to the heavy mobilization of resources. The Northern government spent roughly $3.4 billion during the war years; the direct costs of the Union war effort were an estimated $2.3 billion, of which the federal government paid $1.8 billion. In the four prewar years (1857–60), the entire federal budget only totaled about $274 million. Or, to phrase the point in a different way, the Northern war expenditures over the four years amounted to nearly three-fourths (74.4 percent) of the region's 1859 output, while the Confederacy—at all government levels—actually spent more ($1.03 billion) than the value of its 1859 output.[7]

Both the scale and organization of this vast mobilization are central to our understanding of the economic aspects of total war. The lively debate over wartime strategy in general, and on General Sherman in particular, is perhaps best left for others to continue. But at the very least, the record offers substantial ammunition to support the claim that numerous tacticians on either side recognized the military benefits of destroying enemy resources and undercutting the "will" of civilians.[8] When we turn to war aims, we enter another battlefield that is beyond our present purview. If we take prewar claims at face value, the North simply sought to preserve the Union, and Jefferson Davis insisted in April that "all we ask is to be left alone." Neither goal seems particularly dramatic until they are set side by side. After Lincoln's Emancipation Proclamation, the recognized aims of the North had shifted and with them the stakes had risen, guaranteeing that a Northern victory would have a tremendous impact on the South.

We have also suggested that a proper understanding of total war should take us into the postwar period. The pursuit of the elusive "economic impact of the American Civil War" requires that we follow several of the aforementioned threads beyond Appomattox. In institutional terms, many of the most centrist aspects of mobilization failed to survive into the postwar years. Nineteenth-century Americans, it seems, were quick to take advantage of their "peace dividend." Similarly, the quantitative data do not support the conclusion that the war's economic demands launched the United States into a period of accelerated economic growth. One of the strongest cases for the war's economic legacy emphasizes the lasting impact of the wartime financial legislation. But even if we can identify such an impact, we must mull over the relationship between such acts and our understanding of total war. What, for instance, do we make of the passage of Republican initiatives that predated the conflict and were only tangentially related to the war's economic needs? Finally, the war's economic impact must consider the varied effects on the South, ranging from physical damage to the emancipation of slaves, to the shift in political dominance to the North.

The discussion that follows will concentrate on those aspects of our definition of total war that are most closely tied to economic concerns. The first section examines the economic evidence itself, which is followed by a discussion of the various mobilization policies and their ramifications. It becomes evident in each section that the conclusions are largely dependent on the particular measure selected. Moreover, as we shall see, a separate analysis of each region yields the rather surprising conclusion that the South—the less "modern" of the two combatants—became more fully committed to total war than the North.

## III. The Civil War and Economic Change

As with many historical questions, the debate on the economic aspects of the Civil War includes a number of distinct but related issues. Their analysis rests upon various assumptions both as to the causes of what did happen and as to the probable patterns of change that could have occurred in the absence of the war. While the full set of issues and arguments cannot be dealt with adequately in this limited space, some distinctions may usefully be made at the start. Of particular concern are separating those changes that occurred in the period of the war itself from those long-run changes that reflect subsequent developments attributable to the war.

In describing the war's immediate effects, attention is paid to various measures of aggregate economic activity—as indicators of the nature of economic change in the wartime period—and to their implications for those other economic, political, and social changes that had continuing effects. The links between the short-run and long-run effects relates the latter to specific changes introduced in pursuing the war, and the nature and magnitude of the effects may appear quite different depending on the particular time span analyzed. While it may seem relatively straightforward to describe the aggregate economic change in the war interval, it is rather difficult in the absence of annual censuses of production. The data that are generally available for the war years are limited to partial indicators, which are difficult to interpret as indicators of aggregate behavior. Since there may be offsetting movements in different sectors, and sectors often may change at different rates, partial data make any projection somewhat uncertain. Moreover, some traditionally used indices are based on inferences derived from presumed economic connections that may not be appropriate. To use real wages as an index of profits has limitations, while the use of date on changing prices to indicate changes in real outputs can also be misleading. In short, use of partial indicators and theoretical inferences cannot provide as definite an answer to the question of the nature of the Civil War economy as would be possible with the more complete data available for the twentieth century.

The basic problems in analyzing long-term changes are of a rather different nature. The problems are in the drawing out of the precise relations to explain the causes and consequences of specific changes over time. One aspect of the complexity arises from the need to differentiate several possible forms of relationship between the war and the subsequent changes, meaning that the specific questions asked may be quite diverse. There are (at least) three possible relations. First, basic changes may have resulted from particular wartime operations and patterns of change, with the implication that the specific circumstances of the war led to changes that otherwise would not have occurred. Second, basic changes may have resulted from the outcome of the war, and the policies imposed upon the losing side by the winners, whether to the subsequent benefit of the winners, of the losers, to both, or to neither. Third, is the introduction of policies implemented as a result of the political changes brought about by the war and its outcome, policies that might have been sought earlier and possibly accomplished within a reasonable time, even without the military conflict? To Charles and Mary Beard, the triumph of the industrial economy was inevitable, even without a war.[9] Thus, many post–Civil War changes might be argued to have been the result of basic trends that had earlier emerged, changes that no doubt would have occurred in the absence of the war. These trends were not, it can be argued, directly related to the war and to wartime needs. The presence of similar developments of economic, social, and political patterns in other countries might suggest that the links drawn, in the American case, to the Civil War do not reflect necessary conditions. All of these variants have been argued for, and all have some plausibility. We, therefore, shall examine some of the posited mechanisms.

While we would obviously prefer data for the war years themselves to describe short-run changes, it will be easiest to set the context by using decadal estimates comparing 1860–70. We will generally compare the antebellum years with the decade 1860–70—a comparison that is, however, sensitive to business cycles, since the 1850s were generally a period of rapid growth, particularly in the South (with the cyclical downturn of 1857 being particularly sharp in the North).

Thomas Cochran was one of the first historians to question the contention that the Civil War period had been one of significant economic expansion to the Northern economy.[10] But it was only in the late 1950s, with the presentation of Robert Gallman's estimates of commodity output from 1839 to 1899, that a systematic analysis of the war decade become possible.[11] Gallman presented estimates based on the decadal censuses, with various production series used to interpolate output levels, but no estimates were presented for years in the period between 1859 and 1869. Nevertheless, the pattern found for the war decade was sufficiently dramatic that it permitted some clear interpretations of the earlier years of the decade.[12]

First, at the national level, overall economic growth was relatively low during the Civil War decade, the slowest nineteenth-century growth subsequent to the onset of economic expansion after the War of 1812. The pattern of the Civil War decade thus differed quite dramatically from the rapid expansion seen during World War II, with the latter's coming out of a prolonged depression, but it resembled more closely the experience of most other American wars. By using the census data and Richard Easterlin's regional income estimation, Stanley Engerman pointed out the extent to which the national change was influenced by the decline in output in the Southern economy in the decade.[13] The Southern decline was attributed to the wartime destruction and, more importantly, the dramatic effects of the ending of slavery and the virtual disappearance of the plantation system in Southern agriculture. Yet, looking at the North alone, this decade was a period of relatively slow growth, compared to that in prior and subsequent decades. Thus, unless there was a severe postbellum depression, the war years were a period of relative economic stagnation in the North.

There are two basic economic aggregates for which we have recently obtained more reliable measures for the nineteenth century. Gallman has presented detailed estimates of capital stock, and Thomas Weiss has modified and extended Stanley Lebergott's labor force estimates.[14] The growth pattern of the capital stock at the national level mirrors that of national income for the decade between 1860 and 1870. The war decade was one of slower growth of the overall capital stock, as well as of each of its major subcategories: structures, equipment, land, inventories. Suggestive of the impact of the war on the Northern economy was the slow growth of structures and equipment, components of capital considerably more important in the Northern than the Southern capital stock. There was an accelerated growth of capital stock in the subsequent decade, but the overall growth of the national capital stock in the period 1860–80 was below that of 1840–60, suggesting that any impact of debt finance and repayment in increasing the savings rate of the postbellum period may not have offset the shortfall generated during the period of the war itself.

Weiss's recent labor force estimates also suggest a marked slowing down in growth in the decade 1860–70, with possibly an overall decline in measured Southern labor input. Even for the North, however, the labor force growth slowed down. In part, this reflected a decline in immigration in the war period, reductions in the manpower pool owing to wartime deaths and injuries, an increased mortality for civilians in this decade, which was probably related to the circumstances of the Civil War and, for the South and some border states, the loss of control over slave labor, with slave runaways (often to fight for the North), and then legal emancipation.[15] Deaths were high in this war, equal, in the North, to about 10 percent of white males aged 18–45 in 1860, while for the South, deaths were equal to about 25 percent of all white males in that age bracket. During the war, the male labor force was reduced owing to military needs. At any given moment, about 10 percent of the total labor force was lost in each region owing to military service, with the South suffering even greater losses owing to the loss of slave labor.[16]

There was some increased participation of women and children in the labor force during the war, but this increase apparently did not continue to affect significantly the postbellum situation.

Nor did the Civil War decade lead to dramatic changes in the basic occupational structure of the labor force.[17] For the South, there was little change in the share of the labor force in agriculture between 1860 and 1870—indeed, little change until after 1880. For the Northern regions, there was some decline in the agricultural share in the labor force, but the decline was less than in the preceding decades (although greater than in the next decade). Thus, the pattern of change in the decade was not unique, nor was it continued. Nevertheless, the maintenance of the share of agricultural output in the North, combined with a reduction in the agricultural share in the labor force, did mean a sharp increase in measured labor productivity in agriculture in that region—and for the national average as well. The South did experience some relative growth in manufacturing output over this decade, since the war led to a more rapid expansion and ensuing smaller decline in manufacturing than in agriculture. Nevertheless, the Southern manufacturing sector did not experience a continued postbellum increase, nor, when Southern manufacturing subsequently developed, was it on the basis of industries whose growth was accelerated by military needs or wartime exigencies.

While the decadal estimates suggest that it is doubtful that the war period itself, even in the North, could have been one of rapid economic expansion, it is possible to use some recent economic observations as well as some of the available fragmentary measures to isolate the changes within the years 1861–65. One of the major reasons for the belief in economic expansion during the war years was the reliance on a specific economic model to infer the relation between the known changes in prices and the unknown movement in the level of output. Reflecting patterns generally observed in the expansion phase of business cycles, it was widely argued that the price rises indicated output increases. We now have more recent information on the price–output relationship, and a useful set of models with which to interpret this period. Our recent experience with inflationary periods demonstrates that these can yield price rises with limited output growth. Evidence of rising prices, of some individuals getting wealthy, and of some sectors expanding, all can occur without there necessarily being increases in the overall level of output for the economy. Vietnam was a war with periods of sharply rising prices and relatively slow output growth, while the oil shock of the 1970s similarly led to rising prices with slow growth. Unexpected shocks to the economy (as in the Civil War) can lead to such patterns of behavior. We should be more cautious than in the past in the arguing for economic growth from price changes. Indeed, we are quite aware for the South that rising prices occurred with falling output, and while the Northern pattern was not so dramatic, the price increases by themselves need not imply rapid economic growth.

It is also useful to remember that part of any increase in Northern output after the start of the war may not have reflected only new demands from prewar levels but were in part offsets to the disturbances to the Northern economy that came with the loss of Southern markets at war's start.[18] Frequently discussed by contemporaries were problems owing to the inability to collect financial debts from Southerners, and in various industries, particularly textile and shoe manufacture, there were believed to have been increased levels of unemployment owing to the removal of Southern demand. Within agriculture, some losses also resulted from the ending of Southern markets, and the shifting patterns owing to the war also affected various commercial and service industries. Thus, some of the North's subsequent output growth marked the replacement by new Northern demand sources for disappearing Southern demands.

Much of the fragmentary data available for the war years in the North suggest that the output of those sectors measured either declined in the North or else grew less rapidly than it had in prior or subsequent periods. Censuses of manufacturing for New York and Massachusetts indicate declines in output over the war period, as do the overall data for the manufacturing center of Philadelphia.[19] The decline in cotton textile production with the loss of its raw materials is quite clear, but it should be noted that this decline was greater than the marked expansion of woolen textiles that the war brought about. Shoe output fell—as did the level of patent activity in the industry.[20] The production of pig iron declined early in the war, but even after recovery, this five-year span represented the slowest growth of any period after the War of 1812, with slower growth for the overall industry as well as for the newly emerging sectors using coal fuel.[21] DuPont's production of explosives also grew less rapidly in the war period than previously, and the employed labor force did not increase.[22] Thus, for many of the key sectors of industry producing military output, decline or slowed growth was the general pattern, not rapid expansion. This pattern is consistent with the suggestion of the one index of overall manufacturing production for the period.[23]

While less is known about the pattern of output within agriculture, by linking the decadal censuses with the data collected after 1866 by the Department of Agriculture, some inferences are permitted. The expanded output of wheat and corn in the North was generally post-1866 rather than during the war years.[24] The pattern of change within agriculture thus resembles that in manufacturing, with a postwar boom developing after some wartime declines in output.

In what way did the Civil War economy of the North differ from that of the South, and why did the wartime demands have an apparently limited measured effect on Northern production? In regard to the latter question, there are two considerations to discuss. First, in the period prior to the start of the war, the Northern economy was at a near full-employment level, with output at peak amounts. There was relatively little unemployment or excess capacity, and with limited amounts of new entrants into the labor force or enhanced ability to invest in the private sector after the war started, the rising war demands for military purposes to a large extent meant primarily some diversion of output and investment from other uses rather than increased outputs. The ability to accelerate technical change in such a short period in order to increase productivity was limited, as was the ability of innovations to have a substantial effect on the economy. Second, the military demands in many ways were not those of what we have come to regard as those of a modern war, requiring production of a set of new goods or greatly expanding the output of goods earlier produced by simpler means of technology. Rather, in the Civil War, the primary goods purchased by the army were foodstuffs, textiles (for uniforms), and boots and shoes, and even those purchases of arms and explosives involved limited amounts of new materials relative to prewar uses. The closing down of Southern exports of cotton did mean that textiles would need to be produced with woolens, but woolen output had been about three-fifths that of cotton textiles in 1860, wool textiles already being a large producing sector.

Thus, while there were considerable military purchases, these generally replaced civilian demands for the same commodities, limiting any overall net increase in the demand for these products. The demand for iron for military uses was only a small part of total iron output, and these increases did not fully offset the declining growth in demand for iron for railroad construction, for agricultural implements, and for use in construction.[25] Similarly, the military use of explosives needed to offset changing demands from railroad construction and mining. It is this similarity in demand patterns and amounts from the prewar pattern that limited the magnitude of overall change in both the war period itself and then in the postwar era. The changing magnitudes of demand and the imposed degree of standardization did not lead to the dramatic changes in size of firms and in methods of production that some later wars did.

The similarity in Northern demand patterns before and during the war had one further set of implications, pointing to a major difference in the nature of the necessary economic readjustments that the war generated in the two regions. Given the nature of military goods demanded, and the antebellum pattern of relatively limited imports of manufactured goods, there remained a greater compatibility of goods demanded and goods produced within the North than was possible in the Southern economy of that period. The Northern military needs did not require a dramatic change from the normal prewar production pattern. There was little need to develop new industries to fight the conflict. Thus, it was possible to acquire more of the necessary goods by budget policies and increased expenditures. The existing production structure provided the possibilities of rapid response with basic financial incentives, and the North could make use of taxes, borrowing, and money creation to pay for the goods. In addition, it was possible to place primary reliance upon contracting with already existing firms, and there was little need to provide specific aids to create new firms or new productive technologies. There was some flexibility in choosing among alternative suppliers. Despite these advantages, however, it should be noted that there were frequent charges of scandal and corruption in procurement and contracting, particularly in the conflict's early years (these not being a characteristic separating the Civil War from any premodern or modern war).

For the South, however, the situation of meeting wartime needs was somewhat different. These wartime demands required a quite different production structure from that previously existing, which had been based on expectations of ongoing trade with the Northern states and with England—trading patterns that had yielded a high level of consumption to the Southern states over the previous decades. The South was not, however, backward in the magnitude and nature of its manufacturing output prior to the Civil War, and it ranked high among the developed world in the production of some basic industrial goods.[26] Once the war began it was clear that the North would not remain a major supplier of needs to the South, meaning either that there had to be increased imports from England or increased production of manufactured goods within the South. Given the time required to reorganize the Southern production structure, it is not surprising that the initial focus was upon increased imports from England.[27] The South attempted to influence England to provide more exports by measures made more familiar and (done more successfully) in recent years—by restricting the export of its key commodity.[28] The fact that King Cotton diplomacy was less successful than was to be King Oil diplomacy led to a Southern need for foreign borrowing to finance its import needs, a tactic that met with only limited success. It was not only in manufacturing that structural reorganization was required. The Southern strategy meant that the output of cotton would be reduced in the interest of greater production of foodstuffs, but with food production still primarily based upon the slave labor on plantations.[29] All of this dictated a larger governmental role in the war for the South, with more direct controls and a larger use of subsidies to encourage industry.[30] However, with the major conflicts regarding the role of the central Confederacy in contrast with the rights of state governments, this enhanced governmental role was undertaken with a weakened tax system. Yet the fact that the South was able to produce sufficient materials to fight for four years does suggest that there was sufficient flexibility in adjusting the production structure when necessary, as well as enough direction to ensure the flow of goods to the appropriate segments of the military. There had been some iron furnaces in the South prior to the Civil War, and these expanded production to meet military needs, while the textile sector required considerable expansion. The war demands led to what the historian Raimondo Luraghi has described as a form of "state socialism" in the South, which permitted a prolonged war, relative, at least, to some post-dictions of Southern capacity, but this type of industrial expansion did not have any carryover into the postwar period.

While the war may have led to a slowing of the rate of Northern economic expansion, the war period and the outcome of the war led to actual declines in the regional income of the South. The weakening and then ending of slavery meant a fundamental change in the nature of the Southern economy, leading to the effective disappearance of the system of plantation agriculture that had been the principal basis of Southern production and economic growth in the antebellum period. The losses in the productive efficiency that had been achieved with plantation production led to a sharp decline in production, particularly by black labor, and it took decades for the Southern economy to recover.[31] These declines had been foreshadowed during the war, with slave runaways, slaves held captive by the North, and a weakened ability to control the remaining slave population. Thus, the effective input of labor from the slave population fell during the war, even before the granting of legal freedom at the end of the war.

In addition to the losses in labor input because of the reduced number of effective slave laborers, the military drain of white adult males also lowered the available labor supply within the South. Further, the impact of the Northern army, particularly in the latter part of the war, was to force losses upon the capital and land used by Southerners. Railroads were destroyed, land and machinery were ruined, and livestock were killed, which, with the reductions in labor, meant that considerable amounts of land were withdrawn from production. While the destruction of land and capital did not necessarily lead to prolonged postwar problems, recovery to earlier levels not always taking a very long time, it did serve to set back the wartime economy. Neither agriculture nor manufacturing can easily be undertaken in an area when military action is taking place.

The South also suffered in the wartime from the disruption of its trading patterns. The limits, ill-conceived as they now seem, on cotton production and sales reduced import possibilities, even while they permitted increased production of foodstuffs within the South.[32] While the causes of the decline in cotton production remain debated, given the absence of any centrally enforced prohibitions, the sharpness of the wartime decline is quite clear.[33] The total cotton output of years 1862 through 1865 was below that of 1861 (which had been planted at the very start of the war), a clear sign of the adjustments in agricultural production to the changing needs and possibilities of war. The Northern blockade appears to have been generally successful, but some merchandise did squeeze through. Nevertheless, the interference with Southern trade did have an impact, lowering Southern incomes. While the Northern states experienced difficulties in their trade with Europe and suffered from a deterioration in the terms of trade, their problems in international trade were not as severe as those confronted by the South.[34]

Thus, the costs to the white South of the Civil War were large, as were the long-term consequences of the major institutional changes coming out of the war—the ending of slavery and the plantation system. By the end of 1865, the Southern economy was severely weakened. Yet this decline in the war and with slave emancipation was a once-and-for-all change in the position of the South vis-à-vis the North. Over the next three-quarters of a century, the per capita income of the South grew about as rapidly as did the Northern, and Southern manufacturing also expanded. Despite the late nineteenth-century impacts of racism, colonialism, and sharecropping, the Southern economy was able to expand as rapidly as did the North and, after 1880, did so with significant declines in the importance of the agricultural economy and increases in manufacturing. And to argue that the South should have had a higher income and grown more rapidly than did the North after the war overlooks the basic factor that had permitted high incomes in the antebellum era—the slave plantation. Whatever difficulties the war caused the South, it did not mean, once the initial adjustment was made, that prospects for continued economic growth did not persist.

Discussions of the long-term effects of the Civil War on the economy usually focus on the Northern states, with the arguments that the North was the source of modern development as well as the locus of political power for the nation. Yet, in many ways, the most dramatic changes occurred within the Southern states, and the postbellum Southern economy differed more dramatically from that of the antebellum years than did the Northern.

In the North, the postbellum structural changes in output, capital, and the labor force represented a basic continuation of the prewar patterns. The war neither initiated nor accelerated these changes, although, in many cases, the actual growth or changes over the period 1860 to 1880 were lower than that in the last two antebellum decades. There was no unusual expansion in the size of firms or the structure of industries for over a decade—certainly none that seems directly linked to the wartime economy. The large firms of the late nineteenth century were not those uniquely affected by wartime military needs. Clearly, it is possible to visualize alternative events that might have occurred post-1860 without the war, so that even this slower growth might seem to represent a major economic step forward (such visualizations are always possible), but we wish to avoid such conjectures for the present.

It was in the relation of the federal government to the overall economy that the wartime Northern changes were most dramatic. It was not because of any introduction of direct controls, since these were limited. Rather, the major changes were in the increased share of resources taken by the Northern government, and the tax, expenditure, money, and debt policies that led to this. There were also significant new policies regarding tariffs, land, and immigration passed early in the war, but these were generally not war related, in terms of its financial and military needs, and will be discussed later. (The revenue effect of the tariff was itself small. Tariffs fell from over 90 percent of tax revenues in 1861 to about 25 percent by 1865, changing little in real terms during the war.) These changes could, presumably, have had longer-term impacts upon the centralized operation of the economy, and the development of a military-industrial complex, through their effects on debt policy and subsequent financial market and investment behavior.

While the increased federal budget during the war meant a rise to nineteenth-century peaks, the postbellum reaction was quite different from that experienced in the twentieth century, particularly after World War II. With the ending of the Civil War, there was a sharp decline in the size of the federal budget, absolutely and as a ratio to gross national product (GNP).[35] There was a dramatic decline in military expenditures (and in the size of the military as measured by dollar expenditures and by manpower), while federal civilian expenditures as a share of GNP soon began to decline from postbellum levels. Within the expenditure categories, there were few changes in expenditures on resource-using components relative to prewar, and the main structural changes in federal expenditures came in the category of transfers among taxpayers not in government purchases of goods and services. The primary categories of expenditure growth were veteran's payments (which, however, increased greatly in amount only several decades after the war), interest payments to holders of the debt, and debt repayments. The revenues to pay for these items came in part from tariffs but also from various excise taxes introduced during the war. The net effects of this system of taxes and transfers is still not clear, but it is probable that its overall effects on savings and investment were limited. Indeed, in the post–Civil War decades, as in the antebellum years, most resource-using governmental expenditures occurred on the state and local, not the federal, level.[36] The direct impact upon government, as measured by the federal budget, did not point to an accelerated increase in the degree of governmental centralization. Several decades were to pass before the expansion of those various federal agencies and commissions that were to influence so strongly the economy in the twentieth century.

Similarly, the impact of debt issues during the war and their retirements after the war, and of the overall postbellum tax and expenditure system, were somewhat mixed.[37] To determine their effects requires consideration of the circumstances both at the time of debt issue and debt retirement, as well as the incidence of taxes and of the transfers upon their recipients. While government debt retirement may promote further capital formation, this might not offset the impact of its creation in "crowding-out" private investment. There might be to some redistribution of the pattern of investment over time, but with possibly limited effects on the magnitude of long-term capital formation. And the net impact of the system of compulsory bond sales via the National Bank Act's creation of new banks is not clear. We now know more how well financial and bank systems have operated in the absence of such centralized controls as imposed by the National Banking System (as well as how poorly centrally controlled banking systems can operate). The specifics of National Bank Act measures, designed to support the Civil War bond issue for the

North, need not have done much to promote investment in the private sector. Further, while it is clear that its terms were used to favor Northern banking after the Civil War, the manner of its operation was not costless to the Southern economy and its attempts at financial recovery to its antebellum levels.[38]

The effects of the Civil War on the overall tax system were somewhat limited in their economic consequences. While income taxation was introduced to a limited extent during the war, it did not survive one decade and thus had no permanent impact on the nature of taxation. The introduction of excise taxes, primarily on alcohol and tobacco, did lead to increased revenues relative to tariffs; indeed, their presence may have helped to maintain a lower tariff structure than might otherwise have existed if tariffs had remained the primary source of federal revenues. The full effect of tariffs on income distribution and relative output structures remains uncertain, both because of their limited quantitative magnitude and because, for many manufactured and agricultural goods, the United States was already a net exporter in the world markets.

There were a number of significant policies introduced by the Northern Congress after the Southern secession, policies that had been previously discussed in Congress and whose passage apparently reflected nothing specific to the economic *needs* of war. The war permitted the Northern Republicans to implement their prewar agenda, and the outcome of the Civil War permitted its maintenance—at least for some limited period of time. There remains some question, however, as to whether these measures did much to promote growth, and if they did so in a desirable manner for the long-term development of the economy. In some cases, policies had diametrically opposing effects: For example, the raising of tariffs to promote industry offset the greater availability of land via the Homestead Act, which drained labor from the eastern manufacturing centers. Some policies were of limited importance and were terminated before the end of the century—the contract labor laws were inessential, used primarily for union-busting, and ended in 1885; land grants to transcontinental railroads apparently served primarily to subsidize investors and came to a scandal-ridden end in 1871.[39] And, as always, banking and financial matters are difficult to disentangle. While praise by some is given to the limitations on note issues that, in part, led to the price fall prior to Resumption by 1879 (thus returning the United States to the gold standard), others complain that the slow monetary growth permitting this price fall restricted output growth and had perverse distributional effects. None of this is meant to deny the political importance of the passage of wartime measures nor the significant symbolic effects that they may have had. Rather, it is meant to suggest that the nature and magnitude of their presumed growth effects remain somewhat uncertain. (For example, what percent of the governmental economic measures of the past decades would we believe were significantly growth-promoting and of a large magnitude, despite the promises at the time of passage that they would have such an impact?)

It was in the South, of course, that the social, political, and economic changes were most pronounced, starting with the pivotal change of the ending of legal slavery—immediate and with no compensation to either former slaveowners or ex-slaves. Whatever the limitations to a more complete freedom then, and with the more virulent racism after the 1890s, there was a dramatic reduction in the ability to control and coerce the black population.[40] Similarly, with the outcome of the war, there was a loss in Southern political power nationally and an increased inability to restrict Northern policy preferences. While much legislation favorable to Southern elites emerged in postbellum decades, particularly in regard to racial matters, these were, generally, at the sufferance of the North. The South lacked the political opportunity to independently set pro-Southern policy.[41]

In some ways, there was modernizing economic change within the South after the Civil War. Nevertheless, the share of the labor force in agriculture did not decline until after 1880, and cotton remained the primary crop in Southern agriculture. Indeed, cotton accounted for a higher Southern agricultural output in the postbellum than in the antebellum era. Yet the end of slavery had led to dramatic changes in the level and efficiency of Southern production. The decline of the plantation system (a characteristic of almost all areas where slavery had ended) meant a sharp reduction in the output per black agricultural worker. While there may have been some declines in black labor force participation and in hours worked, clearly the decline in efficiency in the production of cotton, as well as the sharper reduction in the output of sugar and of rice, led to a lowered measured Southern output (but with obvious, albeit unmeasured, gains in utility to those now freed and able to avoid gang work.)

The maintenance of Southern cotton output, even with the reduced output from ex-slave labor, resulted from major changes in the production pattern of white yeoman farmers. Unable to compete with the more efficient slave plantations before the Civil War (except perhaps during boom periods such as the 1850s), white farmers in the postbellum period came to dominate cotton production. This movement meant that Southern staple production could continue to expand, without the need for contract labor from Asia or Africa that characterized those areas of the Caribbean in which sugar production expanded in the late nineteenth century or for the subsidized southern European migrants that accounted for continued coffee production in Brazil once slavery there had been ended.

In describing the economic effects of the Civil War on Southern growth, it is useful to remember that the Southern decline, steep as it was, was basically a one-time decline resulting from wartime damage and the ending of slavery. This decline was then followed by what was, by American and world standards, a relatively rapid rate of long-term economic growth. It did take some years for the South to achieve the levels attained when the economy was dominated by the economically productive slave plantation system, but it does not seem that the institutions in the South in the postbellum era precluded economic expansion, either within agriculture or later when, after several decades, there was a shift out of agriculture into manufacturing.

## IV. THE NORTHERN ECONOMY: HOW CENTRALIZED IS CENTRALIZED?

Although the Civil War did not dramatically reshape the American economy, it may still meet our larger understanding of *total war*. Let us shift our emphasis from matters of economic impact to questions of economic policy. We start with the assumption that the totality of a nation's war effort may be gauged by considering two variables: (1) the degree of economic mobilization of the population, and (2) the level of centralized direction imposed by the state. Thus, a nation moves toward total war as it shifts economic production to the war effort and as the direction of that war effort moves into the hands of a centralized government. In this sense, the relative modernity of a nation's military is not necessarily the best measure of the totality of its war effort. Nor does the movement toward total war imply a concomitant shift in political ideology.

In the antebellum decades, divisions over the role of the federal government in national development repeatedly broke along regional lines, with Northern congressmen supporting legislation aimed at stimulating growth and development while their Southern counterparts, carrying the banner of states' rights, resisted such statist initiatives.[42] Following secession, the Confederate states—far from rejecting the Constitution—claimed to be the Founding Fathers' proper heirs.

Soon the Southerners discovered that their dedication to individual liberties and states' rights, which may have served them well in peacetime, presented major obstacles to the developing war effort.[43] Less than a year following the firing on Fort Sumter, Davis asked the Confederate Congress for a military draft. Many Rebels resented this federal imposition; state governors undercut its effect with wholesale exemptions; and poorer Southerners, objecting to the legislations class biases, actively resisted. But despite the controversies and inefficiencies, the Confederate draft proved a much heavier—and earlier—imposition than did the North's version.[44]

Similarly, the cost of supporting the war effort led Confederate Secretary of the Treasury Christopher Memminger to issue repeated calls for taxation legislation. In the war's first months, the Confederates had passed a modest tax on real estate and personal property, but the government relied on the individual states to collect their quotas; only South Carolina did so by enforcing the legislation. Rather than accept the impositions of taxation, Southerners preferred to turn to the sale of bonds; when the sources of funds dried up, the government eventually joined cities and states in relying on printed notes, which quickly depreciated in value. Finally, in April 1863, with Southern finances in turmoil, the Confederate Congress levied heavy taxes on agricultural products, bank deposits, commercial paper, and various other goods.[45]

The Confederate government proved particularly aggressive in taking on the task of providing materiel for its army. At the outset of the war, the South supplemented its inadequate manufacturing sector with imports from abroad. But soon unpaid foreign debts and the Union blockade forced the Confederacy to seek internal solutions. Where possible, the War Department turned to indigenous Southern businesses. But apart from Richmond's Tredegar Iron Works, there were few Southern factories able to answer the call for heavy industrial goods, forcing the Confederate War Department to open up government manufactories. The war industry system that emerged combined equal parts private enterprise and government armories, with both halves under the centralized control of a handful of military officials. By 1863, Josiah Gorgas was able to report that his Ordnance Bureau was able "to respond to all calls made upon it."[46]

In its zeal to supply the military, the Confederacy did not stop at issuing government contracts and opening new establishments. In the name of military necessity, planners directed the movements of Southern railroads. And time and again the Confederates took advantage of the 1863 Impressment Act to seize goods to support the war effort. The military authorities even periodically impressed slaves—who stood at the heart of the South's commitment to private property—for government labor. And in the war's waning months the

Confederacy nearly turned to the unthinkable policy of offering slaves their freedom in exchange for taking up arms for the government.[47]

In the United States Congress, Northern Republicans—long-time advocates of a more aggressive central government—suddenly found the seats of their most persistent opponents vacant and the call of patriotism providing new support for their larger agenda.[48] The best case for the Civil War's long-term economic effect emphasizes the legislation passed by the Republican-dominated War Congress. While the Confederacy relied on inflationary currency to finance most of its war expenditures, the Union raised 21 percent of its funds through taxation, including the revolutionary federal income tax passed in 1861 and expanded in subsequent years.[49] In February 1862, Congressional Republicans overwhelmed Democratic resistance to push through the Legal Tender Act, allowing for the printing of greenbacks.[50]

This early financial legislation expanded the government's economic role while furthering the war effort. In the war's second year, Congress went well beyond military necessity in passing a series of bills distributing public lands. The May 1862 Homestead Act, granting 160 acres of public land to settlers who stayed on the property for five years, fulfilled a long-term Republican goal. A few months later, Justin Morrill successfully steered legislation through Congress legislation that paved the way for the establishment of state land-grant colleges. And in a series of measures, Congress granted 120 million acres of public land to various transcontinental railroad companies.[51]

Perhaps the Civil War Congress's most important piece of financial legislation was the National Bank Act of February 1863. This act, which created a national banking system, also established a mechanism for the distribution of federal war bonds. But in a larger sense, it answered the longstanding Whig (and then Republican) call for effective regulation of banking. The roll call on the Bank Act revealed a clear partisan split, with nearly all Democrats lining up against the Act and three-fourths of Republicans voting for its passage.[52]

Taken together, this array of economic legislation—taxation, currency, banking, land, land grants—suggests a newly active Congress expanding the role of the federal government in everyday life.[53] Such legislation certainly supports the view that the war led to long-term economic change. But, as suggested earlier, many of these measures—the land grants, for instance— owed less to military goals than to political opportunity. Others, such as the National Bank Act and the Internal Revenue Act, were important precedents but not necessarily vital to the war years. What of the larger matter of wartime mobilization? Let us consider three aspects of Northern mobilization: recruitment, military contracting, and voluntarism.

The North's controversial conscription system, and the series of mid-war draft riots, tends to distract attention from the larger reality: The vast majority of Union soldiers served as volunteers. Fewer than 10 percent of the Union army was made up of draftees and hired substitutes; one in five Confederate soldiers followed one of these two routes.[54] Of course, this may distort the larger point. The draft laws were designed to be spurs to recruiting; as such, they were a critical component in the North's manpower policies.

On the one hand, the conscription legislation points to a growing federal presence in daily life. This is particularly marked when we note the transition from the state military drafts of 1862 to the four federally administered call-ups following the 1863 Enrollment Act. Still, the North's manpower policies essentially relied on local initiatives and free-market principles. Throughout the North, the approach of draft day drove communities to frenzied recruiting campaigns aimed at filling local quotas. The quota system assured energetic grassroots recruiting. A successful effort enabled a ward or community to relax as draft day passed; those who had failed to meet the quotas faced tense public drawings and the specter of violent rioting. After the war's first year, recruiting efforts relied not so much on appeals to patriotism or federal imposition as on the baser and more privatized pull of cash bounties. Thus, even in the midst of heavy military demands, the North pursued policies based on market principles.[55]

If the mobilization of men depended on local initiatives and market forces, what of the mobilization of materials? Once again, the case for total war seems to weaken under close inspection. As we have seen, the war left only a modest impact on long-term patterns of manufacturing output. The organization of that output also revealed a continued reliance on the private sector and market forces rather than on the sort of government control regularly employed in the Confederacy. Several observations point to this conclusion. First, the Union consistently chose to contract with private firms rather than engaging directly in war-related production. The most prominent exception to this pattern was probably the federally administered arsenals that produced goods such as tents and uniforms. But even these establishments contracted out portions of the work and ran at below capacity when local entrepreneurs could fill the military's demands.[56]

Second, even those policy areas with a strong government presence did not reveal a commitment to centrally directed mobilization. Lincoln had a hand in policies ranging from recruitment and emancipation to battlefield strategy, but he generally left economic policies to the legislature.[57] The nation's railroads, often cited as one of the most prosperous and strategically important sectors of the wartime economy, responded largely to market demands rather than to official controls. Only rarely did the government step in and take over Northern lines threatened by labor strife. And even when the military engaged in its own transportation construction, it relied on the direction of key experts from the private sector, such as Herman Haupt.[58]

The example of the railroads underscores the distinctions between a war that is strategically modern and one where heavy mobilization suggests total war. The North's superior railroad system is often portrayed as an important key to its military success. Moreover, the demands on that system stimulated important technological modernization in the midst of the conflict.[59] Yet despite the military importance of railroads, the war years saw a decline in the annual production of new mileage; and in their dealings with military officials, the railroad officials tended to play the role of profit-minded partners rather than helpless cogs in a government-controlled military machine.

Third, the contracting system that men like Edwin Stanton and Montgomery Meigs perfected was based on open bidding rather than ongoing relationships between private business and military purchasers.[60] And whereas other economic forces may have accelerated the wartime concentration of capital, the contracting system does not appear to have favored large manufacturers. The result was that the military procurement system was grafted onto an existing world of small manufactories with only minimal adjustments. Thus, the wartime procurement system left the Northern economy largely in the hands of small entrepreneurs who responded to market incentives rather than government directives.

A final case for the widespread mobilization of total war can be made by shifting our attention to private initiatives. Perhaps the Northern war effort fueled the emerging forces of centralization but simply outside of the realm of governmental controls. The strongest support for this argument can be found in the workings of the two national benevolent bodies: the United States Sanitary Commission (USSC) and the United States Christian Commission (USCC). Both bodies spanned the entire North, far outstripping the South's most ambitious voluntary societies. And at least the founders of the USSC claimed to be pursuing rational organizing goals while bringing comfort to the soldiers at the front.[61]

As a mobilizing force, the two national bodies were certainly quite important: Thousands of volunteers, mostly women, labored under their banners throughout the North. But two factors argue against the importance of these efforts as episodes in total warfare. First, the rank and file in these bodies had only tenuous connections with the national leadership. Thus, the mobilization may have been under a single name, but it is best seen as an upsurge of localized activism. And second, the national bodies in each locality competed with a host of entirely local groups engaged in similar pursuits. Although benevolence certainly became a rallying cry that mobilized an enormous portion of the Northern population, their actions did not reveal the centralized direction that we would expect out of true total warfare.[62]

What can we conclude about the North's wartime experience? Certainly mobilization was extraordinary, if measured by the proportion of citizens who became wrapped up in some aspect of the war effort.[63] But if the test for total war includes some consideration of the level of governmental direction, the case weakens. After examining a wide array of wartime legislation, Richard Bensel concluded that in most areas "the Union relied on an unregulated capitalist market to supply resources and manpower."[64] Federal activism definitely grew during the war, but private efforts remained dominant. Similarly, the evidence for the war as a centralizing force in the private world is not convincing, either if measured by wartime voluntarism or economic activity. Northerners became heavily involved in the war effort, but much of what they did fit within antebellum patterns of behavior.[65]

Perhaps in institutional developments, as in economic growth, the best way to understand the Civil War as a total war is to contemplate the conflict's postwar legacy. Certainly some pieces of wartime legislation—banking, currency, taxation, land—left an impact on patterns of economic development. But many of these developments should be viewed as a legacy of secession, which left the Republican forces guarding the nation's economic chicken coop (and the successful outcome of the war), rather than as true war measures. Moreover, the postwar history of these legislative initiatives does not suggest a steady growth in the government's role. For instance, as described earlier, the expansion of the federal debt and the growth of taxes and expenditures only lasted until the war's conclusion. During Reconstruction, Congress reduced taxes while striving to bring down the (to them) disturbing debt.[66] Similarly, whatever relationships developed between government and business during the war did not leave behind a formidable military-industrial complex.[67]

And while the costs of the Civil War did remain a persistent budget item long into the postwar years, as Congress worked to retire the debt while taking on the costs of dramatically expanded military pensions, most of these involved taxes and transfers among individuals, not government provision of goods and services.[68] But even if the government's role shrank with peace, the organizational skills developed during the conflict may have left their mark. The leaders of the USSC, for instance, went on to remain active in public life.

And several Union generals, such as George B. McClellan, took their expertise from the field and applied it to postwar political and economic challenges.[69]

## V. CONCLUSION: "THE FIRST MODERN WAR" OR "A LAST PREMODERN WAR"?

Where does all this leave us? Despite casual references to the Civil War as a "turning point", military history has no such right angles. For instance, the Spanish-American War over a generation later seems in many senses more "traditional" than its predecessor. That conflict certainly required a much more limited commitment of men and resources, triggering fewer economic or political adjustments.[70]

If we turn our gaze in the other direction, we can find ample evidence that the Civil War was, if not a watershed, at least a major departure from earlier experience. The casualties alone—whether measured by the bloodiest days, the harshest campaigns, or the awesome totals spanning four years—place the war in a distinctive place in our (and any nation's) history.[71] Similarly, the enormous cost of the war and the legacy of debt left an enduring mark on federal fiscal policies. To these weighty effects, we must add the dramatic changes accompanying the destruction of slavery and the damage—both economic and psychological—that the defeated South suffered. It comes as no surprise that so many participants looked back on the war as the nation's formative episode.

Nonetheless, we have seen that the Civil War left only a modest mark on long-term patterns of economic and political development, arguing against the notion that it was the first modern war. Many aspects of the war effort remained entirely or partially in private, voluntary hands. And where military purposes expanded the government's role, demobilization allowed private citizens to reclaim most of their lost autonomy.[72] While the costs of outfitting the armies was unprecedented, those business consolidations that marked the late nineteenth century were not clearly linked to the early military spending or to the ensuing financial policies.

Let us return to our initial paradox: How can a conflict of this scale leave such a modest mark on the nation's political and economical world? Three observations may help to explain this problem. First, if we are interested in the war's economic impact, we should look at the *nature* of the demand as well as the quantity. Even if the Civil War foreshadowed a modern emphasis on heavy military technology, we have seen that much of the expenditure on this war went for more traditional items—animals, wagons, clothing, food—that differed little from peacetime products. Thus, much of the military needs could be met by the private sector, with only modest adjustments to meet government specifications. Even that proportion of military spending that went into heavy industrial products—arms, railroads, ships—did not necessarily require the sort of enormous military factories that characterized later conflicts.[73] The war's economic impact was broad rather than deep, involving thousands of entrepreneurs while leaving the shape of the economy largely unchanged.

Our second observation builds from the first. There is no reason to believe that Americans would have welcomed the changes that we have associated with total war. For generations, they had prospered in a world of limited government encroachment that valued localism, privatism, and market forces over centralized control or public management. This is not to suggest that such values would have blocked the successful prosecution of the war, but they certainly informed the way that policy makers on both sides went about their tasks. Conscription is an excellent case in point. The initial objective, particularly in the North, was to provide incentives for rigorous local recruiting efforts. Those efforts, in turn, hinged on cash bounties rather than forced service. Similarly, by emphasizing open bidding for government contracts, the North took advantage of established market forces rather than relying on the existing federal arsenals. Even the national benevolent organizations prospered by working within familiar local associational patterns. In 1862, Lincoln declared that he would free no slaves, some slaves, or all slaves in order to preserve the Union. He could have made a similar pronouncement about localism and privatism. Such values would be sacrificed if necessary, but only if they did not serve the cause.

This leads, finally, to our third observation. The key to unraveling the war's modest impact may rest in the differences between the two combatants. Whereas Charles and Mary Beard claimed the Civil War as a victory for the modernizing industrial North, it may be that the war exerted stronger modernizing forces on the Confederacy. If so, perhaps the direct legacy of change—as caused by war measures—was muted by the Northern victory (leaving us with the indirect effects resulting from the victory of the more modern North). Thus, we have traded one paradox for another. The South—the bastion of tradition—embraced the techniques of modern warfare more fully than did the industrializing North, which engaged in a more familiar form of limited war.[74]

Consider the war measures passed by the two competing governments. The South turned to conscription and taxation before the North. Southerners, much more so than Northerners, suffered from federal impressment of their property. While Union officials worked largely with private manufacturers, the Confederacy relied heavily on government-run manufactories. Despite states' rights rhetoric, the Confederate government entered the daily lives of its citizens more than did its Northern counterpart.

The reasons for these differences are clear. The Confederacy was forced to fight a long war with far fewer usable men and only a fraction of the North's resources and industrial might. Moreover, the antebellum South lacked the industrial, transportation, and financial infrastructure necessary to support such a huge war effort. Thus, Confederate policy makers had to become more directly involved in munitions making, railroad building, and the like.[75] Union officials could work through an existing industrial and financial system. In April 1861, the term *total war* had yet to enter the military lexicon. But the ideas that we associate with the phrase—complete mobilization, centralization, federal control—would not have been welcomed in Washington or Richmond, and certainly not in the state capitals, North and South. On the other hand, as the first armies began drilling, neither side recognized the scale of the conflict to come. In the years that followed, the Union and the Confederacy turned to various controversial policies—conscription, taxation, arbitrary arrests, impressment—in the pursuit of victory.

The North's economy and society was certainly the more modern of the two. And the eventual Northern success owed much to that modernity. But it was that modernity, coupled with the obvious numerical advantages, that allowed the North to carry on the war without fully turning to total war. The South—although more resistant to such changes—took on more of the trappings of total war, grafted onto a traditional agrarian economy. In short, the North fought a technologically modern war but organized around traditional assumptions and limitations. It did not embark upon total war because it did not have to. The South, on the other hand, moved toward total war because it had to.

### NOTES

1. America's Civil War casualties far surpassed those of any other war, both in absolute terms and—even more dramatically—as a share of the total population. See Claudia D. Goldin, "War," in Glenn Porter, ed., *Encyclopedia of American Economic History: Studies of the Principal Movements and Ideas,* 3 vols. (New York, 1980), 3:935–57; and Maris Vinovskis, "Have Social Historians Lost the Civil War? Some Preliminary Demographic Speculations," in Vinovskis, ed., *Toward a Social History of the American Civil War: Exploratory Essays* (Cambridge, 1990), 1–30.

2. For a discussion on the use of "modernity" in describing wars, see Mark E. Neely Jr., "Was the Civil War a Total War?" *Civil War History* 37 (March 1991): 5–28.

3. The classic statement on Sherman is John Bennett Walters, "General William T. Sherman and Total War," *Journal of Southern History* 14 (Nov. 1948): 447–80. See also Edward Hagerman, *The American Civil War and the Origins of Modern Warfare: Ideas, Organization and Field Command* (Bloomington, Ind., 1988), xiii–xiv, 207–9; and Charles Royster, *The Destructive War: William Tecumseh Sherman, Stonewall Jackson, and the Americans* (New York, 1991). For an excellent review of the literature on the Civil War, see Neely, "Was the Civil War a Total War?" (Chapter 2, this volume).

4. James M. McPherson, "Lincoln and the Strategy of Unconditional Surrender," in *Abraham Lincoln and the Second American Revolution* (New York, 1990), 69–91. Mark E. Neely Jr. disagrees with this reading of Lincoln's war aims in his "Was the Civil War a Total War?" See also Richard A. Preston, Sydney F. Wise, and Herman O. Werner, *Men in Arms: A History of Warfare and Its Interrelationships with Western Society* (New York, 1956), 243.

5. Raymond Aron, *The Century of Total War* (Garden City, N.Y., 1954), 19.

6 James M. McPherson, *Battle Cry of Freedom* (New York, 1988), 306–7; Vinovskis, "Have Social Historians Lost the Civil War?" 9.

7. On the direct and indirect costs of the war, see the estimates in Claudia D. Goldin and Frank D. Lewis, "The Economic Costs of the American Civil War: Estimates and Implications," *Journal of Economic History* 35 (June 1975): 299–325. For a broader comparison, see Goldin, "War." On federal government expenditures, see U.S. Bureau of the Census, *Historical Statistics of the United States, Colonial Times to 1970*, 2 vols. (Washington, D.C., 1975), 2:1114.

8. In addition to the aforementioned sources on Sherman, see Michael Fellman, *Inside War: The Guerrilla Conflict in Missouri During the American Civil War* (New York, 1989). Of course, some of the strategies commonly associated with total war—the destruction of resources on the home front, for instance—were staples in traditional warfare as well.

9. Charles A Beard and Mary R. Beard, *The Rise of American Civilization* (New York, 1930), 2:115

10. Thomas Cochran, "Did the Civil War Retard Industrialization? *"Mississippi Valley Historical Review* 48 (Sept. 1961): 197–210. Cochran had, however, raised this same point in earlier writings. For a recent survey of the debate on the effects of the Civil War, see Patrick K. O'Brien, *The Economic Effects of the American Civil War* (London, 1988).

11. Robert E. Gallman, "Commodity Output, 1839–1899, "in Conference on Research in Income and Wealth, *Trends in the American Economy in the Nineteenth Century* (Princeton, N.J., 1960), 24: 13–71.

12. We should note that Robert E. Gallman has subsequently presented national income estimates for the non Civil War years after 1834 and that these provide some modest revisions to the basic commodity output pattern. The newer estimates, nevertheless, indicate the same basic patterns and conclusions pointed to in earlier writings. Robert E. Gallman, "Gross National Product in the United States, 1834–1909," in Conference on Research in Income and Wealth, *Output, Employment, and Productivity in the United States after 1800*, Studies in Income and Wealth, vol. 30 (New York, 1966), 3–76.

13. Richard Easterlin, "Regional Income Trends, 1840–1950," in Seymour Harris, ed., *American Economic History* (New York, 1961), 525–47; Stanley L. Engerman, "The Economic Impact of the Civil War," *Exploration in Economic History* 3 (Spring/Summer 1966): 176–99.

14. Robert E. Gallman, "American Economic Growth before the Civil War: the Testimony of the Capital Stock Estimates," in Robert E. Gallman and John Wallis, eds., *The Standard of Living in Early Nineteenth-Century America* (Chicago, 1993), 79–115; Thomas Weiss, "Long-Term Changes

in U.S. Agricultural Output per Worker, 1800–1900, " *Economic History Review* 46 (May 1993): 324–41; and Thomas Weiss, "U.S. Labor Force Estimates, 1800–1860, " in Robert E. Gallman and John Wallis, eds., *The Standard of Living in Early Nineteenth-Century America,* 19–75. Some of the discussion on the labor force is based on worksheets underlying Weiss's published estimates, and we wish to thank Weiss for permission to use them at this time.

15. For data on these issues, see Thomas L. Livermore, *Number and Losses in the Civil War in America 1861–65* (Boston, 1901); Goldin and Lewis, "The Economic Cost of the American Civil War," Clayne L. Pope, "Adult Mortality in America before 1900: A View from Family Histories," in Claudia Goldin and Hugh Rockoff, eds., *Strategic Factors in Nineteenth Century American Economic History: A Volume to Honor Robert W. Fogel* (Chicago, 1992), 267–96; and U.S. Bureau of the Census, Historical Statistics of the United States, 2:1140.

16. See Livermore, *Numbers and Losses;* Weiss, "U.S. Labor Force Estimates," and underlying worksheets.

17. See Weiss, "U.S. Labor Force Estimates," and underlying worksheets. See also the claims in Lee A. Craig and Thomas Weiss, "Agricultural Productivity Growth During the Decade of the Civil War," *Journal of Economic History* 53 (Sept. 1993): 527–48, who argue that the growth reflected increases in labor impact more than the increases in conventionally measured productivity.

18. Victor S. Clark, *History of Manufacturers in the United States,* vol. 2: *1860–1893* (Washington, D.C., 1929), 7–53; Paul Gates, *Agriculture and the Civil War* (New York, 1965), 10, 224; and J. Matthew Gallman, *Mastering Wartime: A Social History of Philadelphia During the Civil War* (Cambridge, 1990) 251–328.

19. Engerman, "The Economic Impact of the Civil War"; J. Matthew Gallman, *Mastering Wartime* and Philip Scranton, *Proprietary Capitalism: The Textile Manufacture at Philadelphia 1800–1885* (Cambridge, 1983). See also Raymond H. Robinson, *The Boston Economy During the Civil War* (New York, 1988); and James A. Huston, *The Sinews of War: Army Logistics 1775–1953* (Washington, D.C., 1966), 176–87, for a description of wartime purchasing.

20. Ross Thomson, *The Path to Mechanized Shoe Production in the United States* (Chapel Hill, N.C., 1989) 161, 183.

21. Peter Temin, *Iron and Steel in Nineteenth-Century America: An Economic Inquiry* (Cambridge, Mass., 1964), 264–6; and Clark, *History and Manufactures,* 2:15–16.

22. Harold B. Hancock and Norman B. Wilkinson, "A Manufacturer in Wartime: DuPont, 1860–1865," *Business History Review* 40 (Summer 1966): 213–36.

23. Edwin Frickey, *Production in the United States, 1860–1914* (Cambridge, Mass., 1947).

24. U.S. Department of Agriculture, Agricultural Marketing Service Statistical bulletin no. 56, "Corn: Acreage, Yield, and Production by States, 1866–1943" (Washington, D.C., 1954); and U.S. Department of Agriculture, Agricultural Marketing Service Statistical bulletin no. 158, "Wheat: Acreage, Yield and Production by States, 1866–1943" (Washington, D.C., 1955).

25. Richard Wacht, "A Note on the Cochran Thesis and the Small Arms Industry in the Civil War," *Explorations in Entrepreneurial History* 4 (Fall 1966): 57–62.

26. Robert William Fogel and Stanley L. Engerman, *Time on the Cross: The Economics of American Negro Slavery (Boston,* 1974).

27. See Richard D. Goff, *Confederate Supply* (Durham, N.C., 1969); and Raimondo Luraghi, *The Rise and Fall of the Plantation South* (New York, 1978). See also Richard E. Beringer et al., eds., *Why the South Lost the Civil War* (Athens, Ga., 1986).

28. On the failure of this policy, argued for quite different reasons, see, most recently, Stanley Lebergott, "Why the South Lost: Commercial Purpose in the Confederacy, 1861–1865," *Journal of American History* 70 (June 1983): 58–74: Douglas Ball, *Financial Failure and Confederate Defeat* (Urbana, Ill., 1991); and David G. Surdam, "A Case of Regicide: The Strange Demise of King Cotton," unpublished paper, University of Chicago, 1991.

29. See Stanley Lebergott, "Through the Blockade: The Profitability and Extent of Cotton Smuggling, 1861–1865, "Journal of Economic History 41 (Dec. 1981): 867–88; and Gates, Agriculture and the Civil War, on Southern wartime agriculture. On the antebellum Southern economy, see Fogel and Engerman, Time on the Cross, and the subsequent debates in the American Economic Review between 1977 and 1980. See also Robert William Fogel, Without Consent or Contract: The Rise and Fall of American Slavery (New York, 1989).

30. See, e.g., Mary A. DeCredico, Patriotism for Profit: Georgia's Urban Entrepreneurs and the Confederate War Effort (Chapel Hill, N.C., 1990); Luraghi, The Rise and Fall of the Plantation South; and Emory M. Thomas, The Confederate Nation: 1861–1865 (New York, 1979). On Confederate financing of the war effort, see Richard Cecil Todd, Confederate Finance (Athens, Ga., 1954).

31. Roger L. Ransom and Richard Sutch, One Kind of Freedom: The Economic Consequences of Emancipation (Cambridge, 1979); Jon R. Moen, "Changes in the Productivity System of Southern Agriculture between 1860 and 1880," in Robert William Fogel and Stanley L. Engerman, eds., Without Consent or Contract: The Rise and Fall of American Slavery; Technical Papers (New York, 1992), 1:320–50; and Robert William Fogel, Ralph A. Galantine, and Richard L. Manning, eds. Without Consent or Contract: The Rise and Fall of American Slavery: Evidence and Methods (New York, 1992).

32. See Ball, Financial Failure and Confederate Defeat.

33. See Lebergott, "Why the South Lost."

34. See Reuben A. Kessel and Armen A. Alchian, "Real Wages in the North during the Civil War: Mitchell's Data Reinterpreted," Journal of Law and Economics 2 (Oct. 1959): 95–113.

35. M. Slade Kendrick, A Century and a Half of Federal Expenditures, NBER Occasional Paper no. 48, revised (New York, 1955); and U.S. Bureau of the Census, Historical Studies, 2:1106–15. On the costs of the war, see Goldin, "War," and Goldin and Lewis, "The Economic Costs of the American Civil War." See also Bert W. Rein, An Analysis and Critique of the Union Financing of the Civil War (Amherst, Mass., 1962).

36. Paul Studenski and Herman E. Krooss, Financial History of the United States: Fiscal, Monetary, Banking, and Tariff including Financial Administration and State and Local Finance, 2d ed. (New York, 1963), 6–8; and Lance E. Davis and John B. Legler, "The Government and the American Economy, 1815–1902: A Quantitative Study," Journal of Economic History 26 (Dec. 1966): 514–52.

37. Jeffrey G. Williamson, "Watersheds and Turning Points: Conjectures on the Long-Term Impact of Civil War Financing," Journal of Economic History 34 (Sept. 1974): 636–61; and John A. James, "Public Debt Management Policy and Nineteenth-Century American Economic Growth," Explorations in Economic History 21 (April 1984): 192–217.

38. Larry Schweikart, Banking in the American South: From the Age of Jackson to Reconstruction (Baton Rouge, La., 1987); and Richard Sylla, "Federal Policy, Banking Market Structure, and Capital Mobilization in the United States, 1863–1913," Journal of Economic History 29 (Dec. 1969): 657–86.

39. Lloyd J. Mercer, Railroads and Land Grant Policy: A Study of Government Intervention (New York, 1982).

40. Stanley L. Engerman, "The Economic Response to Emancipation and Some Economic Aspects of the Meaning of Freedom," in Frank McGlynn and Seymour Drescher, eds., The Meaning of Freedom: Economics, Politics, and Culture After Slavery (Pittsburgh, 1992), 49–68.

41. How these North-South compromises evolved, and the extent to which the coalition of Northern and Southern whites served to limit the power of Southern blacks and poorer whites—North and South—will not be discussed here.

42. Richard Bensel argues that the South's antebellum states' rights rhetoric was largely tactical rather than ideological, designed to protect their own legislative agenda, but it is not clear that

such a distinction does not apply more widely in the political arena. Richard F. Bensel, *Yankee Leviathan: The Origins of Central State Authority in America, 1859–1877* (Cambridge, 1990).

43. For a comparison of the Confederate and Union political systems, see Eric L. McKitrick, "Party Politics and the Union and Confederate War Efforts," in William Nesbet Chambers and Walter Dean Burnham, eds., *The American Party Systems* (New York, 1967), 117–51.

44. Thomas, *The Confederate Nation*, 152–254, 260–1; McPherson, *Battle Cry of Freedom*, 430–2; see also Armstead Louis Robinson, "Day of Jubilo: Civil War and the Demise of Slavery in the Mississippi Valley, 1861–1865," Ph.D. diss., University of Rochester, 1976.

45. Thomas, *The Confederate Nation*, 196–8; McPherson, *Battle Cry of Freedom*, 437–42, 615–17.

46. Frank E. Vandiver, *Ploughshares into Swords: Josiah Gorgas and Confederate Ordnance* (Austin, Tex., 1952), 207; Thomas, *The Confederate Nation*, 206–17; Roger L. Ransom, *Conflict and Compromise: The Political Economy of Slavery, Emancipation, and the American Civil War* (Cambridge, 1989), 200–1; and Raimondo Luraghi, "The Civil War and the Modernization of American Society: Social Structure and the Industrial Revolution in the Old South Before and During the Civil War," *Civil War History*, 18 (Sept. 1972): 230–50.

47. Thomas, *Confederate Nation*, 196, 209–10.

48. Allan G. Bogue, *The Earnest Men: Republicans of the Civil War Senate* (Ithaca, N.Y., 1981), 330. For the antebellum debates, see McPherson, *Battle Cry of Freedom*, 193–5.

49. The use of an income tax was new for the Americans but not unheard of. The British had introduced an income tax in 1799 to help finance the Napoléonic Wars. On the history of the income tax, see John F. Witte, *The Politics and Development of the Federal Income Tax* (Madison, Wis., 1985).

50. McPherson, *Battle Cry of Freedom*, 442–8.

51. Ibid., 193–5, 450–3.

52. Ibid., 593–4. Although we have questioned (earlier in this chapter) the economic value of this financial legislation, its passage was certainly a victory for major forces within the Republican Party.

53. For a detailed analysis of wartime voting patterns, see Bogue, *Earnest Men*. On wartime politics in general, see Allan G. Bogue, *The Congressman's Civil War* (Cambridge, 1989).

54. McPherson, *Ordeal By Fire*, 182–3, 357.

55. The quota system imposed governmental coercion on the community rather than on the individual. The communities, in turn, relied on the market-based strategy of aggressive bounty fund raising. Meanwhile, the federal policy of accepting substitutes allowed draftees to enter a different market—for hired replacements—in order to avoid service. The Northern legislation allowing draftees to pay a $300 commutation fee in lieu of furnishing a substitute may have placed a ceiling on the market price for substitutes, but public outcry over commutation led to its repeal in 1864, removing this one modest government infringement on free market principles. On recruitment and conscription, see J. Matthew Gallman, *Mastering Wartime*, 11–53; and James W. Geary, "Civil War Conscription in the North: A Historiographical Review," *Civil War History* 32 (Sept. 1986): 208–28.

56. In Philadelphia, sewing women petitioned Lincoln to get the arsenal to run at capacity because they preferred the higher federal wages to working for private subcontractors. J. Matthew Gallman, *Mastering Wartime*, 245.

57. Phillip S. Paludan, *"A People's Contest": The Union and the Civil War 1861–1865* (New York, 1988), 107.

58. Paludan, *"A People's Contest,"* 139–42. The Union did run a substantial railroad operation in conquered portions of the Confederacy. See Bensel, *Yankee Leviathan*, 151.

59. Long-distance movement of men and materials encouraged competing railroad companies to move toward a standardized gauge. The heavy wear on iron rails accelerated the transition to steel. Paludan, *"A People's Contest,"* 140.

60. This is in direct contrast to America's contracting experience in World War II, when two-thirds of the government's $240 billion in military spending went to roughly 100 corporations, with nearly 18,000 smaller companies splitting the remainder. James L. Abrahamson, *The American Home Front: Revolutionary War, Civil War, World War I, World War II* (Washington, D.C., 1983), 149. See also Harold G. Vatter, *The U.S. Economy in World War II* (New York, 1985), 57–66.

61. See George M. Fredrickson, *The Inner Civil War: Northern Intellectuals and the Crisis of the Union* (New York, 1965), 98–112.

62. J. Matthew Gallman, *Mastering Wartime.*

63. Of course, even by this measurement, the Northern mobilization was much less than that in the South.

64. Bensel, *Yankee Leviathan,* 233.

65. For a discussion of these continuities in Philadelphia, see J. Matthew Gallman, *Mastering Wartime.*

66. Ransom, *Conflict and Compromise,* 267; and Morton Keller, *Affairs of State: Public Life in Late Nineteenth Century America* (Cambridge, Mass., 1977), 107. See preceding discussion in this chapter of the economic legacy of these measures.

67. Although Northern manufacturing prospered during the war years, it appears that the effect of military contracting was broad, with many businesses sharing in the profits. Moreover, the immediate postwar years saw a wave of business failures, particularly among firms most closely tied to military contracting. J. Matthew Gallman, "Entrepreneurial Experiences in the Civil War: Evidence from Philadelphia," in Thomas Weiss and Donald Schaeffer, eds., *American Economic Development in Historical Perspective* (Stanford, Calif., 1994), 205–22.

68. Ransom, *Conflict and Compromise,* 287–8. As late as 1893, 40 percent of the federal budget was devoted to pensions for Civil War veterans and their dependents with interest on the debt accounting for another 7 percent. (To retire two-thirds of the Civil War debt, the federal budget was in surplus every year from 1866 through 1893). See Vinovskis, "Have Social Historians Lost the Civil War?" 21–8. See also Amy E. Holmes, "'Such Is the Price We Pay': American Widows and the Civil War Pension System," in Vinovskis, ed., *Toward a Social History,* 171–95. For a discussion of the postbellum medical experience, see Dora L. Costa, "Height, Weight, Wartime, Stress, and Older Age Mentality: Evidence from the Union Army Records," *Explorations in Entrepreneurial History* 30 (Oct. 1993): 424–49.

69. For instance (and whether to be regarded as a plus or a minus), many of the Northern "carpetbaggers" who rose to political and economic power in the postwar South had served in the Union army. Richard Current, "Carpetbaggers Reconsidered," in *A Festschrift for Frederick B. Artz* (Durham, N.C., 1964), reprinted in Kenneth M. Stampp and Leon F. Litwack, eds., *Reconstruction: An Anthology of Revisionist Writings* (Baton Rouge, La., 1969), 223–40.

70. The five-month-long Spanish-American War had a direct cost of only $270 million, or roughly 2 percent of the GNP. But even this relatively minor war absorbed roughly 60 percent of federal expenditures for the year. Goldin, "War," 938.

71. Vinovskis, "Have Social Historians Lost the Civil War?" 3–7.

72. See Keller, *Affairs of State.* 1–33.

73. Abrahamson, *The American Home Front,* 48–9, 91, 148–9.

74. Bensel argues that the requirements of war pushed the Confederacy to much more substantial centrist legislation than the North. *Yankee Leviathan,* 94–237.

75. Ransom, *Conflict and Compromise,* 200–1. See also Thomas, *The Confederate Nation;* and Vandiver. *Ploughshares into Swords.*

# Entrepreneurial Experiences in the Civil War

## Evidence from Philadelphia

In early 1990 Tom Weiss and Don Schaefer, two of my father's doctoral students, contacted me about a planned conference to honor my father, Robert E. Gallman. My father had been among the cohort of scholars who really created "cliometrics" and the new economic history. He counted people like Bill Parker, Doug North, Stanley Engerman, Robert Fogel, Lance Davis, and Lou Galambos among his closest friends, colleagues, and dining companions. The plan was to do a conference and festschrift volume including both his students and his old friends. And his son.

I was thrilled to be part of this project and agreed to host the conference at Loyola College the following September. We did the whole thing as a grand surprise party. I invited my father to give a lecture at Loyola and told him that I was going to put him up at a charming local bed and breakfast. When we walked into the lobby of the inn, he was amazed to see the room packed with one of the most impressive groups of economic historians ever assembled. As was always the case with this group, there was much drinking and dining to be done, but the scholarship was very serious stuff.

My own contribution, which was published in a volume edited by Weiss and Schaefer, is based on research in the R. G. Dun papers housed at Harvard's Baker Library. As the essay explains, R. G. Dun and Company was a credit rating agency that sent agents across the country assembling reports on businesses large and small. During my dissertation research, I spent months reading through the massive folio volumes for Philadelphia Country, recording information from any report that mentioned the Civil War while also creating a control sample of 452 firms. Some of that research found its way into my first book, but this essay gave me the opportunity to make further use of this rich source. Essentially, I was shooting for an article that would combine case studies illustrating the diversity of entrepreneurial experiences with a quantitative analysis comparing the war contractors with the control group. My chief goal was to test the common notion that war contracting was a popular route for the rich to get richer. In fact, the range of experiences was vast, and in many cases, it was the most desperate—not the most powerful—who turned to government contracting

This essay's use of quantitative data was quite typical of the new social history. In fact, in preparing this essay, I found myself revisiting methodological approaches I had used in demographic studies many years earlier.

. . .

The debate over the economic impact of the Civil War is familiar to most economic historians. While an earlier generation saw the conflict as triggering substantial economic growth, later scholars—responding to Thomas Cochran's provocative essay, "Did the Civil War Retard Industrialization?"[1]—usually agreed that whereas much of the northern economy prospered during the war years, the Civil War's impact on long-term economic growth was slight. The case for more substantial economic change has generally concentrated on a particular sector of the economy or on the effects of specific legislation—banking, tariffs, taxes—passed by the Republican-dominated war Congress.[2] Much of this literature has approached the Civil War as a brief episode in the long-run development of the nineteenth-century American economy. The evidence has been mined for significant, measurable "impacts."

But the war also provides an excellent opportunity to address a more general set of issues concerning the influence of government policies—in this case, military spending—on economic behavior.[3] Here the critical concern is not so much to gauge the net impact of war on economic growth as it is to consider the economic ramifications of an expanded federal role as a purchaser of goods and services. Such an analysis can contribute both to our understanding of nineteenth-century economic growth and development and to larger discussions of the impact of military spending on economic development.[4]

My purpose is to consider the effect of the Civil War on Philadelphia entrepreneurs as revealed in the credit reports assembled by R. G. Dun and Company. When the war began, Philadelphia's Schuylkill Arsenal housed all the uniforms for the nation's 16,000-man regular army. As the conflict progressed, the city's central local and manufacturing diversity assured its businesses an integral position in the developing war-contracting system. These characteristics make Philadelphia particularly well-suited to this study.[5]

In 1841, New York wholesaler Lewis Tappan established the Mercantile Agency to gather credit information for sale to subscribers. Tappan collected his information from correspondents—mostly lawyers—who were well acquainted with local businesses. In 1859, R. G. Dun assumed ownership of the rapidly expanding Mercantile Agency.[6] R. G. Dun's agents typically filed semi-annual reports on local businesses. Any business that had applied for credit or appeared likely to seek loans was liable to fall under R. G. Dun's net. A complete report of a business included the names of all partners, an estimate of the establishment's net worth, any unusual activities that might affect its credit, a comment on the character of the owner, and a credit rating—usually "poor," "good," "very good," or "excellent." In practice, the entries varied tremendously. In some cases, the reporter submitted complete updates every six months; in other instances, reports came years apart.

The reports lend themselves to rudimentary quantitative analysis, but they are particularly valuable because the individual accounts often provide glimpses beneath the data. This analysis concentrates on the wartime histories of 138 Philadelphia firms that the R. G. Dun reporters described as having government contracts.[7] Their collective experiences are compared with those of a control sample of 491 firms.[8]

Several conclusions will emerge. First, Philadelphia's war contractors were a numerous and diverse lot. Thus, wartime profits were distributed over many sectors of the local economy. Second, eventual war contractors clustered in two groups: fairly large, established firms that were well situated to meet the government's needs; and new, often small, companies established specifically to fill government contracts. Many of the established firms sought war contracts following declines in their private business. Third, in most cases, established firms made only slight adjustments in their peacetime products to fill military needs. Finally, although war contracting helped some struggling companies survive, it was rarely a route to riches. Often, in fact, firms performing military work ran into trouble owing to slow government payments. Each of these findings points to the larger conclusion that the Civil War contracting system served to minimize the impact of government spending on economic growth and development.[9]

## PHILADELPHIA'S WAR CONTRACTORS

The evolution of the Union Army's supply system is an excellent metaphor for the North's wartime experience. When the war began, state and regimental quartermasters scrambled to outfit a hastily assembled army. Soon, under the guidance of Quartermaster General Montgomery C. Meigs, a multitiered supply system emerged in which some goods were produced in government arsenals while private contractors provided a wide array of raw materials and finished products. Following the conflict's first chaotic months, Congress passed legislation requiring open bidding for all government contracts. Often those who secured contracts passed on the work to subcontractors. For the purposes of this study, "military contractors" include all firms reported as producing goods to fill contracts for some war-related government agency.[10]

The R. G. Dun records generally noted the type of war contract held by each firm. More than a quarter of these businesses (Table 10.1) supplied uniforms to the army, and an additional 16 percent furnished boots, shoes, haversacks, and canteens. The firms trading with Philadelphia's vast network of military hospitals suggest the war's diverse economic opportunities. George Snowden sold surgical instruments to the Army's Medical Department; druggists J. Wyeth and Brother supplied medicine to local hospitals; the hardware firm of W. W. Knight, Son and Company did "a large bus in the Mfr of Hospital Bedsteads for [the] Govt"; grocer George D. Moses fell upon hard times in 1863 but recovered by "supplying the Hospitals with Groc[eries]"; 25-year-old Charles W. F. Calvert kept his new embroidery business afloat through "the Manufr of shirts & draws for Army Hospital purposes"; lumber dealer Warren F. Ferguson shared in the wartime building boom by selling materials for the construction of "2 or 3 hospitals and the Arsenal."[11]

Table 10.1. Philadelphia War Contractors in R. G. Dun

| Type of contract | N[a] | % |
|---|---|---|
| Clothing | 31 | 27.4 |
| Haversacks and canteens | 11 | 9.7 |
| Guns/rifles | 8 | 7.1 |
| Boots/shoes | 7 | 6.2 |
| Blankets | 6 | 5.3 |
| Saddles | 5 | 4.4 |
| Tents | 4 | 3.5 |
| Swords/bayonets | 4 | 3.5 |

| Type of contract | N[a] | % |
|---|---|---|
| Cannons | 3 | 2.7 |
| Ships | 3 | 2.7 |
| Bread | 2 | 1.8 |
| Wagons | 2 | 1.8 |
| Saddle trees | 2 | 1.8 |
| Food | 2 | 1.8 |
| Coal | 1 | 0.9 |
| Brushes | 1 | 0.9 |
| Drums | 1 | 0.9 |
| Mint acids | 1 | 0.9 |
| Lumber | 1 | 0.9 |
| Stockings | 1 | 0.9 |
| Hospital bedsteads | 1 | 0.9 |
| Ship timber | 1 | 0.9 |
| Hay and feed | 1 | 0.9 |
| Stoves | 1 | 0.9 |
| Potatoes | 1 | 0.9 |
| Gun locks | 1 | 0.9 |
| Propellors | 1 | 0.9 |
| Surgical instruments | 1 | 0.9 |
| Horses | 1 | 0.9 |
| Locomotives | 1 | 0.9 |
| Caps | 1 | 0.9 |
| Ship engines | 1 | 0.9 |
| Drugs | 1 | 0.9 |
| Shot and shell | 1 | 0.9 |
| Shipping | 1 | 0.9 |
| Harness leather | 1 | 0.9 |
| Artificial limbs | 1 | 0.9 |
| Total | 113 | 100.0 |

Source: The R. G. Dun and Company Collection, Baker Library, Harvard University Graduate School of Business.

[a]Includes ten war contractors with assumed "type of contract" based on antebellum activities rather than a specific statement indicating the nature of the contract. These ten cases include seven clothing, two saddles, and one boots and shoes. In twenty-five other cases, the type of contract was not given and could not be determined.

Others profited in more unorthodox ways. German immigrant C. M. Zimmerman sold drums to the army, and bought a farm with the proceeds. John Livesey's dry goods company failed shortly before the war, but by late 1865 he had "made considerable money by furnishing potatoes to [the] Govt" and was worth an estimated $20,000. By April 1864, Condit Pruden reportedly had sold the government 100,000 saddle trees, at a profit of between 50 and 75 cents each. And, in one of Philadelphia's oddest instances of profiting from the war, Dr. B. Frank Palmer grew wealthy by earning "the Govt contracts and patronage for supplying disabled soldiers & officers with artificial limbs."[12]

Pruden's case is also unusual in that his wartime saddle tree contract continued an antebellum relationship with the government. Coal dealers George F. Tyler and W. E. Stone, blank-book manufacturer James B. Smith and Company, and wheelwright Henry Simons also maintained established government contracts into the war years. But, as we shall see, most Philadelphia war contractors made adjustments to meet military demands.[13]

In addition to those military contractors who are the focus of this essay, the R. G. Dun records describe numerous local traders who found other ways to profit from the war. After leaving the 88th Pennsylvania Volunteers, William H. Shearman opened a hotel on Race Street catering to "officers and soldiers awaiting discharge."[14] Book dealer J. W. Bradley failed in May 1861 and then tried (unsuccessfully) to recover by "getting up a history of the war."[15] Several local tradesmen closed their shops and became sutlers, selling goods to the soldiers in the camps.[16]

Philadelphia's war contractors were, on average, larger and older than firms in the general sample. Table 10.2 compares the size of the war contractors with the general sample. Of 128 war contractors with estimated sizes, 39 percent were worth $100,000 or more. Only 11 percent of the sampled firms were this large. Conversely, 57 percent of the sampled firms and only 14 percent of the war contractors had an estimated worth under $15,000.[17] This difference in average size could indicate that larger firms were more adept at securing contracts, but the data also reflect the fact that contracting companies were often manufacturers, whereas a large share of the sampled establishments consisted of small retailers.[18]

In 104 of 138 cases, the reports reveal the approximate age of the firm. These "years of origin" are compared with the general sample in Table 10.3. Thirty percent of the contracting businesses were organized before 1851, compared to 25 percent of the firms in the general sample. Conversely, 32 percent of the companies in the general sample and only 19 percent of the war contractors began

Table 10.2. Estimated Firm Size: War contractors Versus the General Sample

| Estimated worth | Contractors (N) | Sampled firms (N) |
|---|---|---|
| $99,999 or more | 50 | 49 |
| $50,000–99,999 | 24 | 32 |
| $25,000–49,999 | 28 | 50 |
| $15,000–24,999 | 8 | 61 |
| Less than $15,000 | 18 | 257 |
| Total | 128 | 449 |

Source: R. G. Dun and Company Collection, Baker Library, Harvard Graduate School of Business.
Note: This table includes only those cases where the value of the firm could be estimated. These estimates relied on both dollar estimates of net worth and qualitative descriptions.

doing business in the five prewar years. Among established companies, older firms were apparently somewhat better prepared to win war contracts. Table 10.3 also indicates, however, that a disproportionate number of military contractors first opened their doors between 1861 and 1865 (29 percent as opposed to 20 percent in the general sample). This difference reflects the substantial decline in new firm starts during the war. In the five prewar years, 135 businesses opened in the general sample, compared to 71 between 1861 and 1865.[19]

Table 10.3. Age of Firm: War Contractors Versus the General Sample

| Year founded | Contractors (N) | General sample (N) |
|---|---|---|
| Before 1851 | 31 | 89 |
| 1851–55 | 23 | 80 |
| 1856–60 | 20 | 114 |
| 1861–65 | 30 | 71 |
| Total | 104 | 354 |

Source: R. G. Dun and Company Collection, Baker Library, Harvard Graduate School of Business.
Note: This table includes only firms with estimated years of origin. Twenty-one firms from the general sample that were founded between 1856 and 1860 but went out of business before 1861 are excluded.

Philadelphia's war contractors can be divided into established companies that shifted their activities to fill war contracts and firms founded to meet the military demand. The R. G. Dun reports often noted that firms had begun specifically to produce military goods. H. G. Haedrick and Company formed in 1862 to manufacture "cartridge boxes & bayonet sheaths"; J. W. Watson made tents; and J. C. Bower went into business in 1864 producing haversacks.[20] Twenty-two-year-old Adolph Hochstadter quit his father's firm and borrowed $6,000 from friends to manufacture uniforms.[21] W. F. Hansell left another establishment in 1862 and quickly "made money" selling army clothing to the government.[22] In a wartime atmosphere of economic caution, in which Philadelphia saw relatively few new business starts, war contracting presented attractive options for hopeful entrepreneurs.[23]

The combined evidence from Tables 10.2 and 10.3 shows that at least some contractors came from the ranks of Philadelphia's oldest and wealthiest firms. But Table 10.1 suggests that most types of contract were not monopolized by one or two local establishments. The records of contracts signed in Philadelphia confirm this apparent breadth of participation. For instance, the 278 contracts for equipment signed between 1862 and 1864 were filled by 101 different companies.[24] Moreover, the R. G. Dun reports indicate that some established firms that turned to war contracting did so less out of strength than out of weakness.

R. G. Dun's agents occasionally noted unusual changes in the fortunes of a business. Taken collectively, these "ebbs and flows" shed further light on the characteristics separating war contractors from other Philadelphia firms. Table 10.4 groups the agents' annual comments into three categories—those having a good year, those having a bad year, and those in serious trouble—and compares the experiences of war contractors with those of the general sample.[25] The evidence from the general sample indicates that when the Civil War broke out, business suffered through an initial year of hardship, followed by several years of recovery, and then a second decline near the end of the conflict. Beneath this pattern lay great diversity. In 1862, for instance, 14 of 342 companies (4 percent) were in serious trouble; another 13 (4 percent) experienced difficulties; but 11 other firms (3 percent) had begun expanding. The war contractors followed a similar chronology: a high percentage of firms ran into trouble in 1861, whereas roughly a fifth improved their standing in both 1862 and 1863. Although the timing of peaks and valleys is essentially the same as in the general sample, the war contractors' experiences were far more volatile. A higher percentage of firms that eventually became war contractors ran into trouble in 1861 than did firms in the larger sample. And a much greater share of war contractors experienced substantial gains in the mid-war years. This suggests that war contractors turned to the government when their normal activities ran into trouble. The high percentage of war contractors enjoying good years in 1862 and 1863 demonstrates that supplying the army was a profitable occupation. But it also could indicate that many of these companies were "down" in 1861, making their later successes particularly noteworthy to the credit reporters.[26]

Table 10.4. Evidence of Annual Fluctuations: War Contractors Versus the General Sample

| | Total[a] (N) | Good year | | Bad year | | In trouble[b] | |
|---|---|---|---|---|---|---|---|
| | | N | (%) | N | (%) | N | (%) |
| | | War contractors | | | | | |
| 1860 | 97 | 0 | 0 | 4 | 4 | 4 | 4 |
| 1861 | 112 | 6 | 5 | 5 | 4 | 10 | 9 |
| 1862 | 120 | 26 | 22 | 9 | 8 | 2 | 2 |
| 1863 | 122 | 23 | 19 | 0 | 0 | 7 | 6 |
| 1864 | 125 | 10 | 8 | 2 | 2 | 0 | 0 |
| 1865 | 110 | 2 | 2 | 4 | 4 | 4 | 4 |
| 1866 | 88 | 1 | 1 | 5 | 6 | 1 | 1 |
| 1867 | 73 | 0 | 0 | 1 | 1 | 4 | 5 |
| 1868 | 62 | 0 | 0 | 0 | 0 | 1 | 2 |
| | | General sample | | | | | |
| 1860 | 364 | 0 | 0 | 4 | 1 | 8 | 2 |
| 1861 | 341 | 4 | 1 | 9 | 3 | 21 | 6 |
| 1862 | 342 | 11 | 3 | 13 | 4 | 14 | 4 |
| 1863 | 339 | 10 | 3 | 2 | 1 | 2 | 1 |
| 1864 | 336 | 8 | 2 | 10 | 3 | 9 | 3 |
| 1865 | 321 | 3 | 1 | 4 | 1 | 4 | 1 |
| 1866 | 293 | 0 | 0 | 3 | 1 | 1 | 0 |
| 1867 | 253 | 3 | 1 | 7 | 3 | 4 | 2 |
| 1868 | 224 | 1 | 0 | 3 | 1 | 4 | 2 |

Source: R. G. Dun and Company Collection, Baker Library, Harvard Graduate School of Business.
Note: This table records the frequency of unusual comments recorded by the R. G. Dun agents. See text and note 25. See Table 10.5 for companies that went out of business each year.
[a]Total includes all businesses definitely in existence that year.
[b]"In trouble" means the company experienced serious trouble (e.g., suspension, etc.).

The reports offer a wide assortment of cases in which firms turned to government contracting out of desperation. The (aptly named) Phoenix Iron Company suspended payments during the Panic of 1857 and had barely returned to good standing when the secession crisis brought on another wave of suspension. In September 1861, while still under extension, the firm received a favorable report from R. G. Dun's agent because of "large [cannon] contracts with the Government which will help them very materially." Although Beggs and Rowland, wheelwrights, were "a little tight" in May 1861, they remained good for credit because of a government contract which, it seemed, "will ultimately place them in a gd position." On April 19, 1861—only days after the firing on Fort Sumter—an R. G. Dun agent reported that he "could not advise cr to any amt" to jeans manufacturer Bolton Winpenny because of "little if any demand" for his product; two months later the firm had reportedly "obtained a contract from [the] Government for Kerseys." By early 1865, Winpenny's firm was valued at over $100,000.[27]

Frequently, companies with economic ties to the South turned to military contracting when their normal operations fell into disarray. A survey of the R. G. Dun records on Philadelphia's wartime businesses yielded 53 firms, engaged in a wide range of enterprises, with prewar southern ties. Nearly all experienced some difficulties as the war commenced, and 30 of these either suspended or failed before 1866.[28] At least nine of the firms with southern ties turned to government contracting; nearly all of these cases fit the proposed profile: a firm seeking the military's business when familiar avenues closed. Philadelphia tailor Robert Clifton had a prosperous antebellum business with stores in Nashville and Norfolk. With the outbreak of war, Clifton's business failed, and he "settled at 50%" with his creditors. By 1864, he had earned $50,000 from government contracts and had settled his old debts. Michael Magee saw a $100,000 saddlery business fall apart when he lost his trade with New Orleans, but successful government contracts allowed him to retire a wealthy man in 1865. George Evans and William Hassall enjoyed a thriving Ladies Dressing Trimmings business before the Civil War; when the conflict cut off their southern market, they began manufacturing knapsacks and haversacks for the Union Army.[29]

The characteristics of contractors and the range of their products suggest the diversity of Philadelphia's war-contracting history. Some contractors were old, established firms, others came together simply to fill a military demand. Many clearly proceeded from strengths, whereas others turned to government production when the uncertainty and dislocation of secession brought them to the brink of failure.

## WARTIME EXPERIENCES

As we have seen, many companies were formed specifically to meet government demands. Of the remainder, some continued established relationships with the government, and most continued to produce their familiar products, perhaps with slight adjustments to meet the military's needs. Whereas some entrepreneurs threw their energies into war manufacturing, filling government contracts was often a minor portion of a firm's wartime activities. Dry-goods merchant Abraham Ritter sold blankets to the military to supplement his retail trade; woolen manufacturer Martin Landenberger had "good & very profitable Govt contracts," but also "made money rapidly by introducing fancy woolen articles for ladies wear"; and wealthy architect and builder John Rice picked up some extra profits in 1861 by "manufg muskets for the government."[30]

The credit reports offer ample evidence of manufacturers adjusting their operations in response to military demands. In October 1861, the report on George W. Simons and Brother, manufacturers of gold chains, thimbles, and pencils, noted that "they have altered thr machinery for the mfr of swords & are dg a large & profitable bus." The partnership of George Richardson and William Overman had been variously engaged in selling grain and manufacturing umbrellas when the war began. In March 1861, before the outbreak of hostilities, a skeptical R. G. Dun agent reported that they had leased a mill and bought $35,000 in equipment in preparation for the production of "patent rifles." By early 1863, they were "said to have made abt $200,000." In mid-1864, the agent noted that the firm owned a large factory, enjoyed good government contacts, and although "not popular . . . are perfectly good." Allen Ridgeway and Company's manufacturing concern specialized in making coffee mills before the war. In order to shift to the production of sword bayonets, they "expended considerable money on Machinery etc," which resulted in temporary financial difficulties in 1862.[31]

Such adjustments among Philadelphia's metal industries were widespread. Philip S. Justice shifted from the production of railway spring machinery to muskets and rifles; in 1861, the Fair Mount Fork Works began "altering & having machinery made for the purpose of mfg cavalry sabres" and bayonets; North, Chase and North—a leading Philadelphia iron foundry—recovered from the secession crisis by selling shot and shell to the government.[32] Similarly, many of Philadelphia's textile manufacturers shifted their factories over to war work. Carpet manufacturer James Lord, Jr. began producing blankets; cotton-duck trader John W. Everyman earned over $100,000 supplying tents to the government; necktie maker E. Oppenheimer survived the war by subcontracting work in various military goods.[33]

Most of these shifts apparently required only modest alterations, but in several cases firms underwent substantial retooling to meet the new wartime demands. Such adjustments could have had a far-reaching effect on the local economy as manufactories invested in machinery or constructed new buildings. And although the evidence is scanty, several credit reports hint at the importance of war contracting as a stimulus to technological development. Among the most noteworthy are the reports on C. Sharps and Co. In June 1861, the R. G. Dun agent noted that "he has lately invented a Rifle which is said by those who have examined it to be superior to anything of the kind in the world." Four months later, R. G. Dun reported that "we understand they have a Government contract to mfr. 500 stand of arms of his [Sharps's] new patent. This contract will not pay them any profit as they have been to a large expense in altering thr machinery."[34] Both Jesse Butterfield's blacksmith-shop-turned-arms-manufactory and the Cooper Arms Manufacturing Company also reportedly profited from wartime arms patents.[35]

Whether they simply sold their traditional wares to a new buyer or reshaped their operations to fill the military demands, Philadelphia's war contractors—like its other businesses—had to navigate a volatile wartime economy. Although they are not consistently sensitive to subtle shifts, the R. G. Dun reports contain sufficient information to offer a broad comparison of the "failure rate" of the war contractors with that of the general sample. Table 10.5 compares the failure rate of war contractors with that of the general sample using two measurements.[36] The first calculation for each group, "complete cases," includes only those firms where the report gives an exact year of failure. The second calculation, "estimated cases," includes the final year of operation where the evidence is less exact.[37]

The long-term failure rate for the 131 war-contracting firms with known or estimated final years appears quite similar to the general sample of 452 wartime cases. Sixty-five of 131 war contractors (49.6 percent) survived until 1870, whereas 50.2 percent of the larger sample lasted through the war decade. But this apparent similarity masks a clear difference. Only 25 war contractors (19.1 percent) failed between 1861 and 1865, whereas 29.6 percent of the overall sample failed during the war years. This does not necessarily indicate that trading with the government was a wise buffer against wartime turbulence. Many war-contracting firms were formed following the disruptive secession crisis. Moreover, the war contractors that weathered the war's first winter were,

Table 10.5. Final Year in Business: War Contractors Versus the General Sample

| | War contractors | | | General sample | | |
|---|---|---|---|---|---|---|
| | Complete cases[a] | Estimated cases[b] | All cases | Complete cases[a] | Estimated cases[b] | All cases |
| 1861 | 0 | 0 | 0 | 15 | 10 | 25 |
| 1862 | 4 | 0 | 4 | 15 | 27 | 42 |
| 1863 | 3 | 0 | 3 | 8 | 12 | 20 |
| 1864 | 4 | 1 | 5 | 13 | 3 | 16 |
| 1865 | 13 | 0 | 13 | 28 | 3 | 31 |
| 1866 | 9 | 4 | 13 | 19 | 4 | 23 |
| 1867 | 9 | 3 | 12 | 10 | 8 | 18 |
| 1868 | 3 | 8 | 11 | 12 | 27 | 39 |
| 1869 | 2 | 3 | 5 | 5 | 6 | 11 |
| 1870 and after | 51 | 14 | 65 | 215 | 12 | 227 |
| Total | 98 | 33 | 131 | 340 | 112 | 452 |

Source: R. G. Dun and Company Collection, Baker Library, Harvard Graduate School of Business.
Note: See note 33 for a discussion of methods.
[a]Cases in which an exact year of failure is given.
[b]Cases with an estimated final year.

on average, larger and older establishments than their counterparts in the general sample. Under normal circumstances, such characteristics provided protection against abrupt failure in crisis.[38] In fact, larger war-contracting firms fared slightly worse than those in the general sample. Only 4 of 43 sampled firms (9.3 percent) worth over $100,000 (with known or estimated final years) went out of business during the war, and one of these folded during the 1861 panic. In contrast, 7 of 38 large war contractors (18.4 percent) closed between 1861 and 1865. Similarly, "young" war-contracting firms were less likely to survive the war than similar establishments in the general sample. Ten of 29 war contractors (34.5 percent) established between 1861 and 1865 went out of business before 1866, whereas only 16 of 71 such establishments (22.5 percent) in the general sample did so. (Neither group managed as well as the businesses formed between 1856 and 1860. Despite the Panic of 1857, only 21 [15.6 percent] of these young antebellum firms failed before 1861.[39])

The case histories suggest the range of wartime experiences. Although many new firms flourished by concentrating on government contracts, others found the road more rocky. C. W. Williams and Company, gun-lock manufacturers, opened their doors on September 1, 1861, to provide gun locks "for parties holding Govt contracts." The following March, R. G. Dun's agent reported that they had spent $12,000 on machinery with an additional $8,000 earmarked for future investment. These capital outlays had left them "a little short in money matters owing to the expensiveness of the machinery." Eight months later, they had sold out to a Connecticut firm.[40] In December 1861, R. G. Dun's reports listed Charles A. Edwards as owning a new concern with "a large contract for the Manufr of shoes for the Government." After seven months, the firm had "no known means," and that December it was out of business.[41] The clothing firm of Rosenberg and Bohm opened in early 1863 with an estimated worth of $40,000 and a claim that it had $500,000 in government contracts. But R. G. Dun's agent could not corroborate that assertion, and within ten months it had closed its doors.[42]

Among the established firms that turned to government work, the reports offer various cases in which war contracting left healthy companies even better off. In 1860, William G. Mintzer had a solid business producing fly nets and other items. Throughout the war he profited from the "Manufr of military goods." By 1864, his estimated worth had risen from $40–50,000 to $50–60,000. Saddler W. V. Wilstack was "well off" before the war and grew rich through "a large contract to furnish the Govt with cavalry equipment." The saddlery firm of William S. Hansell and Sons was known as "one of the best in line" in 1861; by 1864, it had "added largely to their means" through military contracts. The firm of Wilson and Childs stood among Philadelphia's leading wheelwrights before the Civil War; in 1864, R. G. Dun's reporter noted that the 30-year-old company had profited from "an excellent govt bus & made money rapidly since the war."[43]

Some firms certainly grew rich through war contracting. Emanuel Hay and his brother ran a modest woolen-and-worsted shop valued at $10–12,000 in 1859. By 1862, government work had left the seventeen-year-old partnership in "a better position than ever." In February 1865, an R. G. Dun agent estimated their worth at $100,000.[44] But despite contemporary claims, war contracting does not appear to have thrust many new names into the ranks of Philadelphia's wealthiest men. At the close of the war, local bookdealers sold a printed summary of the "Rich Men of Philadelphia" based on income-tax returns for the year ending April 20, 1865.[45] The list included 36 men who had annual incomes of over $100,000. A search of the R. G. Dun index yielded reports on 26 of these prosperous Philadelphians. The reports suggest that ten of these men did not grow appreciably more wealthy during the war, and only four clearly became rich because of the conflict. Of seven with wartime government contracts, only one, William L. Hunter, Jr.—who engaged in a wide range of war-related activities—gained great wealth thereby.[46]

Rather than helping the rich get richer, government contracts appear to have enabled struggling companies to turn their fortunes around. As we have seen, many who sought military contracts did so out of weakness, if not desperation. The credit reports indicate that this strategy often succeeded. G. Hoff ran a modest cap establishment for over a decade until the secession crisis forced him to suspend payments. Hoff eventually settled with his creditors at 50 percent and rebuilt his business selling uniform caps to the military. Clothiers Rockhill and Wilson suspended payments during the Panic of 1857 and fell upon hard times again in 1861, but by 1862, uniform contracts had left them in "better condition than they have been for some time," and in 1864 the partners were worth an estimated $75,000 apiece. Leather dealer John A. Evers lost credit judgments in 1863, but recovered by securing "a large contract for making 16 inch cavalry boots"; W. W. Knight, Son and Company's hardware establishment was valued at over $75,000 in 1861, ran into serious troubles in 1862, and recovered—under the name Knight and Son—in 1863 by selling hospital bedsteads to the government. The fancy-goods business of W. T. Fry and Company struggled when the war began, but survived by manufacturing "canteens, haversacks and fancy articles for officers in the Army." Reeves, Buck and Company, iron manufacturers, failed in 1854, 1857, and 1861, before turning to the production of rifled cannons.[47]

These cases help explain the midwar improvements described in Table 10.4. But the agents also described more war contractors as "declining" or running into "trouble" (16 percent) in 1862 and 1863 than they did their counterparts in the general sample (10 percent). The differences are not great, but if military contracting guaranteed prosperity, one would anticipate less (rather than more) frequent trouble among war contractors. One explanation is simply that some firms did not turn to government contracting until the middle of the war. But the R. G. Dun reports also demonstrate that government contracting was not always a sure cure.

Sometimes government contracting proved insufficient to restore firms to their antebellum health. Tailors F. Sarmiento and Thomas McGrath ran a "gd & profitable" business in mid-1861, but over the next several years they fell behind in payments and repeatedly lost credit judgments. In June 1862, R. G. Dun's reporter noted that the partnership had "been engaged on [a] Govt contract with Henry Simons and are not supposed to have made much if any money." Three years later they remained "pretty well covered up" with debts. Sarmiento and McGrath managed to return to prosperity in the postwar years, but fellow clothier Granville Stokes was not so fortunate. In July 1863, his report read: "Has been dg a good & paying bus. [and] has had several Govt contracts for clothing by which it is supposed he made considerable money." Nevertheless, five months later Stokes lost several credit judgments and was no longer deemed safe for credit; by September 1864, he had sold out his business. Commission merchant Henry W. Scott's problems began during the Panic of 1857. Finally, in 1862, R. G. Dun reported that he "has given up the Commn bus and is now engaged in filling Army clothing contracts." Within a year, that effort had failed, and Scott had "rent[ed] a mill & machinery at Norristown, Pa and [was] Manufg goods for Govt contractors."[48]

It is not really surprising that some struggling firms were unable to parlay government contracts into renewed success. The recurring source of their troubles is less expected. Repeatedly the R. G. Dun records describe marginal firms suffering from slow government payments. Stove manufacturer Samuel Hill seemed to have recovered from the secession crisis when he signed a government contract "amounting to some 10 to 15 [thousand] $s" in 1861. But two years later he was still losing credit judgments while awaiting a "pretty large balance due to him." Blacksmith Jesse Butterfield opened a small gun-making establishment with his son in early 1862, and they immediately turned to government work. By the middle of the year, they ran into difficulties be-cause "their cap[ital] is sm and the Govt being rather slow in payments they are unable to meet thr bills as promptly as heretofore." Although the agent expressed confidence in the "hardworking hon[est]" pair, they lost several credit judgments the following year and were out of business by early 1865. George Richardson and William Overman made a successful transition from umbrella-making to arms manufacturing, but they had to sell out to the more wealthy American Arms Company in early 1865 because they had been "unable to collect promptly a large amt due them by the Govt."[49]

More stable companies managed to keep in business despite slow payments from the government. The clothing firm of Strauss and Goldman earned an excellent credit rating in 1860 and 1861; therefore, in 1862, the R. G. Dun agent remained confident despite reporting that they were "a little short at present not having received thr money from the Govt."[50] Bishop, Simons and Company profited handsomely by shipping goods for the military, although in early 1862 their future had appeared in doubt because of slow government payments. Neafie and Levy, a large engineering firm, secured substantial wartime profits in naval production and apparently did not miss the "large amount of back monies due them by [the] Govt" that they received in 1866. The shipbuilding firm of Hillman and Streaker fared similarly. From early in the conflict they built gun boats for the navy and maintained a strong credit rating; in mid-1866 they "received considerable back pay due from [the] Govt."[51]

The diverse experiences of Philadelphia's war contractors mirror the range of companies that sought to trade with the military. Some were quite large and well established, others relied on very modest capital. Many made only minor adjustments to meet the new wartime demand, often maintaining an established business with war contracting as a mere sideline. Other firms were organized specifically to meet military needs or invested heavily in new machinery to meet military demands. Although the credit reports suggest no single pattern, the war contractors generally had more volatile wartime histories than their counterparts in the general sample. Several factors explain this volatility. First, the sudden military demand presented opportunities for rapid success. Second, war contractors appear to have come disproportionately from firms weakened by the secession crisis. Third, though the lure of government revenues attracted many Philadelphia entrepreneurs, the reality of slow payments often proved crippling.

## POSTWAR EXPERIENCES

Although our focus has been on wartime entrepreneurial choices, the postwar histories of war contractors shed light on the war's economic legacy. The transition from war to peace after the Civil War—like the transition after all such conflicts—sent a destabilizing shudder through the economy. Many war contractors took that shift in stride, as they had the mobilization for war. Machine manufacturer Alfred Jenks ran a firm valued at $250,000 in 1860; in 1865, having spent the war filling large contracts for rifled muskets, his company was valued between $250,000 and $300,000. For some, the shift to peace meant a return to old activities, but other war-related businesses had to change to survive. No arms manufacturers were reported as shifting to the production of ploughshares, but sword manufacturer William H. Gray turned to gas fixtures, and the Cooper Arms Manufacturing Company made a successful postwar transition to making hinges.[52]

Not all war contractors fared so well (see Table 10.5). While the wartime failure rate was low, 49 of the 119 war contractors (41.2 percent) with known or estimated final years that survived to 1865 went out of business between 1865 and 1868, as opposed to 31.8 percent (111 of 349) of the general sample.[53]

Often these postwar failures occurred shortly after contractors lost their military customers at the war's end. This was particularly true of companies established to meet military demands. Only 8 of 30 (27.6 percent) war-contracting firms founded during the war survived until 1870, compared to 40.8 percent among the general sample. W. S. Robarts went into business in 1861 to manufacture woolen army stockings. In 1865, after recording four years of prosperity, R. G. Dun's agent noted that Robarts had failed after "[losing] heavily on Army contracts lately which has irretrievably embarrassed him." J. H. Purdy and Company opened their doors in December 1864 and immediately prospered by selling corn vinegar to the Commissary Department. The following July, an R. G. Dun agent reported that they "did a good bus & made money until the war closed . . . but are not dg much now." By the following May they were out of business.[54]

Established companies that enjoyed substantial wartime contracts were also particularly susceptible to postwar declines. Cloth dealers DuHadaway and Dodson grew from a "modest" business in 1860 into a $75,000 firm in 1865 by earning "considerable money on Govt contractors." The first two postwar credit reports noted that the business had "made no money," and in April 1867 the two dealers sold out. Even Philadelphia's largest manufactories were not immune from postwar disaster. Locomotive builders Richard Norris and Son suffered discomfort in 1861. But the firm soon returned to prosperity with the aid of "an immense Govt & regular business." Nevertheless, in March 1866, an R. G. Dun agent reported that it had been closed for most of the previous year and then reopened on a smaller scale. The following year's report noted that all of Norris's shops were closed.[55]

Whereas lost credit judgments or slow payments often foretold the postwar demise of a war contractor, some firms closed their doors without reported discomfort. W. F. Hansell went into business for himself in 1862 to manufacture army clothing. The enterprise profited throughout the war and went out of business, with no reported explanation, soon afterwards. Sailmaker Charles E. Miller shifted to tent production when the Civil War began and "was supposed to have made money." In April 1865, within weeks of Lee's surrender, R. G. Dun reported Miller as out of business.[56] Certainly these postwar closings may have been accompanied by unreported financial embarrassment, but it is also possible that savvy entrepreneurs simply moved on to other things when the shooting stopped. This was clearly Joseph F. Page's story. In 1859, Page left

a coal-trading partnership to go into the clothing business. By 1862, he had received "some good contracts from the Govt" and had soon "made a large amt of
money" manufacturing army blouses. By mid-1864, Page's business was valued
at $100,000. Two years later, after the close of the war, R. G. Dun reported that
Page was "not dg any bus now, investing his surplus in Govt securities" and was
"well off." The next report noted that Page was "out of bus."[57]

These postwar histories, although quite diverse, support the general impression that Philadelphia's war contractors can be divided into two camps: those
who acted out of strength, often dedicating only a portion of their resources to
military production; and those who either formed to fill war contracts or turned
to military contractors out of desperation. Within either group the likelihood
of postwar difficulties was great. But for those entrepreneurs who relied heavily
on military contracts, the transition to peacetime was particularly rocky.

## CONCLUSION

I have argued elsewhere that whereas the Civil War touched most aspects
of Philadelphia's economic life, its lasting effect on the structure of the local
economy was not great.[58] The entrepreneurial responses to military demands
followed several patterns, each of which shaped the war's impact on Philadelphia's economic development. First, a tremendous number of Philadelphians
sought to turn the diverse military requirements to their advantage. Profits
could be earned by trading with the various branches of the Army and Navy,
with individual regiments, or even with local military hospitals. Other tradesmen sold their wares directly to individual soldiers or their families. A second
pattern of behavior indicates which entrepreneurs decided to become war contractors. More than a quarter (30 of 104) formed new companies during the war,
generally to produce military goods. Such decisions presumably recognized
the lure of government dollars as well as the relative lack of opportunities in
the private sector. Among established businesses, there were certainly many
strong firms that took advantage of military profits. But war contracting was
often a haven for the weak. Companies left reeling by the secession crisis or
in jeopardy after losing their southern contacts repeatedly sought refuge in
supplying the military.[59] The sorts of enterprise chosen suggest a final pattern of response. Most established firms seeking contracts were able to fill a
government demand with only minor adjustments, and often new companies
were formed by entrepreneurs with some related experience.

How do these patterns of individual decision-making help explain the war's limited impact on the longer-term process of economic development? First, the diverse array of businesses receiving contracts (as well as the large number of companies only marginally involved in government contracting) undercut any tendency for federal spending to speed the process of economic centralization. Second, by attracting new businesses and weakened firms rather than relying on the city's strongest establishments, government contracting presumably had a balancing effect on the distribution of wealth. Finally, the preference shown by entrepreneurs to stay close to their familiar areas of endeavor—and the high rate of postwar failure among those firms established solely to meet war contracts— helps explain the minimal long-term sectoral changes within Philadelphia.[60]

Certainly much of this entrepreneurial behavior depended less on individual reactions to federal spending policies than on circumstances peculiar to the Civil War or to Philadelphia's economy. The mix of arms, equipment, and food required by a mid-nineteenth-century war did not strain the capacities of a peacetime economy as much as modern warfare does. That is, much of the material required to support an army in the field was not strikingly different from what the same individuals might consume at home. Philadelphia, with its large manufacturing output produced largely by small establishments, was particularly well suited to make the necessary adjustments. But it is also appropriate to see the Civil War as an early episode of major federal spend- ing that had some influence on shaping behavioral patterns. Certainly the quartermaster general was in a position to limit access to war contracts, but by filling individual contracts through public bids he left room for widespread involvement. More importantly, while Philadelphia's entrepreneurs recognized the potential benefits of war contracting (R. G. Dun's credit agents clearly saw a war contract in hand as reason for enhanced public confidence), it appears that they also viewed such activities as a gamble. Businesses that turned to the government out of weakness also acted in desperation. Those which only filled the occasional contract hedged their economic bets by maintaining a private trade. Why might the more conservative entrepreneur have steered clear of excessive government work? One explanation may lie in the limited nature of the demand. Philadelphians did not anticipate a long war, and the peacetime government had had little use for military contractors. A further reason was simply that after 1861, most sectors of the economy boomed. War contracting aided this reversal, but profits in producing for the private sector were ample for established businesses.[61] But the most telling evidence is the relationship that many contractors had with the government. Frequently the

R. G. Dun agents reported businesses struggling under accumulated debts while they awaited delayed government payments. Even firms that did not fall into serious trouble must have been inconvenienced when reimbursement did not arrive until many long months after Appomattox. When considering the decision to bid for military contracts, Philadelphia's wartime entrepreneurs had to weigh such uncertainty against the anticipated gains.

## NOTES

I would like to thank Charles Cheape, Stephen Hughes, Thomas Weiss, Lou Galambos, and Stanley Engerman for their comments on earlier drafts.

1. Thomas Cochran, "Did the Civil War Retard Industrialization?" *Mississippi Valley Historical Review* 48 (Sept. 1961): 197–210. Some of the material contained in this essay appeared in J. Matthew Gallman, *Mastering Wartime: A Social History of Philadelphia During the Civil War* (New York, 1990).

2. For an excellent recent survey of the literature, see Patrick O'Brien, *The Economic Effects of the American Civil War* (London, 1988). For two other review essays, see Stanley Engerman, "The Economic Impact of the Civil War," *Explorations in Entrepreneurial History* (now *Explorations in Economic History*) 3 (Spring 1966): 176–99, and Harry Scheiber, "Economic Change in the Civil War Era: An Analysis of Recent Studies," *Civil War History* 11 (Dec. 1965): 396–411. Also see Ralph Andreano, ed., *The Economic Impact of the American Civil War* (Cambridge, Mass., 1962), and David Gilchrist and W. David Lewis, eds., *Economic Change in the Civil War Era* (Greenville, Del., 1965). Cochran's initial article and much of what followed relied on the data compiled by Robert Gallman. See Gallman, "Commodity Output 1839–1899," in *Trends in the American Economy in the Nineteenth Century,* vol. 24 of *Studies in Income and Wealth* (Princeton, 1961).

3. For an analysis of the impact of a different sort of wartime legislation, see Jeffrey Williamson, "Watersheds and Turning Points: Conjectures on the Long-Term Impact of Civil War Financing," *Journal of Economic History* 34 (Sept. 1974): 636–60.

4. On the study of nineteenth-century economic growth and its application to modern developmental economics, see Barry Poulson, "Economic History and Economic Development: An American Perspective," in this volume. The implications of military spending for modern economic development are a source of continuing discussion. See, for instance, John Nef, *War and Human Progress: An Essay on the Rise of Industrial Civilization* (Cambridge, Mass., 1950); Claudia Goldin, "War," in Glenn Porter, ed., *Encyclopedia of American Economic History,* 3 vols. (New York, 1980), 3: 935–57; Saadet Deger and Somnath Sen, "Military Expenditure Spin-off and Economic Development," *Journal of Development Economics* 13 (Aug.–Oct. 1983): 67–83; James Cypher, "Military Spending, Technical Change, and Economic Growth: A Disguised Form of Industrial Policy?" *Journal of Economic Issues* 21 (Mar. 1987): 33–59; Paul Kennedy, *The Rise and Fall of the Great Powers: Economic Change and Military Conflict from 1500 to 2000* (New York, 1987), pp. 444–46 and passim. For an analysis of the relationship between military spending and private investment in recent American history, see Michael Edelstein, "What Price Cold War? Military Expenditures and Private Investment in the United States, 1890- 1980," *Cambridge Journal of Economics* (forthcoming).

5. For a discussion of Philadelphia's antebellum and wartime economy, see Gallman, *Master-*

*ing Wartime,* chaps. 10 and 11; chap. 12 there contains a broader analysis of die evidence from the R. G. Dun and Company reports.

6. Sydney Ratner, James Soltow, and Richard Sylla, *The Evolution of the American Economy* (New York, 1979), p. 230. Also see James Norris, *R. G. Dun & Co., 1841–1900: The Development of Credit-Reporting in the Nineteenth Century* (Westport, Conn., 1978). The Philadelphia branch of the Mercantile Agency opened in 1845. The records of R. G. Dun and Company are housed in the R. G. Dun and Company Collection, Baker Library, Harvard University Graduate School of Business.

7. These firms were identified by scanning the twelve folio volumes from Philadelphia with at least some cases spanning the war years. This "sample" is flawed in two ways. First, it is impossible to be sure that all such reports were identified. Second, we cannot be sure that R. G. Dun's reporters noted every war contractor.

8. This sample includes all businesses that were established after 1855 or were in operation during the war years appearing on every twentieth page of the twelve "Philadelphia" volumes. Most of the quantitative comparisons in this essay will focus on the cases that existed during the war years. For a more detailed discussion of the sampling procedure, see Gallman, *Mastering Wartime,* appendix.

9. The R. G. Dun and Company data also offer small pieces of information relevant to the discussion of the importance of military procurement for technological development. For an excellent entry into the extensive scholarship on military technology, see Merritt Roe Smith, ed., *Military Enterprise and Technological Change: Perspectives on the American Experience* (Cambridge, Mass., 1985). For an application of this approach to an individual enterprise, see Merritt Roe Smith, *Harper's Ferry Arsenal and the New Technology* (Ithaca, N.Y., 1977).

10. Though it would be interesting to compare the characteristics of contractors and subcontractors, the R. G. Dun and Company data do not consistently differentiate between the two. On the contracting system, see Russell Weigley, *Quarter-master General of the Union Army: A Biography of Montgomery C. Meigs* (New York, 1959), and Gallman, *Mastering Wartime,* pp. 283–91.

11. R. G. Dun and Company Collection, Baker Library, Harvard University Graduate School of Business (hereafter RGD), Pennsylvania vol. 131: 275, 131: 284NN, 131: 284W, 139: 231, 140: 171, 141: 84.

12. RGD 134: 557, 136: 527, 133: 183, 140: 180.

13. RGD 136: 495, 136: 509, 136: 528, 133: 183.

14. RGD 139: 51.

15. RGD 135: 204.

16. For cases of businesses turning to sutling, see RGD 138: 11, 131: 270, 136: 394, and 137: 715.

17. These figures are partly a product of the estimation procedure, which typically evaluated firms based on their 1864 worth and therefore inflated the value of prosperous war contractors.

18. Nearly half (220 of 463) of the firms in the general sample with identifiable types of enterprises were either retailers or hoteliers. Gallman, *Mastering Wartime,* p. 308.

19. Philadelphia's wartime building rates indicate a dramatic decline in retail-store building compared to the five prewar years (387 new stores between 1856 and 1860; 176 between 1861 and 1865). New factory building increased, however, from 159 between 1856 and 1860 to 259 between 1861 and 1865. The latter increase may reflect the expansion of existing establishments rather than the formation of new manufacturing enterprises. See Gallman, *Mastering Wartime,* pp. 274–76.

20. RGD 141: 21, 141: 147, 147: 238.

21. RGD 140: 157. In 1863 Hochstadter took on an equal partner, and in 1866 they added several other new names. By early 1866, the company was worth over $50,000.

22. RGD 141: 11.

23. Presumably war contracting directed some investment away from nonmilitary activities, but the overall decline in new business starts, coupled with the disproportionate number of new

firms among military contractors, could indicate that entrepreneurs interested in founding businesses saw few openings in the nonmilitary arena.

24. "Abstracts of Contracts, 1862–1864," no. 2226, RG 92, National Archives, Philadelphia Branch. This phenomenon is discussed more fully in Gallman, *Mastering Wartime*, p. 291.

25. Although it is useful to compare the frequency of different sorts of qualitative comments, we should not assume that all other firms experienced "normal" years. The R. G. Dun agents did not always file annual reports on each firm. Table 10.4 only measures those occasions when agents chose to make unusual comments.

26. The data in Table 10.4 are not conclusive on these points because the reports do not always identify when a firm began doing government work. Therefore, a firm that rose before securing a contract (or without much aid from the contract) would be included in this table. The reports often attributed renewed success to war contracts, however.

27. RGD 134: 545, 134: 645, 139: 131.

28. Of course, the R. G. Dun reporters might have been more likely to mention businesses with southern ties that had run into troubles because of those connections.

29. RGD 132: 471, 137: 657, 137: 612.

30. RGD 131: 284WW, 135: 38, 135: 172.

31. RGD 132: 381, 136: 516, 136: 393.

32. RGD 135: 320C, 133: 296K, 136: 585.

33. RGD 133: 296BB, 137: 455, 141: 98.

34. RGD 137: 507.

35. RGD 140: 156, 141: 201.

36. Firms went out of business for many reasons. Although the terms "failure" and "out of business" will be used interchangeably, some of the firms listed on this table closed their doors without running into financial difficulties, and others stayed in business despite continual problems. In Table 10.5, a firm is listed as "out of business" when one of the following occurred: the business failed; the owner or owners sold out; the owner died (if there were no partners); the establishment moved out of the city; or, in a few cases, a struggling firm only survived when a new partner stepped in with a substantial amount of capital. Conversely, in the following situations, firms were not listed as "out of business": when new partners joined established businesses (even though the name may have changed); when firms relocated within the city; when establishments lost credit judgments or suspended payments but stayed in business.

37. The estimated cases for the final year occur when there is more than one year between the entry noting that the firm was out of operation and the previous entry. If the firm was healthy in one entry and reported as "out of business" in the next, the estimated final year is the midpoint between the two entries. If the next-to-last entry reported that the firm was in trouble, the "final year" was recorded as the year *after* the next-to-last entry.

38. See Gallman, *Mastering Wartime*, pp. 300–308, for a discussion of the relationship between both age and size and business failure.

39. All figures include only firms with known or estimated final dates. Note that by including all 1861 and 1865 failures, the data cover roughly three prewar months and eight postwar months.

40. RGD 140: 152.

41. RGD 140: 142.

42. RGD 141: 61.

43. RGD 131: 36, 131: 121, 132: 603, 132: 431.

44. RGD 134: 603.

45. "*The Rich Men of Philadelphia*"—*Income Tax of the Residents of Philadelphia and Bucks County for the Year Ending April 30, 1865* (Philadelphia, 1865).

46. See Gallman, *Mastering Wartime,* pp. 324–26. In the course of the war, the resourceful Hunter profited from the government's demand for uniforms, railroads, shipping, and coal, while also trading in Treasury notes.

47. RGD 132: 481, 132: 583, 133: 138, 131: 284W, 137: 416, 137: 554.

48. RGD 132: 623, 133: 285, 136: 380.

49. RGD 132: 456, 140: 156, 136: 516.

50. RGD 138: 15.

51. RGD 138: 15, 132: 495, 140: 165.

52. RGD 134: 626,142: 6,141: 201. Gray's company went out of business in 1867; the Cooper Arms Manufacturing Company survived only until 1872.

53. Note that these figures include failures in 1865, the final year of the war.

54. RGD 134: 630; 139: 81.

55. RGD 134: 630, 139: 81, 134: 644, 138: 87.

56. RGD 141: 11, 141: 13.

57. RGD 136: 325. The R. G. Dun reports include several examples of partnerships valued at $100,000 and more that closed in the years after the war with no reported difficulties.

58. See Gallman, *Mastering Wartime,* pp. 257–65.

59. In several cases, wartime sutlers had experienced similar hardships in 1861. See RGD 138: 11, 131: 270, 136: 394.

60. Although government demand determined the mix of goods produced, entrepreneurial choices helped guarantee that the individual firms' adjustments involved minimal instability.

61. And some businesses profited from the reduced competition as firms turned to government contracting. For instance, Edmund Hindle and Son's Good Intent Factory enjoyed unusual profits when their chief machine-making competitor turned to war work. RGD 135: 145.

# An Inspiration to Work

## Anna Elizabeth Dickinson, Public Orator

As I was wrapping up my comparative study of the Irish famine in Liverpool and Philadelphia, I decided to return to the Civil War era, while exploring my growing interests in gender. With the aid of an NEH summer fellowship, I started a project on Anna Dickinson, the Civil War orator. Originally I thought I might just focus on Dickinson as a public woman in wartime, but before long I concluded that I wanted to write a full biography. Along the way I wrote several shorter pieces on Dickinson, aimed at different audiences.

This essay appeared in a collection on civilians during the Civil War, edited by Joan Cashin. Whereas Maris Vinovskis had compiled a small volume of essays by very young scholars, Cashin had taken on the more ambitious task of assembling a much larger volume, relying largely on the work of established scholars. A comparison of these two highly successful volumes—separated by about a dozen years—illustrates how rapidly the field had expanded and evolved. My contribution is one of my first efforts at sketching out Dickinson's extraordinary career to an audience that presumably had never heard of her. The focus here is on how Dickinson, who became a celebrated woman at a very young age, navigated her public and private identities in the midst of the Civil War. This is one of my first efforts at exploring these intertwined threads in a single piece of writing.

. . .

In 1869, S. M. Betts and Company of Hartford, Connecticut, published *Eminent Women of the Age; Being Narratives of the Lives and Deeds of the Most Prominent Women of the Present Generation*. It was indeed an impressive volume, featuring biographical sketches of forty-nine leading activists, authors, educators, actresses and physicians, illustrated with fourteen engraved portraits of the collection's most celebrated women. Among the longest entries was Elizabeth Cady Stanton's thirty-four-page life of Anna Elizabeth Dickinson, who was—at twenty-six—also among the youngest women in the volume.[1]

Born in 1842, Anna Dickinson was the youngest of five children of Philadelphia Quakers. Her father, John, died when Dickinson was two, only hours after speaking at an antislavery meeting. Following in her father's abolitionist footsteps, Dickinson published an essay on "Slavery" in William Lloyd Garrison's *The Liberator* when she was only fourteen. According to Stanton, the defining moment for Dickinson came in January 1860 when she attended two public meetings on "women's rights and wrongs." Long bothered by gender inequities, the seventeen-year-old rose to speak at the first meeting and then returned the following Sunday when she delivered a withering attack on a man who had presumed to discuss women's inherent limitations. "Never," according to Stanton, "was an audience more electrified and amazed than they were with the eloquence and power of the young girl."[2]

During the next year, as the nation was absorbed in sectional crisis, Dickinson developed a reputation in the Philadelphia area as a fiery young orator, speaking largely on abolitionism and women's rights. With the outbreak of war, Dickinson took a position at the United States Mint, but she was fired shortly after accusing Union General George McClellan of treason for his failures at the Battle of Ball's Bluff. In 1862 Garrison arranged for Dickinson to deliver a series of lectures on "The National Crisis" to New England audiences. By this point Dickinson had dreams of supporting herself, and aiding her family, through lecture fees. The crucial step came early the following year when New Hampshire Republicans invited her to stump in the 1863 campaign.

Dickinson spent much of 1863 traveling across New Hampshire, Maine, Connecticut, Pennsylvania, and New York, attacking Democrats and supporting Republican candidates. She proved an extremely effective partisan speaker, attracting large audiences—sometimes several thousand paying customers—and earning the praise of party loyalists, who were happy to pay $100 or more, a remarkable fee for the day, for a single campaign appearance. One of Dickinson's most celebrated moments came on April 4 when she delivered the Connecticut Republican Party's election eve address at Hartford's Allyn Hall. Between campaign appearances, Dickinson made high profile— and well paid—appearances in New York City, Philadelphia, and Chicago. Her unusually high six-hundred-dollar fee for two lectures at the Northwestern Sanitary Fair in Chicago raised some eyebrows, particularly since the event was a patriotic fund-raiser, but the feisty Dickinson answered her critics by pointing out that in making the trip she had sacrificed nearly twice that amount in lost speaking fees in the East while the paying audiences in Chicago had netted the fair a healthy profit.[3] Stanton, who was present when Dickinson spoke at New York's Cooper Institute, recalled that "on no two occasions of my life have I been so deeply moved, so exalted, so lost in overflowing gratitude, that woman had revealed her power in oratory." In January 1864 Dickinson accepted an invitation from more than a hundred senators and representatives to speak before them in the nation's capital. Stanton recalled the moment with deep satisfaction, declaring that Dickinson "was honored as no man in the nation ever had been." In the weeks to come she repeated the address to audiences in Philadelphia, New York, and Boston. During the 1864 campaign, Dickinson spoke out against George McClellan and the Democrats, while having little direct praise for Abraham Lincoln and his cautious policies towards reconstruction. Anna Dickinson, Stanton concluded, was no mere parrot of radical male ideas; rather, "[h]er heroic courage, indomitable will, brilliant imagination, religious earnestness, and prophetic forecast, gave her an utterance that no man's thought could paint or inspire."[4]

Dickinson's prominent treatment in *Eminent Women of the Age* is an indication of her fame in the immediate postwar years. The following year *Harper's Bazar* republished eight of the volume's etchings in a composite image honoring "The Champions of Woman's Suffrage," with Dickinson's image appearing in a place of prominence at the bottom center, balanced by portraits of Stanton and Susan B. Anthony on the top row. Still shy of her twenty-seventh birthday, Dickinson was truly one of the nation's most famed public women.

The public praise and private emotions that Anna Dickinson inspired in 1868 must have been heady stuff for the young Philadelphian, but by then she had established herself as a national celebrity. This essay will examine Dickinson's experiences during the war years, when she first emerged as a national sensation. Her fame presented fascinating challenges to a society that had little experience with women speaking in public before mixed audiences and almost no familiarity with partisan politicking by those generally consigned to "the weaker sex." The handful of mid-century women who appeared on public platforms commonly spoke on the reforms of the day, specifically women's rights and abolitionism, and only rarely had access to more explicitly partisan stages.[5] Dickinson, a strong advocate of both reform causes, stretched the received gender boundaries both by her excursions into an explicitly political arena and by her powerful, dynamic mode of speech. A small woman with striking dark eyes and short-cropped hair, Dickinson captivated—and enraged—civilian audiences across the wartime

North with a combination of eloquence, sarcastic wit, and bold, occasionally outrageous statements. Although physically frail, and periodically silenced by throat problems or other ailments, Dickinson spoke with a powerful voice that managed to fill large halls. Contemporary accounts describe her pacing up and down platforms before packed houses of men and women, delivering prepared remarks without notes and often spiced with clever barbs aimed at local Copperhead editors or unruly hecklers.[6] The published responses to Dickinson's wartime appearances fell along a political spectrum. Northern Democrats were quick to dismiss both the message and the messenger, assailing Dickinson as a "sexless" gender transgressor, an attractive sideshow, or a mouthpiece for radical men. Republican newspapers embraced Anna as an eloquent, charismatic advocate, even while some editors exhibited discomfort with her fame, often selecting language that stressed her distinctive—even otherworldly—persona, thus differentiating her from the rank and file of American womankind. Whatever their political perspective or their opinions about the propriety of Dickinson's public appearances, Northern observers agreed that Anna Dickinson was one of America's most celebrated women.[7]

Before long, this celebrity took on a life of its own, delivering to Dickinson a fame that few Civil War–era Americans could duplicate. She was, in a sense, the equal of the nation's most famed actresses. Like famed actress Fanny Kemble before her, Anna Dickinson became a popular commodity, featured in newspaper stories, engravings, and the various trappings of national celebrity.[8] Like the Civil War's greatest military heroes, Dickinson became a popular subject of the latest in photographic technology: the commercially distributed *cartes de visite*.[9] Dickinson sat for numerous portraits, both during and after the war, including at least one visit to Mathew Brady's New York studio. These reproduced images became a major contributor to Dickinson's burgeoning fame, as Northerners placed her carte de visite in their personal albums alongside pictures of Lincoln, Grant, and the nation's leading political and military figures.

How did Dickinson deal with both her wartime celebrity and the trappings of life as an unmarried woman on the road? As her fame grew, she constructed a complex, messy web of intimate friends, political advisors, casual acquaintances, and adoring strangers. It was in a sense a private life almost completely defined by her public fame, even while her family ostensibly tried to separate the two. At the center of that world were the members of her immediate family. Dickinson's relationships with her mother, her sister Susan, and her three older brothers were all shaped by her wartime fame and fortune. Long before

Dickinson's trip to Boston, Anna and Susan shared thoughts and schemes about how they would support themselves and their widowed mother.[10] Things changed for the sisters when Dickinson went north in 1862. On April 20 an ailing Wendell Phillips invited her to speak in his stead at Boston's Music. "Think of *that* mum," an enthusiastic Dickinson wrote home, "this small snip,—acting as Wendall Philllipses substitute & at his own request at that." The crowd was large and distinguished, and Dickinson was thrilled to report that her performance had been a smashing success, earning special praise from both Phillips and the revered William Lloyd Garrison, who suggested that more lectures should follow. "I do not expect to be very rich" just yet, she reported, but clearly the future looked bright, and soon new offers would indeed follow."[11]

Before long Dickinson was traveling from town to town throughout New England, giving lectures for modest fees to enthusiastic audiences. Susan and her mother tracked Dickinson's progress through her periodic letters and reports in local newspapers. In the process, their relationships became curiously recast. Letters from home inquired about Dickinson's new friends and her sometimes precarious health, but those sisterly and maternal concerns were interspersed with increasingly urgent reports on overdue bills and other house expenses. As winter fell in 1862, and Dickinson's lecturing pace slowed, Susan told her younger sister that "I hope . . . both for thy sake and ours that thee will be pretty well paid for what thee gets to do, both for thy sake and ours. What a weight would be taken off if we were only fairly out of debt."[12] Such was the pressure on the twenty-year-old orator.

The invitation to campaign in New Hampshire the following year was a crucial step for Dickinson's speaking career, but it was also an important boon to the Dickinson family finances. Throughout 1863 Susan kept up a regular correspondence with her campaigning sister, peppered with references to new bills and other fiscal woes. In July, when ill health and physical exhaustion forced Dickinson to postpone several Connecticut lectures, Susan responded with characteristic mixed messages, urging her sister to rest up and protect her health, while dropping hints about the financial strains that she and her mother faced when Anna's checks failed to arrive.[13] This confusion of roles was typical of Dickinson's family correspondence. Although the youngest child, her successes had placed her in the peculiar position as family provider, leading to an unusual recasting of traditional roles.

Susan and Anna were clearly close, frequently exchanging gossip about friends or potential love interests, but one wonders how they navigated this new relationship. While Anna was off basking in the adoration of crowds,

Susan—nine years her senior—was at home in Philadelphia taking care of their mother, running the household, and—increasingly—attending to Anna's correspondence and other bureaucratic needs. As Christmas 1863 approached, Susan responded to a note from Anna with these words: "Thank thee for the money and for what thee so kindly says about money matters in general. Thee's a dear, good, kind sister—and thee knows I think it none the less that I don't often put my feelings into words."[14] Dickinson's prior note does not survive, but it appears that she had tried to set Susan's mind at ease about the family's dependence on her earnings. On the one hand, this exchange shows the bond between the two sisters, but on the other hand the very need for such a discussion points to the awkwardness of their evolving roles.

Dickinson's relationship with her mother was perhaps even more challenging. The Quaker widow worried about her youngest daughter's physical and spiritual health, while also expressing some discomfort with Dickinson's public life and even greater anxiety at rumors that she might turn to a career on the stage. Still, Mrs. Dickinson appeared proud of her daughter's patriotic contributions, and she realized that her household depended on Anna's earnings. A month after Dickinson's triumphant appearance in Washington, Mrs. Dickinson sent her a wistful note regretting that her peripatetic daughter had "no home of thy own to rest at," while also declaring that "my own precious child . . . thou art the chief burden bearer for us all and nobly have thou born it." The letter was full of motherly concern for daughter's well-being, but it closed with a familiar reminder: "When thee [send] funds for home expenses please send $11.75 to pay the bill for the blankets."[15]

Dickinson was in less regular contact with her three brothers. The two eldest, John and Edwin, each spent part of the war years living in California. Both suffered from poor health and apparently provided little if any financial support to their mother and sisters. Samuel, two years Anna's senior, began the war as a clerk in a store until he eventually won a position in Washington with his sister's assistance. Samuel was drafted in 1863 but was able to secure an exemption, probably on medical grounds. Although her three brothers ranged from two to seven years older than she, Dickinson ended up providing each with some form of professional or financial assistance during the 1860s, even footing the bill for Samuel's funeral when he died of tuberculosis late in the decade.[16]

As her family's chief "burden bearer," Anna Dickinson was hardly living out the roles typically defined by her age and gender. Her hectic speaking and travel schedule could have posed further challenges to Dickinson's gender identity, but at least for the war years she mediated the public character of her itinerant status by playing the role as perpetual house guest: wherever she traveled local residents were happy to take her in, sometimes competing for the honor of having Anna Dickinson under their roof.[17] When she first went to Boston in 1862 Dickinson stayed with William Lloyd Garrison and his family, reporting that "Mr Garrison has treated me like a father since I came—his family are delightful." Later that year she moved from the Garrisons' to the Sargents', a transition that she hoped had been achieved without undue tensions.[18]

Wherever she journeyed in the wartime North, Dickinson became almost the adopted daughter of one or more host families. Subsequent letters revealed a growing list of correspondents who shared an intense affection for the young orator. When she visited New Bedford, Massachusetts, in the spring of 1862, Dickinson stayed at the home of Joseph Ricketson. Shortly after her brief visit, Ricketson sent Dickinson a long letter declaring that words could not properly express the impact that she had had on him and his family. Months later, frustrated by his inability to secure her a return invitation, Ricketson declared: "I want not only to hear you lecture but I want to see you 'dreadfully'—& so do Fanny & Ruth who send their best love."[19] Connecticut minister Nathaniel Burton hosted Dickinson when she passed through Hartford in 1863, and later introduced her to an audience at Allyn Hall. Two years later the overwrought (and married) minister declared, "I yearn for you like a thirsty ox for the brookside. I do Anna, I solemnly do."[20] During her wartime visits to both Boston and Hartford's Nook Farm, Dickinson split her time between several families, rapidly becoming the center of an exciting social whirl, with residents competing for the privilege of hosting the young orator.

When she traveled further from home, Dickinson was more likely to be taken in by a single family. Shortly after the election of 1864, she accepted an invitation to deliver her "Plea for Women" in Pittsburgh. Dickinson stayed for just a few days with the Irish family there, but long enough to make a large impact on the entire family while winning the heart of Elias Irish. Less than a week after her lecture, Irish wrote Dickinson a touching, flirtatious letter declaring that "there has been a world of sighing about this house since you went away. Have the goodness when next thee comest to Pittsburgh, to leave the quiver of arrows at home." In Milwaukee she stayed with R. N. and Sallie Austin, who both corresponded with Dickinson into the postwar years. In response to an unexpected note after a lengthy silence, Sallie Austin wrote asking if Dickinson had found peace and wisdom in her hectic life "or if you still give some people who love you heartaches on your account because of your recklessness."[21] In quite different ways these letters suggest the immediate—and ongoing—intimacy that so often characterized Dickinson's relations with her numerous hosts. Anna Dickinson was simultaneously both a powerful heroine who drew those around her into her orbit and a fragile young woman whom many sought to protect from the world's ills. Hers was a charisma shared by only a handful of public figures.

In her travels Dickinson befriended quite a few younger women who saw in her a role model and an inspiration. The patterns in these relationships suggest something about Dickinson's own personal experiences and the chord that she struck in others of her sex. Long before she became famous, Dickinson was close friends with Lillie Atkinson, a young Quaker from Cherry Lawn, New Jersey. Atkinson, a year younger than Dickinson, filled her letters with personal news and commentary on abolitionist doctrine, occasionally expressing frustration when older men failed to take her opinions seriously. In preparation for a debate on women's rights in early 1861, Lillie wrote to Anna—already a veteran of several such platforms—for a few pointers, vowing to take her older friend's ideas and "clothe them in my own language." Two years later, when Dickinson had become a national celebrity and their correspondence had waned, Atkinson went to hear her old friend speak but had no opportunity to shake her hand after the performance. Instead, she sent a teasing, slightly melancholy, note. "Please, dear Anna," she wrote, "I dont know how to write properly to persons who have become so great and famous, and find myself looking back with a sigh at those dear old days of years agone, when I could talk to thee without fear of thy *greatness.*" Following the lecture Lillie had spent her evening reading their old letters and remembering their past friendship with teary eyes about what had once been. But beyond the sadness of friends who had drifted apart, Atkinson seemed particularly pained by measuring herself against Dickinson's achievements and worried that her old friend would conclude that she had been "standing still" rather than developing her own skills and commitment. From Lillie's perspective the relationship with Anna had evolved from one of personal intimacy and shared political passion to an unequal relationship in which she followed Dickinson's success from a distance while finding her own public activism diminished in comparison. Meanwhile, by the middle of 1863 Dickinson was receiving stacks of mail from across the country, generally arriving in packets forwarded to her by her sister in Philadelphia. Whatever her thoughts about Lillie Atkinson, it is a safe bet that they no longer consumed much of her attention.[22]

Even the most loyal companion would have found old relationships crowded out by the new attachments that Anna Dickinson developed on the road. In her first trip to Boston Dickinson became fast friends with young Fanny Garrison, who shared her bed with the visiting abolitionist. Soon after Dickinson left, Garrison wrote declaring that "I missed my soft pillow so many times, and have wished some how or other I might wake up and find a pair of some body's dear arms around me." The intimacy of their nights together clearly had an important impact on Fanny Garrison, elevating Dickinson to a special place in her consciousness. "Remember Fanny longs to hug and kiss you & tell you how much she loves you," she declared at the close of one letter. And with Dickinson's November 1862 return to Boston only a month away Fanny was thrilled that "soon I will hug and kiss you really."

What did the two talk about in their nights together? Judging from the subsequent letters they shared an expected amount of personal gossip (Dickinson had developed a particular interest in Garrison's brother Wendell), but their correspondence was really much more about abolitionism, party politics, and women's rights. With her school's graduation just around the corner, Garrison revealed ambivalence about her approaching independence and the challenges that awaited. After sketching her recent visit to Cambridge for Harvard's "Class day," Garrison reflected the gender sensibilities that Dickinson had encouraged in her, announcing that "it is so mean that we are only allowed there on that day, as though we were only dolls to help their enjoyment when they pleased to want us." And anticipating Dickinson's upcoming lecture, Garrison declared that "[i]t makes me so happy when a woman does something grand and noble. The act is so fine a plea for woman's rights."[23] It is unlikely that her brief visit produced such ideas where there heretofore had been none, but the example of Dickinson's public activism probably expanded Garrison's thinking about woman's proper place. Like Lillie Atkinson, Fanny Garrison seems to have measured her own life as a politically engaged young woman according to the impressive yardstick presented by Anna Dickinson.

During her first trip to New England, Dickinson was befriended by the Chace family in Rhode Island, and particularly Lillie Chace, who was roughly five years younger than the orator. Lillie Chace also became a regular correspondent, providing detailed commentary on state politics and national abolitionism. Chace also shared the belief that Dickinson's success served as a gender beacon. "I am very glad of thy success," she wrote "both because I love thee, and because I am a *woman*, and as much I thank thee from the bottom of my heart for the great work thee is doing for *us*, while laboring for the country, and the Liberty of the black man." And she, too, found that Dickinson's success forced her to look inward, openly wondering if she had the "necessary 'brass'" to be a public speaker like her friend while announcing that "I want to *succeed* in whatever path of life I choose." But for the time being she was content to live vicariously through Dickinson's public successes. In this she was hardly alone. One afternoon, while writing a letter to Dickinson from her boarding school, Chace was interrupted by a roommate who sent Dickinson her love, adding that "'I dont ever expect to lecture myself, but I *feel*.'"[24]

The year after the war ended, a nineteen-year-old Lillie Chace sent Dickinson a particularly long, reflective letter. "I sometimes think you were the first girl I ever really loved," she mused, and "I am thankful I may yet see thee again 'face to face,' and in thy presence feel how true it is that womanhood and womanhood's glory and charm are inherent in her nature, not the forced growth of her hot-house seclusion." Chace went on to admit that she lacked the power "to break the bonds that hold me," and thus she—and women like her—depended on the strength of powerful advocates like Anna Dickinson.[25] There are certainly similarities between this letter and Dickinson's earlier correspondence with Lillie Atkinson and Fanny Garrison. Each young woman came from a highly political, abolitionist household and saw in Dickinson an ideological kindred spirit as well as a powerfully charismatic, slightly older woman. Enduring bonds were built in brief private moments together, and kindled through regular correspondence. In each case, Dickinson came to represent an example of what women could accomplish in public, while also seeming to have achieved the unachievable.

Numerous other women recalled similar closeness with Dickinson, often developed in nights sharing a bed together. Hartford's Isabella Beecher Hooker's niece, Lilly Gillette, first met Dickinson during a Christmas visit to Nook Farm in 1863. The following February, Lilly urged her to stay at her family's home during an upcoming visit to Cincinnati. "When you come you will sleep with me, & when you sleep with me we will have a splendid talk," she promised. Shortly after Appomattox, Lilly—who had married Charles Dudley Warner's brother—wrote her old friend from Nook Farm, urging Dickinson to visit Hartford while the Hookers were out of town and "won't gobble her up." "We'll sleep together & I promise not to make you talk all night," Lilly vowed.[26]

In other cases the affection for Dickinson seemed shared between married spouses. Louise and Walter Brackett had a distinctive relationship with Dickinson, marked by an extraordinary, bantering correspondence. "When you again write do write some *love* to me," Lou demanded in May 1863, "dont waste it all on the *men*, I can appreciate it better than they can, believe me I can." Two weeks later she asked: "How do you live without seeing Lou? Ah! I know, with your lovers, numerous as they are." Lou closed her next letter, a chatty note about how much General Ben Butler wanted to meet Dickinson, by adding a postscript: "How I want to see you visibly—and tangibly before me so that I can *touch you*." As Dickinson's next trip to Boston grew imminent, Lou's enthusiasm for her friend grew. "I scarce can wait to see you," she wrote. "[T]he very thought of seeing your genial and magnetic face once more—makes my heart leap with pleasure—do you love me the same? Has no vile woman torn your heart from me? I fear *no man*." She went on to provide an update on Butler's interests in her young friend and on the more promising prospects from one of Butler's young colonels who apparently had expressed a serious interest in kissing Dickinson, an interest that Lou would gladly have accepted herself "if Walter was willing." The following March, Lou reported that Walter was so taken with Dickinson that he had declared his plan "to make love to you when you came to Boston again. You wont let him darling will you?" she asked. "[Y]ou are mine and belong to me, until you get married—say it is true?" The irrepressible Lou revealed that she had "an irresistible desire all through this letter to make love to you in down right earnest" but instead opted to weave a complex tale about a visit from a soldier on furlough—probably James Beecher—who had asked Walter for permission to kiss Lou, although in truth he really hoped to kiss Dickinson. She had been happy to accept the kiss, and promised that "when I next meet you—and God speed the time—I'll give you a 'Beecher kiss.'"[27]

It is hard to know what to make of this lively correspondence. Certainly both Lou and Walter were very fond of Dickinson, a fondness that continued well into the postwar years. Lou, like Dickinson's various younger friends, spoke tenderly of kisses and physical intimacies, insisting that she merited a special role in her friend's life, at least until the young orator took a husband. Perhaps the most interesting aspect of Lou's letters was her clear presumption that no man could truly replace her in Dickinson's affections, even while she assumed that Anna would eventually select a male lover.

Fanny and George Ames, of Newcastle, Delaware, developed a similar joint relationship with Anna Dickinson. In May 1864 Fanny addressed an affectionate letter to "My Dear Beasty," assuring Dickinson that her husband—"The Dominic"—was perfectly pleased that she and Anna had spent a week together eating oranges and "pet[ting]" and that "all the tenderness shown his wife by the dear little lady of Locust St only makes him love her more." A month later Fanny admitted that "I want to write you a love-letter, especially after that formidable sheet from the Dominic to tell you firstly how much I love you."[28] Most of Dickinson's relationship with the Ameses remains undocumented, but these two letters suggest another couple who had a special bond with Dickinson built on only limited contact together.

As a young woman Anna Dickinson traveled in a world that presumed that she would eventually settle down with a man, while in the meantime it appears that during the Civil War her deepest personal—and physical—intimacies were with other women. For women and men in the mid-nineteenth century, intense homosocial friendships were not uncommon and certainly not understood as evidence of sexual preference, a term that itself would have had made little sense to Dickinson and her friends. Nonetheless, as she journeyed from town to town, and home to home, Dickinson probably had greater opportunities to develop deep bonds with women and young girls—often established in late nights sharing a bed together—than she had with the multitude of boys and men who crossed her path and tried their hand as suitors within the more rigid confines of heterosexual gender interactions.[29]

Dickinson's wartime correspondence are thick with references, generally in jest, about young men who were smitten with her. For a time, Wendell Garrison—Fanny's brother—seemed to be the object of her affections.[30] Dickinson also developed a romantic relationship with Judge Joseph P. Allyn, a Connecticut politician, or at least the judge had that impression. For several months in the spring of 1863 Allyn sent Dickinson long, lovesick letters, making references to stolen moment sharing cherries during one of her visits to Nook Farm. But Dickinson lost interest or perhaps never shared the judge's ardor. At the end of July Allyn's tone changed dramatically. "God spare you from the pain you have inflicted on me these last few days and in those cruel lines," he wrote in answer to one letter. "I love you as I never loved woman before else it be the dead only sister that sleeps in yonder cemetery."[31] This brokenhearted letter speaks to the effect that the twenty-year-old Dickinson had on the poor judge, but although there are occasional references to Allyn in other letters to Dickinson, there is no indication that she reciprocated his passion.[32]

Dickinson had a more serious attachment to Pittsburgh's Elias Irish. This relationship developed during her December 1864 visit and grew when she returned to Pittsburgh shortly after the war, and the two spent time together hiking and picking blackberries. But once again the relationship evolved into one of unrequited love. One remark in an August 1865 letter seems particularly telling. In that note Irish commented on how "wondrous strange" it was that they had grown so close "on paper," but claimed that if the prickly Dickinson were in Pittsburgh with him she "shoulds't not have one pleasant word—not one—not if they were as plenty as black berries on the mountain slopes of

Fayette Springs." Irish, it appears, had hoped for loving words but instead received the same sort of biting sarcasm that had made Dickinson such a celebrated speaker. Several months later he sent Dickinson a sixteen-page missive, representing several hundred pages of discarded drafts, in which he admitted that he had "gone 'clean daft' about" his "matchless black-haired Gipsey" and recalled listening as "my silver tongued enchantress builded castles in the air, and beguiled, enthralled my fancy, enthralled my heart, my soul and fancy, through many a golden hour." But, alas, these were—he acknowledged—the words of "despised love," not to be reciprocated. This story ended tragically when Irish died of tuberculosis in December 1866, leaving Dickinson feeling both sad and perhaps remorseful about her failure to accept Elias's love.[33]

Elias Irish and Joseph Allyn were in most senses quite different men, who shared a deep attachment to—even an obsession with—Anna Dickinson. Their letters to Dickinson both chastize her for her sharp tongue and perhaps for her refusal, or inability, to utter the words that they hoped to hear. Both men wrote most fondly of sweet moments with Dickinson, sharing fruit—cherries with Allyn and mountain blackberries with Irish. Although each was certainly infatuated with Dickinson, and for a time at least she felt a fondness for each suitor, we are left to wonder how well either knew her during their short visits, particularly as compared with her numerous female correspondents.

Dickinson never married, although for decades after the war the press persisted in linking her name with various public figures, including Whitelaw Reid, Ben Butler, and Senator William Allison. Other men who never met Dickinson developed strong emotional attachments based solely on her public appearances. Thomas Seville, of Elmira, New York, penned a lengthy poem praising the "woman who stands brighter than her sex." Chicago's W. M. Boucher was so struck by a Dickinson lecture that he was moved to write, declaring that "My soul longs for a companion whom I can respect for her goodness & wisdom & whose body & spirit I can love with an absorbing emotion," adding that since Dickinson was single, he wondered if she would "permit a correspondence with the view of becoming acquaintances." Six months later an E. M. Bruce of Middleton, Connecticut, penned a two-page poem dedicated to Anna, including these memorable lines: "Oh noble girl! Oh peerless queen! The world hath never known, What struggles woman's heart hath seen, What trials undergone." The following year Cincinnati's R. P. Minier proposed marriage by mail.[34]

Women periodically wrote simply to thank Dickinson for representing their gender so proudly. "*Good bless you* Anna Dickinson," one Massachusetts woman wrote, and "thank you for every word you said [and] . . . for the good your lecture did for me personally."[35] Shortly after the war, Harriette Keyser, a twenty-five year old New York schoolteacher who lived alone with her father, heard Anna speak. "I am trying to educate myself," she explained in a long autobiographical letter, "and when God calls me to any work, I shall step out of the ranks, if need be, and obey His call." Although Keyser insisted that she did not need Dickinson's words to point her in the right direction, she acknowledged that they did "encourage and strengthen" her. This letter suggests the multilayered responses that Dickinson elicited from her peers. Her words and deeds inspired both friends and strangers to action, but ironically Dickinson's refusal to bow to contemporary gender constraints also seemed to prompt some women to rationalize why they were not living out their larger dreams. Another correspondent—the mother of eight daughters—was so moved by a Dickinson lecture on prostitution that she vowed to "rescue" two prostitutes by hiring them as servants, explaining that she only had to figure out how to do so without her husband learning of their background. Other women wrote seeking advice on how to launch a career in public speaking or in other ways follow Dickinson into the public arena.[36]

Various strangers, generally men, sent Dickinson unsolicited words of advice. After Pennsylvania Quaker Amos Gilbert heard her speak in January 1861, he wrote Dickinson a long, grandfatherly letter praising the young orator for her political stances while worrying that all the love and admiration heaped upon her would threaten her own "self respect and self approval." The following month a correspondent volunteered that Dickinson lacked proper schooling "in the sternest order of reason" and thus she had learned the lower art of pandering to an audience. Such uneducated techniques, he insisted, would eventually be her undoing. By taking on "great and intricate questions requiring *time, genius* and a *masculine calibre*" she was setting herself up as a "target for the laughter and pity of all truely educated citizens," he warned. Albany's Henry Homes generally praised Dickinson, but he found her language sometimes unladylike for mixed company, citing phrases such as "'making to eat dirt'" or "'a filthy sheet'" as particularly inappropriate.[37]

These three men—all strangers—had different perspectives on Dickinson's early excursions into the public arena, but they shared a fundamental conviction that they had some insights that their age and gender afforded them. Whatever the source of her public success, in her private life Anna was barraged with words of advice from all manner of self-proclaimed experts, both friends and strangers. In fact, Dickinson's political mentors included some of America's most accomplished politicians, journalists, and reformers. This elite company led Dickinson's most virulent critics—particularly those who were offended by the very notion of a woman entering the public arena—to conclude that she was merely parroting the ideas of familiar radical minds. But even a cursory glance at her voluminous correspondence demonstrates that Dickinson's advisors were hardly of one mind, and none controlled hers.

Dickinson found a long series of advisors as soon as she left home. Garrison sent her charmingly detailed advice on travel arrangements in 1862. Later that year Bostonian Samuel May Jr. wrote offering suggestions about how she should spend her summer, including advice on sleep, exercise, conversation, and the right sort of books to read. That winter, May was pleased to pass Dickinson on to the hands of the other advisors and mentors who would try their hand at controlling her actions and shaping her career.[38] As she became more involved in partisan politics, Dickinson often turned to Philadelphia judge William D. Kelley. Following her April 1863 address at New York's Cooper Institute, the Republican congressman congratulated Dickinson for "illustrat[ing] the folly of that prejudice that excludes women from any sphere of usefulness." Still, Kelley seemed to see Dickinson as a precocious daughter rather than a political equal, routinely addressing her as "dear daughter" or "dear child" and occasionally signing his letters with "papa." Their friendship grew strained when Kelley served as an intermediary in arranging Dickinson's January 1864 appearance in Washington, only to have his protégée balk at some of the preliminary plans, leaving him frustrated that she no longer accepted his fatherly guidance without question.[39]

The events surrounding the 1864 campaign illuminated the relationship between Dickinson and her various mentors. With the war dragging on, and no clear end in sight, President Lincoln faced a strong threat from the Democrats—who nominated General George McClellan—and a series of challenges from radicals in his own party. Dickinson was personally dissatisfied with Lincoln's policies, particularly his moderate stance toward postwar reconstruction, but she was unwilling to damage the Union cause by abandoning the president and unhappy about the prospect of sitting out the campaign. In the first months of the year Dickinson grew increasingly hostile to the president, backing off from her January endorsement of his renomination and abusing Lincoln from the stump, but she also steered clear of a radical movement—led by her friend Kansas senator Samuel Pomeroy—to draft Treasury secretary Salmon P. Chase and a subsequent effort to nominate General John C. Frémont at a late May convention in Cleveland. For Dickinson, these months in 1864 were full of conversations and correspondence about national politics. The fatherly Judge Kelley was deeply distressed with her attacks on Lincoln (and particularly her sarcastic accounts of a meeting with Lincoln that Kelley had arranged). At the other end of the Republican spectrum, Senator Pomeroy sent her a copy of his notorious "circular" supporting Chase for president and unsuccessfully tried to entice her into the movement. Republican journalist Whitelaw Reid shared Dickinson's unhappiness with the president but was equally unimpressed with the strategies of the party's insurgents and disturbed that Dickinson—whom he had recently befriended—was tempted by their appeals. "It can do no good now for you to get tangled in the stripes of personal politics, & it may do much harm," he counseled in early April."[40]

The push for Frémont posed a particular dilemma for Dickinson because her idol Wendell Phillips was at the center of the movement while most of the other leading abolitionists, including Garrison, saw Frémont's candidacy as an unacceptable compromise with the Democrats. Susan B. Anthony, who had grown increasingly fond of the young Dickinson, wrote in early July surveying the political terrain and wondered what had become of "the good old doctrine 'of two evils choose neither,'" adding that "it is only safe to speak & act the truth—& to profess confidence in Lincoln would be a lie in me." The purest strategy, Anthony concluded, would be to continue espousing the radical cause without bowing to political expediency. Anthony did her best to persuade Dickinson to "keep close to the 'still small voice' that has thus far safely led you on." A few weeks later Theodore Tilton, the editor of *The Independent*, sent Dickinson an eight-page letter devoted largely to politics and her political conundrum. Tilton, too, was highly critical of Lincoln but declared that, given the president's popularity and Frémont's shortcomings, "you have no other choice but Lincoln." Tilton urged Dickinson to use her skills to rouse popular patriotism, "teaching the masses a nobler idea of Liberty." In the months until the election, and particularly after Lincoln was renominated in Baltimore, more and more of Dickinson's advisors weighed in with their opinions. Radical Republican B. F. Prescott acknowledged that the president left much to be desired, but expressed his hope that Dickinson would not be blinded by her hatred of Lincoln and abandon the party. Lillie Chace wrote that she was thoroughly engrossed in electoral politics, but could not see her way clear to support Lincoln.[41]

Finally, in September Dickinson issued a formal statement called "The Duty of the Hour" in Tilton's *The Independent*. The content of this widely discussed public letter is a valuable window into Dickinson's thinking. The mere fact that she saw fit to make such a statement and that the public gave it such attention demonstrates her highly unusual status, even among political women. In "The Duty for the Hour," Dickinson acknowledged that she would have preferred a different candidate and declared that "I shall not work for Abraham Lincoln; I shall work for the salvation of my country's life" by campaigning for the Republican ticket. Tilton assured Dickinson that the letter had been well received, at least within his political circle. But Lillie Chace was less pleased, suggesting that having failed to raise the Republican Party up to her own level Dickinson had opted to sink down to theirs. The always ironic Reid sent a congratulatory note from Cincinnati, but noted that he would only "vote for Mr Lincoln, if at all, very much as he has swallowed pills." True to her word, Dickinson campaigned more enthusiastically *against* the Democrats than she campaigned for the administration, and in fact she rarely spoke of Abraham Lincoln at all.[42]

Dickinson's correspondence in 1864, like that of the previous three years, shows how her public utterances were consistently cast within various private contexts. Personally charismatic and politically formidable, Dickinson attracted an assortment of willing advisors among close friends, professional acquaintances, and interested strangers. And every indication is that she actively solicited such advice from a wide circle of Republicans of various stripes. Meanwhile, Dickinson also weighed complex career considerations: What decisions would best enable her to build upon her fame while also continuing to be her family's burden-bearer? The accumulated weight of this diversity of voices pushed Dickinson in various directions, lending further support to the argument that she was not a mere pawn of specific older advisors. In fact, although Dickinson's words and actions often pleased her most ardent supporters, she repeatedly demonstrated an independent spirit driven by her own conclusions rather than the agendas of others.

Anna Dickinson's public and private worlds converged around the emerging trappings of her fame. As she became a household name, friends and strangers sought souvenirs of Dickinson's celebrity, illustrating the nature of renown in the North during the Civil War era. Even before she had made her splash in Boston, cartes de visite featuring young Dickinson were already finding their way into albums across the country. In March, a Quaker woman wrote from Iowa, thanking Dickinson for her picture and asking the young orator for two more inscribed photographs for friends. A few months later Joseph Ricketson sent a gushing letter, celebrating her "womanly and sympathetic appeal" and thanking her for the photograph that she had sent. Fanny Garrison's brother Frank was thrilled that Dickinson had mailed him a carte de visite and wondered if she had seen her likeness in the latest *Frank Leslie's Illustrated*. And, in a fascinating—and galling—combination of paternalism and admiration, New York editor Oliver Johnson wrote to Dickinson shortly after the war asking for an autograph for a friend, adding that he had never made such a request before "so pray be a good girl, and comply promptly."[43]

Closer to home, Dickinson's fame gradually crept into her family relationships. Dickinson's sister and mother carefully collected newspaper clippings, periodically exchanging commentary on particularly glowing or harsh reports. Susan relished the stream of visitors who dropped by their Locust Street home, and on one occasion she was pleased to report that she and her mother were met with "remarkable affability" from several social acquaintances who were especially impressed with Anna's fame. Even Lillie Chace became swept up in her friend's celebrity. In September 1863 she wrote asking for a picture to show off to friends. A few months later Chace reported that she had recently met an attractive young man—"a true blue abolitionist"—and wanted Dickinson to send several autographs, for both the young man and his sisters.[44] We can only imagine how this sort of request reshaped the relationship between these two young women who, in other circumstances, had interacted as peers.

Strangers who had seen Dickinson speak felt a special bond with her that was the true mark of celebrity. Shortly after the war Emma Fisher, of Roxbury, Massachusetts, sent a long letter suggesting the power of these passions. Earlier in the summer she had written asking Dickinson for an autograph and a lock of hair. Dickinson had sent along her signature but deflected the more personal request with the explanation that her hair had recently been shorn and she had no locks to spare. Several months later Fisher was writing back to point out that she had recently seen Dickinson lecture once again and was pleased to discover that the orator's hair had grown long enough to spare a lock or two. Fisher went on to explain that when she had first heard Dickinson speak—on working women—it had moved her to new resolutions, promising herself that she would follow Dickinson's example in helping others. She hoped to make a ring from the lock of hair to serve as a reminder of that evening's commitments, adding that "there is nothing in the world I so covet as your love and friendship but though we shall probably never meet, I earnest pray that Heaven may give you friends true and sincere."[45] Once again a woman who had never met Dickinson had developed a special attachment to her public persona, prompting a note and a highly personal request.

How might all this attention have affected Anna Dickinson? How might she have internalized the accumulated weight of family pressures, political influence, public celebrity, and a seemingly endless string of private passions and infatuations? What was the true connection between that famous public speaker portrayed by Elizabeth Cady Stanton and the charismatic young woman who seemed to touch all who met her? It is hard to imagine that all the adoration would not have had some impact on Dickinson's own sense of herself. And in fact some who met her during the war worried that Dickinson was falling prey to her own celebrity. Following Dickinson's first trip to Boston, Samuel May and Lillie Chace's mother, Elizabeth, shared their concerns for Dickinson's future. "It must be a great trial, and even danger," wrote May, "to so young a person, to be the object of so much interest, to receive so much applause, and to possess so great and happy a talent for holding and swaying the minds of large audiences."[46] As early as November 1862 Dickinson's mother, religiously conservative and personally savvy, wrote her wandering daughter a brief note: "[B]eware my dear child of being carried away by the voice of adulation. Remember under all and every circumstance, thee has an immortal soul to be saved or lost, and a frail tenement of clay, which must sometime return to its native element the earth."[47] In the years to come Mrs. Dickinson continued to worry about her daughter's physical and spiritual health, but—as we have seen—those maternal concerns were periodically muddied by her hopes that her youngest child would continue to earn enough money to maintain the Dickinsons' Philadelphia household.

We know much less about Dickinson's own private thoughts than we know about the praise that she received on a daily basis. One letter to her friend James Beecher, written a month before the Battle of Gettysburg, does offer a fascinating window into the mind of the twenty-year-old abolitionist. "Dear Friend," she wrote:

> I am tired, &—low be it spoken—cross.—I get nothing done,—all sort of people come to me on all sorts of trivial business,—visits of curiosity, flattery—what now?—letters pour in upon me, till I cry out in despair, remembering they are to be read & *answered*—meantime my work, actual work—study, thought, preparation, suffers—and so the other day—when the carrier had called, & Sue (that is my sister) came up with divers ominous looking missives, I cried out—"Heaven preserve us,—no more letters," . . . People tell me I have done thus & so,—give me great meetings, run after,—flatter, praise, caress me,—ah well!—then beg my heart not to be spoiled—There is too great a need of work,—too terrible danger,—too absolute necessity for all the labor of every head, & hand,

& heart—to leave place for any selfish or personal failing. And when one thinks of great hearts, & noble souls, the brave men,—fighting, suffering, dying for the cause,—the greatest cause, the dearest cause that ever stood at stake,—what an inspiration to work.[48]

How we choose to read this revealing letter will say much about how we understand the woman they called America's Joan of Arc. It is evident that Dickinson felt a powerful impulse to work for the Union cause. Although a political partisan, she saw herself foremost as a patriot doing her part to support the armies in the field. But are these also the words of a young woman with an overblown sense of her own importance? Had the deluge of praise from close friends and perfect strangers gone to her head? It is certainly true that Dickinson was quite aware of her own popularity, but her comments to Beecher suggest that she recognized the dangers of empty flattery. Moreover, the attention that Dickinson received really confirmed her importance to the war effort. The letter reveals emotional exhaustion, but less from the work itself than from the trappings of fame. But perhaps Dickinson protested too much. The letter also hints that by 1863 the taste of fame had entered her marrow, not crowding out the higher ideals but shaping her daily personal life. In short, at twenty years of age Anna Dickinson was really doing important patriotic work, but she was also becoming used to her public celebrity—and influence—to a degree that might one day yield frustrated disappointment.

Anna Dickinson's wartime experiences, as reflected in her extensive correspondence, fits into several different narratives. This essentially private evidence provides a different perspective on how Civil War America—or at least Northern society—dealt with, and responded to, a highly unusual public woman. Predictably, some portion of her correspondents viewed Dickinson in the context of her gender and age, and sought to advise and control her accordingly, even while encouraging her in her transgressive life as an itinerant female orator. For others, Dickinson stood as a charismatic icon. Her example clearly had a shaping effect on a host of young women, both those she befriended and those who merely watched from afar. For these women Dickinson presented an alternative model for civilian women in the public arena, one that was quite different from the Sanitary Commission volunteers and female nurses on the one hand, and the celebrated spies and cross-dressing female soldiers on the other. We might also place Dickinson into another home-front narrative, stressing that she—like so many other wartime civilians—was forced into economic adjustments in the midst of the conflict. Although driven by her political passions, Dickinson was also acting as a material provider for her sister and widowed mother. (Of course, in this case the war did not create the financial need—Dickinson's father had died more than a decade earlier—but the politics of the conflict did create a window of opportunity.) Moreover, while her specific wartime actions were quite distinctive, Dickinson's impulse to engage in a useful form of "war work" was very much in keeping with many of her peers on the home front.[49]

Dickinson's wartime experiences are obviously also a crucial early component of her own life's narrative. Her postwar history is beyond the scope of this essay, but a few observations are in order. After Appomattox, Dickinson remained in the public sphere, pursuing a variety of reform agendas while continuing to support herself, her mother, and her sister. Immediately following the war she toured the country as a highly successful lyceum speaker, and when lecture fees began to dry up, she tried her hand as a playwright, actress, and author.[50] Although perhaps best known for her lecture on Joan of Arc, Dickinson's postwar lectures commonly tackled political themes, often focusing on the economic and political status of women. Despite brief returns to the stump in 1872—campaigning for Liberal Republican Horace Greeley—and 1888, Dickinson never recaptured the partisan political voice she enjoyed during the war years.

In her quarter century of celebrity Dickinson also found herself embroiled in a string of bitter legal disputes and public disagreements involving—among others—critics, editors, politicians, and people in the theater. Along the way, Dickinson suffered through private rifts with numerous friends and allies, including Susan B. Anthony, Whitelaw Reid, Fanny Davenport, and Ben Butler. Dickinson's relationship with Anthony, twenty-two years her senior, was particularly complex. In the immediate postwar years they developed a closeness which combined both political passion and some level of physical intimacy.[51] Anthony took personal delight in the younger woman's company, but the two parted company, apparently because Dickinson—although consistently in favor of woman suffrage—refused to accept a prominent leadership role in the movement and in fact endorsed the exclusion of women from the Fifteenth Amendment, which extended suffrage to African American men.[52]

Anna Dickinson's public career ended sadly, but with characteristic flare. In 1891, with her sister's health failing and her behavior seemingly growing erratic, Susan Dickinson arranged to have Anna committed into a state asylum for the insane. This began a final, intricate chapter that would last for most of the decade and remain something of a puzzle a century later. Dickinson won her freedom with the aid of a team of lawyers and a sympathetic doctor, and then launched a series of celebrated lawsuits against the people responsible for her commitment and, later, against four New York newspapers that had reported that she was insane.[53] After achieving some measure of vindication, Dickinson retired to a life out of the public eye, eventually dying in Goshen, New York, at age eighty-nine.

How much might Dickinson's wartime celebrity have shaped her life in the quarter century to come? Like many soldiers and civilians who rose to fame during the Civil War, Dickinson's popularity endured into the postwar years, enabling her to craft a successful public career while also providing her with numerous opportunities to weigh in on the political issues of the day. But one could also write the narrative as one of frustrated ambitions. For a woman with an essentially political orientation, it must have been discouraging to be relegated to the lyceum circuit and the stage while men were directly shaping public policy. And having achieved such success—and praise—in her early twenties, Dickinson was ill prepared for the negative reviews and financial failures that accompanied some of her later efforts. In that sense, her wartime fame left Dickinson with a more difficult postwar road in that even her substantial postwar successes and public influence never quite matched her earlier accomplishments. But regardless of the challenges that lay ahead of her, at the close of the Civil War Anna Dickinson was widely recognized for her contributions to the war effort and to the Republican Party. And—for dozens of friends, hundreds of acquaintances, and thousands of anonymous admirers—Dickinson's wartime career served as evidence of what women could, given the opportunity, achieve in the public arena.

## NOTES

1. James Parton et al., *Eminent Women of the Age; Being Narratives of The Lives and Deeds of the Most Prominent Women of the Present Generation,* (Hartford, Conn., 1869). Stanton's essay on Dickinson is on pp. 479–512.

2. Parton et al., *Eminent Women of the Age,* 486. The only published biography of Dickinson is Giraud Chester, *Embattled Maiden: The Life of Anna Dickinson* (New York, 1951). James Harvey Young, who also wrote a dissertation on Dickinson's wartime career, authored a more scholarly Dickinson biography that has never been published. I am indebted to Dr. Young for permission to inspect both this manuscript ("Anna Elizabeth Dickinson") and his notes in the James Harvey Young Papers, Special Collections, Emory University, Atlanta, Georgia (hereafter JHY Papers). For my own brief overview of "Anna E. Dickinson's Civil War," see *The Human Tradition in the Civil War and Reconstruction,* ed. Steven E. Woodworth (Wilmington, Del., 2000), 93–110.

3. *Chicago Tribune,* November 12, 1863.

4. Parton et al., *Eminent Women of the Age,* 500, 505, 512.

5. Glenna Matthews, *The Rise of Public Woman: Woman's Place in the United States, 1630–1970* (New York, 1992), 108–19; Mary P. Ryan, "Gender and Public Access: Women's Politics in Nine-teenth-Century America," in *Habermas and the Public Sphere,* ed. Craig Calhoun (Cambridge, Mass., 1992), 259–88. See also Elizabeth R. Varon, "Tippecanoe and the Ladies, Too: White Women and Party Politics in Antebellum Virginia," *Journal of American History* (September 1995): 494–521; Varon, *We Mean to Be Counted: White Women and Politics in Antebellum Virginia* (Chapel Hill, 1998); Rebecca Edwards, *Angels in the Machinery: Gender in American Party Politics from the Civil War to the Progressive Era* (New York, 1997), 12–38.

6. J. Matthew Gallman, "Anna Dickinson, America's Joan of Arc: Public Discourse and Gendered Rhetoric during the Civil War" (unpublished essay, 1999).

7. Gallman, "Anna Dickinson, America's Joan of Arc." See also Joanna Russ, *How to Suppress Women's Writing* (Austin, 1983).

8. Faye E. Dudden, *Women in the American Theater: Actresses and Audiences, 1790–1870* (New Haven, 1994), 40–42.

9. On wartime *cartes de visite,* see William C. Darrah, *Cartes de Visite in Nineteenth Century America* (Gettysburg, 1981).

10. Susan Dickinson to Anna Elizabeth Dickinson, January 27, 1861, Anna Elizabeth Dickinson Papers, Library of Congress, microfilm (hereafter AED Papers). (All dates of letters will hereafter be cited in month/day/year style.)

11. Anna Elizabeth Dickinson (hereafter AED) to Susan Dickinson, 4/28/62, 5/27/62, AED Papers.

12. Susan Dickinson to AED, 12/6/62, AED Papers.

13. Susan Dickinson to AED, 7/28/63, AED Papers.

14. Susan Dickinson to AED, 12/23/63, AED Papers.

15. Mrs. Mary Dickinson to AED, 2/11/64, AED Papers.

16. AED family correspondence, AED Papers; JHY Papers, Box 5, folder 21.

17. See, for instance, AED to Susan Dickinson, 4/15/62, AED Papers.

18. AED to Susan Dickinson, 4/28/62, Susan to AED, 11/21/62, AED Papers.

19. Joseph Ricketson to AED, 11/15/62, AED Papers.

20. N. J. Burton to AED, 8/8/63, 8/10/65, AED Papers. (This file is labeled "W. J. Burton" but James Harvey Young identifies the author as Nathaniel, [JHY Papers].)

21. Sallie Austin to AED, 11/12/65, AED Papers.

22. Lillie Atkinson to AED, 9/23/[60?], 3/12/61, 6/1/63, AED Papers. (Note: some of Lillie Atkinson's letters are incorrectly filed among Lillie Chace's letters.)

23. Fanny Garrison to AED, 6/23/62, 9/14/62, 10/12/62, AED Papers.

24. Lillie Chace to AED, 2/3/63, 3/30/63, 4/17/63, 3/12/64, AED Papers.

25. Lillie Chace to AED, 12/17/66, AED Papers.

26. Lilly Gillette to AED, 2/1/64, AED Papers (this is a portion of a note filed in the letters from Isabella Beecher Hooker); Lilly G. Warner to AED, 7/17/65, 1/16/68, AED Papers.

27. Louise Brackett to AED, 5/29/63, 6/15/63, 7/11/63, 7/24/63, 3/4/64, AED Papers.

28. Fanny Ames to AED, 5/2/64, 6/13/64, AED Papers.

29. The letters to Dickinson suggesting physical intimacies with other women raise a sequence of questions. First, what was the actual nature of these actions? Second, how, if at all, should the historian categorize these activities? And third, to what extent would answers to the first two questions contribute to our understanding of the events under examination? Historians agree that nineteenth century notions of friendships, for both men and women, differed substantially from contemporary norms, rendering the rigidity of modern labels anachronistic. Dickinson's

wartime letters certainly indicate that she shared unspecified physical intimacies with several women, but none suggest that Dickinson—or her correspondents—understood their actions as being atypical, or secret, or calling into question a heterosexual future. Both her male and female friends apparently assumed that Dickinson would eventually marry a man. In modern terms Dickinson might have defined herself—either during the war years or later in life—as a bisexual, but I would argue that her actual sexual preference was less crucial than popular perception in shaping wartime responses to her. For the classic discussion of nineteenth-century female friendships among middle-class Northern white women, see Carroll Smith-Rosenberg, "The Female World of Love and Ritual: Relations between Women in Nineteenth-Century America," *Signs* 1 (Autumn 1975): 1–30. For a recent discussion of female culture among white Southern women, see Joan E. Cashin, ed., *Our Common Affairs; Texts from Women in the Old South* (Baltimore, 1996). This collection of documents includes various examples of homosocial relationships comparable to those reflected in the Dickinson letters (see pp. 91–96). The letters of African Americans Rebecca Primus and Addie Brown, edited by Farah Jasmine Griffin, illustrate a more explicitly erotic romantic relationship between two nineteenth-century women *(Beloved Sisters and Loving Friends: Letters from Rebecca Primus of Royal Oak, Maryland, and Addie Brown of Hartford, Connecticut, 1854–1968* [New York, 1999]). In her book *Surpassing the Love of Men: Romantic Friendship and Love between Women from the Renaissance to the Present* (New York, 1998) and in several other volumes, Lillian Faderman has established herself as leader in the pursuit of a *"usable past* for contemporary women who call themselves 'lesbian'" (p. 20). Although she casts her net more broadly than many of her colleagues, Faderman's work represents a valuable survey of attitudes and actions.

30. AED to Susan Dickinson, 4/28/62; Fanny Garrison to AED, 6/23/62; Susan Dickinson to AED, 11/21/62, AED Papers.

31. Joseph Allyn to AED, 7/21/63, AED Papers.

32. Louise Brackett to AED, 7/11/63, 7/21/63; Susan Dickinson to AED, 1/8/63, 8/13/63, AED Papers.

33. Elias Irish to AED, 8/20/65, 1/21/66, AED Papers.

34. Thomas Seville to AED, 6/12/63; W. M. Boucher [?] to AED, 4/6/64; E. M. Bruce to AED, 10/20/64; R. P. Minier [?] to AED, 11/27/65, AED Papers.

35. Emma F. Foster to AED, 4/15/65, AED Papers.

36. Harriette A. Keyset to AED, 2/20/66; Charlotte Garrique to AED, 11/1/65, AED Papers.

37. Amos Gilbert to AED, 1/7/61; Anonymous to AED, 2/27/61; Henry Homes to AED, 11/28/63, AED Papers.

38. William Lloyd Garrison to AED, 3/16/62, 3/22/62, 3/27/62, 3/30/62; Samuel May Jr. to AED, 6/19/62, 1/13/63, AED Papers.

39. William D. Kelley to AED, various letters (quote from 4/22/63), AED Papers.

40. Samuel Pomeroy to AED, various letters; Whitelaw Reid to AED, 4/3/64, AED Papers.

41. Susan B. Anthony to AED, 7/1/64; Theodore Tilton to AED, 7/13/64; B. F. Prescott to AED, 9/4/64, 10/2/64; Lillie Chace to AED, 8/21/64, AED Papers.

42. *The Independent,* September 8, 1864; Theodore Tilton to AED, 10/4/64; Lillie Chace to AED, 9/19/64; Whitelaw Reid to AED, 9/11/64, AED Papers.

43. Ruth Duzdeely [?] to AED, 3/29/62; Joseph Ricketson to AED, 6/24/62; Frank Garrison to AED, 9/12/62; Oliver Johnson to AED, 7/6/65, AED Papers. On fame, see Leo Braudy, *The Frenzy of Renown: Fame and Its History* (New York 1997), 491–514.

44. Lillie Chace to AED, 9/14/63, 3/12/64, AED Papers.

45. Emma Fisher to AED, 10/15/65, AED Papers.

46. Samuel May Jr. to Elizabeth Buffum Chace, 4/17/62, quoted in Lillie B. Chace Wyman and

Arthur Crawford Wynaan, *Elizabeth Buffum Chace, 1806–1899*, 2 vol. (Boston, 1914), 1:236.

47. Mary Dickinson to AED, 11/28/62, AED Papers. This note is written at the end of a letter from Samuel Dickinson to AED.

48. AED to James Beecher, 6/2/63, Schlesinger Library, Cambridge, Massachusetts.

49. Jeanie Attie, *Patriotic Toil: Northern Women and the American Civil War* (Ithaca, 1998).

50. On the nineteenth-century theater, see Dudden, *Women in the American Theater.*

51. See Lillian Faderman, *To Believe in Women: What Lesbians Have Done for America—A History* (Boston, 1999), 25–27. As Faderman notes, the Anthony-Dickinson correspondence has an erotic air, but the available evidence does not fully illuminate the nature of their relationship.

52. Young, "Anna Elizabeth Dickinson," chap. 7. See also Jean V. Matthews, *Women's Struggle for Equality, The First Phase, 1828–1876* (Chicago, 1997); and Barbara Goldsmith, *Other Powers: The Age of Suffrage, Spiritualism, and the Scandalous Victoria Woodhull* (New York, 1998).

53. The trial reports and court testimony provide contradictory evidence, supporting the notion that Dickinson might have been—at the time of her commitment—quite ill, while also leaving open the possibility that she was indeed badly treated by her sister and the other defendants.

# Anna Dickinson, America's Joan of Arc

## Public Discourse and Gendered Rhetoric during the Civil War

I wrote this paper for a conference honoring my graduate mentor, Morton Keller. I was pleased to be included in the project and found it particularly interesting to think about how my current project was influenced by Keller's very different sort of scholarship. Following the conference, three of Keller's other students—Wendy Gamber, Michael Grossberg, and Hendrik Hartog— took on the task of steering the volume into print.

As I prepared this piece, I saw it as a companion to the essay in Joan Cashin's collection, although with the knowledge that few readers would stumble upon both essays. Whereas the former is largely about Dickinson's own wartime actions and relationships, this article concerns Dickinson as the subject of public discourse. The starting premise is that by entering into the public arena in such dramatically unfamiliar ways, Dickinson became the subject of illuminating gendered discourse. And as a highly partisan speaker, she posed interesting rhetorical challenges for both her supporters and her opponents. This essay, more so than the contribution to the Cashin collection, foregrounds the theoretical discussions about gender and about public rhetoric. Although Keller was not known for work on gender, I thought that the discussion of the public sphere was a proper tribute.

Like the essay in the Schaefer-Weiss volume honoring my father, this article is the only contribution in the collection about the Civil War. Civil War historians would have to be pretty dedicated to discover either piece. But Dr. Keller read it and seemed pleased. And that was good enough for me.

. . .

In January 1864 Anna Elizabeth Dickinson, a twenty-one-year-old Philadelphia Quaker, entered the hall of the House of Representatives, with the speaker of the house and the vice president flanking her on the makeshift platform, and

President Abraham Lincoln and Mary Todd Lincoln in the audience.[1] Two months earlier Dickinson had journeyed to Chicago, where she delivered two lectures—for a substantial fee of $600—at the Northwest Sanitary Fair. Some Chicago newspapers questioned the propriety of Dickinson's accepting money for a charitable event, but the *Chicago Tribune* celebrated Dickinson's appearance: "Anna Dickinson is a born orator. She has a mind that can grapple with the most subtle arguments—a voice of rare sweetness, strength and endurance—and a combination of powers that never fails to magnetize the most careless audience. . . . And yet amid all this, she is still a woman—has a woman's way of thinking, and a very womanly way of saying what she thinks."[2]

By the time she appeared in Chicago, Dickinson was one of America's leading orators and one of the nation's most celebrated women. This fame had come quickly. Dickinson delivered her first invited lecture before the Pennsylvania Anti-Slavery Society in the fall of 1860. The following February the teenage prodigy addressed a large audience at Philadelphia's Concert Hall where she spoke on "The Rights and Wrongs of Women." In early 1862 William Lloyd Garrison arranged for her to deliver a series of lectures in the Boston area. The next year the secretary of New Hampshire's Republican State Committee invited her to visit the Granite State to speak for the party's candidates. Although much of her early reputation was built on abolitionist and women's rights speaking, Dickinson proved to be an exceptionally effective partisan stump speaker, attracting enthusiastic Republican audiences in Maine, Connecticut, Pennsylvania, and New York.

As a wartime orator, Dickinson stands at the confluence of two major streams in the recent scholarship in women's history. One considers the various ways in which women entered the public arena. Central to that literature has been a reexamination of the notion of rigidly dichotomized separate gender spheres in antebellum America as well as a rethinking of what we mean by "public" activity. Despite a host of cultural messages and legal restrictions emphasizing that a woman's proper place was in the home, there is ample evidence that middle-class white women ventured into the public arena in various ways: organizing voluntary societies, publishing books and articles, running small businesses, pursuing reform agendas, appearing in civic rituals, and engaging in public discourse.[3] Moreover, recent scholarship has demonstrated that the concept of public and private spheres had less clear resonance beyond the white middle classes.[4] Still, there remains a kernel of truth, encoded in northern society's prescriptions about the proper roles of women in public life, and enforced through both law and custom. Although some northern antebellum women were actively engaged in the crucial reform debates of the time, and some leading figures stepped to the podium before mixed audiences, the rough and tumble world of partisan politics remained a male-dominated world. Anna Dickinson, it would appear, transgressed that line with impunity.[5]

The second scholarly stream concerns the history of women during the Civil War. Immediately after the conflict various tomes celebrated the contributions of the "noble women" on both sides.[6] More recently, scholars have examined the wartime experiences of women in both the North and South.[7] Some of this work has emphasized the underexplored experiences of women who served as soldiers, spies, and the like, but nineteenth-century women's historians have fairly recently discovered the war years as an important episode in the history of women's public activism.[8] Thus, the two interpretive streams come together in the war years.

In her study of women's "warwork," Jeanie Attie examined the activities of women in northern voluntary societies and their tensions with the male leadership of the United States Sanitary Commission. Attie observed that "Although legal and social codes prevented women from performing their loyalties in the same manner as men, war mobilization nevertheless presented women with ways of exploiting the very structures of gender inequality to demonstrate their loyalties." Wartime women, Attie argues, supported the war effort while chafing at the constraints imposed by a cultural world that limited their public actions and a male leadership intent on circumscribing their role to a largely symbolic, passive, form of patriotic support and fund-raising.[9]

Anna Dickinson moved in this same world, but she hardly seems of that world at all. Dickinson's "war work" does not fit under Attie's umbrella in that she worked completely outside the normal constraints defined by her gender. Dickinson has received some scholarly attention as an outspoken abolitionist and advocate for women's rights, but such an iconoclastic nonjoiner does not fit well into analyses of organizational developments or emerging ideological debates. Could it be that she was so distinctive that her wartime experiences are only of limited historic significance? One might reasonably set aside the highly idiosyncratic diarist or the obscure author, but Anna Dickinson was the most public of gender transgressors. If she truly violated accepted gender norms, she did so before hundreds of wartime audiences, often speaking in halls of a thousand or more paying customers.

This essay examines how those audiences made sense of this charismatic female orator. The analysis is really doubly about public discourse. On the one hand, the focus will be on Dickinson as a public orator and contemporary responses to those appearances. And, on the other hand, the evidence is from a wide array of newspaper accounts, which taken together suggest an ongoing public discussion on the propriety of women entering the partisan political arena, and of course a public discourse constructed to shape—and not merely reflect—popular opinion. The reporters and editors who participated in that discourse fell along a spectrum generally reflecting each newspaper's perspective on Dickinson's politics. Although some commentators celebrated Dickinson as a pioneer for women's entrance into the public arena, far more adopted some stance that allowed for no such transforming legacy. Although Anna Dickinson was celebrated as a woman in the public arena, the responses to her celebrity had within them the seeds for future constraints.

Of course these published accounts and editorial comments must be read with care, rather than being accepted as literal depictions of contemporary gender norms. They certainly reflect an ongoing dialogue between newspapers and their readers, with the partisan press endeavoring to simultaneously reflect, exploit, and shape readers' responses about gender roles *and* political policy. In highly competitive publishing markets (even in the smaller cities where Dickinson spoke there were commonly two or even three competing local journalists in the audience), the press could ill afford to offend readers' sensibilities about gender while trying to maintain a political following and an economic base. Mid-nineteenth-century Americans certainly had no universal notion of the proper role for women in public life, but the responses to Dickinson's appearances, and the language of those responses, provide a telling sketch of the parameters of popular thought.

In his magisterial study of the postwar American polity Morton Keller underscored the "ambiguous inheritance of the Civil War." The powerful forces of change unleashed by the Civil War, Keller argues, soon gave way to the more enduring values of racism, localism, and laissez-faire. This essay will argue that the political rhetoric surrounding Anna Dickinson's wartime career suggests a similar ideological conservatism organized around gender roles. As is commonly the case, the crisis of war opened the door for a woman to go beyond familiar practices, but the responses to Dickinson's wartime efforts helped limit their broader impact.[10]


## "SHE HAS A RIGHT TO SPEAK IN PUBLIC"

Although already a celebrated public speaker, Dickinson emerged as a Republican force during the 1863 and 1864 campaigns. Pundits acknowledged that her performances played an important role in the party's successes;

Connecticut Republicans dubbed her "the heroine of the triumph."[11] Rather than only praising the party (she was in fact highly critical of the moderate Lincoln administration), Dickinson specialized in biting attacks on Democratic candidates and Copperhead newspapers, interwoven with discussions of rebel misdeeds, critical analyses of unsuccessful Union generals, and calls for uncompromising patriotism. Observers found that Dickinson speeches were grand performances. She paced the stage like a caged tiger, speaking for an hour or more without notes. Although working from carefully constructed texts, she was at her best responding to a heckler or taking on a local editor, thus ensuring that each appearance had its own unique quality.

Whatever their political perspective, the nation's newspapers took Dickinson's lectures quite seriously, publishing extended summaries of her texts. Even those accounts that did not expressly discuss women in public routinely included detailed, highly gendered discussions of Dickinson's clothing, appearance, mannerisms, and rhetorical style. After her first appearance before the Pennsylvania Anti-Slavery Society, one Philadelphia paper made much of the seventeen-year-old's age and appearance as well as her speaking ability, concluding "the beauty and talent of the young woman exercised a talismanic effect upon even the rudest."[12] Later the examinations of Dickinson's appearance became more clinical, as observers seemed to look for clues to her great success. Following a March 1862 "Lecture on Behalf of the Contrabands," The *Philadelphia Press* reported, "In person, she is rather under the medium height, with a fine, intellectual-looking countenance, large nose, with distended nostrils, which, as she spoke, moved with a sort of nervous twitching. Her mouth is rather large, with arching lips, which gives it an expression of firmness, and, although we cannot say that the general contour of her face is pretty, we must say that, in her general appearance, she is rather prepossessing." Another reporter concluded that "Miss Dickinson, unlike most ladies who speak in public, is young, and made a narrow escape from being pretty."[13]

The *New York Herald* attributed Dickinson's success to her "youth and good looks" as well as her oratorical skills, noting that "[s]he has a full, gracefully rounded figure, is of the medium size of women, has a well balanced, firmly set head, round oval face, a fresh, healthy complexion, inclining to the hue of the brunette, and wears her dark hair in full, heavy clusters about her neck." The *Chicago Tribune* adopted a phrenological approach, reporting, "Her head seems to be perfectly well made, and balanced in all of its parts. The forehead, however, is upon a closer examination capacious, and of a fine intellectual architecture; broad in the regions of ideality, and, what the phrenologists call 'the top head,' is grandly developed. The back of the head is proportionally large, and the whole physique, so far, gives to a careful observer the assurance of a vigorous intellect and a high moral nature, based upon a splendid animal background."

Such detailed physical descriptions, even when accompanied by glowing accounts of her rhetoric, established Dickinson as a physical object whose appeal was not purely about oratorical skill.[14] As she became more financially successful and began abandoning her staid Quaker roots, Dickinson took to wearing custom made dresses and pieces of jewelry. By the end of the war the newspaper accounts began including detailed examinations of her clothing and ornaments, as well as her short-cropped curls and physical appearance.

This emphasis on Anna Dickinson's appearance suggests that she was dismissed by some as little more than a charmingly attractive curiosity, but other reporters—even while noting her appearance—celebrated Dickinson as a woman in public. As early as April 1862 the *Providence Press* was applauding Dickinson as an orator in the abolitionist tradition of William Lloyd Garrison and Horace Greeley, who "with the tongue of a *dozen women* . . . combines the boldness of forty men."[15] Following Dickinson's "A Plea for Women" in late 1862, a New Hampshire newspaper declared, "There has been and still is great prejudice against female lecturers, but all reformers in all ages of the world have met with opposition. Fair minded men and women are willing to listen to all, and then act their pleasure."[16] The radical *Independent* celebrated Dickinson's April 1863 appearance at New York's Cooper Institute as a great display of women's abilities. "Those who have prejudices against women who speak in public ought not to see Miss Anna E Dickinson of Philadelphia, if they mean to keep those prejudices," the paper warned. "*She* has a right to speak in public. . . . Miss Dickinson is not a woman speaking like a man. She is a woman. She thinks and feels like a woman. And she proves beyond all controversy that there are elements of truth, and phases of public affairs, important to be known, that can be given from no other stand-point than the heart of a true woman."[17]

In June 1863, while working for the *Cincinnati Gazette*, Whitelaw Reid ventured to Philadelphia to meet the popular young orator. "Of course she is radical," Reid told his readers, "as all women of culture are likely to be . . . and, of course, like all other women, she sometimes jumps to illogical conclusions without any bother of reasoning on the road. . . . But enough! This young girl, so brilliant, so magnetic, so wonderfully gifted, is a real Genius; and God gives us so few of these, we may be pardoned the rudeness of talking about them in the newspapers."[18] Reid's comments are characteristic of many supportive responses to Dickinson's public role. On the one hand, her allies often embraced the notion of women tackling political issues at public podiums, but, on the other hand, many evaluated her performances through a distinctly gendered lens. In Reid's eyes Dickinson was both "brilliant" and "gifted" but also typically "illogical" and thus "amusing."

These efforts to place Dickinson into some received gender paradigm periodically yielded contradictory results. The *Republican* approved of her public appearances, finding that "Miss Dickinson is preeminently a woman, with nothing but a woman's artillery to conduct and propel electric forces."[19] A Philadelphia paper agreed that Dickinson's skills were distinctly feminine. She was, "[a] perfect mistress of her art, a modulated voice—no declamation, that's schoolboyish—no gesture, that's mannish—for the most part with clasped hands, clenched at times, pacing the stage when the words came too fast for her—with an occasional impatient tap of her foot—a most womanly way of rendering a speech, and, just because it is womanly, utterly incomprehensible to masculine critics."[20] And a correspondent to a San Francisco newspaper added that "Miss D. is a good reasoner . . . but still apparently delighted to leap from the slow approximations of reasoning to the swifter flights, and perhaps truer results, of a keen, womanly intuition."[21]

But other favorable accounts used distinctly masculine language to describe—and praise—her rhetorical powers. A correspondent to the *Philadelphia Press* reported that "[s]he handled her subject in a most masterly, and, I might add, statesmanlike manner, giving facts, figures and dates in such a compact and harmonious whole as to impress all with her wonderful power of memory, and intelligent comprehension of her subject."[22] Claremont, New Hampshire's *National Eagle* added that "[t]o the true woman's natural wit and readiness, she adds a masculine vigor of thought and generalization, [and] a memory never at fault."[23] A letter to another New England newspaper concluded, "She is evidently a *masculine* mind."[24] And a Pennsylvania newspaper found Dickinson "[q]uite passably handsome, with short curling hair, large and expressive eyes, a loud, ringing, masculine voice, a distinctive and forcible enunciation" but concluded that "[h]er address was *womanly* as far as logic and accuracy were concerned."[25]

Some reporters seemed to disagree about whether Dickinson's gender was a strength or a liability. The Rochester *Evening Express* declared that "Miss Dickinson has far more of this real womanhood than the thousands of Fiora McFlimseys, who would affect to despise or sneer at her for violating their rules of false delicacy in publicly laboring for human welfare."[26] Dickinson's February

1865 appearance in Portland, Maine, provided the local press with "the strongest illustration of woman's power on the platform—and the power carries with it the *right* to be there—that we ever witnessed," but the account added, "Her faults as a speaker are characteristic of the feminine mind . . . a propensity to use the tongue *as a lash*" and "the feminine propensity to run to extremes."[27]

These stories all shared the conviction that Anna Dickinson was an effective speaker who had every right to a public audience, and they all measured her strengths and shortcomings in gendered terms. But they shared no consensus about whether Dickinson was distinctly feminine or some masculine-like gender-transgressor who had the ability to apply male logic and masculine oratorical skills to the political problems of the day.

Although Dickinson's supporters were divided on this topic, they seemed to agree that she was unique, perhaps even Heaven-sent. Following a triumphal appearance in Hartford the *Daily Post* announced that she was "[n]ot a woman but a girl 20 years of age, a Joan of Arc that God sent into the field, as many half believed, to maintain the cause of the country at this dreadful and last crisis." The neighboring *Courant* found that Dickinson was "a noble, patriotic woman—a woman who is using the great talents given her by God for the salvation of her country in its day of trial."[28]

These themes persisted throughout her wartime career. No normal process of education and intellectual development could have produced such a young woman. Instead, her supporters seemed certain that Dickinson was sent by God to attend to the nation's urgent needs. "When the country was in its darkest," one report began, "when occupied with an infuriate foe in front, a craven, treacherous band 'assailed her in the back.' A Philadelphia woman, another maid of Orleans in youth, in chivalric daring and grave forecast, in sweet womanly grace and lambent genius . . . went forth with . . . her country-loving and God fearing womanhood—and stood among the people." In so doing Dickinson was following long established patterns: "Ever since the nation had life, women here and there, in different stations, periods and crises, have broken conventional shell or crust, peeped and piped their little hour, and disappeared."[29]

The *Chicago Tribune* adopted a similar historical perspective. "Society at large has an honest horror of the assumption by women of the functions which belong strictly to men," the paper explained. "The feeling is laudable, and ought to be respected." In recent years this concern for gender differences had taken on a new urgency "because of the dissemination amongst us of exaggerated notions concerning woman's sphere, rights and duties, and in consequence of which many good but mistaken women were induced to make very unwomanly exhibitions, much to the scandal of the sex." Nonetheless, the *Tribune* acknowledged, "Nature has endowed some women with genius and power equal to those qualities which are the chief pride of the male sex; and it will not do to shut our eyes and allow our prejudices to entirely overcome us." Anna Dickinson, the Chicago newspaper concluded, was just such a woman, capable of answering the great national need.[30]

In a similar vein, a San Francisco correspondent admitted, "I must acknowledge that I am not, in theory, predisposed to favor female oratory. We cannot afford to let the finer edge of the female character be dulled by the collisions of public life; and yet when a lady can speak as Miss Dickinson does, why, it seems to me her gift is proof of her mission."[31] So many found parallels between young Anna's great success (and combative flair) and Joan of Arc that it became commonplace for reporters to compare her with "the Maid of Orleans," thus underscoring the notion that she was some sort of spiritual, sainted phenomenon rather than merely a young woman speaking her mind.[32]

These responses to Dickinson's public appearances suggest preliminary answers to our central question. True, a radical handful witnessed Anna Dickinson's public appearances and concluded that they illustrated what women could accomplish, but far more of her political supporters selected language which seemed to explain away Dickinson's larger significance. Some attributed her fame to her physical charms, despite feminine shortcomings of logic; others explained her success as evidence that she successfully aped masculine traits. But for many Dickinson was simply a unique aberration, whose appearance on the scene reflected divine will but no larger challenge to contemporary gender roles. In this fashion Dickinson's political supporters were able to profit from her popularity without challenging their essential patriarchal world view.

## The Female Termagant

Anna Dickinson's adversaries faced a different task in coming to terms with her popularity. Both her controversial words, and the fact that they were delivered by a woman, produced widespread outrage among northern Democrats. And the resulting rhetorical battles in the press were only fueled by Dickinson's fondness for selecting targets in the local media.

The early Democratic responses to Dickinson's lectures were dismissive but generally not too biting. After she called General George McClellan "either a traitor or a doughface," one reporter sheepishly acknowledged that "we have seldom heard a more eloquent speaker" whose "musical voice . . . together with her youthful appearance and winning address, make it a pleasure to listen, even though she advanced the most unwelcome sentiments."[33] Or, as a New Jersey newspaper summed up a March 1862 lecture: "It was the words of mediocrity spoken through the lips of genius."[34]

Others opted for the paternalistic assumption that Dickinson was merely a mouthpiece for the abolitionist male leadership, or worse, that the radical Republicans were shamelessly swept up by Dickinson's beauty and charm and thus unable to discern her true mediocrity.[35] These critics commonly blamed the Republicans for leading the innocent Dickinson astray. Following her 1863 appearances in Hartford, where Dickinson had received top billing at the party's election eve rally, several local papers reprinted an editorial from the *Journal of Commerce* which noted that "[p]olitical partisanship sometimes blinds men to the most ordinary rules of common sense. . . . our Republican friends . . . have forgotten the purity and delicacy that attaches to the female character."[36] The following month the *New York Herald* essentially absolved Dickinson from blame for her own actions: "The pretty face, tuneful voice and pleasant manners of the new Joan of Arc contrast ludicrously with the bloodthirsty sentiments she expresses and the reckless vituperations in which she indulges. For a young Quakeress to make such orations might be considered strange, did we not know that she is only the sweet mouthpiece through which the abolition politicians, reverend and irreverend, address the President and the public."[37]

Two years later the *Herald* was singing a very similar tune, with a bit more bite. The "gaseous matter" of Dickinson's latest speech, the James Gordon Bennett newspaper proclaimed, "from masculine lips would be dreadful enough; but coming from a woman's lips, formed only for kisses, smiles and sweet, sympathizing speech, they strike us with a nameless horror. . . . The war has produced many revolutions; but we had no idea that it could so revolutionize a woman's holy nature." But once again the *Herald* concluded that "Miss Dickinson is really much more to be pitied than blamed [whereas] . . . those contemptible cowards who hide behind her petticoats and bid her utter the black and bloody sentences which their craven tongues, less defiant than their reckless minds, dare not frame in public" were the true villains.[38] In this fashion Dickinson's political adversaries used her gender to dismiss her, while also calling into question the manhood of those supporters who had thrust her into the public eye.

The language selected to belittle Dickinson is quite telling. In addition to claiming that she merely rehashed the words of her male Republican handlers, several commentators tried to portray Dickinson as a mentally unstable spiritualist.[39] The highly partisan *World* dubbed Dickinson the "Political Witch," claiming that she was the latest in a recent proliferation of practitioners of "feminine astrology."[40] Such comments on Dickinson's otherworldly nature present an interesting parallel to those of her supporters who contended that she was sent by God. Either perspective implicitly dismissed Dickinson's significance as a pathbreaking woman in the public sphere.

Others openly attacked Dickinson as a gender transgressor. Many joined the *West Jersey Pioneer* in opining that "[t]he young lady in question cannot do better than exchange the harassing duties of public life for those serener and domestic walks so befitting her sex."[41] Or, as another paper took pains to point out: "The province of woman is too well understood to need explanation now. She is the home angel, not the politician. . . . we should disgrace the gentle and noble character of our American women if we encourage them to the public exhibition of political preferences."[42] Even observers who were sympathetic to Dickinson's positions expressed reservations at her actions. A correspondent to the *New York Evangelist* admitted, "We have no patience for the twaddle for 'woman's rights,' and no especial liking for the itinerant Amazons who have gone crusading through the land." Still, within minutes after Dickinson begins speaking "you forget whether it were a man, or a woman, or one of Mary Wollstonecraft's 'third sex' who was pulling at your heartstrings." Nevertheless, after much back and forth about women in public, the author declared his fervid hope that Dickinson's actions would not be duplicated: "We are no more anxious to hear a woman's voice in our Church-meetings, or on the political rostrum, than we ever were. We are fully persuaded that 'woman's mission' is quite in another direction."[43]

By the time she appeared at the Cooper Institute in 1863, Anna Dickinson's fiercest Copperhead adversaries were ready to take the gloves off. "Someone has said that a woman's name should appear in print but twice—when she is married and when she dies," declared the *World* in a lengthy editorial. "Miss Anna E Dickinson, of Philadelphia, is evidently of the contrary opinion, as likewise are Henry Ward Beecher and Senator Morgan, who countenanced a female of that name, night before last, in indecencies of speech which would have disgraced a pot-house brawler of the other sex."[44] Many of the *World's* critiques mined familiar veins. Dickinson had merely offered "the hack arguments of male politicians reiterated in tones an octave higher." But the New York paper went much further in attacking Dickinson's womanhood and the masculinity of her supporters: "Mirrors, it is said, are unlike women, inasmuch as they reflect without speaking, while women are apt to speak without reflecting; but Miss Dickinson in speaking mirrored her audience. Divested of the grace of her sex, as they of the humanity of theirs, stripped of the gentleness and charity and puremindedness of woman as they of the dignity and sobriety and wisdom of men, she unsexed and they without sense, the exhibition was one which no woman of refinement and no man of good sense could witness without blushing for her kind."[45]

These attacks proved too much for Dickinson's supporters to swallow. The *Philadelphia Press* charged the editor of the *World* with having sunk to new lows by "abusing a woman" thus "relinquish[ing] all claim to the consideration of gentlemen." The *Press* admitted some discomfort with "the propriety of Miss Dickinson's appearance before the public as a speaker" but concluded that "she has followed what seemed to her to be a holy and conscientious mission." The essence of the *Press*'s defense was that the *World* had treated a lady in an "unmanly manner." Thus, even her political supporters in the press—presumably mirroring the sensibilities of their readers—fell back on gender paradigms in defending Dickinson.[46]

This sort of highly gendered rhetorical battle between Democratic and Republican newspapers, often involving bitter rivals within the same city, followed Dickinson wherever she traveled. After the *Hartford Times* published a particularly unflattering account of her March 1863 lecture, the *Courant* responded, "We had supposed that the editor of the *Times* had some little spark of manliness left in him, and that when he found he had been convicted of grossly maligning a woman he would have had the decency to retract, and make the apology due from a gentleman."[47] When the Portland *Argus* criticized the orator for accepting a fee for her Chicago performances, the Portland *Press* declared that its adversary had "cowardly and ruffian-like, *dealt a blow at a woman,* whose only shield is her virtue; whose only defense is her spotless purity and good works."[48]

Following an appearance in upstate New York, the Copperhead *Courier and Union* published a particularly virulent attack on "Short Haired Anna." The report, full of explicit gendered imagery, is worth extensive quotation:

"SHORT HAIRED" ANNA—The female lecture termagant, who is now doing the dirty work for the Radicals, in the usual 'spread eagle' style of the strong-minded, brazen-faced sex who eschew womanly dignity, and make the rostrum take the place of the cradle and baby-jumper, is just now in great favor with the admirers of the unsexed; and, as a natural consequence, she flutters her plumage of feathers in the face of the community, and in this way makes a very pitiable effort to bedaub a certain class whom she is hired to abuse, with the slime from her unclean nest. The strong-minded of her sex applaud her when she says anything remarkably smutty and out of place in a woman.

The *Courier and Union* paid particular attention to "the notices which Miss Dickinson has received from that portion of the admiring press that best appreciates her mental capabilities." The Copperhead paper quoted extensively from a detailed physical description in the admiring *Standard* which praised "the 'symmetrical young creature'" and her "'well knit agility of frame'" all the way down to "the *lower fold* of her plain, Quaker-brown dress, which was so intently gazed upon by the strippling reporter of the *Standard,* whose craven and lasivious [*sic*] tastes rivited [*sic*] his huge owlish eyes in that direction!" These attacks followed familiar lines, with special barbs aimed at Dickinson's supporters in the press, but notice how the editorial has sexualized the young orator, both in its physical description of her "'spread eagle' style" and in the detailed characterization of the *Standard*'s fawning portrayal. Moreover, this account is free with condemnation of Dickinson's "slime," "filth-throwing," and general vulgarity. By way of explanation, the author noted, "We are not ordinarily in the habit of criticizing women; but when leaving the sanctity of their home retirement and the privacy of womanly pursuits, they assume manhood's tasks and enter the political arena" where rough and tumble debate was the norm. "For ourselves," the editorial continued, "we believe that woman in her household sphere, discharging faithfully its duties of love, training, sympathy and protection, and purifying and ennobling her home and social circle, has a diviner mission and a nobler and brighter, if a more humble sphere." Dickinson's male supporters, the newspaper concluded, should "consult the New Testament and see what it says as to women talking in public meetings."[49]

Anna Dickinson's triumphant appearance before Congress in January 1864 pushed some of her most dedicated critics to new heights of outrage. The *New York World*'s response was particularly inflamed:

There is really nothing remarkable about this young woman. She is a very ordinary-looking person, with a harsh voice, an unfeminine manner, and a parrot-like flow of words. What she says is merely a rehash of the loose and violent assertions of the extreme radical journalists and orators. She attracts crowds when she speaks, by appealing to the same love of the marvelous and monstrous which Barnum has made his fortune in exhibiting woolly horses, dwarfs, Feejee mermaids, and other queer fish. Yet this silly young person was allowed the use of the hall of Representatives last Saturday to make one of her unwomanly displays.

This critique combines many of the Copperhead strategies for marginalizing Dickinson: as unfeminine, as a "parrot" for the opinions of others, and as little more than a sideshow. After Dickinson repeated her Washington lecture in New York, the *Rochester Union* suggested that "she ought to be pointed to the famous woman order of Gen. Butler, whom she so much admires, and be made to understand that with suitable variations it meets her case exactly. So long as she mounts the political stump so long she will be treated as 'a woman plying her vocation.'"[50]

The *Geneva (N. Y.) Gazette* ran a long essay attacking "Anna E. Dickinson and the Gynaekokracy." This extended diatribe built on the established theme that Dickinson represented a larger evil in social development. Applying a fascinating variant on familiar anatomical metaphors for political life, the *Gazette* argued that periodically "idiosyncracies . . . originate and throw to the surface certain manifestations of disease more or less loathsome and distressing; just as in a morbid state of the human body, boils and carbuncles are produced upon the surface by insidious causes seated perhaps in the vital forces of the system."

"Among the excrescences upon the body politic," the article continued, "is one which may be best described by its Greek name Gynaekokracy, which manifests itself in the absurd endeavors of women to usurp the places and execute the functions of the male sex. It is a moral and social monstrosity—an inversion, bouleversement of the laws of nature, which have assigned to each sex its appropriate relations and duties; and a subversion, so far as it prevails, of some of the fundamental principles of morality and social order." The author—who apparently had never heard Dickinson speak—summarized her lectures as "entirely political, intensely partisan and objugatory, made up chiefly of extracts from Wendell Phillips, Charles Sumner and Horace Greeley, loosely put together, and delivered with great self-possession, flippancy and boldness." Her successes had encouraged "many rivals" to "[spring] up from among the young girls of the country" but the article was pleased to note that "to the credit of the sex . . . so far as is known to the writer, she has not been encouraged in this career by respectable ladies. Her sphere is with the men, and all sensible and modest women, who have a regard for the proprieties of the sex, will be content to leave it there."[51]

By early 1865, as the war was winding down, the venom of the attacks on Dickinson seemed to increase. In February, only days after the *New York Herald* had attacked her "gaseous" performance at the Cooper Institute, the *New York Daily News* added further reflections on the Dickinson phenomenon:

> The war has, in fact, rallied to its support all the social radicalisms of the country, and from Abolition to miscegenation, free love and woman's rights, they have been let loose to rush shrieking through the land to the horror of all decency and common sense. Miss Anna Dickenson [*sic*] is . . . one of the illustrations of the revolution that rules the hour. As a woman she would command the charity of our silence; but in discharge of our duty as a journalist we are bound, very sorely against our will, to deal with her as an advocate and example of a dangerous system of ethics.

Dismissing her, like many of its Democratic colleagues, as a mere "parrot" to abolitionist ideas, the *Daily News* concluded, "The factionists by whom the lady is thrust into a position so false are evil counselors for a woman, and, we can assure Miss Dickinson, have placed her outside the sphere proper to a true woman. This blunt speaking is not only a duty to society in her case, but is a duty of manly frankness to the lady herself."[52] A few days later the *Providence Daily Post* concluded that "Miss Dickinson is a good specimen of a very useless sort of woman."[53]

## CONCLUSION

Only a few weeks before the end of the war Dickinson traveled to Lawrence, Massachusetts, to deliver her new lecture on "Women's Work and Wages." Both local papers praised the performer and the performance, but the *Lawrence Sentinel* still concluded that "[w]e trust she will refrain from political discussion. There are other softer and more womanly themes in the intellectual storehouse—that sit more gracefully on her lips."[54] That is, the newspaper was perfectly willing to grant that Dickinson had earned her place at the public rostrum, but it still wished that she would maintain ladylike decorum by steering clear of partisan political topics, thus suggesting a different take on separate spheres, defined by topic rather than place.

Throughout the Civil War, northern newspapers had divided over Anna Dickinson's political messages, and, to a lesser extent, over the propriety of her public appearances. Many of Dickinson's supporters joined the *Sentinel* in admitting that they were happiest when she steered clear of the masculine world of partisan politics. During the crisis Republicans needed Dickinson to support their cause, but only the radical minority suggested that Dickinson's public appearances should be viewed as evidence of woman's larger capacity. Others, at least implicitly, marginalized Dickinson and thus minimized her gender significance by emphasizing her physical characteristics or her masculine oratorical skills, or by linking her to the sainted Joan of Arc or some other otherworldly imagery. In so doing, Dickinson's political allies could profit from her celebrity and oratorical power while avoiding the taint of woman's rights.

In the meantime, Dickinson's adversaries grew bold in attacking her femininity as a means of dismissing her message. They portrayed Dickinson as the worst sort of "unsexed" gender transgressor, thoroughly beyond the bounds of proper human discourse. Her supporters were happy to fight the battle along gendered lines, blasting Copperhead editors as unmanly for their crude comments about the lady orator. In this fashion they were able to set themselves up as the defenders of womanhood—and separate gender spheres—while at least implicitly supporting Dickinson's political content.

Although today largely forgotten, or historically marginalized, Anna Dickinson's wartime career sheds new light on the two intertwined issues that shaped this essay: the role of women in nineteenth-century public life and the Civil War experiences of American women. Dickinson's stump-speaking career dramatically exceeded the midcentury public political appearances of her most celebrated female contemporaries, suggesting, on the one hand, the breadth of possibilities for Civil War–era public women, and, on the other hand, demonstrating the rule that is best illustrated through the exception. My emphasis here has been less on the activities of this exceptional woman than on what can be learned by examining the range of responses to her public oratory.[55] These responses demonstrate that midcentury gender assumptions were neither fixed nor universally held. The various newspaper reports show that there was a commonly accepted notion of separate gender spheres, but that the shape and rigidity of those spheres was subject to continual negotiation. By pushing at the edges of what was familiar and—to many—acceptable, Dickinson provided the context for an ongoing examination of the proper roles for both women and men. And as I have argued, those who favored her opinions but were uncomfortable with her public role found various strategies to circumscribe the enduring effect of her gender transgressions.

It is perhaps fitting that Dickinson emerged as a public figure in the midst of the Civil War. After all, the demands of war drew thousands of women into unaccustomed roles in both the North and the South. It may even be the case, as some reports suggested, that the sectional crisis made some listeners particularly receptive to the wisdom of a woman's perspective. Dickinson's own wartime correspondence and speeches do not provide much support for the idea that she felt called, *as a woman,* to enter the public arena in this time of crisis. In other guises Dickinson was a strong public advocate for women, both during and after the war, supporting suffrage and delivering powerful speeches defending the interests of working women, prostitutes, and Morman wives. But in her wartime political stump speeches Dickinson did not suggest that she was offering a woman's perspective on politics, nor in any sense advance the idea that she was bringing the domestic sphere into political discourse. Dickinson's motivations for becoming a Republican stump speaker appear to have been threefold: She felt a deep passion for the war effort in general, and the interests of African Americans in particular; she was under tremendous financial pressure to support herself, her older sister, and her widowed mother, and lecturing promised excellent financial returns; and she clearly loved public speaking and national celebrity.[56]

Dickinson's own motivations and sense of self further complicate our understanding of nineteenth-century gender assumptions. Although a public advocate for women, Dickinson did not go onto the Republican stump as part of that agenda and apparently did not claim, either in her public statements or in her private correspondence, that her gender identity gave her a distinctive voice. In no sense was she claiming to bring a domestic perspective to the political platform.[57] But regardless of her own sense of identity, Dickinson's audiences observed her performances through a gendered lens, absorbing her words in the context of her appearance, clothing, haircut, and mannerisms. And the press—friend and foe alike—refracted her words through their own version of that lens as well. Thus, the public discourse about her lectures commonly devolved into debates predicated on gender distinctiveness, even while Dickinson asserted no such claim to a particular woman's voice.

Following the war Dickinson became one of the nation's most active, and best paid, lyceum speakers. When the support for the lyceum circuit waned, she turned to the theater, as both an actress and playwright. She also published three books, including a controversial novel about miscegenation.[58] In 1872 Dickinson returned to the political arena to campaign for Horace Greeley and the Liberal Republicans. Sixteen years later she made a brief, ill-fated, venture back into the political arena as a Republican stump speaker. In 1891 her sister, Susan, had Anna committed to an asylum for the insane. Dickinson eventually won her freedom and then sued those responsible for her incarceration—and the newspapers that had reported her insanity—in a series of celebrated legal battles, before retiring to obscurity in upstate New York.

Although she remained in the public eye for nearly three decades after the war, Dickinson's reduced political voice supports Morton Keller's argument that there was a conservative process of postwar retrenchment: Public activity that was accepted in 1864 was no longer as permissible in peacetime, leading Dickinson to turn to the popular lyceum circuit. But Dickinson's brief return to the stump during the unusual election of 1872 does suggest a postwar political world in flux. Once again political crisis opened the door for an expanded role for women. With the Republicans divided, and the notorious Victoria Woodhull throwing her own hat in the ring, the Greeley and Grant forces competed mightily for Dickinson's support. But this time Dickinson was hardly alone as a partisan public woman. Grant, ostensibly an advocate of women's suffrage, lined up an impressive list of female orators and public figures on his side, while Greeley only succeeded in garnering the support of his old friend and ally Anna Dickinson.

The contrast between the campaigns of 1864 and 1872 was striking. Although women were still disenfranchised and would remain so for another half century, in this election both major parties were anxious to trumpet endorsements from the nation's leading public women. Between Woodhull's flamboyant campaign and Susan B. Anthony's arrest and trial for voting in the presidential election, 1872 is recognized as an important benchmark in the history of women in public.[59] But too often forgotten is the role that Anna Dickinson played two elections earlier when she campaigned for Lincoln and other Republican candidates while most of her peers in the woman's rights movement remained on the sidelines or behind the scenes.[60] Dickinson's unpopular decision to support Greeley, who died shortly after losing the election, cost her quite a bit in political friendships, in future lecture fees, and perhaps in her place in historic memory. But one wonders how much her bold political speech during the Civil War paved the way for the modest gains of the next decades.[61]

# NOTES

1. This essay is part of an ongoing biographical study of the life of Anna Dickinson. The only published biography of Dickinson is Giraud Chester, *Embattled Maiden: The Life of Anna Dickinson* (New York: Putnam, 1951). James Harvey Young, who also wrote a dissertation on Dickinson's wartime career, authored a biography that has never been published. I am indebted to Dr. Young for permission to inspect both this manuscript ("Anna Elizabeth Dickinson") and his extensive research notes in the James Harvey Young Papers, Special Collections, Emory University, Atlanta, Georgia (hereafter JHY Papers). For brief treatments of Dickinson's war years see Elizabeth Cady Stanton et al., eds., *History of Woman Suffrage*, 3 vols. (1881; New York: Arno Press, 1969), 2:40–50; Young, "Anna Elizabeth Dickinson and the Civil War: For and Against Lincoln," *Mississippi Valley Historical Review* 31 (June 1944): 59–80; and Wendy Hamand Venet, *Neither Ballots nor Bullets: Women Abolitionists and the Civil War* (Charlottesville: University Press of Virginia, 1991), 37–56 and passim. For my own overview of "Anna E. Dickinson's Civil War," see Steven E. Woodworth, ed., *The Human Tradition in the Civil War and Reconstruction* (Wilmington, Del.: SR Books, 2000), 93–110. For Dickinson's personal responses to her wartime career, see J. Matthew Gallman, "An Inspiration to Work: Anna Elizabeth Dickinson, Public Orator," in *The War Was You and Me: Civilians in the American Civil War*, ed. Joan E. Cashin (Princeton, N.J.: Princeton University Press, 2002).

2. *Chicago Tribune*, November 18, 1863, Dickinson Scrapbook, art. 125, Anna Elizabeth Dickinson Papers, microfilm reel 25, Library of Congress, Washington, D.C. Hereafter, Dickinson Scrapbook.

3. The literature on women in public is vast. See Mary P. Ryan, *Women in Public: Between Banners and Ballots, 1825–1880* (Baltimore: Johns Hopkins University Press, 1990); Lori Ginzberg, *Women and the Work of Benevolence: Morality, Politics, and Class in the Nineteenth-Century United States* (New Haven, Conn.: Yale University Press, 1990); Glenna Matthews, *The Rise of Public Woman: Woman's Power and Woman's Place in the United States, 1630–1970* (New York: Oxford University Press, 1992); Mary Ryan, "Gender and Public Access: Women's Politics in Nineteenth-Century America," in *Habermas and the Public Sphere*, ed. Craig Calhoun (Cambridge: Harvard University Press, 1992), 259–88 and note 4.

4. For an excellent overview of the discussion, see Linda K. Kerber, "Separate Spheres, Female Worlds, Woman's Place: The Rhetoric of Women's History," *Journal of American History* (June 1988): 9–39.

5. There are scattered examples of women giving political speeches during the 1850s and into the war years. Elizabeth Varon has uncovered cases of Whigs inviting women to speak before mixed audience in antebellum Virginia. Abolitionist Clarina Nichols spoke for Kansas Republicans in 1856. As Dickinson's wartime popularity grew, Democrats periodically countered with female orators to support their own candidates. Nevertheless, no wartime (or antebellum) woman approached Dickinson's fame as a political orator. Elizabeth R. Varon, "Tippecanoe and the Ladies, Too: White Women and Party Politics in Antebellum Virginia," *Journal of American History* 82 (1995): 494–521; Varon, *We Mean to Be Counted: White Women and Politics in Antebellum Virginia* (Chapel Hill: University of North Carolina Press, 1998); Robert J. Dinkin, *Before Equal Suffrage: Women in Partisan Politics from Colonial Times to 1920* (Westport, Conn.: Greenwood Press, 1995); Rebecca Edwards, *Angels in the Machinery: Gender in American Party Politics from the Civil War to the Progressive Era* (New York: Oxford University Press, 1997). See also Janet L. Coryell, "Superseding Gender: The Role of the Woman Politico in Antebellum Partisan Politics," in *Women and the Unstable State in Nineteenth-Century America*, ed. Alison M. Parker and Stephanie Cole (College Station: Texas A&M Press, 2000), 84–112.

6. Frank Moore, *Women of the War; Their Heroism and Self-Sacrifice* (Hartford, Conn.: S. S. Scranton, 1866); Linus Pierpoint Brockett and Mary C. Vaughan, *Woman's Work in the Civil War: A Record of Heroism, Patriotism and Patience* (Boston: R. H. Curran, 1867).

7. For a recent summary of this scholarship, see Drew Gilpin Faust, "'Ours as Well as That of the Men': Women and Gender in the Civil War," in *Writing the Civil War: The Quest to Understand,* ed. James M. McPherson and William J. Cooper Jr. (Columbia: University of South Carolina Press, 1998), 228–40. A few important books have appeared since that essay was published: Jeanie Attie, *Patriotic Toil: Northern Women and the American Civil War* (Ithaca, N.Y.: Cornell University Press, 1998); Elizabeth D. Leonard, *All the Daring of the Soldier: Women of the Civil War Armies* (New York: W.W. Norton, 1999); Judith Ann Giesberg, *Civil War Sisterhood: The U.S. Sanitary Commission and Women's Politics in Transition* (Boston: Northeastern University Press, 2000).

8. See Venet, *Neither Ballots nor Bullets;* Attie, *Patriotic Toil;* Giesberg, *Civil War Sisterhood.*

9. Attie, *Patriotic Toil,* 25.

10. Morton Keller, *Affairs of State: Public Life in Late Nineteenth Century America* (Cambridge: Harvard University Press, 1977).

11. *Springfield Republican,* June ?, 1863, Dickinson Scrapbook, art. 79.

12. Unknown newspaper, n.d. [October 1860?], Dickinson Scrapbook, art. 19. Of course, contemporary accounts of male orators also reported on their appearance and physical bearing.

13. *United States Gazette?* [handwritten notation], n.d. [roughly March 26, 1862], Dickinson Scrapbook, art. 11.

14. *Press,* March 26, 1862, Dickinson Scrapbook, art. 10; *New York Herald,* n.d., quoted in *National Anti-Slavery Standard,* April 25, 1863; *Chicago Tribune,* November 5, 1863.

15. *Providence Press,* [April 1862], reprinted in unknown newspaper, n.d., Dickinson Scrapbook, art. 20.

16. Unknown newspaper, December 15, 1862, Dickinson Scrapbook, art. 98.

17. *Independent,* [April 1863], reprinted in unknown newspaper, n.d., Dickinson Scrapbook, art. 76

18. *Cincinnati Gazette?* June 22, 1863, Dickinson Scrapbook, art. 92. The newspaper is unlabeled but the story is identified as from a correspondent to the *Gazette.* The story is signed by "Agate," a name used by Reid. A letter from Judge William D. Kelley to Dickinson confirms that this letter was written by Reid. Kelley to AED, August 20, 1863, container 9, Dickinson Papers.

19. *Republican,* April 23, 1863, Dickinson Scrapbook, art. 84.

20. Unknown Philadelphia newspaper [May 1863], Dickinson Scrapbook, art. 116.

21. Unknown San Francisco newspaper [October 1864?], Dickinson Scrapbook, art. 154–55.

22. "Correspondent to the *Philadelphia Press,*" reprinted in several unknown papers, October 29, 1864, Dickinson Scrapbook, arts. 87, 163, 168.

23. *National Eagle,* March 10, 1863, Dickinson Scrapbook, art. 29.

24. *Greenfield Gazette?* January 4, 1864, Dickinson Scrapbook, art. 157.

25. *Luzerne Union,* n.d. [October 3, 1863?], Dickinson Scrapbook, art. 148.

26. *Rochester Evening Express,* March 15, 1864, Dickinson Scrapbook, art. 210.

27. *[Portland, Maine?] Transcript,* February 18, 1865, Dickinson Scrapbook, art. 227.

28. *Hartford Daily Post,* March 24, 1863; *Hartford Courant,* March 25,1863.

29. *Republican,* April 23, 1863, Dickinson Scrapbook, art. 84.

30. *Chicago Tribune,* November 11, 1863.

31. Unknown San Francisco newspaper, [October 1864?], Dickinson Scrapbook, art. 154–55.

32. See *Springfield Republican,* April 22, 1863, Dickinson Scrapbook, art. 76; "Correspondent to the *Missouri Democrat,*" January 18, 1864, Dickinson Scrapbook, art. 166.

33. Unknown newspaper [late 1862], Dickinson Scrapbook, art. 8. For similar sentiments, see *Luzerne Union,* n.d. [October 3, 1863?], Dickinson Scrapbook, art. 148.

34. Unknown newspaper ["for the *West Jersey Pioneer"*], n.d. [March 1862], Dickinson Scrapbook, art. 23.

35. See unknown Hartford newspaper, n.d., Dickinson Scrapbook, art. 43.

36. *Hartford Times,* April 6, 1863, and unknown newspaper [April 1863], Dickinson Scrapbook, art. 111. Both reprinted an undated article from *the Journal of Commerce.*

37. *New York Herald,* n.d. [May 1863], Dickinson Scrapbook, art. 100b.

38. *New York Herald,* February 15, 1865, Dickinson Scrapbook, art. 255.

39. *Hartford Times,* March 30, 1863.

40. *World,* May 4, 1863. See also *New York Express,* n.d. [May 8, 1863?], Dickinson Scrapbook, art. 101.

41. *West Jersey Pioneer?* n.d. [March 1862?], Dickinson Scrapbook, art. 23.

42. *Journal of Commerce,* reprinted in *Hartford Times,* April 6, 1863.

43. Unknown newspaper quoting "from the *New York Evangelist,"* n.d. [April 1863], Dickinson Scrapbook, art. 164b.

44. Henry Ward Beecher was a celebrated minister and abolitionist; "Senator Morgan" presumably refers to Senator Edwin Dennison Morgan of New York.

45. *World,* n.d. [April 1863], reprinted in unknown newspaper, n.d. [April 1863], Dickinson Scrapbook, art. 72–73.

46. *Philadelphia Press,* April 18, 1863, Dickinson Scrapbook, art. 83.

47. *Hartford Courant,* March 25, 1863.

48, Unknown newspaper, n.d. [November 1863], Dickinson Scrapbook, art. 124. This art. includes a lengthy excerpt from the *Press* which included quotations from the *Argus.*

49. *[Rochester?] Courier and Union,* November 18, 1863, Dickinson Scrapbook, art. 161–62.

50. Unknown newspaper quoting both the *World* and the *Union,* Dickinson Scrapbook, art. 168. The author was referring to General Benjamin Butler's infamous Order Number 28 which he issued while in command of occupied New Orleans. The order threatened to treat the ladies of New Orleans like "women of the streets" if they persisted in insulting the Union soldiers. This comment is particularly interesting given that the women of New Orleans had prompted General Butler's ire by their actions within the public arena. See Ryan, *Women in Public,* 143–45.

51. *Geneva (N.Y.) Gazette* [March 1864?], reprinted in *National Anti-Slavery Gazette,* April 2, 1864.

52. *New York Daily News,* February 20, 1865, Dickinson Scrapbook, art. 256.

53. *Providence Daily Post,* March 16, 1865, Dickinson Scrapbook, art. 245.

54. *Lawrence Sentinel,* April 1, 1865, Dickinson Scrapbook, art. 249; *Lawrence American,* April 1, 1865, Dickinson Scrapbook, art. 389.

55. For some thoughts on the other side of the equation, on how Dickinson navigated the war years herself, see Gallman, "An Inspiration to Work."

56. Ibid.

57. My argument here is not that Dickinson was somehow unaware that her audiences saw her as a woman and therefore distinctive, but that she asserted her right to speak on the implicit grounds of gender equality and not gender distinctiveness. For early analyses of the links between an ideology of domesticity and various aspects of public activism, see Cott, *Bonds of Womanhood;* Kathryn Kish Sklar, *Catherine Beecher: A Study in American Domesticity* (New York: Norton, 1976); and Nancy A. Hewitt, *Women's Activism and Social Change: Rochester, New York, 1822–1872* (Ithaca, N.Y.: Cornell University Press, 1984). In her study of nine women authors, Lyde Cullen Sizer examines how these writers used their prose to engage in political discourse, often from a standpoint of gender difference. *The Political Work of Northern Women Writers and the Civil War, 1850–1872* (Chapel Hill: University of North Carolina Press, 2000).

58. *What Answer?* (1868; Amherst, N.Y.: Humanity Books, 2003); *A Paying Investment* (Boston:

R. Osgood, 1876); *A Ragged Register: Of People, Places and Opinions* (1879; Estes Park, Colo.: Temporal Mechanical Press, 2000).

59. See Kathleen Barry, *Susan B. Anthony: A Biography of a Singular Feminist* (New York: New York University Press, 1988), 249–74; Barbara Goldsmith, *Other Powers: The Age of Suffrage, Spiritualism, and the Scandalous Victoria Woodhull* (New York: A. A. Knopf, 1998).

60. Melanie Susan Gustafson, *Women and the Republican Party, 1854–1924* (Urbana: University of Illinois Press, 2001). This is not to say that women were silent or entirely ignored during the election of 1864. For evidence to the contrary, see Faye Dudden, "New York Strategy: The New York Women's Movement and the Civil War," in *Votes for Women: The Struggle for Suffrage Revisited,* ed. Jean H. Baker (New York: Oxford University Press, 2002), 68–72.

61. For an analysis of the 1872 campaign, and particularly of Dickinson's efforts to recast public memories of the war, see J. Matthew Gallman, "Anna Dickinson and the Election of 1872," in *The Memory of the Civil War in American Culture,* ed. Alice Fahs and Joan Waugh (Chapel Hill: University of North Carolina Press, 2003); Dinkin, *Before Equal Suffrage, 67–70.*

# "Touched with Fire?"

## Two Philadelphia Novelists Remember the Civil War

For years Marquette University has hosted an annual lecture on the Civil War era in honor of famed historian Frank L. Klement. When Jim Marten invited me to give the 2002 lecture, I took the opportunity to explore some themes from both my past and my ongoing scholarship, while experimenting with some approaches that I hope to wrestle with in the years to come.

This essay revisits my earlier interest in the impact of the Civil War on Northern society, but this time I approached the question through the eyes of two Philadelphia novelists. In 1868 Anna Dickinson published *What Answer?* a novel set in New York during the war. Seventeen years later, Philadelphia doctor Silas Weir Mitchell wrote *In War Time,* a romance set in and around a military hospital in wartime Philadelphia. I had long thought that these were particularly intriguing volumes. Both Dickinson and Mitchell had risen to prominence in other fields, yet both wrote novels about the wartime North. In this lecture, I tried to sort through how these two Philadelphians had chosen to portray the impact of the war on Northern society.

I enjoyed my excursion into Civil War literature and memory, and I especially enjoyed my visit to Marquette with Jim Marten. In 2008, Kent State University Press published a selection of the Klement essays, edited by Jim Marten and his colleague A. Kristen Foster. The collected essays nicely map out the diversity of scholarly approaches to the Civil War era.

. . .

## Introduction: Oliver Wendell Holmes Jr.
### Recalls the Civil War

"Through our great good fortune, in our youth our hearts were touched with fire." Oliver Wendell Homes Jr. made this bold declaration on Memorial Day 1884 at a gathering of the Grand Army of the Republic. Before this audience of fellow veterans, Holmes recalled fallen comrades and declared that "the generation that carried on the war has been set apart by its experience." The following Memorial Day the famed jurist took up similar themes when he spoke before Harvard University's graduating class. But to the civilian audience Holmes's 1885 address had a bit more bite. Not only had the war made his generation better men for having endured the traumas of combat, but twenty years of peace had produced a nation that failed to recognize the value of true heroism and sacrifice. Captains of industry and selfish business tycoons had replaced true heroes in the nation's affections now that war was "out of fashion." And the nation was worse for it. Perhaps to startle his young listeners out of their complacency, the orator declared that "I rejoice at every dangerous sport that I see pursued" including fencing and polo. "If once in a while in our rough riding a neck is broken, I regard it, not as a waste, but as a price well paid for the breeding of a race fit for headship and command."[1]

For the historian, such words invite various interpretations. It is at once a strong statement about postwar politics and power and clear evidence of how participants remembered the war a generation after Appomattox. I find the latter theme particularly compelling in light of recent scholarship examining how postwar Americans constructed a usable memory of the Civil War, sometimes at the expense of the conflict's true dimensions and meaning. That rich scholarship has followed various paths. In his award-winning book *Race and Reunion*, David Blight explored how the forces of postwar regional reconciliation often constructed a narrative that muted the significance of racial tension in the sectional conflict. Other scholars have examined the emergence of the myth of the "Lost Cause" in southern historiography. Still others have asked how veterans' organizations, battlefield commemorations, and monument building both reflected and shaped our national memory.[2]

Holmes and a generation of veterans were intent on reminding Americans of the patriotic sacrifices they made on the battlefield, while often stressing that heroism—and even patriotism—knew no particular uniform or ideology. But in addition to celebrating heroic memory and attacking contemporary sloth, Holmes was saying something very important about change, and how change happens. Civil War soldiers were "touched with fire," and in the furnace of warfare new, stronger characters were forged. This is certainly not a unique observation. Many an author has explained—and often celebrated—the ways in which military experiences transform boys into men.[3] As an historian who has spent much of his career considering the northern home front, I have asked similar questions of different Civil War participants and come to quite different conclusions. I have argued that the crisis of war did not really transform the North, so much as the North "adjusted" to the conflict's substantial challenges within the context of long-established experiences and practices.[4] In a sense these findings confirm Holmes's point. The Civil War soldier had the "great good fortune" to be "touched with fire," whereas those who stayed behind—like the men of the postwar generation—were robbed of the war's true transformative effects.

Still, I have always been a bit dissatisfied with these findings, at least insofar as they are applied to individuals on the home front. After all, my previous work emphasized how individuals and institutions *behaved* during the war years, but I readily acknowledged that my research was not likely to uncover the sort of character developments on the home front that Holmes celebrated in his various addresses. That is partially because behavior and character are not the same, and it is not always possible to glean the latter by observing the former. Moreover, there is an important reflective component in the postwar declaration. True, the passage of time distorts memories of the past and historical actors are prone to construct their memories to serve their present. However, we do not always fully comprehend important changes as we experience them, and thus the diarist or correspondent might not fully grasp—or record—her own personal transformations as they are occurring.

With that in mind, I approached the scene of my earlier scholarship—the northern urban home front, and particularly the City of Brotherly Love—from a new perspective. Rather than asking how those noncombatant participants experienced the war, I wish to explore how they made sense of the experience after the fact. Thus, I am paying my only modest homage to the burgeoning field of Civil War memory. But I remain interested in this notion of the war as an instrument of change. How did Philadelphians who participated on the home front recall the war years? Did they claim to have survived their own fiery furnaces, leaving them with stronger characters and souls? Even if I, as a modern historian, waded through their diaries, letters, newspapers, and annual reports and found strong continuities with an antebellum past, what about those people who actually worked in those military hospitals, received those letters, attended those parades, and woke up one day to black-bordered newspaper reports of a president's assassination? How much did they later feel that the war had left them permanently altered?

Like so many interesting historical questions, this one is hard to answer. One strategy would be to consider the postwar memoir. As the nineteenth century came to a close, hundreds—perhaps thousands—of military veterans published their recollections, providing valuable, albeit deeply biased, sources for the military historian. Perhaps partially in response to this flood of military recollection, quite a few veterans of wartime activism and voluntarism told their own tales.[5] But these texts generally have other goals in mind, and they do not strike me as the best place to look for reflections on the war's role in personal character transformation. Instead, I have decided to turn to postwar fiction for some tentative answers.

I am drawn to fiction for various reasons. First, the scholarship on Civil War–era popular literature—like the recent work on memory—is a particularly exciting field these days, so this lecture becomes sort of a double scholarly homage, honoring both historiographic trends.[6] Moreover, if I am interested in how postwar Americans *understood* the war's transformative effects, I am on perfectly sturdy ground working with novels, which offer a window into how the author remembered—or wished to remember—the war years. The novelist (or at least these nineteenth-century novelists) generally creates characters who then navigate various events and circumstances. With the Civil War providing the factual backdrop, the opportunities for dramatic character development are almost irresistible. Or so we might assume.

I wish today to focus on two postwar novels: Anna Elizabeth Dickinson's *What Answer?* which was published in 1868, and Silas Weir Mitchell's *In War Time,* which appeared in book form in 1884, the same year that Holmes delivered his Memorial Day address.[7] Both Dickinson and Mitchell were Philadelphians. The former was born in 1842, the latter in 1829. Dickinson had been a celebrated orator during the war, speaking out for abolitionism and women's rights but earning particular fame as a charismatic and biting Republican stump speaker. In January 1864, while still only twenty-one, Dickinson spoke in the halls of the House of Representatives before an illustrious audience that included President and Mrs. Lincoln and most of the party's congressmen and senators. At the time she was one of the nation's most famous women. *What Answer?* written three years after the war, was Dickinson's first book and only novel.[8] *In War Time* was also Mitchell's first novel. A well-known neurologist, Dr. Mitchell worked as a contract physician in one of Philadelphia's military hospitals during the war and also played a substantial role in the local branch of the Sanitary Commission. In later life he managed to maintain a highly successful dual career, publishing numerous novels and several highly respected medical tracts. His fame was so great that in the late 1880s the economist and author Charlotte Perkins Gilman went to see Mitchell about her growing depression. Mitchell's draconian "rest cure," and Gilman's disgust with that treatment, became the centerpiece of her famous book *The Yellow Wallpaper.*[9]

*In War Time* and *What Answer?* are certainly very different sorts of books, but they are knit together by several common traits beyond the crucial fact that both take place in the North during the Civil War. Both books are the first novels of authors who had achieved substantial professional success in another arena and who lived in Philadelphia during the war years. That shared Philadelphia background is potentially significant. Unlike many Confederate cities, the City of Brotherly Love never faced an invading army, and its citizens did not endure terrible economic hardships. But Philadelphia was close enough to the seat of war that Union soldiers were a familiar sight on its streets, and after each major eastern battle the city's hospitals filled with wounded.[10]

The plots also share common traits. Each story is set in the urban Northeast, specifically in New York and in the Philadelphia area. Both are packed with characters and subplots, but each has a central love story at its core. And in each love story the lovers transgress conventional lines: *In War Time* pairs a southern woman and a northern man, and *What Answer?*—more dramatically—features the love between a white man and a black woman. Although neither book is a superb piece of writing (I am personally most partial to *What Answer?*), each provided the author with a forum for recalling what it was like to live in the Northeast during the Civil War, and each book suggests some set of answers to my central concerns about the importance of the war in transforming individuals on the home front.

How might the historian evaluate these home front novels? Dickinson and Mitchell were both enthusiastic readers, but not professional writers. I would argue that it was quite natural for them to set their first literary efforts during the tumultuous war years. After all, the scenes and events of the war provided an ideal—and familiar—narrative backdrop for an inexperienced novelist, while also suggesting all sorts of possibilities for excitement, tragedy, heroism, and of course character development. The question then is: how did each novelist choose to use the war in shaping his or her plot? Did the Civil War *change* the men and women in the novel, or did it really only provide a context for the story? What sorts of home front scenes did the author elect to portray? Are the main characters regularly engaged in supporting the war effort? In discussing military and political events? Or do they live in a calm and peaceful world largely insulated from the battlefield's tumult?

Of course the point is not to apply a particular analytic template to each book. I have no checklist of anticipated traits that one might expect from a Civil War novel. But by setting their books in the Civil War home front, Weir Mitchell and Anna Dickinson gave themselves the opportunity to present a version of the war years as they understood them, stressing what they wished, omitting what they chose. Let us consider the two books separately, starting with S. Weir Mitchell's *In War Time*.

## In War Time

*In War Time* opens in July of 1863, just days after the Battle of Gettysburg. Some of the wounded who are strong enough to be transported have been taken to the bustling military hospital at Filbert Street in Philadelphia. It is, Mitchell explains in the novel's first paragraph, one of those scenes that "has been lost, in the healing changes with which civilizing progress, no less quickly than forgiving nature, is apt to cover the traces of war."[11] With these words Mitchell promises a recovered wartime memory, but perhaps without the hint of bitterness that surrounded Holmes's address.

Right away we meet four of the novel's central characters. Dr. Ezra Wendell and his sister Ann are transplanted New Englanders from Cape Cod. Ann is an earnest, slightly stiff Yankee who is utterly devoted to her brother's happiness and comfort. Ezra is a contract surgeon, working in the hospital while also maintaining a small private practice. Later we will learn that Dr. Wendell had had a brief stint in the military that ended abruptly by mutual consent. Much later still, we discover that he had been dismissed for cowardice after abandoning two fellow doctors and a group of wounded men in the face of the enemy. But for the moment all we know is that the young doctor is kind and competent but also rather weak and self-absorbed and distinctly not military in his bearing. His flaws are illustrated on that very first day, when a patient under his care dies and Dr. Wendell suspects that his poor advice was partially to blame. This realization leaves him remorseful, but also annoyed and distracted. On his journey home he loses himself in a soothing smoke, but his reverie is broken when he drops his favorite pipe, which shatters on the ground. For a moment Wendell stares in horror as if he had lost a good friend. To his credit, the young doctor recoils in horror when he recognizes that he is mourning his broken meerschaum every bit as much as the deceased patient.

At this stage the cynical reader—particularly one who is familiar with the sentimental popular fiction of the nineteenth century—would be forgiven for sighing out loud. Here we have a character who is torn between his weaker nature and his better self, with two years of warfare and roughly 400 pages to come to a happy resolution. Moreover, the character is clearly the author's alter ego: a contract surgeon in a military hospital. The only dramatic tension, it would seem, concerns exactly what crisis will Dr. Mitchell construct to lead Dr. Wendell to become a better, more courageous, and less self-absorbed man. But as the book unfolds, we will discover such cynicism is unfounded.

The other two crucial characters who appear in that first chapter are among the hospital's many patients. Both Major Morton, a distinguished man from nearby Germantown, and Captain Gray, a Confederate officer from South Carolina, were wounded on the third day at Gettysburg near the famed copse of trees. In fact, Captain Gray eventually comes to suspect that he was wounded by Major Morton's own pistol. The two old soldiers swiftly bond, in a symbolic display of sectional reconciliation. As the captain's health declines, he sends for his fifteen-year-old daughter, Hester, who has been in school in New Jersey since her mother passed away four years earlier. The captain dies soon after Hester's arrival, but not before securing a promise from Mrs. Morton that she would protect his daughter's well-being.

The scene then shifts to Germantown, a manufacturing village north of downtown Philadelphia. The slowly recuperating Major Morton (who has been promoted to colonel) has enlisted Dr. Wendell as his private physician, necessitating almost daily visits. Meanwhile, the Wendells have agreed to take in Hester Gray as their ward, assisted by a $10,000 trust fund sent to her by a distant cousin from the South. Three more important characters enter the mix. Alice Westerly is a lively, quick-witted widow who immediately takes an interest in Dr. Wendell. The Mortons have two sons, both of whom find Hester particularly fascinating. Arty, the youngest, is nearly eighteen and itching to follow his father into military service. Ned, the eldest, is an athletic outdoorsman by nature, but a fall from a horse has left him with a mysterious debilitating illness that is slowly robbing him of his ability to walk and will probably kill him before long.

The central love story proceeds roughly as one might expect. Hester is sent off to school and returns transformed, both mentally and physically, into a terribly attractive young woman. (Mitchell comments on this maturation so often and so effusively that the reader almost blushes for Hester.) Arty goes to Europe with his parents, leaving Ned behind to be treated by Dr. Wendell and bond with the lovely Hester. When Arty returns he promptly enlists and soon joins the siege around Petersburg. While his brother is away, Ned comes to realize that it is not his lot in life to win the love of the fair Hester, and so he does his best to suffer in silence. As he grows progressively frail, Ned exhibits more "womanly" virtues (thus Mitchell exhibits the sort of gender assumptions which would drive Charlotte Perkins Gilman to acts of literary vengeance). Soon the war ends and Arty returns home as an officer, having received a minor wound in his arm but otherwise no worse for wear. Much as Hester had clearly matured, many observers marvel at Arty's physical transformation, repeatedly commenting on how bronzed he has become during his time in uniform.

Soon the young couple acknowledge their love for each other and agree to marry, but of course there are various obstacles to be overcome. Mrs. Morton is not happy that her son wants to marry at such a young age and beneath his social class; Hester's southern uncle appears and resists the idea that his relative should marry a Union soldier; and the ever-conscientious Ann Wendell insists that the couple should be told that Arty's father was perhaps the one who killed Hester's father. But when Colonel Morton telegraphs his consent from Europe (where he has stayed behind, having apparently having taken an Italian mistress) the various barriers dissolve and the couple is eventually united.

Ezra Wendell's romantic life follows a rockier course. Although Dr. Wendell is almost distressingly drawn to long nature walks with his young ward, Hester, he clearly also reciprocates Alice Westerly's more mature and appropriate attractions. The problem for the ever-brooding doctor is that he is mired in financial difficulties and potential embarrassments. When his love of expensive scientific equipment outstripped his meager income, Wendell had dipped into Hester's trust fund, initially rationalizing that he was only spending the profits from wise investments that he had made, and not the principle. But his investments did poorly, and soon he was digging deeper into that fund. These secret developments cause Wendell to question his interest in Alice Westerly: Was he only after her money, he wonders. In the meantime, Alice has secretly learned of Wendell's cowardly military past, but still she resolves to stick with him and help him to a brighter future.

This resolve cannot survive Wendell's final great sin. Here Mitchell turns to a complex, and somewhat murky, plot twist. The sickly Ned, who had already lent his friend Ezra quite a bit of money, agrees to give the doctor an additional $5,000 to cover all his outstanding debts, thus freeing Wendell to marry Alice

Westerly without guilt. But before this money can change hands, Wendell makes a terrible mistake involving two medicine vials. In a characteristically distracted moment, Wendell gives Arty the wrong vial to administer to his brother, and as a result Ned receives a poisonous dose of "tincture of aconite," killing him almost instantly. A distraught Arty assumes that he had made the error, but Dr. Wendell—quickly recognizing his own mistake—assures everyone that Arty had administered the correct medication and that Ned had merely died of his illness. Mrs. Morton and Alice both assume that Dr. Wendell is graciously protecting the young boy, even at the expense of his professional oath, when in fact he is lying to cover up his own error while also allowing his intended bride to believe him something of a hero.

Before he died, Ned had told his mother of his intended gift to Dr. Wendell, and she honored her son's last wishes by sending Ezra a check for $5,000. Alice is sure that the doctor will decline the gift under the circumstances, since it would appear to be a payment for protecting Arty. When Ezra accepts the money, an astonished Alice refuses to marry him, explaining that she could never wed a man she did not respect. At this point the morally obtuse doctor reveals that he was really responsible for Ned's death, and insisted that he had kept it a secret for fear of losing her. Needless to say, this news is the final straw for poor Alice Westerly. She immediately flees to Europe and is not heard from again. Ezra and Ann Wendell return to New England, but not before collecting an additional $10,000 from Ned's will, which of course makes Ezra feel even more guilty. The story ends with a brief epilogue. A year or so after these events Ann Wendell sends Mrs. Morton a note explaining the true circumstances of Ned's death and returning the $10,000. Her brother, she explains, was thoroughly broken in health and spirit.

*In War Time* is in many senses a typical popular novel for its day, and certainly not a bad effort for a first-time author.[12] How did S. Weir Mitchell incorporate the Civil War into this tale that he consciously set "in war time"? The war is certainly present in all sorts of ways: the main characters initially meet at a military hospital; both Arty and Hester are the children of soldiers, and Arty himself goes off to war; a few other minor characters are soldiers; all the women volunteer at the local branch of the Sanitary Commission and various scenes occur in those offices. But although the war is present throughout the narrative, it is hardly a powerful agent for change.

Consider the experiences of Dr. Ezra Wendell, the novel's central character. Here we have a man who experienced the war both as an army doctor in the field and as a contract surgeon in a military hospital. Yet the character flaws that failed him months before the novel opened and continued to mar his behavior in the book's first scenes, remained essentially unchanged two years later. He was, to the bitter end, weak, self-absorbed, and fundamentally clueless about what it meant to behave honorably. Although he witnessed the impact of war around him, Ezra Wendell, unlike Oliver Wendell Holmes, seems never to have been properly touched with fire.

What of Arty Morton, who proudly served his country for the final year and a half of war before returning home to marry his sweetheart? Arty certainly saw combat, he even took a bullet in the arm and was nearly captured by Rebel troops. But he never said anything, either in person or in his letters from camp, to indicate that the profound experiences of warfare had left him a different man. Instead, Arty came home somewhat older and nicely tanned but fundamentally unmarked by the experience. In one particularly revealing letter, Arty acknowledged that he did not really enjoy combat but he did find "something of a wild joy about" the "mad rushes at death" he had survived.[13] It was Ned, Arty insisted, who really belonged in uniform, demonstrating his valor and patriotism and athleticism. Of course elder brother Ned, despite his love of the active life, had been robbed of his chance to serve by an injury totally unrelated to the war. How ironic that fate would have treated him so. Under other circumstances Ned would have followed his father into military service and—so we are led to believe—might well have won the hand of the lovely Hester.

It is certainly significant that S. Weir Mitchell constructed his plot this way. Ned is the only character who truly evolves in the course of the war, and those changes are not driven by the war itself. As his body declines, he becomes increasingly sensitive to the needs of those around him while growing reconciled to his own sad fate. The younger Hester and Arty certainly mature over the two years, but their evolutions seem to owe less to the traumas of the war and more to natural biological processes. How different *In War Time* would have been had Ned's decline and death been caused by a wound or injury suffered while in uniform, thus meaning that the Civil War was the root cause of the novel's great tragedy. And Mitchell could have created all sorts of plot devices so that the two lovers somehow matured because of the war. Hester might have volunteered in the hospital and come away from the experience transformed; Arty could have left for war as a frivolous young man who came home with newfound wisdom born of heroism. But the author declined all opportunities to cast the conflict as a force for good or ill.

## WHAT ANSWER?

Anna Dickinson's *What Answer?* had its own ironies and ambiguities, but there is no doubting that the novel's central tragedy was caused by the Civil War, and it is equally clear that the nation's great conflict had unleashed enormous potential for future change. Contemporary reviewers praised the novel for its powerful scenes drawn directly from the war's history and for the courage of the central love story, but some critiqued Dickinson for her overly complex narrative with its multitude of characters and occasionally awkward plot devices. My summary will try to shave off a few of those rough edges, sacrificing some of the intricacies along the way.

The novel opens in New York City in the fall of 1860, as a handsome young man gazes out a window onto a bustling 5th Avenue. The young man is Willie Surrey, the bright, charming, privileged son of a wealthy foundry owner. As he watches the crowd below, Willie catches a glimpse of a beautiful woman and is immediately smitten. He will meet her soon enough, but first we meet another key character: Abram Franklin. Abe is a young African American man who works as a clerk for Willie's father. Lame from birth, Abe must limp the long walk home each day because the city streetcars are segregated. Much worse, the predominantly Irish factory workers have come to Mr. Surrey threatening to go out on strike unless he fires their black coworker. Willie and Abe are boyhood friends, and in fact Willie had helped Abe get his first position in the foundry. Now, however, our hero is powerless to stop the racist tide and can only do his best to find Abe another position.

The following day, Willie, still stewing over racial injustice, attends a school recital with his best friend, Tom Russell. There he witnesses the woman from 5th Avenue—Miss Francesca Ercildoune—read an impassioned poem attacking slavery. The two quickly begin a courtship and are clearly on their way to falling in love, until Willie tells her the tale of Abe's firing (while foolishly omitting the fact that he had found his friend another appointment). Francesca disappears without explanation, leaving Willie distraught and confused. As luck would have it, at this moment national events intercede as New York becomes overwhelmed with war fever following the firing on Fort Sumter. Willie enlists in the 7th New York Volunteers and leaves for the seat of war without hearing from his beloved Francesca.

Slowly the reader learns Francesca's secret. Although she looks white, and attends a prestigious New York school alongside young white women, Francesca's father is half black, the son of a Virginia slaveholder and an enslaved woman.[14] At a young age her father had been sent to England, where he had married Francesca's mother, an English woman who was long since deceased. Mr. Ercildoune had eventually brought his family home to the United States, intent on joining the battle against slavery, and quickly discovered that northern society was also thick with prejudice and injustice. Francesca now lives in Philadelphia with her father and her brother, Robert, both of whom are much darker skinned. Dedicated to racial justice, and disgusted by the fact that her fair skin enables her to move freely in white society, Francesca has mistakenly concluded that Willie is in his marrow no different from the rest.

For two years the couple is apart. Willie's letters to Francesca are returned unopened. Meanwhile, Dickinson packs the narrative with smaller episodes, several of which demonstrate Willie's true commitment to racial justice. At Chancellorsville in 1863, Willie loses his arm and is sent home on furlough. While riding a Philadelphia streetcar he witnesses an ugly row over efforts to force a one-legged black soldier off the segregated car. Willie intercedes on the soldier's behalf just as we discover that Francesca is also a passenger on the car. Francesca is impressed and agrees to let Willie call on her, and it is just a matter of time before their various misunderstandings are resolved and the two are once again deeply in love. As in *In War Time,* the real challenge is to win the support of family and friends. Francesca's brother and father are initially skeptical but soon accept that Willie's intentions are honorable and that he fully realizes the rocky road ahead. Willie's family and friends are less understanding. Although they had earlier embraced Francesca, when the Surreys learn her true racial identity and the couple's plans to marry, the family summarily disinherits the young war hero and heir. The two lovers marry and move into a home along the Hudson River, largely isolated from white society.

Their bliss does not last long. Now firmly committed to racial equality, Willie agrees to go into New York City to help raise a brigade of free blacks. It is now mid-July 1863. In New York some old friends come up to shake Willie's hand, but more refuse to acknowledge him on the streets, illustrating the limits of progress in the wartime North. Willie takes a break from recruiting to go visit his sickly old friend Abe Franklin, who is confined to his bed. While he is visiting the Franklins, the infamous New York City draft riots rip through the city. Dickinson devotes two powerful chapters to the riots, leveling strong criticisms on the predominantly Irish rioters and the city's disloyal local press and politicians. The rioters, targeting African American homes and institutions, break into the Franklins' house, knock Willie out, and drag poor Abe from his bed. Relying heavily on actual events, Dickinson describes Abe's horrible death at the hands of the mob.[15] Unable to spare Abe from torture and execution, Willie does his best to protect Mrs. Franklin and sets off to warn Francesca. But the mob sets upon the young officer, beating him to death. (This, too, was based on actual events that the reader would have recognized.[16]) Francesca learns of the killing and rushes to her dying husband's side, only to be brought down by a stray bullet. In a touch of heavy-handed irony, the two star-crossed lovers die on the street immediately in front of the Surreys' home.

Dickinson juxtaposes this tragedy on the home front with equally powerful, but far more uplifting, events on the battlefield. Only days after the draft riots, the black soldiers of the 54th Massachusetts Volunteers led the charge on Fort Wagner, near Charleston, South Carolina.[17] This charge failed in its military objective, but succeeded in elevating the status of black troops in many white eyes. Once again, Dickinson places her characters within actual events, casting Robert Ercildoune as the brave soldier who picked up the 54th's fallen colors and returned them to safety despite receiving several wounds. The charge earned the applause of white soldiers on the scene and was also the subject of admiring discussion among the men from Willie's old regiment, including Jim Given, the ex-foreman from Mr. Surrey's factory. After the attack, the injured Robert is carried to a hospital ship for the journey home. On board, the other wounded men, both white and black, cheer the hero of Fort Wagner, and Jim Given—who had been wounded in a different engagement—generously gives the black soldier his own lower berth.

Dickinson devotes the novel's final chapters to tying up a wealth of loose ends involving various characters. Jim Givens, the ex-factory foreman and wounded veteran, comes home to marry Sallie, a seamstress who had fallen on hard times and gone to work for the Ercildounes. The wealthy Ercildounes pay for Sallie's dress and even give the couple a small home as a wedding present. Meanwhile, Tom Russell—Willie's oldest friend—returns home from the war having been rescued from Confederate troops with the assistance of two run-away slaves. In the aftermath of the deaths of Francesca and Willie, Tom Russell and Robert Ercildoune come together in their grief and become fast friends, discovering they share the same "gentle blood" and have "tastes and interests in common."[18] The novel closes on Election Day 1865. Tom and Robert ride a carriage to the polling place. Despite Robert's warnings, a naïve Tom believes that his black comrade will be able to exercise the franchise. But when they arrive a mob is there to greet them. "Challenge the vote!" they cry, "No niggers here!" A melancholy Robert turns to Tom and asks, "1860 or 1865?—is the war ended?" This then, is the question that the book's title challenged the reader to answer. Writing three years after the war, and in the midst of debates over the Fifteenth Amendment—legalizing black male suffrage—Dickinson clearly felt that the black vote was an important step toward permanent change.

The characters in *What Answer?* were "touched with fire" both at home and on the battlefield. How were they transformed by these experiences? Clearly Anna Dickinson wrote with a powerful political agenda, challenging her readers to examine the state of race relations in the North. The individuals navigate the war years with racial dilemmas as a constant backdrop. Unlike Mitchell's conflicted Ezra Wendell or morose Ned Morton, Dickinson's main characters generally lack such nuance, leaving her main themes more transparent.

At the outset, the racially mixed Francesca is suspicious of the kindness of whites who do not know her true identity. With time, she comes to believe that in Willie Surrey she has found a man who sees beyond race. Willie's heart is in the right place in the book's initial chapters as he recoils at the unjust treatment of Abe Franklin. But it is not until he returns from war that he becomes a man of action, supporting the wounded black soldier on the streetcar and risking his life for Mrs. Franklin during the draft riots. Of course the solutions here are not so clear as they might seem. The man of action was a martyr to the rioters, and the reader is uncertain how any sort of action could have saved Abe's job in the face of 272 angry white employees. Thus, Dickinson appears to be suggesting on the one hand that Willie became more committed to racial justice through the course of the war, but on the other hand perhaps no individual man's efforts could have saved Abe's job in 1860 or his life in 1863.

If the two main characters were fundamentally good and strong from the beginning of the novel, various other characters illustrate the sort of social transformation that Dickinson envisioned. Jim Givens, Tom Russell, and various other white soldiers witness the heroism of black men—both the soldiers of the 54th Massachusetts and several escaped slaves they encounter in South Carolina—and return from the war with a new respect for African Americans. At home, Sallie bonds with Francesca and becomes a loyal servant, in a fascinating reversal of more familiar class and race relations. And of course the novel ends with a celebration of the close interracial bonds between Tom Russell and Robert Ercildoune.

Other characters who remained at home throughout the war are less transformed by the conflict. Willie's family and friends reject the interracial couple, despite the larger national context of emancipation and social change. The passengers on the streetcar divide over how to treat the crippled black soldier, but before Willie intercedes the emerging consensus seems—tellingly—to lean toward enforcing the segregationist law despite their moral qualms. Most power-fully, the rioters kill Abe, Willie, and Francesca in a rage that Dickinson portrays as explicitly racist. The message is clear. The war unleashed forces that had the potential to transform both soldiers and civilians, but such positive changes were certainly not preordained, and in fact these events had within them the seeds of disaster. The social chasm between the races could be bridged, but only with the sort of close personal contacts that brought blacks and whites together as equals. Such transitions occurred most readily in the heat of battle, but folks at home could—she implied—overcome their prejudices. Still, as of 1868 the chances of such larger transformations remained distinctly problematic.

## Conclusions

Is it possible to squeeze these two home front novels into a single narrative about the Civil War and memory? There are certainly differences to contend with. Anna Dickinson was only twenty-six when she wrote *What Answer?* Sixteen years later Mitchell was in his mid-fifties when he published *In War Time.* Age and gender, as well as year of publication, certainly helped shape these two distinctive tales. Moreover, Dickinson had dedicated her public life to reform, and she intended her first novel to exhort as well as entertain.[19] Only three years after the war, America was struggling with its racial future in the North as well as in the Reconstruction South when she published *What Answer?* Silas Weir Mitchell wrote from a much more centrist position nearly two decades after the war, reflecting both the times and his own politically moderate inclinations.

Therefore, one way to read these two novels is as books with distinctly different agendas, where in each case the goal was to shape memory to suit contemporary needs. Writing in 1868, Dickinson described an imagined recent past in which the Civil War forced white Americans to rethink their racial prejudices. But true to the actual events, Dickinson also portrayed a parallel history in which those northern whites who were furthest from the battlefield and who had the most limited contact with African Americans resisted racial change, sometimes to the point of violence. If *In War Time* had a larger po-litical agenda, it was certainly not about Civil Rights. No African Americans appear in the novel, and the characters barely mention race or emancipation. The only exception is when Hester's cousin Henry describes a long lost—and happily forgotten—relative who had freed his slaves and moved to the North where he had reportedly been involved in recruiting a black regiment. But this intriguing narrative thread is quickly, and perhaps significantly, forgotten.

According to his biographer, Mitchell shifted his allegiances from the Democratic to the Republican Party in the course of the war but was never particularly engaged in partisan politics. As a northerner with southern family ties (his father was a Virginian), Mitchell clearly supported harmonious national reconciliation.[20] From the outset we see Captain Gray and Major Morton as two old soldiers and not as political or ideological adversaries. When Mitchell does address the sectional conflict, the recurring theme is that the crisis was created by politicians and not the men on the battlefield. After Lincoln's assassination, one northerner worries that the action will reflect badly on other southerners, and Colonel Fox, a crusty old Quaker, tells Alice Westerly that he hopes that the politicians will behave as temperately as the soldiers, adding that the most belligerent northerners are the editors and not the military men. Even Hester's cousin's hostility to his niece marrying a Union officer rapidly dissolves once he meets the charming Arty.

The marriage between Arty and Hester clearly symbolizes the prospect of sectional reconciliation, much as the pairing of Francesca and Willie illustrates the potential for racial harmony.[21] Interestingly, each author seems to devalue the point in the telling. Hester Gray is a southerner but without the regional loyalty or passion of the prototypical southern white woman. Having lived for years in New Jersey, and then in Germantown with the Wendells, Hester's links to the Confederacy are abstract and easily set aside. Similarly, Francesca Ercildoune certainly sees herself as a woman of color, but she looks white and moves freely within white society. Although Willie remained loyal to his love when he learned Francesca's true racial heritage, the reader cannot forget that he fell in love thinking that she was a white woman. Thus, both of these crucial marriages were technically transgressive and thus politically important, but in fact in each case the bride's unclear identity undercuts the symbolic power of the match. Moreover, both young women had long since lost their mothers and had been living apart from their fathers while in school, thus making it that much easier to imagine that they might abandon their pasts to marry across racial or regional lines.

These larger political and symbolic concerns have lured me away from my initial question. Did these two authors portray a Civil War that truly transformed women and men on the home front, or did the four years of conflict leave no mark at home comparable to the "fire" that Oliver Wendell Holmes Jr. recalled from the battlefield? Clearly the answer is a resounding "no." No character in either novel appears to have grown or evolved because of their own war work; none are left emotionally scarred or fundamentally recast by the war's terrible military tragedies. The death of Captain Gray left Hester an orphan, but Mitchell makes no effort to explore the psychological effects of the loss. Instead, the novel's crucial tragedy is the accidental death of poor Ned Morton, who never had the opportunity to show his valor on the battlefield. Dickinson's main characters are victims of wartime violence, but the draft riots are portrayed more as an extension of antebellum race rioting rather than as a domestic front of the Civil War. The men who go off to fight in both novels almost always return with some sort of wound or lost limb, but none seem emotionally scarred by the experience and their loved ones seem able to carry on without any ill effects.

I am particularly interested in how the Civil War affected northern women. How did four years of conflict recast gender roles? Tens of thousands of women threw themselves into war work, but what was the evolving legacy of these efforts, both for those individuals and for the larger society? In her wartime career Dickinson bent all sorts of gender norms, speaking on abolitionism, women's rights, and politics to enthusiastic audiences across the country. She even did a small stint as a hospital volunteer, providing fodder for one of her popular lectures. But gender themes are completely absent from *What Answer?* Dickinson had disappointed many friends and admirers in the women's movement by siding with those male reformers who prioritized the black male vote over woman's suffrage. Her novel, written in the midst of debates that would eventually yield the Fifteenth Amendment granting black male suffrage, underscored her commitment to those priorities.

*In War Time* is in fact much more attentive to gender issues. Mitchell peppered his text with comments about the fundamental natures of different sorts of women, and he set several scenes in women's voluntary societies. During the war the Germantown women all gathered periodically at the Sanitary Commission offices to engage in unspecified war work; after Appomattox the same women organized to assist war orphans. But the novelist is clearly most concerned with creating scenes where various conversations and conflicts can occur, rather than in exploring the war's impact on women. We learn nothing about how these women had assisted the war effort, and there is no indication that their experiences had transformed them politically or ideologically. In fact, the conversations are invariably personal gossip unrelated to national political or military themes. Of course Mitchell's portrayal of women's organizations tells us nothing about what really went on in those meetings, but it does tell us a bit about how the author chose to remember that crucial moment in the history of women. The Sanitary Commission's volunteers ranged from the highly organized and well-read to the empty-headed and silly. The most progressive woman is the articulate, level-headed Miss Clemson, who repeatedly steers the conversation away from destructive gossip toward more elevated topics. Mitchell clearly wants the reader to admire Miss Clemson as a highly educated and morally sound individual. Although she takes part in the Sanitary Commission's work, Miss Clemson neither rises to a position of prominence in the committee nor speaks about the war or any larger political issues in these conversations. Instead, she impresses by demonstrating a knowledge of modern science, quoting the latest medical theories on malaria and vaccination. Perhaps Mitchell had no larger purpose than to have a character be a mouthpiece for some of his favorite medical theories, but it is telling that the woman who seems most "modern" is intellectually engaged in the world of science, rather than the swirl of contemporary events or the pull of woman's rights.

Sherlock Holmes used to tell Dr. Watson to be attentive to the dog that does not bark. Sometimes the best clues are in those silences. It is always easiest for the historian to examine that which is said and written, rather than to try to make sense of the absence of evidence. These two books are too few to support a comprehensive argument, but it is interesting to consider what Anna Dickinson and Silas Weir Mitchell had to say in their first novels, and also to consider the dogs that don't bark. Like many inexperienced writers, they both selected locations that they knew well, and of course the Civil War years provided an ideal backdrop for compelling narratives. Somehow their imaginations and their memories did not lead either Philadelphian to create wartime characters who were truly transformed by their home front experiences.

### NOTES

J. Matthew Gallman delivered his Klement Lecture in 2002. From James Marten and A. Kristen Foster, eds., *More Than a Contest Between Armies: Essays on the Civil War Era* (Kent, Ohio: Kent State Univ. Press, 2008), 250–71.

1. Oliver Wendell Holmes Jr., "In Our Youth Our Hearts Were Touched With Fire," May 30, 1884, address, and Holmes, "The Soldier's Faith," May 30, 1885, address. Both speeches are available at http://harvardregiment.org/holmes.html. This site acknowledges Richard Posner, *The Essential Holmes: Selections from the Letters, Speeches, Judicial Opinions, and Other Writings of Oliver Wendell Holmes, Jr.* (Chicago: Univ. of Chicago Press, 1992), as its original source.

2. See David Blight, *Race and Reunion: The Civil War in American Memory* (Cambridge, Mass.: Harvard Univ. Press, 2001); Alice Fahs and Joan Waugh, eds., *The Civil War and Memory*

(Chapel Hill: Univ. of North Carolina Press, 2003); Lesley Gordon, *General George E. Pickett in Life and Legend* (Chapel Hill: Univ. of North Carolina Press, 1998); Carol Reardon, *Pickett's Charge in History and Memory* (Chapel Hill: Univ. of North Carolina Press, 1997); Jim Cullen, *The Civil War in Popular Culture: A Reusable Past* (Washington, D.C.: Smithsonian Institution Press, 1995); Stuart McConnell, *Glorious Contentment: The Grant Army of the Republic, 1865–1900* (Chapel Hill: Univ. of North Carolina Press, 1992).

3. Various scholars have examined the attitudes and experiences of the Civil War soldier. For a survey of this literature, see Reid Mitchell, "'Not the General but the Soldier': The Study of Civil War Soldiers," in James M. McPherson and William J. Cooper Jr., eds., *Writing the Civil War: The Quest to Understand* (Columbia: Univ. of South Carolina Press, 1998), 81–95. For a study of the World War II soldier, see Gerald Linderman, *The World Within War: America's Combat Experience in World War II* (New York: Free Press, 1997). The soldier's experience has always been a popular subject for the novelist as well. Three of the most celebrated novels are Stephen Crane, *The Red Badge of Courage* (1895); Norman Mailer, *The Naked and the Dead* (1948); and Tim O'Brien, *Going After Cacciatto* (1978). O'Brien, a veteran of the war in Vietnam, has written several powerful works of fiction and nonfiction examining the soldier's experience.

4. J. Matthew Gallman, *Mastering Wartime: A Social History of Philadelphia during the Civil War* (New York: Cambridge Univ. Press, 1990) and *The North Fights the Civil War: The Home Front* (Chicago: Ivan R. Dee, 1994).

5. Perhaps the most famous of these memoirs is Mary Livermore, *My Story of the War* (Hartford, Conn.: A. D. Worthington, 1887; repr. New York: Perseus, 1995).

6. See Alice Fahs, *The Imagined Civil War: Popular Literature of the North and South, 1861–1865* (Chapel Hill: Univ. of North Carolina Press, 2001); Lyde Cullen Sizer, *The Political Work of Northern Women Writers and the Civil War, 1850–1872* (Chapel Hill: Univ. of North Carolina Press, 2000); and Elizabeth Young, *Disarming the Nation: Women's Writing and the Civil War* (Chicago: Univ. of Chicago Press, 1995).

7. Anna Elizabeth Dickinson, *What Answer?* (1868); and Silas Weir Mitchell, *In War Time* (1884). Mitchell's novel was initially serialized in the *Atlantic* in 1884. *What Answer?* was reissued by Humanity Press in Jan. 2003.

8. This portion of this essay is part of a much longer project on Dickinson's life.

9. Ernest Earnest, *S. Weir Mitchell: Novelist and Physician* (Philadelphia, 1950); Lynne Sharon Schwartz, "Introduction" to Charlotte Perkins Gilman, *The Yellow Wallpaper and Other Writings* (New York: Bantam, 1989).

10. Gallman, *Mastering Wartime.*

11. Mitchell, *In War Time*, 1.

12. Mitchell had earlier begun another wartime novel that was not published. Earnest, *S. Weir Mitchell*, 95.

13. Mitchell, *In War Time*, 226.

14. Dickinson clearly modeled Francesca and her family on the family of Robert Purvis, one of the most prominent black abolitionists in Philadelphia. Dickinson and her family were quite friendly with the Purvises, and Dickinson and Hattie Purvis were particularly close. (In a note at the end of the novel, Dickinson refers to, but does not name, the family.) See Gallman, "Introduction," *What Answer?* (New York: Prometheus, 2003).

15. An African American man named Abraham Franklin was lynched during the riots in a manner quite similar to the grisly murder of Dickinson's fictional Abe Franklin. Adrian Cook, *The Armies of the Streets: The New York City Draft Riots of 1863* (Lexington: Univ. Press of Kentucky, 1974), 143.

16. In her "Note" Dickinson explains that Willie Surrey's death is modeled on the murder

of Colonel O'Brien, a Union soldier killed by the rioters. On Colonel O'Brien's death see Cook, *Armies of the Streets,* 118–19.

17. The attack on Fort Wagner happened shortly after the draft riots, but Dickinson describes the attack immediately before portraying the riots. In her "Note" Dickinson explains that she modeled Robert Ercildoune's actions on the heroics of W. H. Carney. (This is the charge that was featured in the movie *Glory.*)

18. Dickinson, *What Answer?* 294.

19. Lyde Cullen Sizer makes a similar point about Dickinson's novel in *The Political Work of Northern Women Writers,* 236–44.

20. Earnest, *S. Weir Mitchell,* 46–48.

21. For a fascinating discussion of intersectional romance in postwar novels of reconciliation, see Nina Silber, *The Romance of Reunion: Northerners and the South, 1865–1900* (Chapel Hill: Univ. of North Carolina Press, 1993).

# Is the War Ended?

## Anna Dickinson and the Election of 1872

The Huntington Library in San Marino, California, sponsors periodic conferences on selected topics. For the participating scholars these are a great treat. The papers are superb, the gardens are wonderful, the Huntington staff are great professionals, and the audiences are appreciative. One of the most successful in the series was the conference on the "Memory of the Civil War," organized by Alice Fahs and Joan Waugh.[1] With so much recent scholarship on memory of the Civil War, the topic was particularly timely and the lineup of scholars was outstanding. When Joan and Alice invited me to take part, I quickly accepted. My only problem was that my current work on Anna Dickinson had barely moved beyond the Civil War, and I had not previously written about Civil War memory.

I settled on an approach to memory that deviated a bit from the more familiar emphasis on monuments, rituals, memoirs, novels, published histories, and other attempts to construct a memory of the war. I chose as my focus the fascinating Election of 1872, and Dickinson's efforts to use the contested memory of the war as a campaign tool. At one level this meant attempting to redefine the collective memory of the two candidates, Horace Greeley and Ulysses S. Grant. Grant, the general, might have been a hero on the battlefield, but Dickinson insisted that Greeley, the editor, had been more instrumental in ensuring Union victory. Dickinson also manipulated the war's memory in a more subtle way, using her own presence on the stump to recall her exploits a decade earlier when she was the heroine of the Republican Party. For me the essay was particularly fun because Anna Dickinson, my subject, had such horrible—and really unfair—things to say about Ulysses S. Grant, who was the subject of Joan Waugh's major project. Joan, a co-convener of the conference and coeditor of the volume, is one of my closest friends and does not take kindly to critiques of General Grant.

NOTE

1. The essays were collected in Alice Fahs and Joan Waugh, eds., *The Memory of the American Civil War in American Culture* (Chapel Hill: Univ. of North Carolina Press, 2004).

. . .

On October 25, 1872, Anna Elizabeth Dickinson walked alone to the speaker's platform at New York City's Cooper Union. The weather was so terrible that evening that even the famed orator could not fill the house. But Susan B. Anthony and Elizabeth Cady Stanton were there along with various colleagues from the woman's rights movement. All the New York papers and most of the leading national journals sent reporters. They had gathered to hear what the woman who had once been dubbed "America's Joan of Arc" had to say about the upcoming election between Horace Greeley and Ulysses S. Grant.

The speech was a particularly dramatic one, delivered with the flair that audiences had come to expect from Dickinson. Historians have not paid much attention to Dickinson's words that day. In political terms she did not break new ground, nor did her words significantly affect the election results the following month. Nevertheless, the 1872 campaign—and the path that Dickinson took to her role in it—are a valuable window into how the memory of the Civil War shaped postwar politics and culture. Only seven years after Appomattox, all public events unfolded with the memory of the Civil War as a powerful backdrop, but the terms of that memory remained subject to interpretation and negotiation. Her audiences recognized Dickinson as a celebrated veteran of the sectional conflict, and thus, like the candidates themselves, the memory of her own wartime career framed the popular perceptions of her 1872 actions. Moreover, Dickinson, ever the clever orator, did her best to shape the popular recollection of the Civil War to support her chosen candidate. Anna Dickinson understood both the power and the potential malleability of historic memory.

Anna Dickinson had her first taste of the public arena in 1860 when, as an eighteen-year-old, she delivered "The Rights and Wrongs of Women" at a public forum in Philadelphia. The following February Dickinson returned to the same themes at Philadelphia's Concert Hall, where the famed abolitionist Lucretia Mott introduced the young orator to her first paying audience. Over the next four years Dickinson emerged as one of the nation's most charismatic, exciting, and controversial orators.[1] In the process she carved out a distinctive role for herself among American public women. Although a handful of female speakers had already broken the cultural barrier to women speaking before mixed audiences, Dickinson clearly exceeded their example, both in her tremendous national celebrity and in her emergence as an explicitly political speaker who covered partisan terrain where her radical colleagues chose not to tread.[2]

Dickinson first honed her rhetorical skills before abolitionist and woman's rights audiences, enjoying the early patronage of William Lloyd Garrison and Wendell Phillips. In 1863 Benjamin Franklin Prescott, the secretary of New Hampshire's Republican Committee, suggested to his colleagues that the fiery young orator might help the party, and soon Dickinson had signed on for twenty engagements across the Granite State. Dickinson proved to be a popular stump speaker and the victorious governor-elect Joseph A. Gilmore graciously credited her with helping ensure his victory.[3] She went directly from her successes in New Hampshire to speak for Republican candidates across the North, weaving radical convictions and political partisanship into performances that were sure to attract large audiences. Observers differed about whether she was beautiful or merely striking looking, but friend and foe alike were intrigued by what they saw. Her clothing, short-cropped curls, striking gray eyes, and almost every gesture seemed to attract comment. Whatever her prepared text, Dickinson was at her best when responding to hecklers, giving each performance its own special character.[4]

Following a celebrated excursion to Chicago's Northwest Sanitary Fair, the twenty-one-year-old received an invitation, signed by more than a hundred senators and members of Congress, to speak before the combined houses in Washington. After much negotiation the historic lecture was staged on January 16, 1864, in the hall of the House of Representatives. Dickinson initially performed true to form: attacking the Democrats, praising the Emancipation Proclamation, supporting the use of black troops, and critiquing the Lincoln administration's conciliatory stance toward the South. But, in characteristically dramatic fashion, Abraham Lincoln and Mary Todd Lincoln arrived in the audience just as Dickinson was itemizing the president's shortcomings. Whatever her initial inclinations, Dickinson opted to support the president for four more years.

The Washington lecture was certainly the highlight of her wartime career. For the next year and a half Dickinson continued to make her living on the lecture circuit, supporting the war effort and demanding racial justice while firing periodic salvos at the Lincoln administration. Despite her misgivings, as the election of 1864 approached Dickinson broke with her radical colleagues in endorsing the party's candidate and once again went on the campaign trail, nominally supporting Lincoln while emphasizing her disagreements with the Democrats and her hatred of the Confederacy.

With the war's end, Dickinson was in a quandary. Still in her early twenties, she was one of America's most famous women. She had come to enjoy and expect the fame, and her family—including her widowed mother, her sister, Susan, and several brothers—had grown dependent on her ample earnings. Moreover, the war had left her convinced that she had an important contribution to make in public life. Barred from elected office—and even access to the vote—Dickinson faced the limited options available to a public woman in postwar America. Between 1865 and 1872 she prospered as a leader on the booming lyceum circuit, delivering hundreds of public lectures across the country. In the process she was part performer, part writer, part business-woman, and full-time ideologue. Each season required a new lecture; audiences measured success by the yardstick of past performances and against the work of contemporary competitors. Most of Dickinson's lectures tackled political topics, particularly concerning the rights of women, workers, and African Americans, but her most celebrated speech was on the life of Joan of Arc, a talk she introduced in 1870 and then reprised periodically for decades to come. Even her political lectures did not generally toe a particular reform line. Dickinson's "Demagogues and Workingmen" spoke up for the worker while alienating union leaders, and while she favored woman suffrage most of her lectures on women's issues concentrated on economic and social problems.

In 1868 as her companions in the suffrage movement battled for the fran-chise. Dickinson published a novel—*What Answer?*—which emphasized racial themes while essentially ignoring gender equality. Set in the midst of the Civil War, *What Answer?* featured a tragic interracial marriage between a white Union officer and a light-skinned Philadelphian who both fell victim to New York City's draft rioters. With this controversial narrative Dickinson was already experimenting with new perspectives on the war's memory. Rather than using her fiction to explore themes of sectional reconciliation or to wave a rhetorical bloody shirt at Northern Democrats or unreconstructed South-ern whites,[5] Dickinson's novel recalled the heroism of black troops and the racial prejudice of Northern whites, calling on her readers to confront those memories and ongoing realities as they contemplated black suffrage.[6]

In the decade after the Civil War Dickinson maintained personal friendships and professional ties with a wide array of radical reformers and Republican Party regulars while following her own muse and her own fiscal needs in crafting her postwar career. An advocate for radical Reconstruction and black suffrage, she repeatedly took aim at President Andrew Johnson. In the meantime Dickinson remained a strong proponent of woman's rights, even while continuing to move out of the woman suffrage mainstream. During the war the leaders of the woman's movement had opted to set aside the suffrage agenda in favor of an emphasis on abolitionism. After the conflict as Congress contemplated legislation and amendments to enfranchise African Americans, the movement's leaders divided over the proper strategy. Should they insist that women, both white and black, be allowed to enter the voting booth alongside African American men or should they accept the argument—as offered by Wendell Phillips—that this was "the Negro's Hour"? Bitterly disappointed over the lost opportunity when the Fifteenth Amendment excluded women and divided by strategy and personality conflicts, suffragists split into two organizations in 1869: the American Woman Suffrage Association and the National Woman Suffrage Association.[7] Throughout much of these debates Dickinson sat uncharacteristically on the fence. Despite increasingly urgent letters from Susan B. Anthony, she refused to come out squarely for suffrage and, worse, she repeatedly dodged invitations to take a major organizational role in the movement.

Wherever Dickinson roamed it seemed as if admirers competed to host the charismatic orator. A dozen correspondents across the country wrote to her as an intimate friend. Among her extended circle were many of the nation's leaders in public life, including editors, publishers, authors, and politicians. When she was in New York she socialized with the brain trust behind the powerful *New York Tribune*, including Whitelaw Reid, Noah Brooks, John Hay, and the editor Horace Greeley himself. Reid and Dickinson were particularly close friends whose names were regularly romantically linked in the press; Brooks and Hay were both devoted admirers. Her Boston circle included the *Springfield Republican's* Samuel Bowles, and during her frequent visits to Hartford she split her time between the home of Charles Dudley Warner, the editor of the *Hartford Courant,* and visits with various members of the extended Beecher clan. When the Beecher-Tilton scandal broke (pitting Theodore Tilton against Rev. Henry Ward Beecher surrounding the charge that Beecher had committed adultery with Tilton's wife, Elizabeth) the muck that flew threatened to stain the lives and reputations of a host of Dickinson's friends, leaving her with a particular hostility to Victoria Woodhull and her sister, Tennie C. Claflin, whose newspaper had originally published the charges that had brought the scandal into the open.[8]

Often the personal and the political became intertwined as Dickinson navigated through her complex worlds. Her reluctance to throw her weight behind woman suffrage rather than black manhood suffrage certainly reflected her political beliefs, but she was undoubtedly also swayed by her loyalties to Charles Sumner and Phillips. In the meantime Dickinson's dealings with Susan B. Anthony were decidedly multilayered. Anthony's letters to Dickinson in the first months of 1868 suggest an urgency and a level of intimacy that is not present in their earlier correspondence. Perhaps their falling out had everything to do with Dickinson's refusal to rise to Anthony's woman's rights challenge, but some clues to Dickinson's reluctance lie in the unknown details of a complex personal relationship between two powerful women separated in age by a generation.[9] Meanwhile, Dickinson's ongoing relationship with her old friend and intellectual sparring partner Whitelaw Reid and his *New York Tribune* cronies meant that Dickinson was hearing the arguments against woman suffrage whenever she journeyed to New York. These and other relationships would come into play as the campaign season got underway in 1872.

The Republican Party was less than a generation old as the 1872 election approached. Thus, nearly all the party's leaders had memories of abandoning an established party and pursuing ideological and political agendas in a new coalition. By the end of his first term in office President Ulysses S. Grant had given many in the Republican Party ample reason to feel alienated and ready to once again turn to some other path. High on the list of Grant's sins was his ham-handed effort to annex Santo Domingo, despite the vigorous protests of Republican senators Charles Sumner—the chair of the Foreign Relations Committee—and Carl Schurz. Worse, upon losing the annexation vote Grant, who had earned his wartime fame by accepting heavy casualties while defeating an outgunned enemy, entered into open warfare with the embattled Sumner. Grant's Republican enemies were also deeply disappointed with charges of corruption and cronyism in the White House and the president's indifferent record on civil service reform. Lastly, news from the reconstructed South seemed unrelentingly bad and Grant's critics questioned whether he had the interest or ability to handle the problems.

Alienated by developments in their own party and unable to wrest control from Grant and his people, a key core of reformers—led by the likes of Sumner and Schurz—bolted from the Republican Party to form the Liberal Republican Party.[10] Convinced that a coalition of the nation's "best men," including right-minded Southerners, could return the nation to the proper path, the new party met in Cincinnati that May. Much to the surprise of most observers, the convention ended up nominating Horace Greeley. Greeley's nomination owed much to a deadlock between the leading candidates and more than a little to the deft stewardship of Greeley's young lieutenant, Whitelaw Reid.[11] Caught up in the desire to unseat the hated Grant, the Democrats nominated Greeley at their national convention, thus creating some particularly strange political bedfellows for the campaign to come. By nominating the highly idiosyncratic and controversial Greeley and allying with the Democrats, the upstart party faced an interesting set of political challenges. Although the former Whig element in the party had placed tariff reductions in the platform, their standard-bearer had an established record as a protectionist, leaving the Liberal Republicans with a two-pronged strategy stressing an end to corruption and reconciliation with the South. This proved a tough task, as the Republican cartoonist Thomas Nast persistently lampooned Greeley's call for clasping hands "across the bloody chasm" of war and the bulk of the abolitionist leadership that claimed the Republican Party's moral center refused to abandon Reconstruction despite their distaste for Grant.[12]

As she observed these developments, Anna Dickinson had to weigh a range of considerations. First, she had grown to dislike Grant with a venom born of public policy, personal distaste, and deep loyalty to the insulted Sumner.[13] Second, Dickinson had personal ties with many of the men who became part of the Liberal Republican leadership. In addition to Sumner (who was really less of a friend than a hero) and Schurz, Greeley, Reid, Theodore Tilton, and Samuel Bowles were all crucial players in the Liberal Republican insurrection. Charles Dudley Warner—one of her most consistent advisors—and most of the old abolitionists, in contrast, refused to abandon the Republican Party.[14] And if Dickinson were to throw her considerable political weight behind the Liberal Republicans she would be almost alone among woman's rights advocates. The notorious Victoria Woodhull had launched a celebrated campaign for the presidency, drawing considerable support from defenders of woman's rights, while Anthony, Stanton, and other suffrage leaders who could not stomach Woodhull eventually agreed to back Grant in exchange for his nominal support of woman suffrage. Meanwhile, Dickinson was acutely aware of the value of her good name and of her enduring public identity as a wartime patriot. Although she always spoke her mind and seemed to welcome controversy, Dickinson recognized that her reputation—built upon the public's memory of her wartime oratory—was her meal ticket and that her mother and sister depended on her earnings. Would there be a cost to backing the wrong candidate? Conversely, might there be substantial rewards to be earned by offering her services to those who could best afford them?

In the months leading up to the campaign Dickinson solicited advice from far and wide. For quite some time she toyed with a European tour, either as a tourist or as a professional speaker. But all the while she kept one eye on the political season to come. In March 1872 Oliver Johnson offered to help arrange a "'political hoot'" in New York.[15] That same week Dickinson's brother John raised doubts about "pitch[ing] into the renomination of Grant 'til all the circumstances [are] considered," although her brother Ed added that if Anna were to get into the campaign she should do so early, "before delegates are chosen[,] otherwise you simply make a fuss, get abused & knocked, lose some influence & achieve nothing." Sister Sue worried that Anna would "only lose [her] popularity for no good by making a speech now."[16] Clearly Dickinson's political future was a hot topic for friends and family alike, with the latter particularly attuned to how a move against Grant might affect her hard-earned popularity.

On April 2 Dickinson temporarily broke her political silence with a public lecture in Pittsburgh. Still a month before the Liberal Republicans' convention, Dickinson surprised her audience by attacking President Grant while praising the efforts of the true Republican leadership of Sumner, Schurz, and Greeley, all converts to the new splinter party.[17] The crowd was large and Dickinson expressed pleasure with its responses despite scattered hissing at her more partisan attacks. Still, she was disappointed by the leading Republican papers—her old supporters—who barely mentioned the lecture, leaving it to the independent Liberal Republican editors and their new Democratic allies to sing her praises.[18] Her friends and advisors split on Dickinson's new stance. A jubilant Samuel Bowles wrote, "I am delighted that you have raised up your voice on this side" and reported that he had contacted Greeley about publishing her new speech. But the *Hartford Courant*'s Charles Dudley Warner—still a die-hard Republican—closed a note on May 11 with "You are now a democrat. I cannot write any more to a democrat now."[19]

The next week Dickinson delivered essentially the same lecture in Carlisle, Pennsylvania, followed shortly by a similar appearance at Philadelphia's Academy of Music. Carlisle's *American Volunteer* found the performance outrageous. "Anna Dickinson must be ruled out," the paper insisted. "She has the effrontery to stand up before a mixed audience, and declare that it was not Grant who saved the country, but the dead blue coats, and that he is not paying off the national debt, but the people. Was there ever such impudence?" In this context, Dickinson's "effrontery" was partially political, partially gendered—how dare she utter such sentiments before a "mixed audience"?—and partially an impudent refutation of the war's memory. Philadelphia's *Evening Bulletin* found the lecture "vastly inferior" to her recent lecture "Demagogues and Workingmen." And in more criticism that smacked of gendered dismissal, the paper suggested that "if the fair protestor desires to achieve any good result from her scolding, she must at least offer a reasonable and well-digested argument which will command respect and not ridicule." The *Evening City Item* was even less charitable, declaring that "a more complete political fizzle could scarcely have been obtained from any political Amazon," adding that perhaps Dickinson's bellicose demeanor was explained by her status as an unattached single woman.[20]

On April 19 Dickinson repeated her attack on Grant at New York City's Cooper Institute, two days after Grant's people had staged a large rally in the same hall. This time Dickinson, dressed elegantly in black silk, was introduced by her old friend Greeley, who proudly sat on the stage behind her as she spoke and soaked up rounds of applause from an enthusiastic audience. Anticipating themes that she would explore more fully on the eve of the election, Dickinson again called on her audience not merely to reflect on their memories of the Civil War but to rethink the meaning of those memories. "The war was only an act in a drama," she instructed. "What men did then they did not for the life or success of a party, but for the life and success of the nation." The question at hand was whether the next act should be left in the hands of the Republicans who gathered at Philadelphia or the new Liberal Republicans, who were really the proper heirs to the war's memory. So long as the Republicans clung to Grant as their man, Dickinson was prepared to seek answers from the Cincinnati convention.[21]

While she publicly attacked the Grant administration, Dickinson privately discussed her political options. Although fond of Greeley, Dickinson truly idolized Sumner and hoped that he would emerge as the Liberal Republican candidate, even while some of her politically savvy correspondents warned that Sumner carried too much baggage.[22] She declined an invitation to attend the Liberal Republicans' convention in Cincinnati that May, but followed the meetings carefully. When the nomination was announced Dickinson seemed ready to cast her lot with Greeley and the Liberal Republicans. "Hurrah for Us!" Dickinson wrote to Whitelaw Reid. "Next autumn I propose to do the best hooting I ever did in all my life in behalf of the good man and the good cause."[23]

Before long Dickinson once again began to have doubts. Family members and some friends counseled against damaging her reputation by casting her lot with the controversial Greeley. Some felt she would be better off sitting out this election, perhaps taking another stab at writing. In fact, in the midst of these political discussions Dickinson corresponded with Charles Dudley Warner for advice on publishers, book contracts, and the like.[24] The pressures came from all over and grew progressively more intense. On June 6 Dickinson barely missed separate visits from Reid and Bowles, two friends who had joined the Liberal Republican movement, and she received an unexpected call from Susan B. Anthony. Contradictory rumors flew. Liberal Republican advocate Laura Bullard heard that Dickinson had "given [her] . . . sanction to Grant & Wilson"; Republican senator M. S. Pomeroy wrote from Washington, "I read that you hurrah for Greeley!" In fact, in early June Dickinson had declined an invitation to speak for the Republicans and was still mulling over offers from the Liberal Republicans. Moses Coit Tyler chimed in from Michigan, "I'm waiting to be electrified by your tremendous Greeley speech—that one which you are working on now." But if she was working on a political speech Dickinson was still resisting any agreement with either party.[25]

In July Laura Bullard sent Dickinson an extended political analysis, declaring that Greeley was "no idol of" hers yet he was the right man for the moment. Moreover, she argued, "I want you to speak, not only for Greeley because of patriotic motives, but because of the woman question. It seems to me that men will be sooner aroused to the injustice of denying us the franchise, by the sight of such a woman as you acting & swaying an election, than in any other way."[26] Bullard invited Dickinson to visit her in Long Branch, New Jersey, but Dickinson recognized this as a ploy to get her to meet face-to-face with Greeley, something she was not yet ready to do. Ironically, by declining Bullard's invitation Dickinson was at her home in Philadelphia when Republican vice presidential candidate Henry Wilson dropped in. As she explained to her sister, "By avoiding one I fall into the claims of the other—By saying no to the would be President, I had to say yes to the would be ('tother) Vice President. By not accepting Mr. Greeley's invitation to spend Sunday at his house I had the pleasure of entertaining Mr. Wilson at my own."[27] The orator and the candidate shared tea while Dickinson heard Wilson's unsuccessful pitch to lure her into the campaign. Two days later Theodore Tilton invited Dickinson to come to New York to visit with Greeley, to which she responded: "Profoundly sorry but cannot come." If she went to see Greeley, she explained to her mother, "I would be in every paper in the country within twenty four hours." But she was not ready for such public pronouncements. "If I want to go with the campaign," she realized, "I will go with it, & get paid for it." If not, she would keep her own counsel.[28]

Faced with such heady invitations Dickinson threw herself into research for a new lecture while continuing to toy with her book project. Bowles could not resist giving her a difficult time: "So you turn aside from Greeley and from the girls and from heroes and martyrs and attack the labor conundrum! Audacious person!"[29] But in truth she had not yet turned aside from anyone so much as she had turned to more aggressive negotiations. "Do you want me to go into it," she asked Reid, "and if you do what will those vampires of the Com[mittee] pay me—the most, *very* most. Mind, I don't know that I will go at all," she added, "but I want to know on what ground I shall tread, if I do walk abroad."[30] In his response Reid recognized that he was at once friend, advisor, and political partisan. He deflected her requests for advice, pointing out, "You have many friends, whose counsels you are accustomed to consider, who earnestly deprecate your getting mixed up with it. . . . For myself, I am, of necessity, profoundly interested in the campaign, & therefore hardly a dispassionate adviser." But that having been said, he insisted, "I don't see how it could hurt you since ours is unquestionably the side that has the future with it." And turning to campaign logistics and fiscal strategy he suggested that Dickinson commit to "one or two elaborate speeches" for Greeley "at any price the Committee would pay, or without price. That is my idea of the political obligation of those who aspire to political leadership—obligation to the country, to their principles, to themselves. After that . . . I'd treat it purely as a business question, & work or not as the terms suited. But I can't reconcile it with my notions of political honesty or patriotism to make one's entrance on great national questions, on one side or the other, or even one's absolute silence depend solely on whether one got paid enough to break silence." Reid continued this extraordinary letter by alluding to their long history of personal squabbles and political bickering, concluding, "You used to rate me for being unsentimental, practical, indifferent to the sentimental demands of this or that Great Cause. Well, perhaps we've changed parts: & what I now write may seem a romantic idea of public duty that has no place in the calculations for a successful season. But it has always been my way of thinking." Thus, the crafty journalist tried to shape Dickinson's political future by calling upon her memories of their shared wartime past.[31] Oliver Johnson—another Greeley loyalist—penned an equally long and high-minded letter drawing on Dickinson's role as a beacon for all women: "I would have you make a speech so elevated and elevating that every one who hears you will be constrained to confess that your part is noble and every way worthy of a woman who aspires to lead and inspire man."[32]

Dickinson delayed her decision into August, assuring Reid that she was busy on other projects.[33] A concerned Greeley sought out Laura Bullard to find out why Dickinson had apparently changed her mind. Bullard explained that Dickinson made her living with her oratory and could not afford such ventures without compensation. The publisher-turned-candidate insisted that he had already authorized generous payment and was only awaiting news from Philadelphia.[34] But the negotiating dance continued for weeks. On August 7 Dickinson told Reid that she was writing a book for "a pot of money" while sitting out the election. But the following day she expressed uncertainty about book deals and admitted that although she lacked enthusiasm for the campaign her affection for Reid and Greeley might still win out.[35] As she continued her Hamlet-like indecision, Dickinson received advice from across the country. Even Dickinson's mother, always a bit unsettled by her public performances, entered the debate: "Dear daughter: please [do] not have any more to do with politicks [sic], political lectures and not much with politicians any more." We can only wonder if Mrs. Dickinson's views were swayed by a visit that afternoon from Wendell Phillips, an old mentor of Dickinson and no friend of the Liberal Republicans.[36]

Dickinson finally agreed to stand up for Greeley and the Liberal Republicans only to find that the party was unwilling to meet her price to speak in Maine, Pennsylvania, or Indiana.[37] For a time it seemed that Dickinson had finally thrown up her hands and abandoned the whole idea. She arranged for several newspapers to print short notices announcing that she would be sitting out the campaign while writing a book and that she would resume lecturing after the election.[38] Meanwhile, she told her mother and sister that she finally had a contract for a new book, promising a ten-thousand-dollar guarantee, which ensured that she would stay out of the campaign.[39]

A month later Bowles confided that he had heard from one of her "personal friends, high up in the Grant administration" that the Grant campaign was really behind the book deal as an effort to keep Dickinson off the stump for Greeley.[40] But if that had been the Republicans' devious plan, they had not properly reckoned on Dickinson's political drive and independent mind. By the end of September Dickinson and Reid were once again deep in negotiations about a Cooper Institute lecture planned for early October. The veteran lyceum speaker was still worried about her reputation, particularly given her recent falling out with James Redpath's speaker bureau and the loss of a few invitations because of her more controversial political stances. But this was no cynical careerist decision. "If you knew just how I stand towards a great many of my business people," she assured Reid, "you would understand that what I do I do with a bit, at least, of my life in my hand. If I pay such price I do it because conscience compels and because I believe I can be made of really great service to Mr. Greeley and a great cause, but to that end I need help."[41]

For much of October Dickinson worked away at the upcoming New York lecture that she was calling "Is the War Ended?"[42] But there was to be one more stumbling block before she reached the platform. The Republican leadership concluded that a full house was the highest priority and thus decided that the Cooper Institute lecture would be advertised with an unusually low twenty-five-cent admission. Dickinson was furious. Not only would the lowered price cut into her fee but the discounted rate also threatened to undercut her reputation as a speaker. Angry letters flew back and forth before Reid managed to talk his colleagues into raising the admission fee.[43] On October 22 the *New York Daily Tribune* published a letter from several prominent Liberal Republicans who officially called on Dickinson to break her silence on the campaign followed by Dickinson's response that she would do just that on the twenty-fifth of the month.[44] And so, after months of back-and-forth, the day of Dickinson's Cooper Institute lecture finally arrived.

Whereas in April Dickinson had been more interested in burying Grant than in praising Greeley, when she returned to the Cooper Institute in November she was playing the role of political partisan. And at the heart of her strategy was an elaboration on her earlier themes about how the Civil War should be remembered. In calling her lecture "Is the War Ended?" Dickinson had adopted a clever rhetorical ploy. If the war was indeed over, then one might reasonably ask why the United States maintained a war footing in the conquered American South. Moreover, if the war was truly over then Ulysses S. Grant could not merely run for reelection on the basis of his war record. Rather, Dickinson insisted, he should be held accountable for his embarrassing record of cronyism and corruption. In short, she intended to challenge the Republican Party both on contemporary political terrain and on its claim to the bloody battlefields of the nation's memory.

Dickinson—the hired rhetorical gun—was at her best firing sarcastic shots at her political enemies and Grant made an easy target for her moral outrage. The president had, she declared, a "greater fondness for the smoke of a cigar and the aroma of the wine glass" than for the proper duties of the White House. After exhausting her ammunition on Grant's foibles, Dickinson shifted to praise for the Liberal Republicans and the Cincinnati convention. "He who runs to extinguish the flames of a house when the house is burning, does well," she acknowledged. But by that same token, "he who checks the flow of water when the flame is extinguished, does also well, because the water, continuing, swamps the house, ruins the furniture, and brings decay and rot into the house."[45] With this imagery Dickinson implicitly introduced another layer of memory into the debate. Four decades earlier William Lloyd Garrison had launched the *Liberator*, his great abolitionist newspaper, by promising that he would be uncompromising in his fight against slavery. "Tell a man whose house is on fire, to give a moderate alarm," he had written in 1831, "but urge me not to use moderation in a cause like the present."[46] Forty-one years later Dickinson seemed to be assuring her audience that the fire Garrison spoke of had been extinguished by emancipation, and thus the postwar years called for a more moderate approach. It was a particularly audacious act of historical appropriation since Dickinson well knew that the aging Garrison himself had refused to join his old abolitionist allies in jumping on the Liberal Republican bandwagon.[47]

As she turned to her central question, Dickinson constructed a complex case that the war was indeed over and that Grant and the Republicans were wrong for continuing to maintain a combative, fiscally wasteful posture toward the vanquished South. But how could the former abolitionist reconcile her calls for Southern home rule with her often-stated commitment to the political future—and physical safety—of the freedpeople? Following the logic of the Liberal Republicans Dickinson declared, "These blacks were slaves, then freemen, then citizens. Before the law they stand on a level with the whitest white man here. [Applause] That being the case there is no need and there should be no excuse for special legislation for any special class of people, since there is none such in the Republic. [Applause]." And following this logic further, "if they cannot defend themselves and exercise their right at the polls, then either we are in a state of war, and actual war power is brought to bear against them, and we ought to declare war and fight it out; or we are at peace, and being so, if millions of voters are unable to defend themselves . . . we might as well confess the experiment of the Republican Union is ended. [Applause]." If her audience wanted a return to war, so be it. If not, let the democratic process work its magic in the South. Let white Southerners craft policies to appeal to black voters, even if that might mean losses for the Republican Party.

In weaving her tale of what could and should be, Dickinson also imagined an alternative future shaped by another sort of memory: the memories that the young white Southerners of 1872 would take into their adulthood. Half the Southern voters, she pointed out, would be casting their first presidential ballot in 1872. Whereas the Southern white leadership remembered secession and war (and, she insisted, had become reconciled to defeat), "the boys, who never did anything, who were not born when the war began, those boys, and those men, have no such recollection, have no memories of combining against the Republic. All that they see is the wrong and bitterness of the Government which rules them." Thus, Dickinson argued, the election of 1872 was not only about how to understand the memory of the Civil War but also about how the next generation would remember what they did at the polls that year.

But the problem of memory was also much closer to home and less abstract for Dickinson and the Liberal Republicans. After all, President Grant was the Union's greatest war hero. Undaunted, Dickinson dismissed the president as "a man whose interest was first centered in a tap-yard; second in the blood he shed; and third in his cigar." As she geared up for more flowery invective, a voice from the audience cried out, "'Who saved the country?'" The quick-witted Dickinson confronted this popular memory head on. It was "the men who fought under Gen. Grant" who won the war, she declared. And in fact those men "had learned their lessons of loyalty through twenty-five years of the columns of THE NEW YORK TRIBUNE." It was Horace Greeley, the *Tribune's* editor, who deserved credit for fighting to break the chains of slavery, and now he stood for Republican constitutional principles. "History," she declared in offering yet another audacious twist on historic memory, "will write the record concerning us."

Dickinson was not content to claim that the nation owed a greater debt to the physically unimposing bespectacled editor than to the cigar-chomping hero of Vicksburg, Petersburg, and Appomattox. Before she closed she had to wriggle out of one other conundrum. How could she back a man who had opposed woman suffrage, when so many in the woman's rights leadership had aligned themselves with the Republicans? Part of the answer was simply that Grant's support of women smacked of cynical opportunism, backed by no real conviction or concrete action, so the suffragists should not hand over their political capital to such a man. But she did not stop there. Instead she turned again to the past, quoting Greeley's own words from 1860: "'When the women of the United States shall desire this, not merely as a privilege, but as a responsibility, then I am willing to give it.'" Dickinson, ever the maverick, endorsed such harsh terms, adding, "We have enough supine and lazy and careless voters already."

The published responses to Dickinson's Cooper Institute lecture followed expected party lines, with several reports focusing on Dickinson's split with the other leaders in the woman's movement. The Democratic *New York World* led with the importance of Dickinson speaking to an enthusiastic audience "in opposition to her sisters of the suffrage-making organizations," while Grant supporters Elizabeth Cady Stanton and Sallie Devereaux Blake looked on from the audience. Conversely the *Boston Post* noted that while the familiar female leaders had ended their "meaningless flirtations" and backed Grant in exchange for a "ridiculously small bone," Dickinson was the "one woman who remains true to her honest convictions" in supporting Greeley.[48] The *Providence Journal* approached Dickinson and her lecture gingerly, noting that "Miss Anna Dickinson is a lady who makes lecturing a profession. . . . While we would treat all opponents with fairness," the *Journal*'s editors explained, "we confess to more than usual hesitation in dealing with a woman who has entered upon the domain of politics." Nevertheless, the newspaper managed to characterize Dickinson's lecture as "the most insipid and oft repeated slanders against General Grant, and an equally ludicrous and false glorification of Horace Greeley." The *Boston Journal* took the *New York Tribune* to task for celebrating "the sensational female declaimer" who was guilty of "demagogism." In contrast, Bowles's *Springfield Republican* celebrated the lecture as an "impressive plea for honest government and true national unity," adding that "in delivering it the most eloquent of American women has performed the noblest and most courageous actions of her life." Other critics found diverse ways to minimize Dickinson's significance. Waterbury, Connecticut's *Evening American* suggested that the only remaining question was "who wrote it?" The mocking *National Republican* attributed the favorable coverage in the *Tribune* to Dickinson's personal relationship with Reid, "whom she rejected some time ago" and who "praises Anna in a gushing way in the *Tribune,* from which we infer that his angelic bosom is still torn by the tender passion."[49]

Dickinson's friends praised her performance even while acknowledging that it came with a cost. She had "[done] a noble thing in coming forward when Mr Greeley's chances seemed to be almost hopeless," gushed Carl Schurz. Laura Runkle, who had been in the audience, reported, "Everywhere I hear praises of your pluck and honesty even from Grant men, and, if it cost you loss, this winter as I hope it may not, it will be more than made up another year." Even her loyal Republican friends were impressed with the gesture. In early December Charles Dudley Warner, the always sardonic editor, wrote, "I thank the lord that I am so constituted that I love even geese, and Greeley people." Senator Ben Butler, who had a long-standing affection for Dickinson, told her that although he was disappointed that she made the speech he still thought it "the *bravest* thing done through the campaign."[50]

But what exactly had Dickinson done, and how and why had she done it? When she took the stage in support of Greeley, the war's memory was present in at least three senses. Most obviously, Dickinson's text was a direct confrontation with the Republican Party's claim to the war's memory. The Republicans' logic was powerful. The Republicans were the party of Lincoln, and President Grant had led the Union army to victory. A vote against the Republicans was a vote against fallen Northern soldiers and a martyred president. Thus, Grant's political enemies were wise to shift attention away from the war and toward his failings in office. Dickinson certainly took her shots at the Grant White House, but she also confronted the war's memory head on and claimed it for her side. If the war had indeed been won—as the Republican conquerors were proud of declaring—then why maintain a military presence in the South? If this was really a war for democratic principles and one of the results was the winning of suffrage for African American men, then why not let democracy run its course? And, most outrageously, Dickinson was not even willing to grant the president credit for winning the war. The soldiers, not the generals, really triumphed, and men like Greeley—who helped shape the popular will—deserved praise for the victory. Here was the old political pro making the best case that she could with the available material. While Greeley was proposing that Americans "clasp hands over the bloody chasm" and put the conflict behind them, thus effectively calling for national amnesia, Dickinson was suggesting new ways of remembering the war and its meaning that made such an approach more palatable.

At a very different level Dickinson's speech—and her tortured decision to give it—was all about her own memories of the war and its aftermath and an assortment of loyalties that dated to the war years. Her distaste with Grant ran deep, particularly because of his treatment of Sumner, and her friendships with Reid and other Liberal Republicans weighed into her decision. Still, Dickinson knew that her decision would disappoint Warner, Phillips, Garrison, and a host of old allies, thus making the decision that much more difficult. At bottom, Dickinson was drawn into the campaign because of her own sense that she belonged in the political arena. And that sense of self was born in her own memories of youthful wartime successes and the recollection of a time when thousands flocked to hear her opinions on affairs of the day. This can be read in various ways. On the one hand, Dickinson had a large ego that thrived on the attention and praise she received as an important political player. On the other hand, she was a woman of powerful convictions that she felt deserved public airing. In a political world that offered her few opportunities to effect change, how could she turn down such a fine pulpit?

This raises a further tier in this tableau of memory. Rather than concentrating on what Dickinson said or why she said it, perhaps we should shift our focus to the collective memory of the people in that New York audience. As a Boston reporter explained, Dickinson's appearance "recalled vividly the days of the war, not so very far away, when her woman's voice rang out through the country in defense of all that was just and noble, and in bitter denunciation of wrong."[51] Dickinson, like Grant, was a veteran of the Civil War. And like many other war heroes she had built her postwar career on her celebrated actions as a patriotic youth. Even those reporters who came to ridicule recognized the political significance of Dickinson's endorsement of Greeley. That both camps battled for endorsements from leading women, and trumpeted those successes, was an acknowledgment of women's expanded public role. That increased political voice was in no small part a further legacy of the Civil War and particularly of Dickinson's celebrated role in wartime politics.

Dickinson's continuing importance as a public woman was not lost on her many female friends. As one friend and admirer wrote, "Don't forget that you owe it to all us women who are dumb, and for whom you speak, who are in obscure places, and for whom you stand, who find in you the ripe, beautiful, missing expression of full womanhood, to be always at your best in all of your spoken and written words—So much of the future of women lies in your white hands, so heavy a burden of the needs rests on your girlish shoulders."[52] Almost a decade after the war Dickinson still played an important symbolic role in American public life.

Things went badly for the Liberal Republicans in the election of 1872 and far worse personally for Horace Greeley. On October 30 Greeley's wife passed away, and within a month a distraught Greeley followed her to his grave, but not before Dickinson visited him one last time at the *Tribune* office.[53] Anna Dickinson was thirty in 1872. She would remain in and out of the public eye for another two decades as a lecturer, author, occasional stump speaker, and—for a time—a celebrated actress and playwright, but she never really recaptured the fame or popularity of her earlier years. By the late 1880s Dickinson was poor, seemingly mentally unstable, perhaps an alcoholic, and generally in terrible shape. In 1891 her sister, Susan, arranged to have Dickinson committed to a hospital for the insane. Dickinson successfully won her freedom and then spent much of the next several years in a series of court battles against those who had had her committed and against an assortment of newspapers—including many of her old supporters—who had trumpeted her insanity. She died in quiet obscurity in 1932, largely forgotten by her contemporaries. In her final years she spent much of her time filling scrapbooks with clippings and writing long letters in a seemingly futile attempt to etch her name more deeply into the nation's memory.

# NOTES

Preliminary research for this project was supported by a fellowship from the National Endowment for the Humanities. I would like to thank Joan Waugh and Alice Fahs and the participants in the Huntington Library's conference "The Memory of the Civil War in American Culture." I would also like to thank two anonymous readers for their suggestions.

1. This essay is part of a larger biographical study of Anna Dickinson (forthcoming from Oxford University Press). For a short essay emphasizing Dickinson's war years, see J. Matthew Gallman, "Anna Dickinson: Abolitionist Orator," in *The Human Tradition in the Civil War and Reconstruction*, ed. Steven E. Woodworth (Wilmington, Del.: Scholarly Resources, 2000), 93–110. Dickinson's papers are housed in the Anna E. Dickinson Papers at the Library of Congress. Washington, D.C., and available on microfilm (hereafter AED Papers). The only published biography is Giraud Chester, *Embattled Maiden: The Life of Anna Dickinson* (New York: G. P. Putnam's Sons, 1951). James Harvey Young, who wrote a dissertation on Dickinson's wartime career and several important articles on various aspects of her life, authored a Dickinson biography in the late 1940s, "Anna Elizabeth Dickinson," that has never been published. I am indebted to Young for permission to inspect both this manuscript and his research notes in the James Harvey Young Papers, Special Collections, Emory University, Atlanta, Georgia.

2. Karyln Kohrs Campbell, ed., *Women Public Speakers in the United States, 1800–1925: A Biocritical Sourcebook* (Westport, Conn.: Greenwood Press, 1993). See also Karyln Kohrs Campbell, *Man Cannot Speak for Her,* 2 vols. (Westport, Conn.: Greenwood Press, 1989).

3. Benjamin Franklin Prescott to Anna Elizabeth Dickinson (hereafter AED), January 29, 1863, AED Papers; Young, "Anna Elizabeth Dickinson," chap. 3, pp. 1–7.

4. On Dickinson's rhetoric and popular responses, see J. Matthew Gallman, "An Inspiration to Work: Anna Elizabeth Dickinson, Public Orator," in *The War Was You and Me: Civilians in the American Civil War,* ed. Joan Cashin (Princeton: Princeton University Press, 2002), 159–82; and Matthew Gallman, "Anna Dickinson, America's Joan of Arc: Public Discourse and Gendered Rhetoric during the Civil War," in *American Public Life and the Historical Imagination,* ed. Wendy Gamber, Michael Grossberg, and Hendrik Hartog (Notre Dame: University of Notre Dame Press, 2003), 91–112.

5. See Nina Silber, *The Romance of Reunion: Northerners and the South, 1865–1900* (Chapel Hill: University of North Carolina Press, 1993).

6. Anna Elizabeth Dickinson, *What Answer?* (Boston: Ticknor and Fields, 1868). See also J. Matthew Gallman, "Introduction" to *What Answer?* by Dickinson (1868; reprint, Amherst, N.Y.: Humanity Books, 2003), 7–28.

7. See Ellen DuBois, *Feminism and Suffrage: The Emergence of an Independent Women's Movement in America, 1848–1869* (Ithaca: Cornell University Press, 1978).

8. See Barbara Goldsmith, *Other Powers: The Age of Suffrage, Spiritualism, and the Scandalous Victoria Woodhull* (New York: Alfred A. Knopf, 1998).

9. Susan B. Anthony to AED, various correspondence, AED Papers. Jean Baker discusses the Anthony-Dickinson relationship in her forthcoming book *Founding Sisters.*

10. The standard history of the Liberal Republican Party is still Earle Dudley Ross, *The Liberal Republican Movement* (1919; reprint, New York: AMS Press, 1971). See also Richard Allan Gerber, "The Liberal Republicans of 1872 in Historiographic Perspective," *Journal of American History* 62 (June 1975): 40–73, and the sources cited below in notes 11 and 12.

11. Matthew T. Downey, "Horace Greeley and the Politicians: The Liberal Republican Convention in 1872," *Journal of American History* 4 (March 1967): 727–50.

12. James M. McPherson. "Grant or Greeley?: The Abolitionist Dilemma in the Election of 1872," *American Historical Review* 71 (October 1965): 43–61.

13. On Dickinson's feelings for Charles Sumner, see AED to Mary Dickinson, February 2, 1871, AED Papers.

14. McPherson, "Grant or Greeley?"

15. Oliver Johnson to AED, March 8, 1872, AED Papers.

16. John Dickinson to AED, March 7, 1872; Sue Dickinson to AED, March 13, 1872; and Ed Dickinson to AED, March 19, 1872, all in AED Papers.

17. *Pittsburgh Daily Post,* April 3, 1872, clipping in Dickinson scrapbook, AED Papers.

18. AED to Susan Dickinson, April 3, 1872, AED Papers.

19. Samuel Bowles to AED, April 5, 1872, AED Papers; Charles Dudley Warner to AED, May 11, 1872, copy in Young Papers.

20. *Carlisle. (Pa.) American Volunteer,* April 11, 1872; *Philadelphia Evening Bulletin,* April 12, 1872; *Philadelphia Evening City Item,* April 12, 1872, clipping in Dickinson scrapbook.

21. *New York World,* April 20, 1872; *Springfield Republican,* April 20?, 1872; *St. Louis Dispatch,* April 20, 1872; *Boston Post,* n.d.; *New York Sun,* April 20, 1872; and several unidentified newspapers, April 1872, all clippings in Dickinson scrapbook.

22. Laura Bullard to AED, April 5, 1872; and Melinda Jones to AED, April 6, 1872, both in AED Papers.

23. AED to Whitelaw Reid. May 11, 1872, Whitelaw Reid Papers as cited in Giraud Chester notes, AED Papers.

24. Laura Bullard to AED, May 31, 1872, July 14, 1872, August 9, 1872; Robert Callyer to AED, July 28, 1872; "Little Brownie" (Ele Brown) to AED, July 29, 1872; and Charles Dudley Warner to AED, May 9, 1872, and May 11, 1872, all in AED Papers.

25. Laura Bullard to AED, June 6, 1872; M. S. Pomeroy to AED, June 7, 1872; Moses Coit Tyler to AED, June 30, 1872; Henry Wilson to AED, June 11, 1872; and AED to "Dicky" (Susan Dickinson), June 7, 1872, all in AED Papers.

26. Laura Bullard to AED, July 7, 1872, AED Papers.

27. AED to "My Dear Badness," July 14, 1872, unidentified letters folder, AED Papers. This letter is almost certainly to Susan Dickinson.

28. AED to Mary Dickinson, July 12, 1872, July 15, 1872; AED to Susan, July 10, 1872; Susan to AED, July 11, 1872; and Theodore Tilton telegram to AED, July 12, 1872, all in AED Papers. All quotations are from Dickinson's July 12,1872, letter to her mother.

29. Samuel Bowles to AED, July 15, 1872, AED Papers.

30. AED to Whitelaw Reid, July 23, 1872, Whitelaw Reid Papers as cited in Giraud Chester notes, AED Papers.

31. Whitelaw Reid to AED, July 30, 1872, AED Papers.

32. Oliver Johnson to AED, July 30, 1872, filed under "unidentified fragments," AED Papers. Identified by handwriting and return address.

33. AED to Whitelaw Reid, August 2, 1872, Whitelaw Reid Papers as cited in Giraud Chester notes, AED Papers.

34. Laura Bullard to AED, August 3, 1872, AED Papers.

35. Ibid.; AED to Whitelaw Reid, August 7, 1872, August 8, 1872, Whitelaw Reid Papers as cited in Giraud Chester notes, AED Papers.

36. Mary Dickinson to AED, August 16, 1872, AED Papers.

37. Whitelaw Reid to AED, August 22, 1872, AED Papers.

38. For the newspaper notices, see *New York Independent,* August 27, 1872; *New York Golden Age,* August 31, 1872; *New York Daily Tribune,* August 30, 1872; *Pittsburgh Evening Chronicle,*

August 28, 1872; and several unidentified newspapers, all clippings in Dickinson scrapbook. For correspondence demonstrating that Dickinson was behind these notices see Wm[?] Hayes Ward to AED, August 26, 1872; Oliver Johnson to AED, August 27, 1872; AED to Susan Dickinson, August 30, 1872; and Susan Dickinson to AED, September 2, 1872, all in AED Papers.

39. AED to Susan Dickinson, August 26, 1872, and AED to Mary Dickinson, August 27, 1872, both in AED Papers.

40. Samuel Bowles to AED, September 27, 1872, AED Papers.

41. AED to Whitelaw Reid, October 3, 1872, Whitelaw Reid Papers as cited in Giraud Chester notes, AED Papers. For lost lecture opportunities, see Sue Warner to AED, September 28, 1872; and Moses Coit Tyler to AED, October 2, 1872, both in AED Papers.

42. AED to "Birdie" Warner, October 4, 1872, copy in Young Papers; Susan Dickinson to AED, October 7, 1873, AED Papers.

43. AED to Mary Dickinson, October 6, 1872, AED Papers; AED to Whitelaw Reid, October 7, 1872, Whitelaw Reid Papers as cited in Giraud Chester notes, AED Papers: Whitelaw Reid to General John Cochrane, October 4, 1872, Whitelaw Reid Letter Books, Whitelaw Reid Papers, microfilm, Library of Congress; Whitelaw Reid to General John Cochrane, October 9, 1872, AED Papers; AED to Susan Dickinson, October 9, 1872, AED Papers; Whitelaw Reid to AED, October 10, 1872, AED Papers; [Laura Bullard?] to AED, October 10, 1872, miscellaneous letters, AED Papers; Susan Dickinson to AED, October 11, 1872, AED Papers; E. P. Bullard to AED, October 13, 1872, AED Papers; Whitelaw Reid to AED, October 24, 1872, AED Papers; AED to Whitelaw Reid, October 24, 1872, Whitelaw Reid Papers as cited in Giraud Chester notes, AED Papers.

44. *New York Daily Tribune,* October 22, 1872, clipping in Dickinson scrapbook.

45. Several newspapers reported detailed accounts of the speech. The excerpts throughout come from the *New York Sun,* October 25, 1872, clipping in Dickinson scrapbook.

46. *Liberator,* January 1, 1831.

47. McPherson, "Grant or Greeley?"

48. *New York World,* October 26, 1872; *Boston Post,* October 30, 1872, clipping in Dickinson scrapbook.

49. *Providence Journal,* October 29, 1872; *Boston Journal,* October 29, 1872; *Springfield Republican,* October 28, 1872; *Waterbury (Conn.) Evening American,* October 26, 1872; and *National Republican,* n.d., all clippings in Dickinson scrapbook.

50. Carl Schurz to AED, November 3, 1872; Laura Runkle, November 7, 1872; Charles Dudley Warner to AED, December 21, 1872; and AED to Mary Dickinson, November 14, 1872, all in AED Papers. Dickinson quoted Butler's sentiments in her letter to her mother.

51. *Boston Post,* October 30, 1872.

52. Laura Runkle to AED, August 27, 1872, AED Papers.

53. AED to Susan Dickinson, November 8, 1872, AED Papers.

# "In Your Hands That Musket Means Liberty"

## African American Soldiers and the Battle of Olustee

This essay, like the piece on the Election of 1872, began as a contribution to a Civil War conference at the Huntington Library, this time hosted by Gary Gallagher and Joan Waugh. The conference's theme was "Wars Within a War." We were interested in exploring conflicts and differences that divided the two sides internally. Once again Joan and Gary assembled a wonderful list of scholars and good friends for several days of papers, good food, and wonderful weather.

I used the occasion to write about several unfamiliar themes that had begun to absorb my attention. Having moved to the University of Florida, I had become intrigued with the Battle of Olustee, the largest Civil War battle in the state. Olustee is also known for the contributions of three separate regiments of men from the United States Colored Troops. When I first read about the battle, I noticed that these three regiments, although obviously similar in that they were all composed of black men, were actually dramatically different in their origins and experience. I wondered about the different paths that brought them to Olustee, and also about how white soldiers might have responded to their very different performances on the battlefield.

Meanwhile, I had long been interested in the recruiting rhetoric Northerners used to recruit black soldiers. How did this rhetoric—speeches and recruiting posters—differ from that aimed at white men, and what did this suggest about soldiers' motivations? I was particularly anxious to explore how gendered notions of manhood and masculinity found their way into this racialized discourse. As luck would have it, one of the Olustee regiments had been recruited in Philadelphia, and Anna Dickinson had in fact had a hand in recruiting them. Better yet, a recruiting poster I had been using in class for years had been produced in Philadelphia only months before the regiment formed. This essay, then, gave me the opportunity to think systematically about some issues and themes that had long been part of my teaching but had never been part of my scholarship.

. . .

The battle of Olustee—or Ocean Pond—was fought on February 20, 1864, about ten miles east of Lake City, Florida, and about forty-five miles north of Gainesville. In the grand military narrative of the Civil War, it was a minor battle culminating a failed Union operation in northern Florida. The original plan, proposed by Maj. Gen. Quincy A. Gillmore, commander of the department of the South, and approved by President Abraham Lincoln, combined an array of economic and political objectives. The idea was to send a small force into northern Florida to cultivate Unionist support, liberate (and enlist) slaves, cut off Confederate supply lines and perhaps acquire some of the state's stores of cotton and timber. On February 7 a division of Union troops under Brig. Gen. Truman B. Seymour captured Jacksonville, in the northeast corner of the state, and prepared to move westward. On the 20th, Seymour's command of about 5,500 men—including three regiments of black troops—faced 5,000 Confederates under Brig. Gen. Joseph Finegan at Olustee. The terrain was flat, marshy, dense with thin grass and weeds, and broken by stands of pines. Ocean Pond limited movement to the north. The tracks of the Florida, Atlantic, and Gulf Railroad ran on an east-west axis along the southern edge of where the armies met.

From the standpoint of the invaders, the best that could be said of Olustee is that it did not go as badly as it might have. In the early afternoon, Union cavalry encountered Confederate pickets in advance of Finegan's prepared entrenchments. At about two o'clock the 7th Connecticut Infantry moved forward with some artillery, driving the Rebel pickets back towards Olustee, but as they did the superior Confederate force threatened to flank and overwhelm the Federals. As the Connecticut troops fell back around 3:00 p.m., the 7th New Hampshire Infantry and the 8th United States Colored Troops moved forward, with the 7th taking the right flank. In the chaos of the moment, orders became garbled and the men from New Hampshire fell apart soon after they arrived, leaving the 8th USCT isolated and facing a superior Confederate force. Within twenty minutes Col. Charles W. Fribley, the 8th's commander, fell mortally wounded. Soon the black regiment was also in retreat and the Union's situation had become precarious.

Seymour had already sent three New York regiments to the right to support the panicked Connecticut troops. Now, as the 8th fell back and the Union artillery was in danger of capture, Seymour called up his remaining reserves. Several miles to the rear, Col. James Montgomery commanded a brigade of two African American regiments, the 54th Massachusetts Infantry and the 1st North Carolina Colored. The two African American regiments rushed into the fray, with the North Carolinians moving to the right and the 54th shielding the 8th on the left as they retreated. The fighting raged as daylight faded and Seymour ordered his men to abandon the field. Most of the Union soldiers made a safe return to Jacksonville. Still, the losses were heavy. The Union suffered 1,861 killed, wounded, and missing; the Confederacy reported 961 casualties.[1]

Although a minor episode in the larger military narrative of the Civil War, Olustee figures more prominently in the wartime history of African American soldiers. Their story illuminates how the history of the Civil War is—in a variety of ways—a story of fundamental similarities amongst diverse people, and at the same time a narrative defined by crucial differences, both demographic and ideological, sometimes revealed in unexpected and ironic ways.

Scholars of Civil War soldiers can be simultaneously splitters and lumpers. Thus, the military historian may speak of a particular "fighting regiment" as contrasted with another that was prone to cowardice or poor discipline. But many Civil War historians have noted the fundamental commonalities in attitude, motivation, and experience bridging the two armies, producing bonds that would facilitate postwar reconciliation among veterans. In these broad discussions the African American soldier commonly stands to the side, the subject of separate monographs and collections but rarely interwoven into that master narrative—and with good reason. The multiple steps that led to the inclusion of black men in the Union Army are a distinctive story. Once in uniform, African American soldiers endured unequal treatment from government officials, a skeptical reception from their white comrades, and threats of execution or enslavement at the hands of their enemies. And even where scholarly questions might span white and black soldiers, the evidence inhibits the analysis. Archives are packed with white soldiers' letters and diaries, but few black soldiers left behind such private writings.[2]

For many Americans, knowledge of the USCT comes from the movie *Glory* (1989), the exciting tale of the 54th Massachusetts from enlistment to the heroic and tragic assault on Fort Wagner in July 1863. As Civil War movies go, *Glory* is recognized as a superb piece of work, albeit one told largely through the eyes of the regiment's charismatic white commander, Col. Robert Gould Shaw. The film's audiences received an excellent sense of military action, even though the filmmakers tinkered a bit with some of the minor details. Moreover, tens of thousands of viewers learned quite a bit about black troops during the Civil War and the multiple inequalities that the 54th faced.

Yet *Glory* seems intent on injecting as much diversity as possible into this single regiment. The result is an interesting cross-section of personality and human experience slowly blended together to produce a cohesive fighting unit, reminiscent of any number of old war movies. Viewers watch as the highly educated, culturally sophisticated man trains and fights alongside the illiterate laborer, the angry ex-slave, the grizzled elder statesman, and a host of men of varied backgrounds who seemingly share only race in common. While this portrayal gave audiences a taste of the diversity among the 180,000 African American men who served in the Union army, it overstated the range within the 54th. As the first regiment of northern black troops, it represented the best and the brightest of the sons of northern black elites. Eighty percent were born as free men. The bookish character Thomas Searles—played by Andre Braugher—was probably close to the norm, rather than the charmingly peculiar aberration suggested by the film.[3]

Those who have seen *Glory* will recall that the audience did encounter one other USCT regiment, providing a stark comparison with the disciplined men of the 54th. In June 1863, Shaw and his men joined Colonel Montgomery and the 2nd South Carolina Infantry in a brief sortie to Darien, Georgia, where Montgomery ordered the sacking of the town. The 2nd was composed of freedmen, and under the cynical Montgomery they are thoroughly undisciplined, to the disgust of Colonel Shaw and his men.[4] The filmmakers might have presented this scene as a contrast between the unruly behavior of the recently enslaved men of the 2nd and the higher ethical standards of the free-born men of the 54th, but—in keeping with the narrative focus on Colonel Shaw—the cinematic emphasis is really on the two white commanders. Shaw and Montgomery articulate different perspectives on what the Union can reasonably expect from black men in uniform. Montgomery is a devout abolitionist, but he has a limited respect for his men, and treats them accordingly; Shaw has greater hopes and expectations. Thus, the moviegoer is left to conclude that the 2nd and the 54th behaved differently at Darien because their white commanders approached their tasks differently.

Turning from film back to history, what information is available about the three regiments of African American troops who fought at Olustee? The first into the fray were the 8th United States Colored Troops. Recently recruited in eastern Pennsylvania and trained at Camp William Penn just outside of Philadelphia, the 8th was under the command of Colonel Fribley. Prior to Olustee, the regiment had seen no action. The 1st North Carolina—which had been redesignated the 35th USCT on February 8, 1864—was another relatively green regiment. Recruited along the eastern seaboard of Virginia, North Carolina, and South Carolina the previous summer and mustered in on June 30, the men of the 1st were freedmen who had made the dramatic transition from slavery, to freedom, to military service. Prior to the Florida invasion the 1st had been engaged in siege operations outside Charleston, but they had yet to see any serious action. They were commanded by James Beecher, the brother of Harriet Beecher Stowe and Henry Ward Beecher, but Beecher was on leave that February and command had passed to Lt. Col. William N. Reed.[5]

The 1st went into battle alongside the 54th Massachusetts, part of a two-regiment brigade commanded by Colonel Montgomery. The 54th, alone among the three black regiments at Olustee, marched across Florida with the confidence of a veteran regiment. Although *Glory* left the filmgoer with the impression that the charge on Fort Wagner had decimated the 54th, the veteran regiment had survived the disastrous assault, assembled new recruits anxious to join a celebrated unit, and returned to battle. The 54th was commanded by Col. Edward N. Hallowell, a Philadelphian who had survived his wounds at Fort Wagner and rejoined his regiment after a brief recuperation.

Many characteristics and experiences forged a bond among these three regiments, making it logical for any observer or chronicler to treat them as a unit. Thirteen months after Abraham Lincoln issued the revolutionary Emancipation Proclamation, the 1st N.C., 8th USCT, and 54th Massachusetts represented a revolution on the battlefield: a significant presence of armed black men. The soldiers of the United States Colored Troops, of which these three regiments represented a small contingent, were collectively a part of at least two sorts of revolutions. First, they were invaluable new recruits at a time when the Union sorely needed reinforcements. As historian Joseph T. Glatthaar has argued, the addition to Union military forces of 180,000 men—arriving on the scene when they did and swelling the Union ranks on strategically vital battlefields—helped ensure a northern military victory.[6] They were not merely symbols, but critical soldiers in the Union cause, helping turn the tide in a war that had become a battle over slavery. The North's black regiments became revolutionary actors as soon as they donned blue uniforms. By fighting alongside white men and against white enemies, black soldiers destabilized a host of assumptions about race and manhood. In this sense, too, the African American soldiers shared a common bond that transcended their diverse histories and circumstances.

While they were collectively changing the military terrain and recasting the nation's racial landscape, the USCT troops also shared the common bond that came from shared discrimination and injustice. Whatever the conditions of their birth or the terms of their enlistment, black soldiers were forced to endure a litany of insults and humiliations at the hands of their government:

they fought under white commissioned officers, routinely drew assignments more as laborers than warriors, and received the poorest equipment and lower wages than the $13 a month paid to white infantrymen.

In all these senses the African American soldiers at Olustee were fundamentally similar to each other, and fundamentally different from their white comrades. But that is only part of the story. Several characteristics distinguished among the regiments of the USCT. Three traits come to mind, all of which were represented among the black regiments that fought at Olustee. First, the Union's African American troops hailed from many parts of the country. The 54th Massachusetts was distinctive in that the original recruits came from across the North and the Border States, but when the regiment sought to replenish its depleted ranks after Fort Wagner it turned to New England: 80 percent of the 286 new men hailed from either Massachusetts or Vermont.[7] The men of the 8th came largely from eastern Pennsylvania. The 1st North Carolina originated along the eastern coast of South Carolina, North Carolina and Virginia. The African American regiments at Olustee were further differentiated by their level of training and combat experience. At one end of the spectrum was the 54th Massachusetts, which was a truly veteran regiment. On paper the 1st North Carolina was a fairly experienced regiment, but in fact its members had had little opportunity to fire their weapons in anger. The Pennsylvanians were an extraordinarily green regiment. The Florida invasion was their first campaign. Although the three black regiments at Olustee had confronted similar barriers, they—just like white Civil War regiments—marched into battle with very different levels of experience.

A further trait that separated the Union's black regiments, and also distinguished them most powerfully from their white brethren, was the array of circumstances and motivations that lured them into uniform. White volunteers left behind a wealth of letters, providing insight into the forces that led them to enlist and enabled them to endure years of warfare. Although each man responded to his own personal impulses, various patterns do emerge. When they enlisted, Civil War soldiers were following the dictates of both masculinity and ideology. War presented an opportunity to demonstrate manhood, and the failure to fight called that manhood into question. But the initial volunteers were not simply following paths determined by culture or testosterone. Their letters—both North and South—revealed a deep commitment to nation and cause.[8] By the third year of the war, the mix of motivations had shifted. New white recruits responded to the persuasive lure of high bounties or the threat of conscription. Other men offered their services as paid substitutes, serving in the place of draftees. Perhaps bounty men and substitutes also embraced the Union's core values, but they required the additional financial incentives to act on those impulses.

What about those black men who chose to shoulder a weapon? The three regiments at Olustee represent distinct points on a spectrum—or really multiple spectrums—as defined by geography, chronology, and servitude. For the men at the extreme poles—the 54th and the 1st—the decision to fight might have come rather naturally and even easily. The 54th's recruiters drew on that pool of the North's free black men who felt most compelled to strike a blow against the South and the slaveocracy. For freedmen along the Carolina coast, the impulse to fight their former masters must have been even more powerful. Moreover, for ex-slaves who sought economic autonomy and a modicum of independence, soldiering represented the best of a limited range of options.[9]

In contrast to the 54th Massachusetts and the 1st North Carolina, the 8th U.S. Colored Troops occupied the geographic center. The 8th mustered in for training at Camp William Penn, outside of Philadelphia, on December 4, 1863, nearly ten months after Massachusetts Governor John Andrews received permission to recruit the North's first regiment of black men, and four and a half months after the 54th Massachusetts led the charge at Fort Wagner. What made these Pennsylvanians join the Union army? The most willing African American recruits had already enlisted in the previous months. In fact, the 54th Massachusetts had an entire company recruited in Philadelphia, and Philadelphia men appeared in most of the other companies of the 54th and 55th Massachusetts.[10] For those African Americans who had not been swept up in the previous winter's war fervor, there was ample reason to remain on the sidelines. By the war's third year the northern economy was prospering and jobs fairly plentiful. And when the men of the 8th enlisted the Pennsylvania recruiters for the USCT had not yet begun to offer bounties to black volunteers.

Moreover, despite the much-celebrated Emancipation Proclamation, northern black men had every reason to conclude that this was still not their war. At home they endured a host of legal, political, and institutional indignities delivering the daily message that African Americans were not equal partners in the nation. In a particularly disturbing ironic twist, when the wives and loved ones of Philadelphia's black soldiers tried to ride the city's streetcars out to Camp William Penn, the conductors refused to let them sit in the covered section, requiring instead that they ride standing on the cars' open platforms. Many women preferred to walk the miles to the training camp, rather than enduring the insult to their womanhood.[11] If their lives on the home front were not sufficient to convince them that this was not their fight, by the fall of 1863 northern black men knew that the Union army hardly promised to be a haven of racial equality. Whereas the men of the 54th had had reason to believe that they were entering a new world of racial equality, or at least equal compensation and treatment, by the time the 8th mustered in all understood that black men were not going to enjoy equal treatment from the Union army, and if captured they were liable to face harsh treatment at the hands of their enemies.

What made these later waves of northern black men enlist? Although few personal papers have survived, there are ways to gain a sense of what spoke to these prospective recruits. By examining newspaper editorials, public speeches, and recruiting broadsides, the historian can piece together a portrait of the considerations that shaped decision-making among Pennsylvania's black men in the fall of 1863.

It would perhaps surprise many modern observers to learn that Civil War Philadelphia had a substantial middle-class black community, with a dense web of institutions and organizations. Black Methodists turned to Philadelphia's *Christian Recorder,* a weekly organ of the A.M.E. Church, for information and commentary on current events.[12] When the war first broke out, many northern blacks—including three companies of Philadelphians—jumped at the chance to offer their services, but the *Christian Recorder* repeatedly dissented from this martial spirit. "To offer ourselves for military service *now,* is to *abandon self-respect and invite insult*" the paper advised.[13] In those first months of the war, Frederick Douglass shared this skepticism. "Nothing short of an open recognition of the Negro's manhood his rights as such to have a country equally with others would induce me to join the army in any capacity," he told a friend.[14]

By February 1863 the terrain had shifted. Lincoln's Emancipation Proclamation had not only turned the Union army into an agent of liberation, but it had also opened the door to the extensive arming of black troops. On February 14, the *Christian Recorder* ran an editorial about "Colored Soldiers," asking "Will They Fight? Should They Fight?" In answer to the first question the paper declared that anyone familiar with the history of black Americans should know that they had never "failed to show their courage when the hour and place has come." The second question was a bit more complicated. Before they enlist, black men "should . . . know whether they are to have all the rights and privileges of other citizens in every state of the Union, and receive as much compensation for their services as any other soldier according to their rank in the army."[15] If the *Recorder* still had doubts, Douglass had already cast his lot with the Union cause, promising the government that "we are ready, and only ask to be called into this service." Before long Douglass had signed on as a military recruiter for the 54th Massachusetts, calling on "Men of Color" to "fly to arms and smite with death the power that would bury the government and your liberty in the same helpless grave."[16]

Within a few months black men had begun to demonstrate their valor on the battlefield, putting more pressure on the northern black leadership. In May 1863, the *Recorder* reprinted a series of resolutions passed by the A.M.E. Church during their annual conference in Philadelphia. Having witnessed the exploits of "those men of color, our brethren, acquaintances, and friends" on the battlefield, the conference formally resolved that "the great political interests of the colored people of these United States are at last thrown into the balances of military equity" and that "no pains be spared by us at home to advance the general interests of our soldiers in the field." The A.M.E. Church and the *Christian Recorder were* now squarely behind the black military effort.[17]

But although the door was now open to black troops, the Philadelphians' frustrations were not over. On June 17, 1863, in the midst of a local fervor over Robert E. Lee's invasion of Pennsylvania, a company of black Philadelphians offered their services for defense of the state. At first it seemed that the government had accepted this new step in an ongoing revolution: city military officials sent the black recruits on to Harrisburg. But that is as far as they got. The Union army promptly sent the volunteers home in disgrace, refusing their patriotic services even while white Philadelphians failed to respond to the crisis.[18]

Meanwhile, Pennsylvania's white Unionists had come around to the idea that the North should recruit black troops. The following week several hundred leading Philadelphians petitioned Secretary of War Edwin M. Stanton for authority to recruit three new black regiments. Stanton quickly granted permission, and the city's Supervisory Committee for Recruiting Colored Regiments swung into action, supported by the efforts of Maj. George L. Stearns, the state's new recruiting commissioner for U.S. Colored Troops. The proposed terms of enlistment underscored the fact that these new fighting men—like their black comrades already in the field—were not going to receive equal treatment. The Supervisory Committee could enlist three new regiments of three-year volunteers, but unlike white enlistees in 1863, these new men would not receive bounties, and whereas white infantry recruits could count on thirteen dollars a month, these men would get ten dollars a month and up to three dollars of that could be paid in clothing. If the men of the 54th had reason to feel misled, these new Pennsylvania recruits would know precisely where they stood.[19]

As it happened, young Cincinnati journalist Whitelaw Reid was in Philadelphia when word of the new recruiting drive reached the city. Reid reminded his readers of Stearns' impressive credentials as an abolitionist. The Boston merchant had supported radicals in Kansas and helped fund John Brown's raid on Harper's Ferry. But Reid pointed out that the gentlemen behind this new initiative were cut from different political cloth. These men were "not Abolitionists" or "Free Soilers" and in fact they were "scarcely . . . Republicans" at all, but rather "Union men" intent on "calling out a valuable element of their military strength, for relieving . . . the burdens of their white population." "What a change!" Reid remarked. "Scarcely six months ago, to advocate the arming of negroes was to horrify all the respectable conservatives in the Union party." But now abolition had become "an accepted fact" and the recruiting of black men "no longer a theory or an experiment" but a policy embraced by the conservative leadership, "in Philadelphia, at least."[20]

While Philadelphia's pragmatic white Unionists calculated that black soldiers could fill recruiting quotas while helping win the war, the city's black leadership saw the turn of events as an important challenge and opportunity. With the secretary of war's authorization in hand, more than fifty prominent African Americans gathered to draft and sign a grand proclamation, addressed to the North's "Men of Color!" "Now or Never!" it declared, "This is our golden moment. The Government of the United States calls for every able-bodied colored man to enter the army for the three years' of service, and join in fighting the battles of liberty and Union. A new era is open to us," they effused. The committee reproduced the proclamation as a broadside to be distributed across the city, and as a spectacular 8-foot banner that hung outside the Supervisory Committee's Chestnut Street offices.

This extraordinary proclamation, whose signers included Thomas Dorsey, Octavius V. Catto, Frederick Douglass, and William Forten (the father of young diarist Charlotte Forten), merits some close examination. By this point in the war, northern citizens had grown accustomed to exuberant recruiting posters. Most in the genre combined patriotic and martial imagery with relatively few words, calling on young men to serve their country while sharing in the glory of war. By mid-1863 recruiting posters had already begun to include promises of considerable bounties and other financial inducements. Some sought to convince white men that voluntary enlistment on their own terms was preferable to conscription. But the men of the Supervisory Committee relied on extended rhetoric rather than simple patriotic imagery. The broadside included nearly 700 words of text.

Several themes ran through this fascinating proclamation, but one core message remained paramount. The fifty-five signers spoke directly to their target audience's sense of manhood. In fact, the word "manhood" appears six times in the text, and terms like "man," "men," "manly," and "freemen" appear another fourteen times. The message was clear. For generations black Americans had suffered the humiliations of slavery and abuse. "Our manhood has been denied, our citizenship blotted out, our souls seared and burned, our spirits cowed and crushed, and the hopes of the future of our race involved in doubts and darkness." Now the Civil War, and the United States government, had provided them with the opportunity simultaneously to strike a blow at a hated enemy and prove their manhood to a skeptical nation. In making the case, the authors played every card at their disposal to challenge the manhood of those young men who had not yet enlisted. A host of immigrant races had already proven their valor on the battlefield they noted. "If we are not lower in the scale of humanity than Englishmen, Irishmen, white Americans, and other races, we can show it now." And this was not merely a matter of black men in comparison to white men. Recently freed slaves, they noted, had already demonstrated their heroism on battlefields like Port Hudson and Milliken's Bend. "If they have proved themselves heroes, cannot we prove ourselves men? Are freemen less brave than slaves?"

Certainly wartime appeals to manhood and masculinity are hardly surprising. But traditionally—and particularly during the Civil War—that rhetoric was cast in the language of individualism. Military service presented the young man with the opportunity to demonstrate his personal honor, heroism, and fundamental manhood, to himself and his larger society. But in the "Men of Color" broadside the manhood in question was collective. The words "our," "we," and "us" appear no less than fifty times in this proclamation. "Our manhood" is in question, and "we" must answer the call, they said. Either that, or admit that "freemen" are indeed "less brave than slaves" and "lower in the scale of humanity" than even Irishmen.

The signers understandably couched their argument in the most positive terms, stressing why young black men should cast their lot with the Union cause rather than contemplating the many arguments against participation in an army in which they would be treated like second-class citizens. But near the close they hinted that negative arguments were in the air. "Stop at no subterfuge," they warned. "Listen to nothing that shall deter you from rallying for the army."

Meanwhile, the Supervisory Committee reserved Philadelphia's National Hall for a grand recruiting rally on July 6, 1863. The mass meeting could hardly have come at a more dramatic moment. Three days earlier Robert E. Lee's Army of Northern Virginia suffered a disastrous loss at Gettysburg, and on July 4 Union commander Ulysses S. Grant captured the vital city of Vicksburg on the Mississippi River. Suddenly the war was going well for the Union, but none of these developments changed the status of black soldiers in the field or of black citizens at home. It would be up to the evening's three speakers to make the case to both the patriotic and the skeptical.

The first to ascend the platform was local congressman Judge William D. Kelley. An abolitionist and friend of the local black community, Kelley began his address by building upon the themes of manhood. "Are you content to spend your lives as boot-blacks, barbers, [and] waiters ... when the profession of arms ... invites you to acknowledged manhood, freedom and honor?" he asked. After two hundred years of oppression, the war had "opened the way for the Africo-American to prove his manhood to the world." But while the broadside spoke to a collective black male identity, Judge Kelley seemed to speak directly to individuals, challenging each man to grasp the moment and assert his own manhood and thus elevate his station in life. As if to reinforce that point, Kelley next turned his attention to the "old men," "mothers," and "girls" in the audience. Fathers should threaten to "disinherit and denounce" sons who "prove cowards"; mothers should demonstrate that they are ready to match white women in their sacrifices; and girls should make it clear that they would "rather marry the wooden leg and empty jacket sleeve of a war-torn hero" rather than a handsome coward.

Military service might promise the glories of manhood and future elevation, but what about the persistent realities of an unequal present? Here the congressmen made no grand promises, but instead he turned to the "white men and women" in the audience and called upon them to flood Congress with petitions "demanding" equal pay and pensions for these brave black soldiers. Meanwhile, they should ensure that black widows and orphans would be cared for if their men folk fell in battle. Kelley's appeals were met with choruses of "Yes, we will" from his white listeners, effectively assuring the predominantly black audience that their claims would not be forgotten. He closed his remarks with a passionate declaration that "the negro is the 'coming man' for whom we have waited" and that the fate of the nation rested in his hands. The congressman took his seat to "Tremendous and long-continued cheering."

As the applause died down the audience turned their attention to the next speaker, Anna Elizabeth Dickinson. Only twenty years old, the Philadelphia Quaker had already established an impressive reputation as a radical orator and patriot. The child of abolitionists, Dickinson had impeccable credentials as an advocate for black rights. Now she had a delicate rhetorical task: how to cajole African American men into uniform, knowing full well that she was asking them to accept a poor deal.[21]

Dickinson took Gettysburg as her starting point. No black troops had fought there, but she argued that Union fortunes had shifted because the nation had embraced emancipation and started arming black men. In the past, she noted, black civilians had been used to assist the nation's military causes, but only with "their brains contracted; their souls dwarfed; their manhood stunted." Now, finally, the people had declared that "we have wronged you enough" and the time had come to "stand aside and let you fight for your own manhood, your future, your race." Dickinson admitted that the nation needed the black soldier to win the war, but at the same time she could not ask them to step forward on those grounds alone. To do so, she said, would cause her to blush with shame. How could she answer the obvious question: If you need us, "'why don't you give us the same bounty, and the same pay as the rest?'" "I have no answer to that," she admitted, as the room erupted in cheers.

Instead of asking black men to fight for a white cause, Dickinson tried to argue that the war was indeed "a war of the races, of the ages." True, equal pay and bounties "are good: liberty is better," she declared. Unequal treatment is bad, "slavery is worse." Although her listeners might reasonably "hesitate because you have not all, [y]our brothers and sisters in the South cry out, 'Come to our help, we have nothing.'" In her rousing conclusion, Dickinson called on her audience to seize the opportunity and claim the gains dangled before them:

> The black man will be a citizen, only by stamping his right to it in his blood. Now or never! You have not homes!—gain them, You have not liberty!—gain it. You have not a flag!—gain it. You have not a country!— be written down in history as the race who made one for themselves, and saved one for another.

Once again, the published accounts reported that the speaker left the platform to "immense cheering."

The evening's final speaker was none other than Frederick Douglass, the eloquent ex-slave and frequent spokesman for the African American community. Douglass had long since thrown his energies into black enlistment, and in fact two of his sons served in the 54th Massachusetts. But it was one thing to tour the North encouraging young men who were predisposed to the fight, and quite another thing to make the case to the reticent and the skeptical. Although Kelley and Dickinson had strong credentials as allies to the African American community, they still spoke across a racial divide. How would Douglass cast his arguments?

Like Dickinson, Douglass opted to confront the elephant in the room: the unequal pay and bounties offered to black soldiers. He promised to be "plain and practical" in his remarks. There were, he reasoned, two views to take on the subject: the "narrow view" and the "broad view." The narrow view would emphasize the obvious fact that men who are all risking their lives should receive equal compensation and treatment, regardless of their race. Douglass readily acknowledged the justice in the argument. But the man who took the broad view would recognize that the wisest path to "manhood, equal rights and elevation, is that we enter this service." The act of fighting would be "ennobling" to the black race, and was thus worth the intermediate humiliations of salaries and bounties.

Stepping away from those narrow material concerns, Douglass asked his audience to consider the two sides that were "today face to face" in the bloody conflict. The question, he insisted, should be "which is for us, and which is against us?" Even if one could argue that the Federal government was not fully invested in making the war about slavery, Douglass pointed out that the Confederacy was dedicated to protecting and expanding slavery. Moreover, whereas the Union cause may have appeared indifferent to slavery two years earlier, Douglass pointed to ample evidence that the worm really had turned and the North was moving towards emancipation, citizenship and racial justice. And in picking up the themes of the "Men of Color" broadside, Douglass announced that "The opportunity is given us to be men. . . . Once let the black man get upon his person the brass letters U. S.; let him get an eagle on his button, and a musket on his shoulder, and bullets in his pocket, and there is no power on the earth or under the earth which may deny that he has earned the right of citizenship in the United States."

Finally, in echoing Dickinson's arguments, Douglass told his listeners that northern whites would likely win the war and abolish slavery without their help. If they wanted future equality and citizenship, "this is no time for hesitation." Indeed, black men received lower wages, had been denied black commissioned officers, and had previously been spurned by Pennsylvania's recruiting officers. But if they hoped for a happier future, they must set aside those past grievances and have faith in a changed future. "Young men of Philadelphia," he declared, "you are without excuse. The hour has arrived, and your place is in the Union army. . . . In your hands that musket means liberty."[22]

At first the combination of patriotic editorials, enthusiastic broadsides, and passionate rhetoric struck a responsive chord among eastern Pennsylvania's African Americans. Many of those who had been spurned in mid-June now stepped forward to join the new regiments, and hundreds of other young men followed suit. By the end of July these recruits had filled the first of the three proposed regiments, and in August the 3rd USCT left Camp William Penn for South Carolina, where they would join the 54th Massachusetts in the assault on Fort Wagner. Two months later the 6th USCT headed south from Philadelphia. But local recruiters worried that the flow of African American volunteers had slowed to a trickle. In September, African American Jacob A. White reported that "recruiting is dull at present." The following month barely half a company of new recruits reported to Camp William Penn. In fact, the city finally agreed in mid-December—not long after the 8th mustered in—to offer $250 bounties to black volunteers, thus following a strategy already widespread in white recruiting.[23]

Even though the men of the 8th USCT shared many fundamental characteristics and concerns in common with their comrades in the 54th Massachusetts and even the 1st North Carolina, the timing of their recruitment and the arguments used to cajole them into uniform underscore fundamental differences. Those men who agreed to enlist in the end of 1863 weighed the arguments that their service would further the interests of black Americans and the multiple challenges to their collective manhood against nagging doubts that accompanied realities in a racially segregated northern society and continuing reports of unequal treatment experienced by their brothers in arms. In fact, shortly after speaking in Philadelphia, a frustrated Douglass temporarily abandoned his recruiting efforts because of the combined weight of discriminatory Union practices and Confederate threats to execute black prisoners.[24]

What made these men hang back in the recruiting frenzy of June and early July, but then step forward in November or December? No doubt these volunteers, like white recruits, responded to a host of entirely personal considerations. Perhaps family members heeded the advice of Judge Kelley and exerted pressure on individual young men. Or, conversely, maybe some had to convince their loved ones that enlistment was the right path or at least the time was right. Still, it seems reasonable to conclude that these men were collectively more reticent about the cause—or the role of black men in that fight—than those Philadelphians who rushed to join the 54th, or even the men who jumped at the chance to join the 3rd USCT several months earlier. If the various recruiters knew their intended audience, which seems likely, it follows that the men who joined the 8th were a particularly contemplative lot. Prior appeals to national patriotism or vengeance against the slaveholding aristocracy had failed to reach them; the martial enthusiasm of blue uniforms and brass bands had not found its mark. Until the Supervisory Committee began offering bounties, the practical arguments for enlisting were not persuasive, or at least no more so than they had been months earlier. The arguments that spoke to those men who enlisted in late 1863 called for a subtle weighing of variables and considerations. They should relent and sign up *despite* all the good reasons not to because in the long run their sacrifice would yield important gains for black Americans. Something in that message struck a nerve, tilting the balance in favor of marching off to war. And so they found themselves wearing the same uniform as the veterans of the 54th Massachusetts and the freedmen of the 1st North Carolina.

The 8th left Camp William Penn for Hilton Head, South Carolina on January 16, 1864. In South Carolina they worked on entrenchments and other fortifications, sometimes alongside the 54th. The 54th's Cpl. James Henry Gooding was impressed with the raw newcomers. "Some say that the 54th has a rival," he reported to the readers of the New Bedford *Mercury,* "the 8th U. S. regiment is indeed a splendid organization, and I may add that no regiment in the department can boast a more healthy-looking, martial bearing body of men."[25] Before long both regiments were ordered further south to Florida, where they would join in the occupation of Jacksonville.[26] On February 20, they found themselves marching west from Jacksonville towards Lake City as part of General Seymour's excursion across northern Florida. With the 54th and 1st bringing up the rear under Colonel Montgomery, the untested 8th had the honor of being the first black regiment in the Union column. Thus when the 7th Connecticut faltered that afternoon, Seymour turned to the green Pennsylvanians. It was hardly an ideal opportunity to learn the art of war. When the 8th rushed forward many still wore their knapsacks and half carried unloaded weapons; the regiment's first sergeants had no opportunity to discard their sergeant's sashes, making them inviting targets for enemy rifles. If that was not hard enough, shortly after the 8th arrived on the scene, the 7th New Hampshire to their right dissolved in a morass of confused orders, hostile enemy fire, and sheer panic.[27]

Contemporary accounts from the battlefield tell a horrific tale. Lt. Oliver Willcox Norton reported that the 8th successfully "formed a line under the

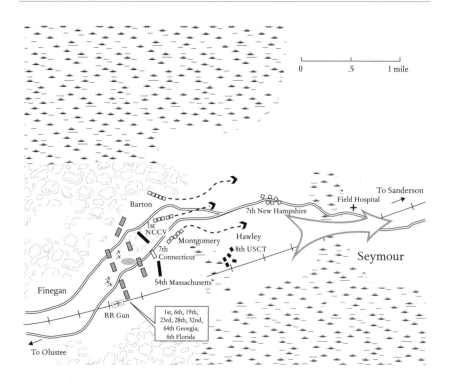

most destructive fire I ever knew." Regimental surgeon Dr. Alex P. Heichold noted that they "wavered at first, but soon recovered themselves, and then commenced the struggle for life and death." Both white observers credited the 8th with almost astonishing bravery for such untried men. Dr. Heichold pointed out that the regiment had "but little practice in loading and firing" and few had ever heard a cannon's roar. As Norton put it, they "could stand and be killed" but they had little chance of taking any toll on the enemy. When the word finally came to withdraw, their inexperience became even more costly, as the retreating regiment gathered in frightened clumps, becoming the perfect target for deadly enemy fire. Even as their casualties mounted Colonel Fribley fell mortally wounded, most of the men of the 8th responded bravely—although largely ineffectually—throughout the crisis. As one Confederate officer put it, "they stood killing d——d well, but they didn't hurt us much."[28]

When the 54th and the 1st appeared on the scene at the double quick, the narrative changed dramatically. Capt. Luis F. Emilio recalled that his comrades in the 54th rushed into the fray with the ironic battle cry, "Three cheers for Massachusetts and seven dollars a month!" The veterans of Fort Wagner formed a battle line with dispatch and opened fire, effectively saving the day for the disorganized Union forces. A correspondent to the *Boston Journal* reported that they "fought like tigers"; the 54th's Capt. James W. Grace agreed that "no regiment fought like it." Meanwhile, according to a *Philadelphia Press* account, the 1st North Carolina arrived "with a yell on the double-quick," cheered on by their white comrades in the 47th New York Infantry. The 1st's Capt. J. S. Croft, who took over for the fallen Colonel Reed, was proud to recall that his men earned "the warmest praises" from all observers. A variety of contemporary accounts shared this assessment.[29] In his account of his failure, General Seymour acknowledged that "the colored troops behaved credibly—the Fifty-fourth Massachusetts and First North Carolina like veterans," in stark contrast to several white regiments, most notably the 7th New Hampshire.[30]

Seymour's comments are telling, both in his praise of his black troops but also in the distinctions that he drew amongst his men. The 8th, 54th, and 1st all behaved bravely, no doubt demonstrating their manhood to all who cared to contemplate the issue. The real differences on the battlefield, and in the way the white observers commented on the scene, had little to do with racial politics. True, the men from Massachusetts adopted a battle cry that pointedly reminded their white comrades that while they were good enough to die for the cause, they were apparently not good enough to be paid the same as the men they were saving. But the irony of their timely appearance and heroic performance was more complex than that. On this battlefield, with its motley assortment of green troops, draftees, and bounty men, the 54th and the 1st behaved "like veterans" because that is precisely what they were. In that moment the Union soldiers from New York, New Hampshire, and Connecticut were probably less concerned with the niceties of racial prejudice, and more focused on the fact that the men in the blue uniforms arriving from their rear seemed to know precisely what they were doing. If they were aware that one USCT regiment was composed of the sons of some of northern black America's leading families, whereas the other black regiment was made up of recently freed slaves, those hugely significant socio-political realities were presumably lost in the confusion. Meanwhile, the intrepid men of the 8th USCT surely demonstrated that "free men" were every bit as brave as "slaves," but they also illustrated that on the battlefield other differences took a back seat to experience. They had mastered the art of dying well, but little else.

If in the hail of bullets Union soldiers really lost track of racial difference, that color-blind moment would not last long. The men from Colonel Montgomery's brigade helped make the difference between a disastrous rout and an orderly retreat, but Olustee was still a Union defeat. As they fled from the scene,

Seymour's men had to confront a new set of grim realities. The Confederacy had threatened to enslave or execute captured USCT troops and their white officers, and Union soldiers were well aware of rumored battlefield atrocities where Rebels had killed black troops on the battlefield rather than taking them as prisoners. With the Union army in retreat, various black soldiers and their white comrades stepped forward to keep the wounded black troops from Confederate hands. Dr. Heichold insisted that wounded USCT troops be given priority in the ambulances, reasoning that white soldiers would fare better at the hands of Confederate troops. Meanwhile, a small detail of men from the 54th who had been held in reserve during the battle stepped forward to cover the retreat. When the men of the 54th discovered several boxcars of wounded left behind in Baldwin—about halfway between Olustee and Jacksonville—they secured ropes to cars and bodily dragged their fallen comrades to safety.

Despite these efforts, numerous post-battle accounts—written by both Union and Confederate soldiers—reported the battlefield execution of wounded USCT soldiers. By one estimate, as many as fifty men were killed after the fighting stopped. Seven months earlier Frederick Douglass had urged Philadelphia's young men that "in your hands that musket means liberty." After the battle, when wounded white soldiers had generally abandoned their weapons, black men clung to their rifles even when they could no longer march. As a sergeant major in the 8th observed, wounded men came "into camp with their arms and equipments on, so great was their endurance and so determined were they to defend themselves till death." On more than one occasion wounded black men died rather than accept capture and execution.[31]

The USCT regiments at Olustee suffered heavy casualties. The two veteran regiments survived with the least damage. The 54th lost 13 men killed, 62 men and 3 officers wounded, and 8 men missing. The 1st lost 2 officers and 20 men killed, 8 officers and 123 men wounded, and 77 men missing, The untested 8th fared the worst, with 48 men and Colonel Fribley killed, 8 officers and 180 men wounded, and 1 officer and 72 men reported missing.[32]

In 1863 the men of the 8th had hesitated to enlist when their brothers in the North and South had jumped at the chance. By wavering they had illustrated the fundamental concerns that divided northern blacks. By finally enlisting before bounties had been added to the mix, they demonstrated that their decisions were probably not dictated by pragmatic financial concerns. It was as if they had collectively subscribed to the arguments articulated by the *Christian Recorder* the previous February. Of course the black man would fight if circumstances warranted it, but reasonable men could—and did—disagree about whether he should fight.[33] Finally, in February 1864 they demonstrated that their reticence had not been from a lack of manhood or courage. They fought bravely, even though they had little sense of the art of war. In both their bravery and their ineffectiveness, the 8th USCT illustrated a fundamental point about the differences among Civil War soldiers. Whatever distinctive traits divided one regiment from another in the paths they took to war, once the shooting started experience mattered more than race, or geography, or ideology.

That leads to one final irony. Although they did not enlist until months after the battle of Gettysburg and saw no action until February 1864, the 8th participated in considerable combat over the next fourteen months. They fought at Fair Oaks, the Bermuda Hundred, Chaffin's Farm, and Hatcher's Run, and saw heavy duty throughout the siege of Petersburg, finally joining in the chase of the Army of Northern Virginia to Appomattox Court House in April 1865. By the end of the war, the regiment had lost 4 officers and 247 men to mortal wounds and disease, with another 245 men wounded and 72 captured or missing. After the war the 8th was honored as one of the celebrated "Three Hundred Fighting Regiments" of the Civil War.[34]

## NOTES

1. On the campaign and battle see George F. Baltzell, "The Battle of Olustee (Ocean Pond), Florida," *Florida Historical Quarterly* 9 (April 1931): 199–223; Arthur Bergeron, "The Battle of Olustee," in John David Smith, editor, *Black Soldiers in Blue: African American Troops in the Civil War Era* (Chapel Hill: University of North Carolina Press, 2002), 136–49; Noah Andre Trudeau, *Like Men of War. Black Troops in the Civil War 1862–1865* (Boston: Little, Brown, 1998), 129–55; Robert P. Broadwater, *The Battle of Olustee, 1864: The Final Union Attempt to Seize Florida* (Jefferson, N.C.: McFarland, 2006); Stephen E. Woodworth and Kenneth J. Winkle, eds., *Oxford Atlas of the Civil War* (New York: Oxford University Press, 2004), 218–20; Luis F. Emilio, *A Brave Black Regiment: The History of the 54th Massachusetts, 1863–1865* (1894; reprint, Cambridge, Mass.: Da Capo, 1995), 148–85; *Christian Recorder,* March 12, April 2, 9, 1864. For a superb web page on the battle of Olustee see http://extlab1.entnem.ufl.edu/Olustee/.

2. For the leading treatments of African American soldiers in the Civil War, see Benjamin Quarles, *The Negro in the Civil War* (1953; reprint, n.p.: Da Capo, 1979); Dudley Taylor Cornish, *The Sable Arm: Black Troops in the Union Army, 1861–1865* (1956; reprint, Lawrence: University Press of Kansas, 1987); James M. McPherson, *The Negro's Civil War* (1965; reprint, New York: Vintage, 2003); Joseph T. Glatthaar, *Forged in Battle: The Civil War Alliance of Black Soldiers and White Officers* (New York: Free Press, 1990); Ira Berlin, "The Black Military Experience, 1861–1867," in Ira Berlin, Barbara J. Fields, Steven F. Miller, Joseph P. Reidy, and Leslie S. Rowland, *Slaves No More: Three Essays on Emancipation and the Civil War* (New York: Cambridge University Press, 1992); Smith, ed., *Black Soldiers in Blue;* and Trudeau, *Like Men of War.* In his prize-winning study of the motivations of Civil War soldiers, James M. McPherson read "at least 25,000" soldiers'

letters and 249 diaries. McPherson reports that black men made up only 1 percent of his sample of Union soldiers. (McPherson, *For Cause and Comrades: Why Men Fought in the Civil War* (New York: Oxford University Press, 1997), pp. viii-ix, 11–12.) For a recent treatment of Union soldiers from North Carolina, including the 1st North Carolina Colored Infantry (35th USCT), see Richard M. Reid, *Freedom for Themselves: North Carolina's Black Soldier in the Civil War Era* (Chapel Hill: University of North Carolina Press, 2008).

3. On the 54th, see Emilio, *A Brave Black Regiment,* and Peter Burchard, *One Gallant Rush: Robert Gould Shaw and His Brave Black Regiment* (New York: St. Martin's Press, 1965). On *Glory,* see Martin H. Blatt, "Glory: Hollywood History, Popular Culture, and the Fifty-Fourth Massachusetts Regiment," in Martin H. Blatt, Thomas J. Brown, and Donald Yacovone, eds,, *Hope and Glory: Essays on the Legacy of the Fifty-Fourth Massachusetts Regiment* (Amherst: University of Massachusetts Press, 2001), 215–35.

4. For a discussion of the actual episode, see Trudeau, *Like Men of War,* 73.

5. On the 1st North Carolina, see Trudean, *Like Men of War,* 114.

6. Joseph T. Glatthaar, "Black Glory: The African-American Role in Union Victory," in Gabor S. Boritt, ed., *Why the Confederacy Lost* (New York: Oxford University Press, 1992), 133–62.

7. Edwin S. Redkey, "Brave Black Volunteers: A Profile of the Fifty-Fourth Massachusetts Regiment," in Blatt, Brown, and Yacovone, eds., *Hope and Glory,* 22–23.

8. See McPherson, *For Cause and Comrades.*

9. For discussions of these divergent attitudes toward black recruitment, see David W. Blight, *Frederick Douglass' Civil War: Keeping Faith in Jubilee* (Baton Rouge: Louisiana State University Press, 1989), 148–74; James M. McPherson, *The Struggle for Equality: Abolitionists and the Negro in the Civil War and Reconstruction* (Princeton, N.J.: Princeton University Press, 1964), 202–04; McPherson, *The Negro's Civil War,* 29–35, 175–85.

10. Frank H. Taylor, *Philadelphia in the Civil War, 1861 -1865* (Philadelphia: The City, 1913), 187.

11. *Christian Recorder,* December 26, 1863; Philip A. Foner, "The Battle to End Discrimination Against Negroes on Philadelphia's Streetcars: (Part I) Background and Beginning of the Battle," *Pennsylvania History* (September 1973): 261–90.

12. McPherson, *Negro's Civil War,* 51.

13. *Christian Recorder,* April 27, 1861; J. Matthew Gallman, *Mastering Wartime: A Social History of Philadelphia During the Civil War* (New York: Cambridge University Press, 1990), 45.

14. Blight, *Frederick Douglass' Civil War,* 99. Blight cites Douglass to Samuel J. May, August 30, 1861, in Philip S. Foner, ed., *The Life and Writings of Frederick Douglass,* 5 vols. (New York: International Publishers, 1950), 3:158–59.

15. *Christian Recorder,* February 14, 1863.

16. Frederick Douglass, "Address Delivered in New York," February 6, 1863, in Frederick Douglass, *The Frederick Douglass Papers,* ed. John W. Blassingame, Series One, 5 vols. (New Haven, Conn.: Yale University Press, 1985), 3:569; Blight, *Frederick Douglass' Civil War,* 159.

17. *Christian Recorder,* May 23, 1863.

18. Taylor, *Philadelphia in the Civil War,* 188; Gallman, *Mastering Wartime,* pp. 46–47.

19. *Address of the Hon. W. D. Kelley, Miss Anna E. Dickinson, and Mr. Frederick Douglass, at a Mass Meeting, Held at National Hall, Philadelphia, July 6, 1863, for the Promotion of Colored Enlistments* (Philadelphia: n.p., 1863), 1, 8, African American Pamphlet Collection, Library of Congress, Washington; Gallman, *Mastering Wartime,* 47.

20. *Cincinnati Gazette,* June [?], 1863, miscellaneous scrapbook, Anna Elizabeth Dickinson Papers, Library of Congress, Washington. This dispatch from "Agate" (Whitelaw Reid) is dated June 22, 1863.

21. On Dickinson's life, see J. Matthew Gallman, *America's Joan of Arc: The Life of Anna Elizabeth Dickinson* (New York: Oxford University Press, 2006).

22. *Address of the Hon. W. D. Kelley, Miss Anna E. Dickinson, and Mr. Frederick Douglass,* 2–7.

23. By the end of the war, eleven regiments of African American soldiers had been trained at Camp William Penn. See Taylor, *Philadelphia in the Civil War,* 189–90; Jeffry D. Wert, "Camp William Penn and the Black Soldier," *Pennsylvania History* 46 (October 1979): 335–46; Frederick M. Binder, "Pennsylvania Negro Regiments in the Civil War," *Journal of Negro History* 37 (1952): 383–417; Gallman, *Mastering Wartime,* 47–49; Jacob A. White to Joseph C. Bustill, September 8, 1863, *Journal of Negro History* 11 (January 1926): 85; *Christian Recorder,* August 1, 1863.

24. Blight, *Frederick Douglass' Civil War,* 167.

25. Virginia M. Adams, editor, *On the Altar of Freedom: A Black Soldier's Civil War Letters From the Front* (Amherst, 1991), 109–10.

26. For a first-hand account by a musician with the 8th USCT, see William P. Woodlin diary, The Gilder Lehrman Institute of American History, New York City.

27. Broadwater, *Battle of Olustee,* 7–33; Taylor, *Philadelphia in the Civil War,* 191; Trudeau, *Like Men of War,* 137–42; Edwin S. Redkey, ed., *A Grand Army of Black Men* (New York: Cambridge University Press, 1992), 41; *Christian Recorder,* April 16, 1864.

28. Trudeau, *Like Men of War,* 143; Bergeron, "Battle of Olustee," 146; Glatthaar, *Forged in Battle,* 145; *Christian Recorder,* March 12, 1864. Praise for the 8th USCT was not universal. Some men from the 3rd Rhode Island Artillery blamed the 8th for failing to support their battery. (Broadwater, *Battle of Olustee,* 93–6.)

29. Trudeau, *Like Men of War,* 145–47; Adams, ed., *On The Altar of Freedom,* 114; Broadwater, *Battle of Olustee,* 123, 127; Emilio, *A Brave Black Regiment,* 163.

30. Cornish, *The Sable Arm,* 268–69.

31. Trudeau, *Like Men of War,* 150–52; Redkey, ed., *A Grand Army of Black Men,* 42; *Christian Recorder,* April 9, 16, 1864. Arthur Bergeron notes that while there were a few atrocities, "no wholesale massacre of the blacks occurred." (Bergeron, "Battle of Olustee," 144.) Robert Broadwater accepts the estimate that roughly fifty wounded black soldiers were executed after nightfall. (Broadwater, *Battle of Olustee,* 141–43.)

32. Baltzell, "Battle of Olustee (Ocean Pond), Florida."

33. *Christian Recorder,* February 14, 1863.

34. Taylor, *Philadelphia in the Civil War,* 191.

# Permissions

"Voluntarism in Wartime: Philadelphia's Great Central Fair." From *Toward a Social History of the American Civil War: Exploratory Essays,* edited by Maris A. Vinovskis. Cambridge University Press, 1990. Reprinted with the permission of Cambridge University Press.

"Preserving the Peace: Order and Disorder in Civil War Philadelphia." *Pennsylvania History* 55:4 (October 1988). Reprinted with the permission of the Pennsylvania Historical Association.

"Gettysburg's Gettysburg: What the Battle Did to the Borough." Coauthored with Susan Baker. From *The Gettysburg Nobody Knows,* edited by Gabor S. Boritt. Oxford University Press, 1997. By permission of Oxford University Press, Inc.

"Urban History and the American Civil War." From *Journal of Urban History* 32:4 (May 2006). Reprinted with permission of Sage Publications, Inc.

"The Civil War Economy: A Modern View." Coauthored with Stanley Engerman. From *On the Road to Total War: The American Civil War and the German Wars of Unification, 1861–1871,* edited by Stig Förster and Jörg Nagler. German Historical Institute/Cambridge University Press, 1997. Reprinted with the permission of Cambridge University Press.

"Entrepreneurial Experiences in the Civil War: Evidence From Philadelphia." From *Economic Development in Historical Perspective,* edited by Thomas Weiss and Donald Schaefer. Copyright © 1994 by the Board of Trustees of the Leland Stanford Jr. University. All rights reserved. Used with the permission of Stanford University Press, www.sup.org.

"'An Inspiration to Work': Anna Elizabeth Dickinson, Public Orator." From Joan Cashin, editor, *The War Was You and Me: Civilians in the American Civil War.* © 2002 Princeton University Press. Reprinted by permission of Princeton University Press.

"Anna Dickinson, America's Joan of Arc: Public Discourse and Gendered Rhetoric during the Civil War." From *American Public Life and the Historical Imagination,* edited by Wendy Gamber, Michael Grossberg and Hendrik Hartog. (University of Notre Dame Press, 2003.)

"'Touched with Fire?': Two Philadelphia Novelists Remember the Civil War." From *More Than a Contest Between Armies: Essays on the Civil War Era,* edited by James Marten and A. Kristen Foster (Kent, Ohio: Kent State Univ. Press, 2008). Used by permission of the publisher.

"Is the War Ended? Anna Dickinson and the Election of 1872." From *The Memory of the Civil War in American Culture,* edited by Alice Fahs and Joan Waugh. Copyright © 2004 by the University of North Carolina Press. Used by permission of the publisher. www.uncpress.unc.edu.

"'In Your Hands That Musket Means Liberty': African American Soldiers and the Battle of Olustee." From *Wars within a War: Controversy and Conflict over the American Civil War,* edited Gary W. Gallagher and Joan Waugh. Copyright © 2009 by the University of North Carolina Press. Used by permission of the publisher. www.uncpress.unc.edu.

# Index